PLATO

The Arguments of
the Philosophers

EDITOR: TED HONDERICH

The group of books of which this is one will include an
essentially analytic and critical account of each of the
considerable number of the great and the influential
philosophers. Each book will provide an ordered
exposition and an examination of the contentions and
doctrines of the philosopher in question. The group of
books taken together will comprise a contemporary
assessment and history of the entire course of
philosophical thought.

PLATO

J. C. B. Gosling

St Edmund Hall, Oxford

Routledge & Kegan Paul
London and Boston

First published in 1973
by Routledge & Kegan Paul Ltd
Broadway House, 68–74 Carter Lane,
London EC4V 5EL and
9 Park Street, Boston, Mass. 02108, U.S.A.
Printed in Great Britain by
The Camelot Press Ltd, London and Southampton

ISBN 0 7100 7664 9

Library of Congress Catalog Card No. 73-83075

Contents

Preface

The terms of reference of this book ensure that it will be an irritant to scholars. It is intended as a critical discussion of some of Plato's central philosophical theses. In order to get enough of what I wished to discuss on the table I have had to curtail the scholarly discussion, though I have tried to supply enough to avoid instant dismissal. This is not done from any contempt for scholarship. Far from it. The prime purpose, however, has been to extract some theses which can plausibly, and in my view truly, be attributed to Plato, which it is of some philosophical interest to discuss. If I aggravate some philosophers into reading Plato more throughly and more seriously, then I think Platonic scholarship will in the end benefit, even though the following is not the most rigorous example of it. For those stimulated to further enquiry I have supplied a number of basic references within Plato, and for the variety of scholarly opinion they could do worse than start on the books mentioned in the bibliography. This, however, contains only books and articles mentioned in the text. It has no pretensions to giving all books and articles that I have found helpful or even most helpful, still less to giving a selection adequate to reflect the present state of scholarly opinion.

Many parts of the book have been delivered in an earlier form to the Southern Association of Ancient Philosophy, the Oxford Philological Society, members of the philosophy or classics departments at the Australian National University, Melbourne, Monash and Waikato universities, and to various undergraduate lecture-goers. It has been impossible to keep track of influences, and changes are often unnoticed or unadmitted by oneself in the absence of clear historical evidence. Frequently, however, the discussions were extremely helpful and I am indebted to those concerned.

One whose influence can be identified is Mr I. M. Crombie. Often what follows started life as an attempt to get clear where I stood on positions put forward in his *An Examination of Plato's Doctrines*, which receives little explicit mention only because I am aware of my powers of distortion. He has also kindly read through an earlier draft and made a number of helpful suggestions.

The main body of the work reached final form during a five-month period as a visiting fellow at the Research School of Social Sciences at the Australian National University. My gratitude is due to the authorities there for appointing me to the fellowship and to my colleagues at St Edmund Hall, Oxford, for giving me leave for that period.

I

Moral Scepticism

Two of Plato's main interests were in science and morality. He thought that if one did the first properly one's problems with the second would be solved. At least, this is what he came to believe. For in his view the main problem in morality is to discover how it is best for a man to live, and a fully developed scientific understanding will reveal how it is best for things to be, where 'things' include humanity. This position seems to have been reached as a result of trying to meet a variety of arguments corrosive of traditional moral standards, and this moral concern pervades the dialogues, cropping up in the midst of apparently abstruse discussions far removed from ethics. It is not always easy to see how his answers to other problems bear on these moral issues, or even, sometimes, how his views are anything but a perversion brought about by moral obsessions. An example of the latter is the constant Platonic refrain that knowledge, true knowledge, is of the good. One can see how a fervent moralist might be carried away to such excesses, holding that only moral knowledge is true knowledge, but Plato seems to apply it over a very broad field, as though all branches of knowledge were really moral knowledge. An example is his treatment of negation and falsity. The topics seem austere philosophical logic, yet in the way Plato talks falsity is somehow allied to sophistry and illusion in contrast with philosophical knowledge which is the underpinning of virtue.

In what follows I propose to discuss this attempt to unite the concerns of science and morality. In a synthesising author like Plato his theses on these topics have repercussions in other areas such as law, politics, education, aesthetics and religion, but I shall only touch on his treatment of these in so far as it is absolutely necessary. This is not to suggest that Plato considered them unimportant – the truth is too obviously the other way – but his views on them are to a very large extent the result of the positions I propose to discuss.

I shall start by trying to establish the form of Plato's reaction to certain brands of moral scepticism and show how this ties in with the view that properly conducted science is concerned with how it is best for things to be. The first six chapters contain the main exposition of the moral position, with a first sketch of the thesis on the sense in which knowledge is of goodness. There are other influential elements in Plato's requirements about knowledge which are developed in chapters VII–XIII. While these chapters contain a certain amount of criticism it is for the most part muted. In the last five chapters, by contrast, there is little or no exposition. I have tried there to take some of the main Platonic themes on morality and knowledge as expounded in the earlier chapters and elaborate and add to the criticisms adumbrated in the more expository sections.

The earlier dialogues, such as the *Laches, Protagoras, Meno, Gorgias, Republic* Book I, *Lysis* show a number of predominant moral themes. To begin with, there is a probing of the shaky rational foundations of traditional morality. Nicias and Laches both admire manliness, but are unable to give any clear account of what they admire, let alone of why it is admirable. The same is true of Polemarchus in *Republic* Book I. He is all for justice, but has no clear idea of what he is all for. In the *Meno* and *Protagoras* the question is raised whether virtue can be taught, and in both use is made of the point that familiar models of moral virtue, such as Pericles, proved unable to teach it, which suggests that they had no clear account or justification to pass on to their children. The picture that emerges is of traditional moral views held unthinkingly by many, with puzzlement by others. On the other hand – and this is the second theme – there are also critics of the traditional morality. These take various forms. At their mildest they raise questions for debating purposes as part of a general training in argument in preparation for a career in law or politics, as perhaps Gorgias and Protagoras. At a more serious level they delight in sceptical verbal gymnastics like Polus in the *Gorgias*. At their worst they openly advocate the abandonment of normal moral standards and the adoption of a more self-centred form of life altogether, as Callicles in the *Gorgias* or Thrasymachus in the *Republic*. In face of such critics the position of someone brought up in the traditional moral norms is extremely precarious. With his confused views it is easy to produce examples of enemies who would be friends by his account, cowards whom he would have to account brave, unjust acts he would have to call just. He may, like Cephalus in *Republic* Book I, turn a deaf ear to the pestering questions of the intelligentsia, but if he consents to think he will be liable to the dangers described in *Republic* Book VII (538c–e), of being shown that what he considers just might as well be called unjust until he loses all faith in moral distinctions.

The sceptical criticisms portrayed not only show differences as regards the seriousness with which they are followed through, they also take rather different forms, and are not always seen as sceptical by their holders. The title 'sceptical' is given because Plato seems to have thought that that was their tendency. Sometimes, the view is a form of relativism, to the effect that norms of what is right and wrong differ from society to society, and there is no such thing as an objective moral norm, if this means a norm that can be shown to be right without reference to any particular society. Such relativism can itself, of course, be developed in various ways. From the fact that there is no particular set of norms that all societies either do or should adhere to, it does not follow that a society could or might as well exist without any set of norms. A person could, therefore, develop a view which looked on moral norms as necessary for the cohesion of society, while also holding that variations in environmental conditions, temperament, state of intellectual and cultural development would obviously make different norms right for different societies. Something of this sort is suggested in the *Protagoras* (cf. 319 seq.). Such a view might allow that man's nature required some norms, but the actual variation in norms between known societies might suggest a plasticity in human nature indicating that the forms the norms take is a matter of convention only. This might tempt a person to a more radical position. So far moral norms have been defined in terms of a type of purpose – the cohesion of society – and this might be felt to put some limits, however broad, on the content of the conventions. Someone impressed by the variations between societies might slip into thinking of moral norms as ones predominant in a given group. Defined in this way, the title 'moral' yields no limits on the content of moral norms. If in a given group a man is admired for his capacity to flourish without depending on others, then that will count as a moral ideal. Now the insistence that morality is a matter of convention is stronger. It is an insistence that there is complete freedom with regard to the content of moral norms, and with this view of morality it becomes a good question whether moral norms have any importance at all. On a general survey they seem often inconvenient to the individual, so why not drop them?

In this way a position that starts off as a form of relativism may develop into a more radical rejection found in Callicles in the *Gorgias* and Thrasymachus in *Republic* Book I. This form of scepticism does not normally bother with relativism, but is a direct challenge to anything resembling a set of norms governing just, honest and generally virtuous behaviour. The objection is that a man who submits to these norms is rather evidently accepting a way of life where he agrees not to get all he wants and not to do as he wants. It cannot therefore be a life that he or anyone else can really want, and only weakness or stupidity can explain his acceptance of it. The characteristic of moral codes seized on is that their rules enjoin or forbid behaviour irrespective of what the agent might want to do. It now becomes a good question why one should accept such restrictions on one's pursuits. The obvious answer is that men cannot get on alone but need the help of others. This necessitates a certain give and take and the acceptance of limitations on one's behaviour that one would do without if one could. All this is an explanation in terms of weakness. It has no persuasive power to a man perfectly able either to get along independently or to master others so as not to have to accept restrictions himself. In such a case we should have to suppose a certain measure of either weakness or stupidity. If we suppose neither defect, then we are left with no reason why such a person should accept the restrictions of moral behaviour. But clearly stupidity and incompetence are defects. Everyone recognises the desirability of competence and intelligence. So it is now clear that without these defects no reasonable man would be moral, and so virtue is only desirable to someone in a defective state. It cannot therefore be part of a human ideal.

In this sort of scepticism the contrast between nature and convention has a different twist. To begin with there is no tendency to undermine the possibility of generalisations about human nature. On the contrary, the view depends on one. What is questioned is that virtue is naturally suitable for human beings. Convention, on the other hand, tends to get a slightly stronger sense, closer to law – which, of course, the relevant Greek word means. Granted what human nature is really like, it would obviously need some near-enforceable agreement or legislation to bring about virtuous behaviour.

What is common to all these forms of scepticism is the doubt they raise as to the possibility of any general argument to the effect that a traditional ideal of life is best. Even the milder form of relativism only supplies an answer, if it does, to why these norms are best for this society. It supplies no means of arguing whether we should try to change the society, nor any answer to the individual who asks 'is it best for me?' The more rampant sceptic supplies an argument for supposing that morality is not really good for anyone.

In Plato's view it is of the utmost importance to know whether the sceptic is right. For the issue is one of how one should live one's life (cf. *Republic* 352d). Any moral code embodies a claim about how it is best to live, and the claim is that this holds indifferently for all men. If that claim can be made good, then morality has a message for everyone; if, on the other hand, traditional morality has the wrong answer, or is wrong in supposing there is any such general answer, that too would be important to know. The problem, of course, is how to go about settling the question.

Plato has a variety of approaches to this, some of which I shall leave aside. Sometimes he relies on portrayal of the admirable moral life to appeal to our better natures. Thus in the *Symposium*, the *Phaedo* and the *Crito*, for instance, considerable use is made of the portrayal of Socrates, an obviously upright man in unwavering pursuit of truth and justice and with no interest in power or wealth. The calibre of the central figure plays at least as important a role as the cogency of his arguments. At other times there is an attempt to show that the position put forward is not clear. This is a common technique in probing common moral positions, but is also evident, for instance, in some of the arguments against Polus in the *Gorgias* or Thrasymachus in *Republic* Book I. A third manœuvre is to take one of the opposition's terms of praise or contempt and try to turn it back on them. Thus, for instance, Callicles obviously despises the ordinary moral man for his lack of self-sufficiency and independence and his fawning consideration of other people's wishes and requirements. Socrates draws out the implications of Callicles' position until he is able to develop a picture of Callicles' ideal man as a fawning slave of his bodily desires with no genuine independence or control of his life at all. It looks as though Plato thinks that Callicles is in part rightly admiring certain qualities, but mistakenly and confusedly supposing that they will be manifested in a certain form of life. The style of argument is *ad hominem* and relies on the 'genuine' admiration surviving the argument and militating against the attraction of the simple pursuit of pleasure or whatever it may be.

All the three approaches mentioned above have the limitation that even when they involve argument and not just rhetoric their application is limited to a particular form of opponent and showing his position either to be unclear or to commit him to what he was hoping to reject. Even if Plato thinks that all men do or should admire the qualities that Thrasymachus or Callicles admire, these approaches supply no argument to that effect. The fourth approach to scepticism differs in just this respect, that it is an attempt to provide a general argument for the desirability of virtue for each individual.

It is important to get clear just what it is that Plato is looking for here. It is possible to try to distinguish moral from other codes or sets of norms by characterising how moral arguments go, what counts as a moral justification. Thus it looks as though one point that many utilitarians wish to make is that moral norms are distinguished from others in that they are aimed at the greatest happiness of the greatest number. Armed with the utility principle we can understand what morality is about. But, of course, if that is all, it seems always conceivable that someone should have no interest in the greatest happiness of the greatest number, and if he asks 'why should I be bothered about it?' we have so far no answer. The principle of utility is of no help at this point as it is precisely what he wants a reason for adopting. While it may (or may not) correctly explain what distinguishes moral from other interests, it is not a reason why someone lacking such interests should adopt them. One can either interpret the question 'why should I be bothered about it?' as 'why (morally) should I be bothered about it?' on the above account of 'moral'. In that case it is like asking why medically one should be interested in health, and collapses into 'why from the point of view of concern for general happiness should one be concerned for the general happiness?' Alternatively, it might be interpreted as 'give me a cogent reason for bothering about it', with no restriction by type of context on what will count as cogent. The challenge now is to produce some reason for taking 'it makes for the general happiness' as a reason in favour of an action or policy. It is this sort of reason that Plato is after. Further, as, in the sort of argument I shall consider, he is wanting to pass beyond *ad hominem* considerations, he needs a reason that can confidently be supposed to apply to all men.

It might be worth pausing at this point to ask what form such a reason might take. Ambitions such as the one that I am attributing to Plato are common in the history of ethics and exercise a perennial attraction, but philosophers' attempts to satisfy them have taken a variety of forms. Some awareness of this variety will help get clearer the lines of Plato's attempts. The variety can be limited by noting that Plato's reactions take a form determined by an assumption about what constitutes a reason in the area of action. This assumption is common to Plato and his opponents and is that to give a reason for a policy or an action is to show it to answer to some desire(s). To show there is no reason is to show what is in question to fail to answer to any desire. The criticism of Thrasymachus and others was that traditional morality only answers to desires under certain undesired conditions of weakness and stupidity, and *therefore* where these conditions do not hold there is no reason to accept it. Clearly in face of such a criticism someone who wished to defend traditional morality might hope to use the assumption in his favour, and its usability for this purpose might strengthen its inherent plausibility in his eyes. The project then will be to show in some way that traditional morality does answer to desire.

Such a project might be pursued, as sometimes by morally minded hedonists, by arguing that to desire is to aim at pleasure, and that strength of desire is a function of the degree of pleasure foreseen from a course of action – degrees, of course, being a matter of intensity, spread, etc. (cf. Bentham, 1789, chapter 4). If it can now be shown that observation of the traditional moral norms conduces to the greatest pleasure, it has been shown that what really meets our desire is a traditionally virtuous life. If we remember the fate of the utilitarian answer to 'why be virtuous?', it is easy to appreciate the attraction of the hedonist move. For the utilitarian answer left itself open to the question 'why should I bother about other people's happiness?' If some hedonist accounts are right the analagous question is blocked in their case. The answer to 'why should I want pleasure?' is simply 'you cannot help it. Pleasure is the only object of all wanting.' This usually amounts to the claim that all successful deliberate behaviour is a function of what the agent believes will be most pleasant. If, therefore, any given agent deliberately avoids virtue, it must be because of some false belief about virtue's pleasure-producing properties. So even if our arguments fail to persuade him, he can at least be convicted of error. We are not left with a collision between rival ideals that cannot in principle be settled because there is simply no question of either side being right or wrong.

This approach is one which notoriously Plato did not, at least in most of his works, favour. Why not will be considered later. For the moment I just want to contrast it with the lines taken, especially in the *Republic*. In particular it is noticeable that neither Plato nor his opponents are offering something of which men's deliberate actions are always a function. The sceptic in question is ready enough to admit that in fact the average fool's deliberate behaviour is a function of what he deems honest or just, and so, in a superficial sense, he may be said to want to be honest and just. The argument is about what he would want to pursue if certain conditions did not obtain. Consequently the sceptic here is not claiming that the traditional moral man is mistaken about the means of obtaining what he is after. The claim is not even that it would be better for him to behave otherwise. The issue is about actual ideals, as to whether every man's ideal is to be able to be other than virtuous, and as to what the right ideal is. It emerges that it is a man's ideal to be otherwise if the only reason why he is not is the possession of certain characteristics such as stupidity or weakness, generally acknowledged to be defects. The argument for virtue is won, therefore, not by showing it to be a requirement of the object of every desire, but by showing it to be a requirement for the satisfaction of everyone's ideal.

It therefore becomes a question how we establish what a person's ideal is. On this Plato takes two quite distinct lines. The first, which will be considered in the present chapter, is to argue that a traditionally virtuous life is the one that best answers to the desires integral to a human person; the second, to be considered in the next chapter, is to win agreement that everyone would admit that the ideal is to get the best out of life, and then to argue that that admission can be used to rule out certain ways of life as unideal. Expressing what a person's ideal is in terms of what he really wants, the second approach takes it that we can discover what he really wants by extracting from him a top-level description under which anything he is to acknowledge as ideal must fall. The first, by contrast, operates without regard to a subject's admissions, and aims, by description of the desires that everyone has, to argue that various ideals of life fail in greater or less degree to meet them fully, leaving only one ideal as adequate. This argument about what men really want, therefore, does not concern that of which all deliberate behaviour can be seen to be a function – the thesis concerns modes of life, not particular actions – but is about what life fits all men's ideals. For this it is important to be able to show that in some sense all men do share an ideal, and the argument now to be considered is that all men share a certain desire structure and only a certain manner of life satisfies that structure. While the style of argument and analysis appears elsewhere, it is at its clearest in the *Republic* and I shall therefore concentrate on that.

The official object of the *Republic* is to decide whether the view that man's excellence consists in being 'just' should be accepted, or whether that ideal should be rejected as Thrasymachus proposes, and Glaucon and Adeimantus fear, in favour of a view of man's excellence as consisting in the ability to do as one wants and satisfy one's own desires without restrictions imposed by the requirements of others. The precise form of the dispute is not easy to determine because at least in Book I there seems to be some vacillation between various forms. When Thrasymachus first states his view at 338 it seems fairly clear that he is giving an analysis of justice in terms of the law. The question 'what is just?' collapses into the question 'what is required by law?' and the law is said always to be geared to the benefit of those in power. Consequently, it is never devised with a view to the benefit of those ruled. Even in a democracy, the laws aim at the preservation of democratic authority, not at the benefit of the individuals who collectively exercise that authority. Invariably justice is the benefit of the stronger.

This is not in any ordinary sense a definition of justice or the law. It is like the slogan 'property is theft' in that it aims succinctly to draw attention to what is believed to hold of the actual operation of the law. The word translated 'just', while the only term to translate the English 'just', is more closely related than is the English word to the notions of law and legality. Thus the Greek for 'the things that are just' is a common expression for 'what is required by law' (cf. e.g. *Protagoras* 327b, *Theaetetus* 172a, Aristotle, *Nicomachean Ethics* V 1129b 11–14, as well as the passages of the *Republic* to be discussed). A positivist view of justice is consequently very natural. At the same time, Socrates' assumption, expressed at *Republic* 348c, that 'justice' constitutes human excellence, would be a natural Greek one at least in many circles.

8

Certainly Thrasymachus, with his wish to equate 'injustice' with human excellence, is being paradoxical. Consequently, there was a tendency to assimilate observance of the law to the conduct of a good man and of what is required by law to what is right, what is required of a good man. Thrasymachus' first point then is that as a matter of fact what is required by law and what is best for the individual are not the same. The law enjoins what is best for the party in power.

At this point Socrates objects that as rulers are fallible they may enjoin what is not to their advantage, in which case it will be right (just, required by law) to do what is not to their advantage. To this there are two obvious possible counters. The first, suggested by Clitophon, is to say that what is required by law is only what the rulers consider to be to their advantage. Thrasymachus rejects this move. It is sometimes said that this is an example of Plato's unfairness to Thrasymachus. Presumably this means that Thrasymachus' position would have been harder to refute if Clitophon's suggestion had been accepted. The difficulty in this is the talk of 'Thrasymachus' position'. It is in fact not clear at first whether his thesis is an historical analysis of the actual tendency of states, or whether it is intended to point out the fact that there is no reason for any individual to enthuse about them. No doubt many people purveying such views conflated these purposes, but the value of inserting a clear rejection of Clitophon's suggestion is to make it clear which form the thesis to be discussed takes. This can hardly be unfair to Thrasymachus. It is not as though there were a single thesis that could be more adequately defended if Clitophon's suggestion were accepted. There are two quite distinct theses and the rejection of Clitophon's suggestion simply makes it clear which is being considered. The result is to make Thrasymachus make the other counter to Socrates' objection, that of holding that mistakes on the part of rulers show them not to be 'stronger' (superior) in the required sense. To count as that they must succeed. The thesis can no longer be about actual rulers and laws. Reference to the historical fact of a general tendency of laws to serve the rulers' benefit focuses attention on the actual ideals of rulers so as to lead us to recognise what constitutes the ideally successful ruler. In consequence 'just' also operates in an ideal context. It doubtless remains true that no legal requirement is aimed at the benefit of the individuals who have to abide by it, but the interest is now in who might value the law and for what reason. The answer is that the person under the law could never have a reason to value it as a benefit *tout court*, but a ruler, someone with power to make the law, granted intelligence, would value it as a means of benefiting himself through the enforced co-operation of others. For a successful ruler will pursue and secure the best for himself (341a–b), and others, obedient to his authority, will ensure that he has the best out of life (343b–d). The word in this last passage, transliterated '*eudaimon*', is an adjective indicating that the person to whom it is applied has received the highest possible blessings. It is the usual word for indicating that a person has achieved the ideal condition, and makes it clear that Thrasymachus considers that a perfect ruler and he only can achieve the ideal life.

So far, then, it seems clear that Thrasymachus is holding that the ideal is to be above the need to obey laws, and that such obedience shows weakness and lack of intellectual ability. The position is elaborated mainly with regard to the law, but seems intended to apply equally to moral standards not enforced by law. For anyone who accepts these is thereby agreeing to forego his own advantage on occasion in favour of the advantage of that section of society whose interests the morality in question serves. If Thrasymachus was to be portrayed as holding a position about the law only then he would have had to be described as making that point especially. The word for 'law' (*nomos*) is the one used to speak of convention (cf. *Gorgias* 482–3, *Cratylus* 384–5), and the word for 'justice' covers the law and sub-legal moral conventions equally.

It looks, however, as though Socrates is taking on a variety of theses. In Book I 351 onwards he argues that 'justice' is necessary both for groups and for individuals if they are to be capable of achieving their ends. The argument for its necessity for groups is that even if you take a gang of thieves (prima facie a group with no concern for 'justice'), it is clear on a little reflection that if the members of the gang wronged each other the gang would fall apart. 'Injustice causes quarrels, hatred and internecine warfare, justice unity of purpose and friendship' (351d). What is not clear is that the members of such a gang must recognise the principles of conduct that Socrates wishes to uphold. Indeed, it is only obvious that they must accept some principles of organisation as distinct from each member operating independently for himself. There is consequently some uncertainty as to whether Socrates is arguing that even thieves must, if they are 'jointly pursuing a dishonest end', have a code of honour, or just that in these circumstances they need some organisation, some rules binding their efforts together. The latter at least is clearly necessary. Even if the first is meant, we only have an argument against someone who rejects any sort of moral code, not against someone who rejects the traditional Greek one. If the second is meant, we only have an argument against someone who wishes to reject the value even of organisation. No doubt the tenor of Thrasymachus' remarks suggests that even the need to co-operate rather than dominate is a sign of weakness, but the fact remains that 'justice' would be given a slightly different interpretation. Once again, because of its closeness to 'law', 'rule', the word could admit of it.

The argument that even an individual needs 'justice' (351e–352a) is developed as though it is an application to individuals of the point just made about groups. It is difficult to interpret notions such as a sense of honour or justice as applied to the individual (or his desires) in relation to himself (or each other). On the other hand, if the point about groups is that for effective operation they need organisation and discipline, the application to the individual would be less bizarre. The picture would be of a person having a number of desires or interests, analogous to individuals in a group with divergent interests. Just as a gang of thieves can be seen as organised for the benefit of its members who accept temporary restrictions on the achievement of interests for their fuller satisfaction in the long term, so an individual may be viewed as having a set of disparate desires and interests and needing to accept some ordering and organisation if they are to be variously met. Without some order of priorities an individual would collapse into a set of warring desires with the strongest at any moment carrying him off. The point may be that any such person is obviously a far cry from the well-organised highly competent Thrasymachean ideal, or it may be the stronger one that even following one desire in preference to others involves, however temporarily, setting aside the pursuit of other goals and accepting whatever organisation of one's immediate future is needed to attain the goal. In either case what is argued for is some degree of organisation or discipline. Yet this is hardly anything that Thrasymachus would want to reject. On the contrary, to satisfy his ideal a man would have to be very clear on his order of priorities and self-disciplined in the pursuit of them. One misplaced orgy could easily be his downfall.

This may simply be fraudulent behaviour on Plato's part, but just as possibly it is an indication of how he sees the issue. For at least the point is now made that anyone who is going effectively to pursue goals of the long-term complexity advocated by Thrasymachus will need some disciplined organisation of his life, some firm views on the extent to which his various inclinations should be satisfied. The issue then is what form this self-discipline should take. As the need for it arises from the complexity of men's desires this can only be answered by seeing what men's desires are, and whether any particular form of organisation of life is needed to satisfy them. This is why Plato's account of 'justice' in Book IV strikes one as so strange. The modern, and perhaps the ancient reader, might well expect some argument to show that it is to a man's advantage to acknowledge the normal obligations of justice. In fact the argument is that it is to a man's advantage to have his various psychic tendencies properly fulfilled, each playing its proper role, and that (cf. 433–5 and 442d–444e) is to say it is to his advantage to be 'just'. In other words 'justice' is being wrenched to mean 'proper organisation of one's life'. It is also true, as I shall argue later, that because of the constitution of the human personality, a person whose life is so organised will recognise the obligations of justice, but that is not what the dispute is in the first place about.

If one moves to the early part of Book II, where the challenge to Socrates is refurbished, this point becomes clearer. Glaucon wishes to be shown what 'justice' does that it should be considered something that we should agree to pursue for its own sake and not just for its consequences. He puts forward the thesis that what is by nature good (i.e. in the context, what we should agree to pursue for its own sake) is to ride roughshod over others. The evil of being on the losing side, however, so outweighs the benefit of winning through that, rather than risk losing, those who cannot be sure of winning contract for a second best. The compromise course is to agree to the laws/conventions of justice, whereby in return for not riding roughshod over others one is saved from similar treatment by others (359a–b).

This shows that men are only unwillingly virtuous (cf. *Republic* 360c), because of their inability to succeed by disregarding morality. If everyone had the power to do as he wanted, then he would act as his desire dictated, not as justice requires (359c). What Socrates has to show is that 'justice' is something that we should want even if it did not bring the benefit of saving us from being wronged by others. If we move on to Book IX where refutation of Thrasymachus is concluded, we find Thrasymachus' emphasis on freedom (344c) and the present passage echoed. The tyrannical state, and the type of personality analogous to it, are less free than any other, considered as a whole (577d–e and 579e); the tyranny-type individual does what he wants less than any other.

This shows that Plato considered the challenge to be to show that 'justice' produces a life that satisfies all our desires, and so is something that we should want for its own sake. But there is a difficulty in this. For surely this is only showing that 'justice' has good effects, in that it ensures that our desires are satisfied, and that is not to show it to be good in itself. To this two points can be made. First, we have to interpret the challenge to show 'justice' to be good for its own sake in the sense given to the terms by Plato. At 357b it is clear that to say something is good for its own sake is to say that *we* should be glad to have it, not because we were pursuing anything else by means of it, but because we were fond of it for itself, and pleasure is the example. In other words, if it answers our desires as their final object it is good for its own sake. So if 'justice' is shown to meet our desires it is shown to be good for its own sake, on this reading of that expression.

Second, although Glaucon makes a distinction between the effects of something and the thing itself, he also (358b) asks Socrates to show what power justice has of itself in a man's life (soul), without regard to various possible rewards, and this seems to be meant just to repeat the challenge. But it is impossible to give the power of justice without reference to the effect it has. Consequently, 'effect' must be being interpreted too broadly for Glaucon's purposes in the above objection. Some indication of his distinction can perhaps be got by an analogy. Suppose a university has been muddling along fairly happily, but is contemplating the introduction of business organisation. Critics ask, 'what will business organisation do for us?' To this there seem to be two sorts of answer. First, it might be claimed that it would produce an efficient system of filing and accounting, regular monthly cheques of the right amount and so on. Second, it might be claimed that it would give the university a better public image, especially in the eyes of business firms from whom it was hoped to attract grants. These sorts of answer differ, in that the first seems to be spelling out what having such organisation amounts to. Absence of these features is proof of the absence of the organisation. It is here impossible to distinguish between saying what business organisation does and saying what it is (or, in Plato's language, giving its nature). The second answer, on the other hand, appeals to effects that are contingent on other people's views, and invites the objection that in that case it is not that business organisation is good in itself that is claimed, but only for its effects.

This is, I think, the way that Glaucon's distinction operates. Considering the power of 'justice', as distinct from its effects, is considering those effects which are necessary conditions of the presence of 'justice' as distinct from others that are not. These effects are that every part of the soul plays its proper role, in the language of Book IV, or that considered as a whole a man's desires are satisfied in the language of Book IX.

The challenge, then, is to show that by adopting 'justice' a man is adopting something desirable for itself, even if it fails to bring in further extrinsic bonuses. To show it to be desirable is taken as showing that it secures the satisfaction of desires. The argument is to the effect that the acceptance of a certain discipline of life (more or less corresponding to traditional norms of virtue) meets this requirement. It is shown to do so, however, by being considered in the first instance as a method of organising a person's life, rather than as, say, a system of obligations. It is only in this way that it can be shown to be desirable for itself. The reason why showing it to be desirable is showing it to answer desires is that Glaucon is arguing that what we all want, left to ourselves, is to do what we want. This is ambiguous as between 'doing as we want' (and so collecting connotations of freedom) and 'doing what will satisfy us'. It is a fair presumption that in Thrasymachus' eyes a man who failed to satisfy his desires would be unideal, so that some expertise about his desires and how to satisfy them would be needed.

13

It would therefore be a natural move to argue that if he knew the truth about his desires he would recognise that only a virtuous life answers to them. This, however, would require some analysis of desires, and if the argument is to apply to all men, the relevant desires must be integral to the human person. This is precisely what Plato aims to supply.

In Books II–IV Socrates sketches the foundation of a city with the purpose of discovering what part 'justice' plays in it. This amounts to asking when and why law is required. While this gives Plato the opportunity for a good deal of political and educational provocation, the official reason is that if we see the conditions that require law in a state we may hope for insight into the conditions needed within an individual. (The translation 'law' makes the transition to the individual less startling, and brings out Plato's point better.) The need in the state arises from the need for different types of person educated to different aspirations which all have to be made to serve the whole. When the question is raised about applying the analogy to the individual, it is argued that the predominant characteristics of the types of person required for the state, are all found to some extent in each individual. That some, as it were personal, law is required is shown by an argument that assumes that the various characteristics are types of desire. At 437b–c it is claimed that for present purposes words such as 'want', 'desire', 'wish', 'be prepared to' come to much the same thing, and that if we are to say that one of this list holds of someone and the negation of one of the list also holds with regard to the same object at the same time in the same respect, then it must be in some sense of different parts of the person that the positive and negative ascriptions hold. There are then illustrations of familiar cases where people do and do not want to do the same thing, so requiring different parts of the person to do the wanting. As it stands the argument doubtless proves either too much or too little, but for the present it is enough that the division into three parts of the soul is at least intended to establish a distinction between three sorts of desire, and three sorts essential to the human person at least during his embodied life. Any man, therefore, manifests three different sorts of desire that at times conflict with each other. Some personal legislation is needed to ensure that each plays its proper role.

So far, then, we have the expected analysis of desires integral to the human person, requiring some ordering. When this is pursued further in Books VIII and IX we find a description of a rake's progress from the ideal situation to a tyrannical state and each portrayal of a state is a model for a condition of the individual. It is clearly brought out that as the degeneration proceeds a person's higher aspirations receive progressively less fulfilment, so that in the final state a person can be described as fulfilling his desires less than anyone, if one considers him in the round.

Some of the details will be considered further later in this chapter and in later chapters. For the moment it is enough to see the direction of the argument, which is clearly to the effect that only a certain form of personal law or discipline gives one a life where all one's desires are fulfilled. How the gap between some law or other and a particular form of it is bridged will be considered later. At present let us suppose that that is satisfactorily done (as Plato must hope). Then the refutation of Thrasymachus takes the form of arguing that if we are to be successful in getting what we want we must first know what we want; an examination of the human personality reveals that all men have three different types of want; the only way of achieving all we want is to accept a certain discipline of life which alone ensures that *all* our wants are satisfied; consequently virtue ('justice') is what we really want and for its own sake (i.e. quite apart from honours and the rest, 'justice' is the answer to our desires).

This answer has an obvious air of relevance to Thrasymachus' position, but it is worth asking how good it is. If the opposition has claimed that the ideal was either to satisfy every type of desire that stirs in a man's breast, or to live a life with no unsatisfied desires, then the argument would be directly relevant; for it is precisely to the effect that in a just life every *type* of desire (but not every instance of every type, for some of these might be distortions of the type or occur at untoward times) is satisfied and a life with no unsatisfied desire is provided. But the position attributed to Thrasymachus and re-furbished by Glaucon and Adeimantus is not clearly of this form. Their argument is to the effect that while men pursue other things, what every man would want if he had the power would be to be free of 'justice'. Even the challenge at the beginning of Book II is that Socrates should show that 'justice' is something that we would agree to have for its own sake if we understood what it was. But Socrates does nothing to show that we would want it. He needs to show that we would all want a life with no unsatisfied desire. But by the time someone has contemplated the long effort needed to secure such a life (see the educational programme, especially Book VII), the sort of desire predominantly satisfied and the short commons given to more interesting desires, he might well think the price too high and prefer a life which, while containing some disappointments and lacking the delights of philosophy, is well stocked with both the quiet and exciting pleasures of ordinary men. To rule out this possibility Socrates would need to show, say, that all desire is in fact aimed at a situation where no unsatisfied desire exists. This would certainly have the strength aimed at by many hedonists in that if true, then the 'just' life would be what alone satisfies the requirements of desire, so that only lack of knowledge or conviction would explain someone's not wanting it. On the other hand it would, on the face of it, be less plausible than the hedonist approach, and there is no sign of it in the *Republic*. Alternatively, he could introduce some further factor that made alternative ways of life clearly not what one would want, and this is what he in fact does.

If we take what Plato considers he has already got, and interpret the argument as one about what men really want, we can consider forms of the claim about real wants that might appear hopeful and try to isolate the one chosen by Plato. In this case, one form such a claim often takes is to the effect that while the life of pleasure, say, or of dutiful citizenship, has its satisfactions, they pale into insignificance compared with those of the form of life being advocated. There is some sign of this approach in the *Republic*. The glowing picture of the central books, the imagery of the sun, the vision of the form of the good, and the argument about the superior pleasantness of the philosophic life in Book IX, are all more or less explicit claims that if people had more understanding or more experience they would want what Plato advocates. It is not, however, a very profitable line for the purpose in hand. For it is not a thesis about what everyone's ideal is, but about what everyone's ideal would be, if he were different. The original Thrasymachus/Glaucon contention was that everyone's ideal already is to be free of the requirements of virtue, and only weakness explains its not being an operative ideal. It is not to the point against this to claim that the ideal would be different if people were different.

A slightly stronger position would be one that claimed not merely that a life of virtue would in fact leave no desire unsatisfied (where a desire that could be aroused and satisfied, but is not, counts), but also that unsatisfied desires make themselves felt in the unsatisfied life, so serving as a constant reminder of its unideal nature. Thus it may be that a man is jealous of one of his colleagues and has a desire to see him fail in his bid for fame and promotion. As he is an upright man, however, none of his behaviour is directed to this goal, and so it is useless for predicting what steps he will take. Nevertheless, it is a desire that needs constant efforts to suppress and accounts for the rigidity of his smile and the slightly forced air of his gaiety at his rival's success. In this way talking of it as unsatisfied is not a claim about the absence of satisfaction of a hypothetical or dormant desire, nor of a present but untroublesome desire. The lack of satisfaction results in some disturbing dissatisfaction.

Of this, too, there are some signs in the *Republic*. The tyrannical city in Books VIII–IX is one where a single man is constantly wracked with fear and having to keep constant watch on possible usurpers. The individual corresponding to this model is dominated by some desire or set of desires and constantly having to be on the lookout for possible influences that would disturb the pattern of domination. The picture is of a man who, say, is dominated by a desire for his home comforts and security. But he is aware that he is vulnerable to appeals to his sympathy and tends in consequence to walk away from conversations about the needs of the poor or the mentally retarded. They are a threat to his equanimity. If he listened he might have to stir himself and give up some of his familiar pleasures which have acquired so strong a hold of him. Such a man would be tyrannised by a lower desire operating in fear of usurpation as required by the tyranny model. The suppression of other desires is something active operating against a tendency that makes itself felt. Such a man might wish not to have such desires at all but if Plato is right some desires are ineradicable, being of the soul's very nature. The only way he could be without the resultant dissatisfaction would be to satisfy them.

This again, however, is too weak a move for Plato's purposes. For nothing has been done to show that faced with the option anyone would choose a life without suppressed desire. After all, the option offered is to enter a somewhat gruelling course of training and study leading to a life largely taken up with philosophy and government for the benefit of others. It is not beyond the bounds of imagination that someone might prefer a life that carried a certain amount of suppressed desire, even granted it was a little troublesome, so long as the desires that received satisfaction were ones that yielded, and more readily, more intense pleasure. The objection is that the philosophic life seems an implausible candidate for the position of most people's ideal, that is, what they would want if they had the power.

Whether deliberately or from some feeling for the inadequacy of the position as so far described, Plato in fact inserts something which, if it held, would make the position stronger. This is the view held on physical desire, the 'lowest' part of the soul in the tripartite division, and the insecurity of any person lacking the full development of reason.

Plato's view of the 'lower' desires is one that is strange, once one reflects on it, although it seems to have had an appeal for many moralists. The picture given of physical desires is one that portrays them as insistent and demanding. They are seen as having a tendency to domination which it requires vigilance and firmness to curb. Thus in *Republic* Book IV (442a–b), we are told of reason and the spirited element in the personality that

with such training, having properly learned and absorbed their
own business, these two will take charge of the desiring part –
which is the most extensive element in everyone and naturally
most insatiable; – they will be on the look out to prevent it from
growing in size and strength by the indulgence of so-called
bodily pleasures until it abandons its own role and tries to

subjugate and dominate beyond its proper sphere, and turn everyone's life upside down.

This part of the soul covers desires for nourishment and increase (436a), love, hunger and thirst being cited as examples (439d). These are considered to require constant vigilance if they are not to take a dominant position in a man's life. They are insistent for satisfaction and grow stronger and more demanding with indulgence. The picture is the same early in Book IX, but more dramatic, with its suggestion of Bacchanalian riot as the lower part of the person gets out of hand. This is reinforced later (588 seq.) when these desires correspond to the head of a wild beast in the image.

Now of course it is a familiar fact that some people do become obsessed with physical pleasures. Some people are slothful, others gluttons, drunkards, lechers and so on, and a given person may display more than one of these characteristics. Further, these are people whom Plato's picture fits in proportion to the extent that they manifest the characteristic. The pleasures that preoccupy them tend to obtain a stronger grip on their lives with indulgence, to make them impatient with other pursuits or with considerations of honourable behaviour, to confine the use of their wits to the discovery of means of satisfying their desires. What is strange is that these states should be considered the natural term of such desires as hunger or thirst, so that the indulgence of these needs careful control if gluttony and drunkenness are to be avoided.

To the oddity of this view I shall return later. For the moment I want simply to note the fact and draw out its importance in Plato's argument. For it is clear that the desiring element in the soul plays a vital role, and indeed is needed to show the necessity of 'justice'. At the beginning of his response to Glaucon and Adeimantus Socrates proposes to construct a city to see where 'justice' enters. At first the city is held together by the bond of mutual need. It is, let us note, a city that requires some organisation to meet the ends of its citizens. At 371e 12–13, Socrates asks if we can as yet discern 'justice' or 'injustice'. Adeimantus suggests we look at the mutual dealings of the citizens with regard to their products. Socrates simply says 'Perhaps you are right. We must examine the matter further.' In fact he does not. He describes the general mode of life of the citizens as sufficiently austere to make Glaucon remark that the equipment is no better than that required for a city of pigs. It is now suggested that some luxury is introduced, and Socrates comments (372e) that perhaps that would be no bad thing as we might then get a chance to see how justice and injustice take root.

The importance of all this is as follows: to begin with it gives Plato a chance to make it clear again that he is not concerned with the question of just dealings, but with law. Second, it is not just with law considered as the rules of organisation in a voluntary association. It becomes clear as the *Republic* develops that the introduction of luxury is what leads to the need not simply for organisation, but for the power to enforce it. Luxury is not given to the guardians in the city, but only to the artisans who are the city's counterpart to the individual's desiring element – they are, in effect, the city's desiring element. They consequently need more than just organisation, they need controlling (431c9–d1). The controlling is done by the legislators whose decisions are enforced by the military. When this happens, when the law/justice is effectively present, the result is a city which is a single city, every class performing its appropriate role. 'Justice' and law over and above mere organisation are needed because the introduction of luxury brings in an element of disturbance. The lower desires of the individual or of the artisan class tend to produce a divided person, or cities within cities. 'Justice' removes the discord, forbids trespass beyond one's proper function and so enforces harmony (cf. e.g. 443c–e, 462).

All this indicates that Plato was clear as to the special disturbing role of 'desire' as the condition that leads to the need for 'justice' or discipline. Further, he feels that 'justice' has a very precarious hold on the average virtuous person because such a person cannot grasp exactly why it is best to be disciplined. The dangers of undermining are described, for instance, at 538c–e, and more dramatically in the rake's progress of Books VIII and IX. It is of some interest that when Plato describes the change from philosopher to timocrat he does not describe an individual who is a philosopher changing. It is the philosopher's son who is worked on at an early age. Now this child cannot possibly be a philosopher – one has to have been through a considerable curriculum for that. The next degeneration is also described as occurring in the philotimic man's son, but we are explicitly told (553a9–10) that the son starts by emulating his father – and as children can manifest 'spirit', this is in order. The corruption here, therefore, and in the subsequent examples is of someone from one condition to a relatively degenerate one. Lacking the clear light of reason, any such person is a ready victim to the blandishments offered, especially if he or his father are also afflicted with misfortune. The picture given is of there being no sure resting place between the condition of philosopher and that of tyrant. Further, all the moves from the philotimic condition are under the influence of the love of money—one of the names for the desiring part – and the story of degeneration is a story of the weakening influence of other inclinations and the growing dominance of the lowest ones. These, as we have seen, are viewed as tending to obsessive extremes if left to themselves, and consequently yield a picture of the personality and life dominated by them as one that not only involves suppression of other desires, but as turbulently ruled by insatiable passions in a way calculated to make it a not unduly attractive option to most of Plato's readers.

At this point one might hope to object that while that option is one that no one would consider ideal, Plato himself gives us others. It is here that the imperialist tendencies of the lower desires and the importance of reason come into play. For what Plato wants to convince us of is that there is no sure option between the two. I cannot, say, decide to be or decide to bring up my child to be, a person who admires rich men and the pursuit of wealth, but draws back from the out and out rule of passion of the tyrannical-type personality. That is to say, if I recognise the facts, I shall realise that I have opted for a mode of life in which I cannot be sure of persisting. For my persistence will depend on my not suffering various misfortunes. External circumstances are needed to keep the balance, and over these I have no control. So while conditions exist between those of the philosopher and those of the undisciplined man, no one can say with any assurance 'I am going to be (remain) a philotimic man, and not bother about philosophy.' If a man becomes a philosopher he can say with assurance that that is how he will go on living, and if he declares himself against philosophy and the ideals of the spirited part, he can be sure of an undisciplined life. In between, it is a matter of chance.

The result of this is that by introducing the desiring part of the personality as a disordered element with a tendency to domination of a person's life, Plato hopes to be able to depict the choice as basically between a philosophical and a totally undisciplined obsessive life. Anyone would want to avoid the latter as portrayed. Consequently anyone in full possession of the facts would want to be a philosopher. The result is produced not by discovering what everyone's ideal is, but by bringing out what is everyone's ideal not to be. This negative approach is necessitated by the fact that to no one but a philosopher could one give any account of a philosophical life that he could readily appreciate. It remains, however, that Plato in fact does something to fill the gap mentioned earlier, and brings some argument for supposing that the only real alternative to undergoing philosophy is a life no one would willingly choose.

It all, however, depends very much on two props: the first, the view of the lower desires, the second, the role of reason. The second I shall leave to a later chapter. The first can be appropriately touched on now. As already mentioned some such view of physical desires has had some vogue with moralists, and it is worth querying it. To begin with, one might well ask what the connection is between hunger and an inordinate interest in food? Plato talks as though we should be sparing of our indulgence of our appetites as indulgence brings increase. I have used the word 'appetite' because of its vagueness. If one substitutes 'hunger' it is far from obvious that the satisfaction of hunger gives rise to a stronger more imperious hunger next time. Similarly, quenching one's thirst regularly does not lead to addiction. In this case the matter is if anything clearer, since the life-dominating desire is associated not simply with drink, but with alcohol. Not even a pint of milk a day will produce drunkenness.

Conversely, it is not at all characteristic of those with inordinate desires for food or drink to feel constantly hungry or thirsty. The Roman vomitorium was intended to produce not hunger, but room. Plato must, therefore, hold the empirical and unsubstantiated thesis that there is a connection between the regular satisfaction of hunger and the development of gluttony. There is at least as much plausibility in supposing a constant refusal to satisfy hunger to be connected with an inordinate interest in food. In practice, of course, it is the disordered interest about which Plato is concerned. On the other hand, it is hunger and thirst (e.g. 437d, 439b–e) that are taken as typical examples of physical desire, and which (442a–b) are considered to have imperialistic tendencies. Since hunger only dominates the lives of the underfed, this last passage must consider gluttony as the development of hunger, or hunger must be an exception in that it loses its domineering tendencies if satisfied. The importance of citing hunger rather than gluttony, however, is fairly obvious. Plato needs desires that can be imputed to everyone as integral to their nature. Only then can 'justice' be shown to be best for everyone. Hunger, thirst and sexual desire are fairly obvious candidates. Gluttony, drunkenness and lechery are not obvious elements in everyone's life. Explanation, however, is not justification.

It is also worth bearing in mind that if one observes one's fellow men the impression given is that large numbers in fact are concerned to produce a life with as many physical comforts and pleasures as they can afford without at all fitting the maniacal picture of Book IX, but yet failing to show that sporadic interest in philosophy or honourable conduct characteristic of the 'democratic' type personality of Book VIII. So long as the pleasures in question are fairly varied it seems possible to live a life wholly devoted to pleasures of this type while remaining sober, temperate and a good husband and father. Indeed, sometimes (cf. e.g. *Phaedo* 69a–b) Plato recognises the possibility – almost. Interestingly, however, what he considers a bastard sobriety is based on a calculation of pleasure and pain – fear of a hangover securing temperance. He does not envisage a man whose appetites are moderate and varied, and whose life fails therefore to show any sign of the febrile anxiety that ought to mark the sybarite.

This brings one to an ambiguity in the notion of physical desire, well obscured by the use of the word 'appetite' in the previous paragraph. A desire may be physical in the sense that its object is either physical well-being or, in Plato's conception, physical pleasure (a notion that must be left as supposedly clear); or it may be physical in that there is some felt physical lack that demands removal. It seems that predominantly at least Plato has in mind, in thinking of the desiring element, the experience of a lack insistent for replenishment. The analysis of physical pleasure in the *Gorgias* (496) concentrates on certain ones (significantly, again, hunger and thirst), supposed typical of the life of pleasure. The analysis is of thirst as a form of distress, caused by a lack, removed by the quenching, a replenishment. In the *Republic* Book IX, there is recognition that some physical pleasures are replenishments of lacks that have not been felt, but most physical pleasures (584c) are releases from felt lacks. (This embodies interpretation: they are first said to be releases from distress; later (585a–b) hunger and thirst are said to be deprivations whose removal is a pleasure.) Hunger and thirst, in fact – typical desiring-element desires – are forms of distress from felt physical deprivation. Later, in the *Philebus* the connection between these felt deprivations (cf. 44–52, desires that are of their nature felt deprivations) and inordinate interest in the related pleasures is made explicit and drawn out in more detail. Plato seems to have felt early on that the disorderly tendencies that he felt to be characteristic of physical desire (cf. e.g. *Phaedo* 64–6, *Phaedrus* 254 seq.) were connected with the 'fact' that such desires were always also cases of felt distress. This gets elaborated as time goes on until in the *Philebus* there is the thesis that such desires correlate with false anticipation (35 seq.) as well as obsession (46–7). While drunkenness and gluttony and so on may not be examples of excessive thirst and hunger, they may plausibly be thought to involve felt physical discomfort that is only removed by indulgence, and so this analysis would hold equally for both, so distracting attention from the differences.

What this account quite overlooks is the possibility of someone being interested in physical pleasures without at the time experiencing any distress, physical or otherwise. Indeed, the object of common observation alluded to above does not usually allow himself to suffer hunger, certainly not in any acute form, nor is he harassed by the glutton's itch. He ensures that his meals are both punctual and pleasurable. He sits down to them and enjoys them. But there is no fever of excitement about them. There are other things in his life. It may be true that physical satisfactions are the only things in his life, but when it is said that that is all he wants the point is not that he is beleaguered by importunate desires, but that these pleasures constitute his objective. This man's desires are what he pursues, Plato's man's physical desires almost pursue him.

The failure to allow for the deliberate hedonist of moderate appetite also makes Plato over-ready to call physical desire and pleasure irrational and hostile to reason (*Republic* 439d 7, *Philebus* 63–4). Even so, there are differences. It is true that hunger in its extreme form may deprive a man of usual moral sensibilities and disable him from thinking of anything but food, and even in its milder forms it simply occurs, quite undaunted by considerations of what is best or most reasonable. This much it has in common with gluttony. But whereas hunger is something it is generally good to satisfy, and extreme hunger something it is unwise to leave too long, gluttony is only good to satisfy if it is a good thing to have such a constant anxiety about food, or if on a given occasion indulgence is the only way of enabling someone to think for a moment of something else. In Plato's view its tendency is to usurp the supremacy of reason not just for a moment, but for the whole of one's life – it distorts a man's conception of what is best in life.

In the above I have concentrated on hunger and thirst, gluttony and drunkenness, and argued that Plato needs to show that the latter are developments from and distortions of the former, bloated by indulgence; and that he also needs to show the impossibility of the apparently common phenomenon of the person whose life is calmly directed to physical pleasures without his being the quivering victim of constant, overpowering physical desires. But these are not, of course, Plato's only examples. A third common one is sexual appetite (cf. *Republic* Book IX 573c–d). Here it is at least more plausible to think of lechery as a disordered form of a desire that can be sedately channelled into marriage. The whole project of an analogy between sexual drive and hunger may, of course, well be questioned, and doubtless should. Plato is not alone in not doing so, however, and it is of some interest that while hunger and thirst are the typical examples when an analysis of physical pleasure/desire is in question, love comes to the fore when the Bacchic potentialities of physical pleasure/desire are the issue. It is a more persuasive example for these purposes, and is arguably Plato's paradigm. Indeed, at one point in the *Philebus* (65–6) Socrates asks whether intelligence or pleasure is more admirable. Protarchus answers that pleasure is so far from being considered admirable that many will only indulge it in the dark. No pleasure is mentioned in Protarchus' statement, but we are clearly intended to understand sexual pleasure which has been mentioned a little earlier and is the example that dominates the passage.

To sum up this chapter briefly: I have argued that one strand in Plato's defence of traditional moral norms is to accept that the norms should take the form of meeting men's desires. If a virtuous life is to be held to make a good man it must be to all men's good. The challenge is to show this in the sense of each man's good where this amounts to showing that it meets each man's desires, even if no extraneous benefits are attached. The general type of strategy is familiar. It amounts to questioning what in fact men want. Plato attempts to show that all men have three distinct types of desire in common, and that they can all be met only by a virtuous life. Consequently, if we consider a person in the round, only a virtuous man really does what he wants. The opposition arguments of Glaucon and Adeimantus appeal to a plausible account of the genesis of societal rules, to our hunch as to everyone's likely action under the hypothetical condition of the power to transgress with impunity, and to the assumed ideal underlying most education. It is fairly clear that showing a virtuous life to be one that meets all desires does not show it to be every man's ideal, or what he would choose if he only had the power. There is no sign that Plato is aware of shifts in the burden of the claim that men really want X, but in fact he supplies an account of the nature of physical desire such that (a) it is all set, unless curbed, to take over a man's life, and (b) a life that is so taken over might be expected to seem unattractive. Even if the account of physical desire were right, he would not have shown that no one does (really) want to be 'unjust' where this means that they would not live that way if they were able. He has only produced a picture such that the chances are that most people would find it unattractive. They might well find the proposed alternative equally unattractive and consider it better to choose an intermediate state with its risks of descent to 'injustice'. So while the claim about the desire-structure of the individual, if right, would be relevant against someone who claimed that satisfying all desires was the ideal – for then any proposed life would be a mistaken solution if it left some unsatisfied – it has no bearing on the question of what everyone would choose. Perhaps Plato was helped by the ambiguity in saying that the ideal is to do what one wants.

I have concentrated on the *Republic* in discussing this argument, but it is not the only source of interest. The view that the ideal is for a man to be able to do what he wants occurs in several places (cf. *Lysis* 207d–e, *Laws* 727a–b). In the *Gorgias* we find Polus (466 seq.) holding that orators are admirable because they can do as they want. Socrates disputes this on grounds to be discussed in the next chapter. Later (489 seq.) Callicles puts forward as ideal a life of intense desire constantly satisfied. To this Socrates opposes an image of Callicles' ideal soul and Socrates'. The point is to underline the impossibility of satisfying Calliclesian desires (a point repeated in different form at *Republic* IX 585–6, *Philebus* 54–5), but there is no development of any distinction of types of desire as found in the *Republic*, nor any attempt to show the superior satisfying power of a virtuous or philosophical life. The hint is there that somehow the one vessel will not be leaky, but elaboration is lacking. At least a twofold division of the soul seems to have been known to Plato at the time of the *Gorgias* (cf. 493), but nothing is made of it. By the time of the *Phaedo* there is more development of the point that there are distinct types of interest. In the *Phaedo* the doctrine of reminiscence, in the *Symposium* the claim that the form of beauty is the proper satisfying object of all love, show that Plato is beginning to make the 'higher' interest characteristic, at least in some embryonic form, of all men. But not until the *Republic, Phaedrus* and *Timaeus* do we get a clearly (though variously) developed view of three types of desire being integral to human beings at least during their physical lives. At least so far as the *Republic* is concerned this is part of the construction of an argument against ideals of the sort put forward by Polus and Callicles in the *Gorgias*, an argument based on a view of the human person to the effect that only a virtuous life can fully satisfy anyone.

In the *Philebus* we do not find the tripartite psychology. It would not, in fact, be directly relevant to the claim that pleasure is the good. There is still, however, an appeal (cf. 21–2) to what men would pursue/want as in some way settling the question of what life is best. The claim that men really want a life containing both pleasure and intelligence, however, is not there based on any claims as to desires they have but do not recognise. It is enough that a given option would patently be rejected as a choiceworthy sort of life by any man. In the *Laws* (733–4), we again find appeal to what men really want and the claim that only the virtuous really do what they want. The psychology of the *Republic* is not, at least explicitly, appealed to, but the style of claim is the same. In all these cases, while there are unacknowledged shifts, the claim is that we can tell what people in some sense really want and thereby determine what life is best, without mediation of the notion of goodness. Plato also often argues that we all really want what is good/best and can then, through the notions of goodness and excellence, determine the content of what we want. This is, even if it is not distinguished, in fact a different argument altogether, and will be recognised as such by a separate chapter.

II

Wanting the Good

Arguments to the effect that all desire is for good are common in the dialogues. That is to say, arguments that meet that rough description are, though they take slightly differing forms and it is not always easy to determine quite how to interpret the conclusion. In the *Gorgias* (466 seq.) Socrates claims that politicians often do not do what they want, although they do what they think best. He argues that people take drugs for the sake of their health, run the risks of a sea-crossing for the sake of profit, and that in general, as in these cases, what the man wants is not what he does (take medicine, sail) but the purpose of these activities. Some things, such as health and wealth are goods, their opposites evils, but a great many things are neither, but take on the character of good or bad or neither according as they are conducive to the first, the second or neither. These neutral things are pursued only for the sake of some good. This is summed up by saying that they are done always 'in pursuit of the good'. A man may, however, be wrong about how to achieve the good, so that while he does what he thinks best he is unable, because of his intellectual failure, to do what in fact he wants to do.

So far this might be interpreted as saying that in every pursuit a man has some goal which he takes as worth pursuing, and that there is a set of goals which men generally consider worth pursuing for their own sakes. There are other activities which men pursue for the sake of some or other of these goals. In general, what a man wants is the goal in question, what he thinks best is what he thinks will achieve the goal. This would be sufficient to indicate that dictators are not all-powerful in that they are liable to error and in that case fail to do what they want.

On the other hand, Socrates does say (468b 1): 'In fact it is in pursuit of the good (*to agathon*) that we walk when we walk.' He could have said: 'In fact it is in pursuit of some good (*agathon ti*). . . .' As it stands, he might well intend the conclusion that everyone, in characterising his goal as good, is showing that there is some objective he has in common with everyone else, and that considerations could be brought to show that his goal was not really good and so not what he really wanted. 'In common with everyone else' is capable of varied interpretation. It may be as weak as 'Everyone wants his own good' (and one man's meat is another man's poison); or it may be 'Everyone wants his own good' (and as all men are basically the same, there is a general account to be given of this); or it may be 'Everyone wants the best state of affairs to obtain.' In any of these cases a person might hope to use the admission that a man wants the good to object to the goals the man in fact has. In this they contrast with two other possibilities: first, that any final goal is in fact a good thing – and that is what gives it its attractive power, though men may not in any way want the best arrangement of goals; second, that when we give a man's goals, as distinct from reporting his inclinations, this is to be expressed in terms of what he considers it good to get as distinct from what he finds attractive. In this case 'Every man pursues/wants the good' might be making a formal point only.

There are signs of some awareness of the formal point on Plato's part. Socrates attributes to Prodicus a distinction between *boulesis* (wanting the good) and *epithumia* (wanting pleasure) at *Protagoras* 340a. This was probably the distinction operative at *Charmides* 167e, where *epithumia* is attached to pleasure, *boulesis* to the good. This looks like distinguishing two notions of wanting, one whereby to say 'Jones wants X' is glossed as 'Jones thinks X is a good thing' and another whereby 'Jones wants X' is glossed as 'Jones considers X would be pleasant.' The *Gorgias* uses the *boulesis* terminology and ties it to the good. The distinction between 'wanting the good' and 'deeming something good' does not rely on contrasting something which really is good with something apparently so, but on distinguishing wanting some goal and considering something to be a good means to it. So Plato could be held to be aware of a three-fold distinction between (i) 'Jones wants Y' = 'Y is Jones's goal' (ii) 'Jones wants X' = 'Jones is after X as the supposed best means to Y' (iii) 'Jones wants X' = 'Jones thinks X pleasant', and he distinguishes the first two in the *Gorgias*. This is not, of course, to say that he always has the distinctions in mind. In the *Republic* he needs a use of 'want' to cover (i) and (iii) indifferently, and ignores (ii). The distinction of (i) and (iii) is there made not by contrasting terms but by talk of different desires, and the difference is not marked by the difference of good and pleasure as objects, at least not in any clear way.

In the *Gorgias*, however, (i) and (ii) are definitely distinguished, and (i) is expressed also as 'Jones considers Y a good thing to aim at.' It is a question whether Plato thinks that that is merely a formal point, or whether he thinks that the use of the word 'good' allows of dispute over the correctness of taking certain goals as objects of pursuit for their own sakes. It seems fairly clear that in the *Gorgias*, however bad the argument, the assumption is that certain conditions of character can be shown to be bad, or must be agreed to be bad. The conclusion at 468e is that tyrants are not necessarily powerful, since they may well not do what they want. Polus remarks that Socrates, like anyone else, would be glad to have a tyrant's power. Socrates objects that this 'power' is only a good thing if the exercise of it is beneficial (470a–b) (i.e. only in that case is it what one wants). The argument then is that injustice is not beneficial, and that, if accompanied by no wish to remedy it, it is the worst of evils (down to 479d). This justifies Socrates' contention that wronging people is not what anyone wants, though it may be what someone mistakenly deems best.

It seems, then, that here Plato treats it as a point yielding substantial conclusions that everyone wants what is best. It is doubtful, however, whether one can attribute to him, as yet at least, any clear grasp of the possibility that 'Jones thinks *X* pleasant' does not entail 'Jones thinks *X* a good thing.' So far as the *Gorgias* is concerned, or the argument at *Meno* 77–8, there is no indication that the point is not meant to hold of any example of desire. There is, indeed, the suggestion from the way each passage runs that Plato has pursuits in mind, examples where a person acts on his desire and does not just yearn; and in the *Gorgias* passage 'pursue' and 'want' seem interchangeable for the purposes of the argument. But there is no suggestion that some desires, such as hunger, are directed to pleasure, not the good. In the *Meno* passage, indeed, the two words '*epithumia*' and '*boulesis*' which at *Charmides* 167e seem to mark some such distinction, are used interchangeably.

By the *Phaedo* (cf. 64 seq.) there is a clear attempt to contrast the pursuits of the intellect/soul with the distracting clamours of the body. The first is directed at the truth about the nature of things, the latter at a variety of pleasures. Bodily appetites are clearly a hindrance to the operations of reason, and it seems (cf. 97–8) that those operations are, at least ideally, directed to the question of what is best. But this seems to be in contrast with 'physical' desires. Since the body is viewed as a temporary appendage of the person, who is essentially his soul, the *Phaedo* seems to show some awareness of the need for some qualification of the thesis 'all desire is for the good'. If we are to say, even, 'all men always desire the good' we shall have to be clear that men are essentially souls, and so preserve the thesis by interpreting counter-examples of drunkards, or hungry men going after food without thinking, as being men driven by their bodily desires. Thus the person becomes identified with the urge to reason/discover what is best. The contrast, however, is not simply between pursuing what is best and pursuing what is most pleasant, but between the former and an interest in 'bodily' pleasure. Plato's language in the *Phaedo*, as at *Republic* 436a 10–b 1, is carefully limited. So even if we take it that he is coming to accept a distinction of the sort marked at *Charmides* 167e, still 'pleasure' has to be interpreted as covering only a limited range of pleasures, as indeed it still seems to for Aristotle's distinction.

In the *Republic* the contrast is both more elaborate and more puzzling. It is not now put in terms of a soul/body war. The distinction is within the soul or person. But the tie between reason and the desire for what is best is more definite (cf. Book VI 505 *ad fin.* where the object of everyone's desire emerges as the object of intellectual endeavour), while the anti-rational tendency of physical desire is at least as clear and it is directed to physical pleasure. What is not so clear is the salvaging of the thesis that all desire is for good by the interpretation 'all men (=rational souls) as such always and only desire the good'. To begin with, where Plato talks of a threefold division of the personality he seems clearly to be attributing to each of us desires which are indifferent to considerations of what is best (cf. especially 439a–b). When, as at Book VI 485, he talks as though we each had an undifferentiated desire-force which can get concentrated on the truth or on honour or on physical pleasures, it still seems that a person can set his heart on (desire) other than what is best, not being interested in that question. But later, 505d–e, we are told that everyone is after the good and does everything for its sake. This seems to be saying that all desire involves conceiving of the object of desire as good, and that physical desires differ from some others in that when dominant they determine a wrong conception of what is best. So the glutton is to be characterised not as pursuing physical pleasure rather than the good, but as being driven by physical desire to take physical pleasure as his good.

It looks, in fact, as though Plato wants to hold two theses. On the one hand, he wants to hold a connection between asking 'what is it best to do?' and reasoning about what to do (cf. e.g. 441b–c, 442c), as contrasted with blind desires for pleasure, or to be avenged. It is at least plausible to suppose that anyone who deliberates will put his deliberation in terms translatable into the terminology of whether it is best to do *A* or *B*. Granted certain views on the term 'good' there might now be the possibility of arguing whether his objective was really good at all, let alone these means or those. In so far as he deliberates, in fact, he shows himself to be interested in (wanting) what is best. But then this contrasts with a blind desire for food, where no questions of what is best are raised. The food is not put in context, or its value queried, it is simply wanted. To say that this desire is nevertheless for the good we need the second thesis. According to this, to say something is *A*'s goal is just to say that *A* treats it as a good. It follows immediately that everything everyone does is for the good. But it follows uninterestingly. On the first thesis, granted a view about 'good', it might seem to follow that there is something that all deliberate behaviour is ultimately aimed at. In putting the question 'is it best to do A?' a man is showing an interest in what is best, and differences are due to mistakes. But the second thesis would only show that all action has its own goal. It seems fairly clear that Plato wants something stronger than this last. He might hope to get it by standing by the first thesis, but there is a price. For now it is false that we all do everything we do in pursuit of the good. For this has to be interpreted as saying that all our behaviour is deliberated, done because it is considered best, and this is not true of a thirsty man seizing a drink. It now becomes possible to envisage someone dominated by his lower desires and so like a wild beast (439b). It will not be true of him that he wants what is best. He is not interested in such questions. All that is true is that each desire of his has an object, goal or good. But these goods may not be a good thing, nor does he conceive them as being so. The consequence is that Plato would lose a point he wishes to retain for his argument with Thrasymachus, Callicles and others. For if he can show that all desire is for the good, and also show that some people are mistaken about what is good, then first he might hope to show that Thrasymachus and others are among those who are mistaken while at the same time being able to block the counter-move of asking why anyone should want, then, to be good. He could block this if he could show that that is all anyone wants – other things are wanted only if viewed as good. There would, of course, still be other possible moves even if he distinguished the two theses and chose the first as what he needed. He could try a *Phaedo*-like approach of attributing some desires to the body and attaching others to the person, but then he would start further from his opponents and would have the uphill task of elucidating and establishing the view that a person is really only a reasoning entity. Alternatively, through the connection between 'good' and reason, he might argue that the intelligent or reasonable man will pursue what is best. Such a line has *ad hominen* force against his opponents and is, as we shall see, followed. But it is not an argument that all men want what is best. It is one thing to show that beings that pursue X show lack of fully developed reasoning power, and another to show that it is not really X that they pursue.

Plato could, no doubt, defend himself against this. He might, for instance, argue that we are discussing men. While it is possible to describe a man dominated by physical desires in the way suggested we should be describing someone indistinguishable from a beast. In that case we should be unable to discuss anything with him. Once we suppose something more human then he will be capable to some degree of expressible calculation, and will at once have to express himself in the terminology of what is a good or bad thing to do. With regard to physical desires one of three things will hold: first, he might temporarily be overwhelmed, in which case temporarily the wild beast model holds; or second, he will pursue physical needs in so far as required by his conception of what is best, where this includes other things; or third, he will, temporarily or permanently, be deluded into thinking that physical pleasure is the good. In the last two cases we are dealing with humans as humans, but their views on what is best are in no way privileged. In short, while a person is not identified with his reasoning powers, persons are identified by them. These (cf. *Republic* Book I 352d–354) opinions are a human person's distinguishing mark. This does not entail a distinction between the person and his lower desires, but between what characterises a person's pursuits and what characterises an animal's. A person's pursuit, even of physical pleasures, will be typically deliberative in that at least he will think it a good thing to pursue what he pursues. So if we are talking of men we are talking of deliberators or pursuers of what is best.

I said above that Plato could defend himself in this way. By this I mean only that some of the things he says are capable of development in this way, and that sometimes his points seem to suppose some such view. The fact remains that he makes the remarks about physical desire mentioned earlier; he does not reconcile his statements about its irrationality with those to the effect that all desire is for the good; he does not elaborate the relation between feelings of hunger and thirst and setting one's heart on pandering to one's appetite for food and drink as a main objective; he also, as I shall argue later, vacillates in what he says about the supposed distinguishing marks of humans, reason. All this suggests that he has a good deal to clear up before he could deploy this defence. But two major points in it he fairly clearly wishes to hold: that in some sense we all want what is best and only what is best, and that it is possible, not to say usual, to be mistaken about what is best. I shall take the second first, and then raise some further questions about the first.

Plato did not, of course, live at a time when there were many sophisticated theories of a subjectivist or prescriptivist variety about the word 'good'. Protagoras, it is true, seems (cf. *Theaetetus* 172, 178–9) to have held that it is sufficient for the truth of '*X* is good' that the speaker thinks *X* good. But this is not a special thesis about the word 'good', but part of a general theory of knowledge in which '*X* is good' is simply typical of all propositions of that form. Plato has, however, statements about how to go about discovering the excellence (goodness) of something which in fact commit him to some views on how the word 'good' operates, and, of course, the rejection of others. So far are subjectivist views from attracting him that it is almost axiomatic with him that where 'good' can truly be applied knowledge is possible, and vice versa. Why this is so and what is meant by it I shall discuss in a later chapter. Nor, as will then become clearer, would he like the view that 'good' stands for a non-natural property, nor that to call something good is to say that it answers to some human desire. He would agree, I think, with some who hold some forms of the latter view, that you cannot choose just any noun to substitute for X in 'X is good' and be sure of coming up with an intelligible sentence, but there the agreement ends.

To see what his view is I shall concentrate on five main passages: *Gorgias* 464–5, 499–506, *Meno* 71–2, *Republic* Book I 352 *ad fin.*, 601d–e, where we find drawn out what is often just taken for granted.

The Gorgias

The two *Gorgias* passages concern Socrates' distinction between a *techne* and an *empeiria*. One of the examples to illustrate the first is medicine, to illustrate the second cookery. Socrates is arguing that rhetoric stands to the enforcement of justice as does cookery to medicine. The second of each part is concerned with the welfare of what it deals with, the first, despite all pretensions, with pleasure. The first (465) has no account to give of the nature of its 'remedies', and so no explanation to offer of their effectiveness. This disqualifies it from the title of '*techne*'. So two marks are given of a *techne*: it is concerned with the good of its subject-matter, and it can give an account of its nature and so explain its operation. These points are elaborated in the second passage, where it becomes clear that they blend in that to know what is best for X and to know its nature amount to the same thing: to know the order that constitutes it. But whereas in the first passage we are only clearly told that anyone who is skilled will know how to tell good from bad situations in the area of his skill, in the second we have added to this the point that where we are committed to talking of better and worse situations we have a topic where a skill is needed (cf. 503c–d, 506d). In short, if we can talk of the excellence of X (or of X being good) then it must be possible to talk of the proper order or arrangement of X, and so of states of disorder that would make it a bad X. Thus if we take a mathematical unit, it will not make sense to speak of it as good or bad, because however much we may approve of it or commend it and all others like it to the attention of others; however much it may answer to men's desires; there is no sense in talking of a disordered state of a mathematical unit which produces a poor, though genuine, specimen. The main model here, that of physical health, readily suggests such an account, and fits with the current view of health as the proper balance of elements in the body. The result is that if X can truly be said to be good, then it is something which manifests order but is capable, without ceasing to be the sort of thing it is, of admitting a certain degree of disorder. Typically, but not invariably, that disorder which makes something bad of its kind leads, in extreme form, to its destruction (cf. *Republic* 608e seq.). The obvious models are organisms and artefacts.

The Meno *and the* Republic

In the *Republic* the model of health is still operative. It is explicit in talking of justice at the end of Book IV and again in the more general context of 608–10. But there is also now another formulation. At the end of Book I (352d seq.) Socrates proceeds to discuss what constitutes human excellence. This he does by talking more generally about excellence, and he argues that certain things have a characteristic activity which they alone perform or which they perform outstandingly. The competent performance of this activity comes with the thing having its own excellence, and lack of excellence results in poor performance. It is not said, in so many words, that always excellence is related to good performance, but only that the excellence of things that have a characteristic activity is so related. The point sounds more general, however, and this is confirmed by Book X 601d (with the substitution of *'chreia'* (use?) for *'ergon'*), where 'of every tool (object), animal and action . . .' seems to be an attempt to cover the range of things capable of excellence rather than limit us to the subset whose excellence is determined by reference to that for which it is naturally fitted (cf. *Gorgias* 506–7 and *Phaedrus* 270c–d).

According to this view if we can sensibly talk of the excellence of *X* it must be possible to specify the acitivity characteristic of *X*. This activity must be one capable of degrees of performance, since otherwise we should have the situation where something simply is or is not an *X*. There would then be no place for something being an *X*, but a bad one. Thus if some empiricists were right, and our empirical concepts were generally to be defined in terms of simple sensible properties, it would not, on Plato's view, be possible to use the terms 'good' and 'bad' of things so defined. Plato is, in fact, stating a view about the proper way to define terms for natural objects that is taken over by Aristotle.

I shall return to this later. For the moment it is worth pausing to consider the significance of this addition. It is not, I think, hard to see. While it is plausible to talk of health as the body's physical order and of disease as its disorder, 'order' and 'disorder' are used to assess the value of a given arrangement. It is a good question, therefore, what determines what arrangement counts as good order, what as disorder. If we take an example like the eye, or a sickle, the obvious answer that suggests itself is that an arrangement that makes efficient seeing or cutting possible is a proper one, one that hinders these activities a bad one. This allows the notion of order to be preserved, with the mathematical possibilities hinted at *Gorgias* 501a 5–7, while providing a means of settling what order is in any case desirable.

This view may be implicit in the *Gorgias* (cf. 503e), with its realisation that different arrangements are proper to different things, but it is not drawn out. It is more strongly suggested by Meno's words at *Meno* 71e–72a. There Meno is answering the question 'what is excellence?' He proceeds to give an account of different excellences: for a man, playing an effective part in politics; for a woman, running a home. In general, if you wish to discover what the excellence of X is, find out what X's role is (72a).

It is not altogether clear what Socrates' objection to this is. It is often supposed that the point is that we ought to be able to define 'excellence', and that Meno fails. Instead he gives examples. But in fact Meno offers, at 72a, a quite general account of excellence, though it is one that would yield different activities as constituting excellence for different sorts of people. Further, Socrates' objection is not that Meno fails to define 'excellence' generally, but precisely that he supposes that excellence is not like health, but may differ from person to person. He argues, in fact, that men and women alike are made good by the presence of 'justice' and temperance. These are hardly responsible for the excellence of my typewriter. So Socrates is not arguing about the definition of excellence in general, but about whether human beings vary in what makes them excellent or whether there is not some characteristic(s) which they must all have to be good. So Meno is at fault not through lack of generality, but because he supplies a general account which would yield lack of similarity between man and man in what is needed to make them good. It is true that Meno is probably interested in the variety and in the recipe for finding the appropriate form of excellence rather than in the generality of the account. The fact remains that the approach found here is at least the ancestor of that applied generally over all instances of excellence, not merely human, in the *Republic*. The reference to Gorgias at the beginning of the *Meno* passage (71d 7) suggests that Plato is tackling a familiar view and one which would prevent a general account of moral virtue of the sort Plato was after by insisting that excellence is relative to role. In the context of the *Meno* it is this last fact that interests him and he seems not to have seen the possibility of developing it for his own purposes by the kind of general application we find in the *Republic*. If he had we should expect a characteristic turning of the tables by asking whether there was not some activity peculiar to human beings as opposed to other things. As it is, he relies upon the traditional use of 'justice' and temperance in talking of a good man.

Indeed, to turn the tables and reject the relativism of Meno's view,

Plato needs a general account of the human person. This is supplied in the *Republic* (Book IV) with the account of the soul and the insistence (but hardly argument) that the only difference between men and women is physical. Any psychological differences do not come from the soul, but from the physical conditions in which it has to operate. Between these two dialogues Plato's views on the soul have developed. Its distinction from the body has been argued, reason has been made its hallmark and the body blamed for reason's lack of development (cf. *Phaedo* 78–80). Thus the differences between men come not from their essential nature – for essentially they are souls – but from the relative success of their reasoning tendencies in winning through against the blandishments of the senses and (by the *Republic*) of ambition. There is now a possible answer to the question 'what is man's *ergon*?' especially if we widen the notion of '*ergon*' from 'social role' to 'characterising activity'.

The notion of '*ergon*', then, in the *Republic* should help fill the gap left by the *Gorgias* account. There is now a thesis about the preconditions of attributing excellence which should enable us to distinguish between an ordered and a disordered person. What was previously a suggestive analogy with health can now be shown to hold. Consequently in the *Republic* we can be given at least first steps in showing that 'justice', temperance and the rest in fact constitute human excellence. I say 'first steps' because at 504 Socrates makes it clear that the final proof would be beyond him. Quite why I shall discuss in a later chapter. For the present I shall discuss the way in which Plato applies his rules about excellence in the *Republic*.

To begin with, it might well be argued that he does not. For despite the passages cited from Books I and X, in the main body of the work there is no reference to *ergon*, and the analysis of the soul is carried through without a mention of the soul's characteristic performance. We are surely justified therefore in taking these remarks as hints that are not developed. An idea that sounds good on simple examples looks more difficult when applied to more complex ones. When it comes to the point Plato falls back on the analogy with health, bolstered by an analogy with the state. This view becomes even more plausible if we suppose, as seems likely, that Book I was originally written as an independent dialogue, and that the first part of Book X was inserted as an appendix to ram home some points against artists. In that case it is hardly surprising that the various parts should not perfectly cohere.

This last consideration can, of course, cut two ways. Especially with regard to Book I, if we suppose that Plato picked it off his shelf as a good first course for the *Republic*, we have further to suppose that he did not read it through. For as it stands it ends with a clear line on how to determine what excellence is, which is then ignored. It is at least as easy to suppose that it was chosen just because it clearly pointed how to interpret the later discussion of the soul. In fact everything hinges on whether the discussion of the soul is in fact in terms of effective performance of characteristic activities despite the failure to recall the terminology. In fact it is.

Towards the end of Book I (353d–e) Socrates declares the characteristic function of the soul to be 'to watch over, direct and deliberate and everything of that sort' and also to live. At the end (354b) he complains that he has been asking whether 'justice' is intelligence or excellence without knowing what justice is. In what follows the interest shifts to the nature of 'justice'. While the question is whether it is good in itself, this is interpreted as meaning whether it is desirable for its own sake (357–8), giving a person all he wants (Book IX 579e). Whether it is really good is not shown (Book VI 504). The question is not: 'what does the soul do?' but 'what does "justice" do to the soul?' We already know what the soul's function is. This function is performed, in the terms of the analysis of Book IV, by the reasoning element with some help from our 'spirited' tendencies. The effect of the operation of 'justice' is to ensure (443d–e) that each part of the person performs its proper function and that only. The preservation of this condition is the role of justice, and intelligence, the excellence of the reasoning part, plays the guiding role. The terms mentioned at 353d–e and their like recur throughout the end of Book IV (cf. e.g. 440d, 441a, 441e, 442b–d, 443b, 444d), to say nothing of their use in discussing the soul's analogue, the city. Always they indicate the function of the reasoning part, and it is clear that the operation of justice is needed to ensure the performance of the proper reasoning function. Consequently it is clear that if Book I is right about the soul's/human person's characteristic activity, then because a person is more complex than just a reasoning entity 'justice' is needed for the proper performance of that activity. In fact, therefore, Books II–IV, in elaborating Plato's view of the human person, bring out how, while deliberation and the rest remain the soul's characteristic function, a person has more to him. This explains why (433c–e) it is a good question in the case of the state, and so presumably also of the individual, which of the four excellencies is properly *the* excellence. On the doctrine of Book I one would expect the answer to be straightforward: intelligence. That would hold of a purely intellectual being, but with man the matter is more complicated, and it is a fuller and more accurate account to cite 'justice'.

The importance of this complexity is not simply that the lower desires have to be controlled in order to allow for the operation of our reasoning faculties. It is the operation of the soul to live, and in this desires for food, drink and sexual enjoyment have a role. This partially determines the area of operation of the reasoning part, for a man has to take thought for his whole life (441e, 442c, 443d–e), and so for the proper operation and satisfaction of each type of desire. Yet while he shares with animals the lower desires and 'spirit', he is characteristically a deliberating calculative entity. To perform these activities a certain ordering is required. The correct ordering is determined by the requirements for the operation of the reasoning faculty. Thus other orderings, such as a life ruled by physical desire, are shown to be disorder by reference to man's characterising activity which determines his excellence.

It seems, therefore, that in fact the discussion of 'justice' in the *Republic* shows its relation to the characteristic function of the soul mentioned in Book I, and also declares the situation where reason rules to be the proper one. It is also this function that enables us to distinguish between order and disorder. So even if Plato does not put out a bulletin to tell us that he is now doing what we ought to have been able to expect him to be doing, he is nevertheless doing it. Perhaps he expected his reader to notice.

Granted this view about how to determine the excellence of any type of subject, it is not surprising that Plato should think it possible, not to say common, for people to be mistaken about what is best. In the case of what all men want, this is usually interpreted as what is best for men. At the least it would be necessary to know what man's characteristic activity is and the conditions needed for its development. Even this brief statement suggests an enquiry which few have pursued far. As I hope to show later, the full project envisaged by Plato is even more daunting.

It is now time to return to the point from which this discussion started. We had reached the position where it seemed clear that Plato wished to say that everyone wants the good, or what is best. Sometimes this is expressed just like that. Sometimes (cf. *Meno* 77) it is put in the form of wanting what is good for oneself, and this can be glossed as wanting *eudaemonia*. These themes are drawn together at *Euthydemus* 279–82, where it is agreed that everyone wishes to do well, that this is achieved by the possession and use of good things; the value of philosophy is argued for and its possession said to make a person *eudaemon* and a good man. In the *Republic* also it is taken for granted that we all want to live the best life possible, that is the best life for men, that is an excellent human life. We therefore want to know what we must acquire to enable us so to live.

Now this can sound either egocentric or implausible. It is plausible to suggest that we all want to live the best life possible, in that this last phrase might be generally accepted as a description of what we want of life. But then it readily receives an interpretation in terms of the agent's good. If interpreted as the most virtuous life possible, it is highly implausible to suggest that that is what would generally be recognised as what is wanted, and it would take a good deal of argument to show that a virtuous life was what alone satisfied the description 'the best life possible'. This comes back to the question of whether one can move from a formal point that anyone who, on a given interpretation of 'want', wants X must consider X the best thing to pursue, to a substantial conclusion that he must really want something of a specific description. What I now wish to pursue is the question whether Plato is committed to an egocentric view of human excellence, and for this purpose it will be as well to pause a moment to get the issue clearer.

Suppose someone says that we all want the best life possible, and this is a claim as to what we would all acknowledge to be a description of our overall aims. It is natural to interpret this as claiming that we all admit that unless we are being unreflective we take our own good as the overriding criterion for deciding how to conduct our lives. Such an interpretation appeals to our natural cynicism in the same way as does egoistic psychological hedonism. It is, however, an interpretation that relies on some contrast between certain gains of an agent's that can be contrasted with the gains of others. On Plato's view as expanded above, what we all want is a well-organised personality, so that it is easy to get the impression that we are/should be all aiming at our own mental health. Something less like a traditionally self-centred account emerges if desire for the best governs the general organisation of life, but is not the determining motive of every action. Thus, if it emerged that a tendency to affection was an integral part of the human personality, then the desire for the best life might lead to the development of affection, on Plato's type of account of excellence, but affection would ensure that at least some behaviour was determined by reference to the welfare of others. The question then is whether Plato's account of the human person does in some such way allow of other-directed motivation and how the desire for what is best is related to the other main desires.

On the face of it Plato seems inextricably committed to an egoistic picture. The two 'higher' parts of the soul are desire for honour and desire for the truth. The first is clearly directed to one's own honour. The second seems to reach its highest satisfaction in academic pursuits, away from the hurly-burly of public life or family responsibilities. Indeed, it looks as though Plato himself feels some difficulty in persuading his philosophers, in the *Republic*, to take up their duties in the state. They are, apparently, already in possession of the best kind of life, and are portrayed as understandably unwilling to leave their pursuits for the confused entanglements of politics. They will agree, we are told, because the request is just, and just requests never go unheeded by just ears. This sounds like the desperation of weakness. If the philosopher rightly wants the best life and the requirements of justice conflict with the pursuit of it, then the conclusion should be that justice is not in this case a good thing. This would not affect the argument in favour of justice where this is proper internal discipline – but it would indicate that that is no argument for behaving justly to others, and so drive a wedge between justice in Plato's sense and justice in a more ordinary sense.

Of course, even in the context of the ideal republic, a philosopher might be able to argue that it is best to give in to justice on the grounds that the practicable alternatives would be worse for him. But it would not be difficult to devise examples where such an argument is not available. For instance, suppose a philosopher with an impediment of speech which does not interfere with his philosophising, but does render him unfit for any public office. Suppose, also, that he knows it to be curable. All he has to do to retain his academic privileges is to keep this knowledge to himself. No lie is required, no strife or scandal in the state is caused, so his own soul will not be damaged, nor his life in the state endangered. So what possible reason could there be for him to reveal his knowledge and accept his responsibilities?

In fact I think the above constitutes misinterpretation. To bring out just how will involve more detailed discussion of the two 'higher' parts of the soul, which will be given in the following chapters. There I shall concentrate once more on the *Republic*, with some reference to later dialogues. The reason is that the problem becomes acute there. In earlier dialogues the argument is more exclusively aimed at the question of what is best for the individual, or what measures up to the ideals espoused by various participants in the dialogue. The latter makes the argument primarily *ad hominem*. The former line emerges in the *Gorgias* with the view that a virtuous life is a satisfied life. In the *Phaedo* the philosopher's withdrawal from the ordinary interests of life seems to be advocated, and a somewhat similar emphasis on personal intellectual fulfilment seems to pervade the *Symposium*. In the *Republic* there are developments. To begin with, it became important for the argument to raise the question of what men really want. This line of attack seems to have led to a view whereby an interest in what is best is not just an interest in intellectual satisfaction. Finally, while the analogy with the state is officially just that, and introduced to make points about the individual, the fact remains that political interests loom large in the *Republic*. The result is a richer view of the human subject, and a greater awareness of the importance of the community with consequent awareness of the importance of education. As a result there is more sense of a strain between the requirements of intellectual satisfaction and those of 'justice'. For education does not occur *in vacuo*, but in community, and education in moral virtue immediately seems both community orientated and not obviously intellectual. This I think leads to further consideration of ordinary moral views and their motivation, and also to a more fully developed view both of the role of reason and its relation to ordinary moral motives. The individual portrayed is one whose potentialities, when fully developed, are for community life, and there is no longer the hostility of soul to body, or simple contrast of intellectual and sensual lives. In the earlier dialogues Plato's position is inchoate. There is a bias in favour of Socrates, and Socrates stood both for intellectual pursuit and general uprightness of character; he also seems to have shown a certain personal austerity in contrast with what contemporary hedonists advocated and if lucky practised. The value of philosophy is stressed in contrast with public life, of the intellect over and against the body. At the same time Socrates is a model of courage (*Symposium* 219–21, *Phaedo* 114d *ad fin.*), self-control and the typical virtues. Arguments tend to defend these latter from attack without making it clear what their relation is to intellectual development, or what their relation is if any to the usual social context of their exercise. By the *Republic* there is a more elaborate position which, because of its breadth of cover, enables one to see how Plato adapted to these stresses. The fact remains, of course, that the *Republic* does not do anything called 'giving us Plato's doctrine', but it does mark a significant stage of development, and one from which, if from anywhere, we might hope to discover the truth on the present question.

III

Admiration for Manliness

First I shall consider the spirited part of the soul and examine the part played by it in the *Republic*. This will entail a fairly detailed treatment. It is not at all obvious what Plato is trying to isolate with the term *'thymos'*, and the problem has not been helped by a tendency to concentrate on a few prominent passages interesting largely for other reasons. The result is to suggest that he is trying to distinguish emotions from, say, intellect and desire, or to distinguish the will from intellect and affective parts of the personality. In neither case can he be considered very successful for reasons that will become apparent. Only one thing seems clear, and that is that either Plato is very confused or else he is using the word *'thymos'* technically to isolate a phenomenon for which there is no term readily available, but a salient characteristic of which this word catches. This last is, I think, the correct alternative, and the concept is both of some interest in itself and important in the development of Plato's argument. Among other things its use gives us Plato's view on the value and argumentative status of ordinary moral ideals at their best.

The problem about the spirited element is, I suppose, fairly familiar: that it seems to be so many things. Thus when it is first introduced in Book II it seems to be an aggressive quality observable in dogs and desirable in men. By Book IV it has become anger – in the particular example – with oneself. But we have been told that spirit needs developing as the main characteristic of the military class, and their main characteristic is said to be not anger but courage. By Book VIII, on the other hand, a man in whom spirit is dominant is remarkable for his love of honours. It is not easy to see why a person given to the pursuit of honour should be particularly irascible – why more so than a miser? Nor is it obvious that a tendency to anger should go with courage or lead to love of honours. Nor again, is it clear why one's aggressive instincts should be thought to be connected either with anger or love of honours. Yet we cannot explain it all away as an inadvertent slip or set of slips on Plato's part, as though he had forgotten by Book IV the precise point of Book II, and by Book VIII had passed through the Lethe of his epistemology. The importance of spirit for courage is openly stated early on (375a 11), and in Book III we are given the connection of the spirited element and anger – not only in Book IV – and again in Book IX (572). In Book IV itself courage, anger and aggressive quality are all spoken of. In Book VIII, again, it is characteristic of the lover of honours to be somewhat aggressive and cruel, and a man is tempted towards philotimia by being led to consider his father *anandros* (unmanly) – not having *andreia* (manliness). Consequently, we must either say that Plato has got into some confusion, or else show how the whole can be made into a coherent view. I shall try in what follows to do the latter, though not without a certain amount of recourse to the former.

To begin with, I want to draw out an apparently clear contrast between the way in which the spirited element is spoken of in Books II–IV, and the way it appears in Book VIII. In Books II–IV it seems to be thought of *primarily* as an aggressive tendency, which can be educated indeed and soothed by a proper dose of culture, until we get a mixture of spirit and gentleness, but which of itself is simply violent. So when in this part of the *Republic* the possibility is entertained of the spirited part becoming dominant, the picture is of a man who 'accomplishes all his ends by violence and fierceness, like a brute beast, and lives in ignorance and ineptitude, devoid of all rhythm and grace' (411d 8). Here spirit seems to be thought of as some sort of aggressive tendency, leading, if unchecked, to senseless violence: but something which could be worked off on useful objects if properly channelled.

By Book VIII the picture is slightly different. For instance, when Socrates draws the picture of a youth turning from possibly philosophic into merely philotimic, we are told that his mother will complain that his father is unmanly, and the servants will encourage him, when he grows up, to avenge his father's wrongs, and to show himself more of a man than his father. Now it is true that he is being encouraged to be tough – but not just as such, but because it is manly. It is held up as admirable; and when the next corruption takes place we are told that the desiring part has subjected the spirited so that now 'it honours only wealth and the wealthy, and seeks a reputation only in the acquisition of money' (553d 4). The uncorrupted thymoeidic man had a militaristic ideal, and this fitted well enough with a violent tendency; but there is no necessary outlet for violence in admiring millionaires. What has happened here is not that the man's violent instincts have got channelled in a different direction, but that he has been attracted by a different ideal

42

of manliness: the real man is the man with a private aeroplane. It looks as though the spirited element is being treated as a tendency to be attracted to certain ideals of manhood, some of which may be soldierly, but others may set up as admirable the clever man, who has succeeded in amassing a large fortune. This same feature characterises the pluto-cratic state (cf. 551) which is the model for the individual.

This shift of emphasis shows even in the picture of the dominantly thymoeidic man (549). He is no longer a savage; he is rather an old-style Athenian gentleman of the hoplite class, not given to philosophy, nor unduly cultivated, but no boor. He is somewhat arrogant, with ideas as to what is his due, and is keen on things military. He is not yet given over to the pursuit of money. Having plenty, he can afford a sense of honour, and his sense of honour, being derived from right views on the good life, is not far off the mark. What is notable about him is not that he is uncontrolledly violent, but that he has definite ideas on how to behave, on what is the conduct expected of a man, which curb his incipient acquisitiveness without, however, being rationally held.

Again, in Book IV, spirit is said to be clearly distinct from reason on the grounds that it is manifest from birth onwards, whereas reason appears on the scene at best late in life. It is doubtless true that there is a clear element of savagery in children from the moment of birth, but it is not so easy to discern in them the lines of the philotimic man of Book VIII, cruel to slaves, gentle with freemen, and assiduously obedient to their rulers. The spirited element as dominant in Book VIII in fact, is that of the early books *as it appears when influenced by literature and the arts.* A man who has received this training becomes dyed in the law (429–30), having been brought up in admiration of the proper gods and heroes, as portrayed in the new bowdlerised version of the old legends. But by Book VIII the spirited part seems to have become rather different, independently of training, and seems rather to refer to some supposed tendency to admire certain conduct as manly; so that when a person is induced to admire the ingenuity and wealth of a financial genius, this admiration is the function of spiritedness (553). Unreasoned admiration seems to have been substituted for unreasoned aggressiveness.

In Book VIII, in fact, Plato seems to have three main possibilities of motivation between which other classes fall. First, there is the man whose first question is 'what is best?' and who can give a reasoned answer to the question. Second, there is the person with definite ideas about the conduct expected of a real man; he has his ideal, which wins his admiration, but of which he can give no reasoned defence, and this ideal dominates his conduct. His first question is 'what should a *man* do in these circumstances?' Third, there is the person whose sole aim is money and the pleasures to which money gives access. There are various intermediate stages, but these are the types where clear domination of one or other part of the personality shows, and the philotimic man is one who accepts a moral code, and more or less the right one, accepts it willingly, but accepts it without being able to give it any rational basis.

The question now is, can this account in Book VIII be reconciled with the earlier account? The answer is, I think, yes, though it has to be allowed that there are some untidy bits which Plato does not tidy up. The characteristic in which Plato is primarily interested is spiritedness as portrayed in Book VIII, and this is clear not only from Book VIII, but also from the treatment in the earlier books. That is to say, Plato is interested in the fact that men are capable of accepting rules of conduct not on the basis of reason, nor yet from fear, but from some sense of what is honourable or manly – an acceptance based on admiration of a type. Further, this is not only possible in individual adults, but is even characteristic in some states such as Sparta.

Now that this *type* of thing is not only possible, but even common, is of course, true. It does not take much prodding of most people's moral position before one reaches some such defence as 'it wouldn't be decent', 'it wouldn't be liberal', 'it would be narrow-minded', 'it's bourgeois', 'it is not the behaviour expected of a gentleman' or some equivalent, which indicates the presence of some admired ideal, too obviously admirable to need defence, at the basis of the accepted rules. This characteristic, then, with a qualification to be added later, is the one in which Plato is interested: it is possible to appeal to a tendency in men which is neither reason, nor desire for physical pleasures, but a leaning towards some ideal of a successful man. That this is so in Book VIII is fairly clear. It is now time to show it also to be so in the earlier books. Here the first and most obvious point is the similarity between the soldier class and the philotimic man of Book VIII. The soldiers are the result of the education outlined in Books II–III, and while it is true that they are examples of *tempered* spirit, still, when in Book IV the state analogy is applied to the individual, the characteristic that the soldiers exemplify is spiritedness. Now it is not typical of them that they are savage; they are cultivated people, with plenty of spirit, and right views on what is to be feared and what not (cf. esp. 430a–b). They are no lily-livered money lovers. Nor yet are they philosphers, from whom they are clearly distinguished (414b). They do not keep the laws through fear, but nor do they keep them because they understand how they are in fact for the best. Their training has made them law-abiding – but how?

The treatment of early education and the criticisms of poetry in the early books are concerned with the development of the spirited part, and so of the lover of honours. The criticisms of poetry, with minor exceptions, fall into two main parts. First, there is the long tirade against false portrayals of gods and heroes, and second, there is the question of imitation. The first is deprecated on the ground that gods and heroes are naturally to be taken as models (cf. 378b). Children reading of their doings naturally aspire to do likewise, and take from them their standards of what is fine and what shabby behaviour. A child brought up on Homeric heroes will tend to imbibe an Homeric ideal, which in Socrates' view is at least morally dubious. The second main objection is to taking the characters of any but good heroes, as a person is likely to become imbued with the outlook of the character he acts. What Plato fears, here, is that a child's admiration may get fixed on a quite unworthy model, so that when he comes to the age of rational criticism the results of reasoned argument will be hard to appreciate, because so foreign to what he instinctively takes as noble and manly. In fact, at this stage too, Plato has in mind a person's capacity for being attracted to an ideal in opposition, possibly, to his desires for physical pleasure, but not because he has reasoned out that this is the best way to behave. The result of the training of the soldiers is correct opinion, not knowledge (429–30 and 522a and cf. *Phaedrus* 253d–c, *Timaeus* 69–70). It is the normal function of legends of gods and heroes to arouse this capacity for admiration and fix, in youth, the general lines of an ideal which may stay with a man for life. It need not. In Book VIII we are told of a man whose ideals take a tumble in face of misfortune, and whose admiration gets transferred from his Raj-type father and all he stood for, to the man who can make money quick and keep it. At this stage, the only sure defence is reason. In Books II–III the fear is of a child getting a false start, so that what it aspires to constitutes little or no bulwark against the allurements of his more fleshly desires. In either case Plato has in mind a tendency to ideals which is not reducible either to reason or physical desire. He clearly thinks that this is a powerful element in human motivation (cf. 551a), and that it can be influenced and trained by proper education in literature and the arts.

Before going on to consider some difficulties, I want to illustrate the connection of this type of motivation with anger, indignation and contempt (three emotions attached to it in the *Republic*), and shame (mentioned in the *Phaedrus* 253d). To begin with, suppose we consider a man who just wants money in order to live a more comfortable life. If his desire is to be described just as that, then we cannot attribute to him certain reactions in relation to it. For instance, it will be neither here nor there to him if someone else fails or succeeds in getting money, except that he might feel frustrated if it lessens his profits, or glad if it boosts them. But contempt for the man who fails will not enter in. Contempt involves not just a judgment of inferiority, but an attitude to success or failure such that a person who fails has not merely not brought off some project, but has shown himself to be an inferior sort of being in failing; he has descended to depths that one would be ashamed of oneself. Contempt indicates something about the person's pursuit of money: possession is not just desirable, but admirable. Again shame: if I merely want money, I may be frustrated if I fail, or disappointed or annoyed; but to be ashamed of failing I have, as it were, to stake my reputation on success; to consider success not just as achieving my purpose, but also as showing my mettle, so that if I fail I lose not only the goal I was after, but also my honour, my claim to be considered of note. A person who suffers from shame after losing a game of tennis shows that he has treated it as more than just a game. He did not just want to win: it was important to him to win, to show his prowess.

Similar things hold of anger and indignation. These reactions are functions of certain views of what is due to persons of a certain sort. I can feel indignant if a student addresses me at first meeting by my christian name only if I think that senior members have a status that demands deference from inferiors, and students are inferiors. The bias of the notion of 'anger' also tends in this direction, so that such things as insults are its most natural object: i.e. behaviour that no *man* will suffer meekly.

In short, there are certain reactions to the achievement, lack of achievement, or frustration of certain desires, which indicate that what is wanted is not simply wanted because, say, it gives pleasure, but that more is at stake. Such reactions as contempt, shame, indignation and so on show that the objective is looked upon in a certain light: the man does not just want money and the comforts it brings; these are also a status-symbol, they show him to be a man of parts. An ideal of manliness is informing the desire. This, I take it, is one aspect of the difference between the oligarchic and the tyrannical man, as also of that between the respective states.

Now if we for the moment consider the truth and not Plato, it must be admitted that it is not possible to give any simple characterisation of the light in which an object must be conceived to make these reactions possible. It is not, in fact, necessary that one should consider one's manliness at stake: it may be one's artistic integrity, for instance, one's name as a wit, one's prowess at producing monster marrows – though doubtless here one must consider the class of artists, wits or gardeners a superior one to belong to. Nor need one's standing as a member of a class, however, be at stake: my trouble may just be that I am glad that I am not as the rest of men so that I am deeply ashamed of any sign of the common touch. Still, Plato may be said to be right in supposing that these reactions do indicate a difference in motivation, and also in thinking that ideals of manliness would tend to give rise to such reactions. Once such ideals are influential, then activities which might otherwise be pursued for fun become a matter of honour. Plato may be too limited in what he allows as a basis for such reactions, but at least they show the presence of some sort of outlook of which the philotimic outlook would be an example, and a philotimic man, as distinct from a purely epithumetic one, could be expected typically to exhibit such reactions.

So far, then, I hope to have shown that in the early books and again in Book VIII, in what he has to say about spiritedness Plato is showing interest in a form of motivation whereby one's actions are regulated by admiration for a type. This gets instilled in childhood by the heroes of one's reading, and may at that stage take the form of open hero-worship but in later life may recede to a background ideal type. The existence of such ideals is rightly supposed by Plato to be shown by the occurrence of certain sorts of reaction; and the type of reaction concerned is at least rightly supposed to be an important indication with regard to motive, showing it not to be of the simple type which mere mention of the goal might suggest.

There remains, however, a difficulty that I mentioned earlier. Spirit and spiritedness are said to occur in animals as well as men, and in children from birth onwards, as well as in adults. Yet it is hard to suppose in these subjects the existence of ideals. Dogs may be ferocious, and children may show a tendency to violent behaviour, but these facts do not seem to indicate any particular attachment to standards of dog-hood or ideals of manliness. No doubt Plato's views on canine philosophy can be taken with a pinch of salt, as what humourless scholars call a jocular episode. The attribution of spirit to children, however, ought not to be in such a light-hearted vein, as it is part of the basis given for distinguishing spiritedness from 'reason'. Yet it is just the difficulty of taking seriously the suggestion that babies are philotimic that inclines one to interpret spirit as a tendency to violence. The suggestions that are rife when philotimia is to the fore: the having of views, devotion to the law, submission to right opinion, are inapplicable to small children, and all we can find are aggressive tendencies. It looks, therefore, as though Plato assumes that it is these tendencies which are educated and elevated by music and poetry, giving on to philotimia proper. Yet this seems a gratuitous assumption at best. The reaction of a dog when you try to remove a bone from it, or the activity of a child destroying one's choicest flowers, do not seem even analogous to the conduct of a philotimic man.

Part of the difficulty here is that we do not know exactly what, in children, Plato is claiming to be the antecedent of philotimia; part of it is that we do not know quite how seriously to take these allusions, and part, probably, that Plato did not stop to ask himself precisely what he was referring to. The most important point for him is that in adults there occurs the sort of motivation in which he is interested, leading to conduct possibly quite against the inclinations to physical pleasure. Something of the sort is observable in children, which shows its possibility at a pre-critical age, and it is probably pressing a sentence too hard to ask whether Plato had done any research on one-day old babies. Granted all this, however, he must have thought there was some phenomenon at least prima facie analogous to the full-blooded development that interests him; and so it is worth pointing out that he does not make it clear what the phenomenon is. I have talked of aggressive tendencies, and liability to violence, because it often gets spoken of this way, presumably because excess of spirit leads to *agriotes* (violence?). Yet, whether Plato realised it or not, a taste for violence is a common concomitant of cowardice, while spirit is taken as obviously the starting point of courage.

Perhaps it is of some help to remember that when the notion of spiritedness is introduced – which is in connection with courage (375a–b) – the characteristics given to spirit are not violence, nor even aggression, but invincibility and fearlessness. This suggests that *agriotes* ('violence') should be interpreted as that fierceness which accompanies these qualities, which shows in a person's being unprepared to sit down meekly under danger or attack, and inclined to stand up for himself, even if the chances are poor. If so, then such behaviour does begin to look analogous to that of the philotimic man. Plato may have thought, with some justice, that some such quality was observable in dogs and children: that it looks as though each considered it unworthy of itself to take certain sorts of treatment, or indulge in certain sorts of behaviour. Many of the stories in Lorenz's *Man Meets Dog* (1954) invite interpretations in terms of shame, sense of dignity, sense that certain behaviour is unworthy of a dog. Thus Plato might be appealing to something which could at least be considered as analogous to the conduct characteristic of philotimia, though he is, of course, still left with the problem of establishing an actual connection.

The point of this last section has been to show that the strain between spiritedness considered as a tendency to violence and spiritedness considered as a tendency to admiration of an ideal type is not so great as it might at first sight seem. For it is possible to interpret spirit, as attributed to children and animals, so that it is at least analogous to philotimia, and so might be plausibly thought of as its prelinguistic counterpart.

There still remains, however, a further peculiarity. In treating of Book VIII I illustrated the sort of thing I thought Plato was getting at with examples of a person relying on some picture of the liberal man, or the broad-minded man, to support his view on conduct. But Plato, if he would allow such examples at all, would clearly think of them as degenerate cases of spiritedness. Throughout the *Republic* it is assumed that the prime example of a thymoeidic man is interested in fighting and similar things. The only case of spirit being excited by any other sort of ideal is the degenerate case of the oligarchic man. Even here, it looks, from the description, as though what attracts about wealth is the fact that it seems to give a position of influence and respect: the life of honour leaves one with no resource against catastrophe and envy. In short, it looks as though for the spirited part to be influenced, the life has to be presentable as 'manly', as not having the appearance of weakness. And not only this, but the *proper* object of its admiration is the type of 'manliness' in a thorough-going old-fashioned sense. In short, Plato is not drawing attention to the general type of motive which I mentioned earlier, but to one form it may take, with certain possible modifications of that form. The reasons for this are probably partly his educational interests and partly the actual historical situation. His educational interests might account for it in that boys do generally pass through a marked gang stage when toughness and roughly physical prowess loom large as ideals, which can with luck be channelled along not too anti-social lines. This is thought by many educationalists to be a quite important stage at which ideas of social responsibility can be inculcated. It is also clear, however, that the ideals of this stage can be grown out of, and others be substituted of a quite different kind. Here Plato was probably influenced by the historical situation, where he seemed to find an old-fashioned morality, relying on a military-cum-citizen ideal, being undermined by more egoistic views on conduct. This might have led him to think, perhaps rather crudely, of ideals as primarily in the hoplite mould, and of deviations from this as always and only moves towards an openly self-centred outlook. Consequently, as ideals in his experience tended to be associated with a certain sort of outlook, and this to be related to an observable educational stage, he seems to have taken it that attraction to ideals is always, if uncorrupted, attraction to ideals of a certain sort. These ideals in fact bear some relation to the proper ideal. That is to say, the perfect man does in fact include more or less the characteristics to which the properly spirited man aspires. So that so long as it does not get misled, a man's spirit will lead him to admire more or less the right sort of man, even before he can understand how it is that that is the right sort of man. This is a happy circumstance, and most people's adherence to moral rules, when not from fear or sheer habit, rests on this sort of basis. The important thing is to develop this potentiality early along the right lines.

It is now time to relate this to the earlier discussion. The question raised towards the end of the last chapter was whether Plato can explain the philosophers' preparedness, in the *Republic*, to enter public life, responding to the 'just requests' made to them. If the above account of the spirited element is right then it seems that Plato thinks that we all have a tendency to admire and aspire after manly behaviour, and this tendency, when satisfied, shows itself in attachment to rules and norms characteristic of the ideal inculcated. If we consider in the round the description of the soldier class in Books II–IV, or of the philotimic state/ man in Book VIII, it is clear that manliness involves far more than military courage. It involves, for instance, resistance to the allurements of pleasure, respect for authority, a sense of duty and generally the virtues admired by Cephalus in *Republic* Book I, or Laches in the *Laches*. The ideal held by such men will in the case of the soldier class of the *Republic* have been critically revised, but it is recognisably out of the same stable. I shall consider later the status of the spirited element as Plato's analysis of traditional morality. For the moment it is enough to note that he considers it an integral part of a human personality, which may be suppressed or distorted, but should be developed in a perfect human being. This means that a perfect human being will be one whose behaviour is in part determined by admiration for a correct ideal of manliness, and will so respond to the norms that form part of that ideal. Among these will be norms of just (law-abiding) (cf. *Republic* 429c–430b, *Phaedrus* 254a–b, *Timaeus* 70b) behaviour. So when, in the context of the ideal state, we appeal to the justice of a philosopher's taking his place in public life, we are appealing to his appreciation of the law on the model of the ideals on which he has been brought up. It would be, in the light of those, mean, base, unmanly, to refuse to shoulder his responsibilities. In short, granted that Plato is right on the desires that he considers attributable to all men, a perfect man will not, or not on all occasions, be self-centredly motivated.

This is not, however, the end of the problem. According to Plato, 'spirit' is characteristically responsive to reason (cf. *Republic* 440). Since reason is concerned with questions of what is best, this is not, on the present account, difficult to understand. For ideals of manliness embody views on how it is best for a man to behave. A change of conviction about what constitutes a good man might be expected to bring about a change of ideal. The lower desires, by contrast, do not involve any conception of what is best that might be corroded by rational argument. But if this is so, it becomes a problem why it should be considered part of what constitutes human excellence, to have the sort of admiration for manly behaviour that might lead one to abandon philosophy for public life. In other words, the problem simply re-emerges at the level of reason. For it looks as though the reasoning element in us is, among other things, a desire for the truth, a desire that can only reach fruition at the end of a somewhat gruelling education. But this desire would seem to be at odds with any desire to be and show oneself to be a real man. It might be argued that it is not at odds, because a perfect man will know when it is best to act in various ways – this is involved in having the correct ideal – and his view of what is the manly thing to do will trim its sails accordingly. Such a man will only feel to be best what he can also show to be best. If Plato took this line, however, he would have to face the original question: why should a philosopher think it his duty to enter public life? If he cannot show it to be a good thing, he cannot show such behaviour to be manly and so his spirited element will not respond to the appeal to justice. On the face of it it is a course that means abandoning the best for an inferior form of life, and so contrary to the desire to live as well as possible. Whether or not this creates a difficulty for Plato largely depends on how we are to interpret the notion of a reasoning element and its relation to the desire for what is best. This makes a suitable starting-point for a new chapter.

IV

Reason and Goodness

In order to deal with the problem posed at the end of the last chapter it will be necessary to examine the way Plato talks of reason, and especially the tie between reason and goodness. Since the final goal of reason is knowledge (*episteme*) an examination of what Plato says on this topic will also be necessary. In all this it is important not to be cumbered by too many prejudices derived from the English terms or from post-Platonic philosophical interests. Thus it is very tempting to take the tripartite division of the person in *Republic* Book IV as an embryonic distinction of faculties. Men have the capacity to reason – a capacity used in learning – they can desire and they have an element resistant to desire. It is, of course, a crude first stumble. 'Desire' is limited to desire for certain objects, and the middle element is an attempt either to isolate that varied area of emotional reaction which can be contrasted with appetite or to isolate the will, our capacity to enforce our decisions as to what is best on our recalcitrant lusts. Still, it is a first attempt at an analysis of mental capacities carried out more systematically by later philosophers.

There are, of course, two theses here, one about the influence of the Platonic passages on later philosophers, the second about the similarity between Plato's purposes and those of his successors when doing their analyses of mental capacities. It is only Plato's purposes that concern us here, and one point worth noticing is that if he is trying to make either of the analyses mentioned above he is making a very bad job of it. In all the main passages where the tripartite division is elaborated (*Republic* Books IV and IX, *Timaeus* 69–72, *Phaedrus* 240–57) the lowest part of the soul is clearly confined to certain pleasures only, and is in conflict with the desires of the other two. The spirited element, on the other hand, is very selective in the emotions it collects – a fact noted by Murphy (1951) and Crombie (1962), who both espouse the emotion view of spirit – and too tied to admiration, respect and love of honour to be very close to a notion of will. Further, in the *Republic* most markedly each division must be considered as at least in part a distinct desire. If the analysis of the challenge that Plato is facing and the form of his answer that was suggested in chapter I is accepted, then of course one would expect this as necessary for preserving some relevance between Socrates' answer and the problem. Even if we only attend to the immediate context of Books IV and IX, however, the conclusion seems inescapable. Thus the description of temperance at 431 is in terms of better desires/intelligence controlling worse desires. Again, when the question of division is raised, Socrates argues that the same subject cannot be subject to opposed modifications in the same respect in relation to the same thing at the same time (436b seq.). It is then established (437) that desiring, wanting, wishing are all opposed to their negations as pursuit to aversion. Next it is established that desires are distinguished by their objects. It will follow that if we seem to have one object, and a subject desiring and not desiring that object at the same time, something will have to give, and Plato opts for the unity of the subject having to be given up. It is important in this argument that the discussion at 437 is intended to establish that 'want' 'wish' 'desire' ('*boulesthai*', '*ethelein*', '*epithumein*') can be treated as equivalent, simply indicating some at least embryonic movement towards their objects. If this is not accepted the argument for distinguishing reason and desire at 439b–c will not work, as one could claim that the 'does not wish to drink' of 439c 2–3 is not the opposite of the 'wants to drink' entailed by 'is thirsty' (439a–b). Only if one allows that these three terms form one side of an opposition whose other side is occupied by their negations must one admit that the example of 439b–c offends the rule at 436b, and so some modification of the description is necessary. But that is to say that the argument is to show opposition of desires. Strictly, perhaps, it is opposition of desires and non-desires. But it seems clear that Plato is using 'does not want p' as equivalent to 'wants that not p', as the interpretation of denials of wanting in terms of rejection at 437c brings out and as is required for any conflict to arise. This fact makes the argument in one way more dubious. As introduced, it looks like an application of the principle of non-contradiction. 'Motion' and 'rest' are most readily viewed as contradictories, at least over the range of possible movers, and 'want' 'not want' *look* like contradictories. Unfortunately even over the range of possible wanters, they are contraries or, rather, operate in Plato's argument as contraries. It is, of course, open to dispute whether they are. In fact, Plato's use of the notion of opposite is by later standards loose and it would be a mistake to read 436b as giving a principle of contradiction or contraries if this would imply attributing to Plato an awareness of the distinction. The fact remains that in this passage 'does not want p' has to mean 'wants that not p', and however damaging that might be to Plato's argument, the result is that each division of the soul has to be seen as a separate desire. This position is still operative at 571b following and 580d.

In none of these passages does Plato argue that reason is a desire, he simply takes it for granted that certain desires that can be isolated can be equated with reason. This can seem very puzzling to a present-day philosopher. He is used to Hume's view that reason cannot initiate action, but is in practical, and perhaps all, contexts the slave of the passions. Even when considering an interest in the truth, he might take for granted a distinction between the desire for it and the intellectual capacities to satisfy the desire. It would be tempting to suggest that Plato thought that the capacity to discover the truth can only be attributed to beings that pursue it, and the desire for the truth can only be had by beings with certain intellectual capacities. This suggestion of high-level conceptual connections would be in line with present-day anti-Hume fashions, but would be quite anachronistic. Plato does not envisage Hume's position. At the same time, it remains a problem how he does think of reason so as to treat it as a desire, and precisely what it is supposed to be a desire for.

One first suggestion might go as follows: Plato clearly speaks of reason as 'that with/by which we learn or calculate' (cf. e.g. 436a 9, 439d 5, 580d 10). Further, when he comes to describe the various degenerations from the perfectly reasonable 'philosophic' man, it is clear that reason is still functioning (cf. 553 d, 590c), though apparently not on its proper subject-matter. One might suggest, therefore, that Plato thinks that all men have some desire to learn, which is manifested by all types of men. Thus even a man who is simply pursuing his own gratification is interested in knowing what things constitute such gratification and how to go about achieving them (cf. also *Philebus* 58d, 63b–c). They have an interest in the truth, although the range of the interest is determined by other, dominant, considerations.

This will not, however, do as it stands, at least as the whole story. To begin with, it as yet contains nothing to suggest an independent desire of the sort required by the *Republic*, and suggested by the *Phaedrus* and *Timaeus*. For these purposes, to be independent means to be capable of coming in conflict. For all that has been said so far reason might just be an extra faculty that men have enabling them to arrange more effectively for the satisfaction of their desires. It might affect the general form or pattern of these desires even, on occasion, leading to some desire being denied in favour of another but would not constitute a separate aim that might by itself conflict with other desires. Second, this account, while it fits the passages cited, and also *Republic* 518–19, does not sit well with the argument at 441a–b for distinguishing reason from 'spirit'. The point made there is that while children show spirit from birth onwards, some never achieve reason and most people only late. There may be senses of 'reason' whereby people mostly only achieve it late, but it must be some sense stronger than 'articulate interest in discovering means to ends'. This last may not be manifest at birth, but is certainly normally evident in early years.

To satisfy the second point above one needs a desire that might well commonly be absent. One obvious candidate is an interest in knowledge or the truth for its own sake, for instance an academic pursuit of answers to questions unrelated to the satisfaction of any desire except that for discovery. Such a desire might well be at odds with one's desire for food or bed, and is arguably a late developer where it develops at all. Further it seems to fit that general tie between *episteme* (the condition aimed at by reason) and truth found in Books V–VII and Plato's preference for high-level abstract intellectual pursuits over mundane practical ones.

Yet this, too, has its difficulties. It is hard to see in what sense such a desire is supposed to govern a man, let alone a state (cf. e.g. 441e). It is also hard to see in what sense such a desire is distorted and subjected to other interests in a man dominated by admiration for wealth or by various lusts. Why should one attribute such a desire, distorted or not, to such a man? There is no obvious reason for connecting his articulate pursuit of his ends with an academic interest in truth for its own sake. And indeed, any such account overlooks a recurrent theme in the *Republic*, and elsewhere. In Book I 353d, the characteristic activity of the soul is said to be not understanding or discovery, but 'caring for, ruling, deliberating and such like' and this is the function of reason in Book IV. In so far as we hear of knowledge, it is made clear that the mark of knowledge is ability to tell good from bad (e.g. 409d), and goodness is the 'cause' of both knowledge and truth (508e). The knowledge of good is the highest peak of learning, without which all else is useless. These are dark sayings, but they none of them suggest the academic pursuit of learning as the ideal, at least not as that idea is familiar to us.

In order to get clearer where Plato stands it will help first to consider the relation of knowledge (*episteme*) to goodness, for this is perhaps the aspect of Plato's position that is most puzzling to the modern reader. One might as well, therefore, face the puzzle at its most gross. It seems, then, that Plato has four strange things to say. He is liable to say first that a person only has knowledge if he can distinguish between good and bad; second, that if one can talk of a good (or bad) X, then X is something of which we can have knowledge; third, an ideal analogue of the first, real knowledge is of *the* good; fourth, an ideal analogue of the second, *the* good is responsible for knowledge. The third and fourth seem to reach the giddy heights of Platonic metaphysics, but the first two are mysterious enough. An obvious possible item of knowledge from which a modern philosopher might start a discussion of knowledge might be that I have a toothache or that the cat is on the mat. Whatever problems there might be about our knowledge of these there is no temptation to suppose that I can only know either of them if I know whether it is a good or bad thing that matters be that way. Conversely, it is the last thing that seems to strike most modern philosophers as obvious that if you can sensibly talk of a good (or bad) X, then it is a thing of which you can have knowledge.

The first two sayings are not late developments. In the *Gorgias* Plato develops a distinction between theory-supported skills (*technai*) and other apparent skills relying on trial and error (*empeiriai*). This last, especially, is an inadequate description, as Plato makes it a mark of this class that they are directed at giving (immediate) pleasure. What is of present interest is the former. In the first passage that treats of the distinction (464–5), *technai* are given two distinguishing marks, first that they are concerned with what is best for, not pleasantest to, their subjects, and secondly that they can give an account of the nature of their treatments. In the second passage (500 seq.) these two points seem more clearly blended as well as elaborated (cf. esp. 501a–b). A *techne* will yield an account of the nature of its subject and an explanation of its activities, and will consider what is best for its subject. This latter (cf. 503d–504e, 506d–e) is a matter of finding the right order and arrangement. For each thing has its proper order that constitutes its excellence, and is investigated by the skill covering it.

In the *Gorgias* the discussion is about *technai*, not by name about knowledge. *Technai*, however, including medicine, which is so prominent in the *Gorgias*, are commonly cited by Plato either as examples of *episteme* or to illustrate points about *episteme*, especially when the requirement that knowledge entails the ability to tell good from bad is being discussed (e.g. *Republic* Book X 601c–e). Further, the way Plato talks of the need for a special *techne* covering the soul's welfare parallels the talk of reason and the health of the soul in *Republic* Book IV, and the later role of *episteme* in that work, as well as, e.g. *Phaedrus* 270. By the time of the *Republic* he has further points to make to distinguish *episteme* from vulgar *technai*, but *technai* still serve to illustrate some of the vital points about the most important form of knowledge. Similar points are found elsewhere. For instance, in the *Phaedo*, Socrates remarks that when he read Anaxagoras' suggestion that intelligence is the orderer and cause of everything, he inferred that in that case everything would be ordered for the best. In short, intelligence and *episteme* are shown in the ability to distinguish good from bad states.

The second point is also found in the *Gorgias*. At 503c–d it is assumed that if Socrates is right in saying that the satisfaction of certain desires makes a man better, of others worse, then it will require a *techne* to tell us which. Later, in 506d–e, it is declared that in all cases excellence is a matter of order, correctness and skill. In other words, it is taken as read that if one can talk of good and bad states of affairs or conditions of things, then there is a *techne* devisable in accordance with which one could discriminate between the good and the bad. This assumption recurs, for instance, in *Republic* Book I, where Socrates moves naturally from the suggestion that justice is a matter of benefiting one's friends to the question of what skills confer various benefits. Similarly in the *Philebus* it is taken that good mixtures are proper subject for intelligence and skill (cf. 23–31 esp. 26a–c and 28a–30c).

The first two points, then, are not early aberrations, but a persistent Platonic theme. The question remains: why? To begin with it will, I think, help to note some linguistic differences between the Greek word '*episteme*' and the English 'knowledge', as a good deal of the mystery derives from their supposed equivalence. A small point of interest is that the Greek word has a plural, while the English does not. One can, indeed, operate on the English to produce a plural, indeed to produce two: 'piece (item) of knowledge' and 'branch of knowledge' each has a plural. It is probably fair to suggest that if one is asked what one knows, or what is known in general, especially if one has come from an English speaking epistemological tradition, any answer will be in terms of pieces of knowledge. Thus I might be inclined to give that William the Conqueror invaded Britain in 1066, or at least that I exist as possible claimants. 'Philosophy' or 'the violin' would not leap to mind. When a Greek is asked to list *epistemai* he does not give items known by him or the population at large, but something nearer to branches of knowledge – geometry, medicine and such like are the *epistemai* – the 'sciences'. The things known are not propositions but, e.g. numbers, shipbuilding and so on.

Further, the adjective from 'knowledge' is 'knowledgeable' (that is, the adjective that connotes having knowledge), and a knowledgeable person is someone with a wide range of knowledge. Not only that, but a wide range of factual knowledge is sufficient for meriting the description. One can also, of course, be knowledgeable in particular areas, but here too, a large collection of facts is enough. I can be very knowledgeable about football if I know the winners of the major competitions in the last fifty years, the main stars and the various records, while being an innocent at the game. Indeed, it is at least plausible to suggest that the bias of the adjective is in this direction. By contrast, the Greek adjective *epistemon* has strong connotations of competence in performance, approximating to 'skilful'. The suggestion of calling someone *epistemon* about football would not at all be the Brain of Britain accomplishments mentioned above, but rather that he was at least worth consulting about tactics and training, and possibly also a good performer. Increasingly, with Plato, there is a tendency to reserve '*episteme*', at least, for skills with a strong theoretical element, but the connotations first of competence, and secondly of practical use are still there. Consequently, the plural *epistemai* does not suggest everything that might count as a branch of knowledge, or come on a university syllabus. Archaeology, for instance, would be a surprising member of the list. On the other hand, it will collect items that would not readily come to mind as branches of knowledge, such as building and flute-playing. It may be that Plato wishes to argue that these should not strictly be included, but he is clearly aware that so far as linguistic naturalness goes they naturally could, not to say would.

It would, of course, be extravagant to suggest that these linguistic differences are enough to explain the contrast between Platonic and modern treatments of the apparently identical questions 'what is *episteme*?' and 'what is knowledge?' respectively. Philosophical and scientific backgrounds also play their part, though the linguistic facts doubtless help. That they are not sufficient is, I think, clear enough in the English case. The use of the word 'knowledgeable' discussed above seems to be a late one (the first occurrence mentioned in the *O.E.D.* being nineteenth-century), so that the problem of the chicken and the egg might well be raised. When it comes to the verb 'know', some explanation is needed of why there is concentration by philosophers on constructions governing that-clauses rather than how-clauses, or ones governing particular items, rather than subject-matters. Even if recourse is had to the view that problems were derived from philosophers with separate knowing – verbs, such as '*connaître*', that in effect pushes the answer back to whatever determined the problems being put in those terms.

Suppose we accept that Descartes was interested in asking what any individual could be certain of, and proceeded in a way that quickly concentrated attention on particular facts and general mathematical and ratiocinative principles. It is also important that in the subsequent period the great scientific advances were in physical sciences, where it was plausible to suggest that in the end results had to be substantiated by factual observation. The whole discussion, in fact, is being conducted in a quite different context from that obtaining in Plato's time. Then we have a society where the most promising of the developing theoretical interests, medicine and music, were closely linked to practical skills. This is not to say that no one was interested in cosmology. Most pre-Socratic philosophers were so. But no school seemed obviously to hold the field in Plato's time, nor was it obvious what was the proper procedure for pursuing them. On the other hand, Pythagorean developments in the theory of music, and Hippocratean ones in medicine might understandably have seemed more hopeful, and so led Plato to concentrate on those suggestions of the word 'episteme' that best fitted these examples.

If this is more or less right, one would expect the question 'what is episteme?' to produce rather different treatment from that given to 'what is knowledge?' This latter has tended to run together two questions: first, 'how do we define "know"?' and second, 'what counts as an adequate substantiation of the claim to know?', a question that has notoriously often been confused with the question 'how do we acquire our knowledge?' Answers to both have tended to concentrate on 'know' when governing that-clauses or simple items. 'What is episteme?', on the other hand, is treated by Plato more like 'what is it to have a skill?' There is no obsession about individual certainty, though there is concern about something that looks like a combination of precision and clarity. The question is rather, what has to be true if it is to be true that there are skills such as medicine, music and so on? If we take the items in a characteristic Platonic list of technai or epistemai used to make general points about episteme, then it looks quite plausible to suggest that it is characteristic of an episteme to distinguish between a good and a bad state of affairs. Thus the exposition of medicine in the school of Hippocrates will start from the description of a certain condition of the body as good, i.e. a healthy condition, brought about by a certain balance of elements, which is thus the correct balance. Similarly an exposition of music will necessitate establishing the scales and the general rules governing the melodious combination of notes. In general the technai that receive mention – strategy, navigation, farming, music, medicine – operate with some notions indicating good formations, times for attack, weather-conditions, conditions of crop, combinations of notes, balance of elements and so on. It would therefore be not an outrageous, but quite plausible account of technai to say, summing this point up, that they are concerned with the good. Each provides, in its subject-matter, a distinction between good and bad, and the exercise of the techne is concerned with production of the relevant good. In the Gorgias, it is true, there are in fact two ways in which the empeiriai concerned are distinguished from technai, first, they are concerned with pleasure, not the good, and second, they do not understand the nature and causes of pleasure, but rely on guess-work. This suggests the possibility of a more effective pastry-cook who did not tailor his cooking-habits to the fashions and whims of the population, who instead of simply trying to please his customers set about giving them the greatest pleasure. It may be that Plato did not notice the possibility, but it may also be that he thought that if you examined the nature of pleasure you would find that it was, say, the experience of satisfied desire or the restoration of natural balance. In either case you would be likely to emerge with some distinction between good and bad pleasures, even if only on the hedonistic grounds of relative fertility. More likely, Plato would want to relate the pleasure to its conditions, and its worth to the worth of the conditions, so that the development of the *techne* would not simply involve the development of *some* criteria of good and bad, but of criteria to distinguish between the good and bad conditions of those whose pleasure was sought.

It is arguable, then, that the first puzzling statement, that any case of knowing is somehow knowing the good, is in fact part of a plausible answer to the question 'what is an *episteme*?' An *episteme* is a theory-supported practical capacity employing centrally some notion or notions of good and bad states of affairs. Even if this is not an adequate analysis of the Greek term, it is at least no more influenced by a combination of language, scientific development and philosophical problem (of which more later), than treatments of 'knowledge' in English-speaking philosophy over recent centuries. What, then, of the converse, that if *X* can sensibly be called good or bad, then there is a *techne* or *episteme* covering it? Here I must recall chapter II (pp. 31–5). It was there argued that Plato considers that certain conditions have to be satisfied if something can be said to be a good or bad *X*. In the *Gorgias* (503a–506e), the emphasis is put on order. Talk of excellence supposes the possibility of distinguishing between order and disorder. Clearly, however, not any ordering is right, and each thing has its own proper ordering (506e), so that a question arises how we are to determine a thing's proper ordering. Possibly the talk of characteristic activity or function, found in the *Republic*, is intended to supply an answer to this question. If, but only if, an object can be brought under a type (or types) defined in terms of a characteristic activity or function can it be said to be capable of excellence, and, of course, only in respect of the function defining that type(s). As I remarked earlier, it certainly seems that some substitutions for '*X*' in 'a good *X*' would yield bizarre results, as e.g. 'natural number' or 'speck'. It may be that other descriptions on occasion hold of given natural numbers or specks which make it sensible to assess their worth in those respects, but at least these don't. It is also true that a wide range of descriptions which do generate respects in which excellence can be assessed seem to fit Plato's account very well, e.g. 'eye', 'typist', 'pencil'. It does not follow, of course, that everything will. 'Picture', 'toffee', 'friend', 'suggestion', 'collection of shells' seem less obviously to fit. Still, it is a common philosophical weakness to be dominated by one's first examples, especially if they are also the most common. In Plato's case, his attention might well have been focused on these examples because he was interested in *epistemai*, and descriptions of which his account held would commonly also give the 'object' of some *episteme* – 'condition of body', 'eye', 'arrangement of notes', 'combination of tide and weather', 'bridle' and so on. By contrast, a present-day philosopher would have no analogous bias from an interest in knowledge or science. Impressed, rather (as indeed was Plato, see *Phaedrus* 263), with the intractability of moral argument, and with no inclination to associate knowledge with goodness, he will be as likely to take 'good' as it occurs in aesthetic contexts or expressions of taste as the model for moral uses. Plato does not, as I hope to bring out, have any temptation to treat moral disputes as basically any different from any others about excellence. Further (a) the analysis that suggests itself in the cases that catch his attention is plausible for those cases, and (b) they are cases where one might well expect some *techne* or *episteme* to be devisable.

It is worth now noting the limitations of this position as developed so far. The first is that in so far as it supplies an account of the claim that knowledge is of the good, it does so only for a summing-up interpretation. In other words, 'knowledge is of the good' has to mean 'any *episteme* employs some good/bad distinction'. If Plato wants to say that there is some overall knowledge covering an overall good/bad distinction this thesis would nowhere near show it. Second, the account of the conditions for attributing excellence that I have fathered on Plato either overlooks a possibility, or is not yet strong enough to produce a conclusion he wants. The possibility is that allowable substitutions for 'X' in 'a good X' should be such as to yield a disjunction of functions, rather than one function. Thus 'part of a clock' or 'tool' might be allowable, but there is not one function that all things correctly characterised in these ways has. So one might hold that allowable substitutions are such that they imply some function(s), rather than that for each there is just one. If, on the other hand, Plato is allowing for this possibility, then clearly it does not follow from the fact that we can talk of a good man that we can talk of *the* excellence of man. This could fail to follow in one of two conditions. First, 'man' could function like 'tool', in that there would be an indefinite range of recognised activities any one of which would constitute a respect for assessing someone as a good man. Thus 'good man' can be used to comment on someone's excellence as a building employee, a sergeant, a business manager and so on. Second, it might function like 'part of a clock', where there are various excellences that are all related to the overall function of the clock. Thus one might consider the human species as essentially social, requiring different capacities from different members who would therefore manifest different excellences all judged as excellences, however, because of their relation to the requirements of the community or species. If either of these conditions held, it would be impossible to talk of *the* excellence of man in terms suggesting a uniform excellence for all men. At least, some further argument would be needed to show that there was at least one excellence that covered all humans or that one deserved the title of *the* excellence.

It is difficult to say whether Plato appreciated this point. That he had come across the possibility is clear from the *Meno* (71e seq.), although which of the two forms mentioned above Meno's position exemplifies is not clear. Socrates' objection there in fact seems to rely on the assumption that one can talk of the excellence of man, an excellence relevant to all men, of which justice and temperance are aspects. His view of the soul is in part a view that certain characteristics hold of all human beings, and ones that, in Plato's view, yield a single ladder of assessment. So this view would justify talking of a single excellence. In fact, of course, the *Republic* also contains the seeds of the second possibility outlined in the last paragraph. It is tempting to suggest that the various classes in the state perform different functions, calling for different types of person with different excellences. 'Justice' might still be required, in the sense of obedience to community requirements, but it would either cash out as something different in each case, or not be related to specific functions. In the latter case, if a man was to be called good in virtue of being just, we should have a counter-example to Plato's general thesis on the discernment of excellence. In fact Plato insists on talking of human excellence, including 'justice', in individual-related rather than species- or community-related terms, with the result that only a few achieve unqualified excellence.

The result of all this is that the account offered of why Plato says that any *episteme* is somehow of the good, and any goodness is a proper subject of *episteme* does not as yet account for the further moves in the third and fourth statements mentioned earlier. We still need to know how he reaches the conclusion that there is an *episteme* of *the* good, and that *the* good is the cause both of the truth and the knowing mind. Further, it would be nice to know what these conclusions might mean. All we have so far is some understanding of why every *episteme* might be held to be concerned with some good, and how on Plato's account of the preconditions for attributing excellence goodness is always a subject of *episteme*.

At this point it has to be admitted that any view is going to be more speculative. A great deal of what Plato says in this area is either extremely gnomic or stated through imagery such as that of the sun or the cave in *Republic* Books VI and VII. On the other hand such views cannot be passed over. Not only in the *Phaedo* and *Republic*, but also in the *Symposium* (with *kalon* substituted for *agathon*) they are given considerable importance in the central dialogues, and the *Timaeus*, *Philebus* and *Epinomis* suggest a persistent life to them. If no sense can be made of them, then an important element in Plato's views remains obscure. In what follows, I shall take it that these sayings are in some way related to and indeed extensions of the sayings that I have tried to elucidate in the foregoing paragraphs. This is, I think, what one would expect, and I hope to show that it yields an account which both makes Plato's remarks intelligible and explains both his resort to imagery and his excitement. The main sketch will be given in the present chapter, some further points will be made later when I consider some objections to this whole interpretation of Plato on knowledge.

How, then, could one move from a collection of unrelated branches of knowledge covering unrelated goods to a single *episteme* covering good in general? First, I shall suggest how it may be done, and then I shall try to indicate how it fits, or is suggested by the things that Plato says. Suppose, then, we take an artefact such as a rack or a thumbscrew, and suppose two people arguing each that his is a better thumbscrew than the other's. We can, of course, readily interpret this as a dispute about relative efficacy, but one could also understand an objection to talking in terms of 'good' or 'better' on the grounds that thumbscrews are not good things at all. In other words, the dispute suggests an assumption that thumbscrewing is a good thing, an assumption which Topcliffe might have accepted, but many would now want to question. At any rate, the objection comes from the feeling that agreeing to talk of a good X is tantamount to agreeing that it is a good thing that there be Xs of certain sorts, and that there is an air of paradox in talking of good murderers, thieves, poisons and generally things considered bad.

In this example it is easiest, though not necessary, to interpret 'good', 'bad' at the higher level in a moral sense. Suppose we take another example. Suppose someone is interested in the development of muscles. He decides that the role of muscles is to provide strength, and that this is a function of the size of the muscle. He sets up criteria accordingly for distinguishing between good and bad conditions of muscle, and thereby an *episteme* of muscle. It might well be objected, however, that he is assuming that it is a good thing for muscles to be as large as possible, whereas in fact it is possible to have overdeveloped muscles which become a hindrance rather than a help. The objection is not that the man has no intelligible criteria, but that they are wrong. The argument that they are wrong claims that the special activity of muscles has to be assessed in a wider context of the operations of the organism. It is this context that determines whether or not it is a good thing for muscle to be developed beyond a given point. The position in this case is not moral, but depends on the view that talk of the proper functioning of parts of an organism is to be assessed by reference to the whole.

Both these examples suggest the possibility of holding that in some way the criteria for distinguishing between good and bad Xs presuppose that it is a good thing to have Xs of a certain sort. The second example suggests a first move that might be made towards questioning or establishing this presupposition. Clearly something analogous could lie behind the first example. The assumption that thumbscrews are a good thing might be questioned by reference to the sort of society in which they have a role. In the second example the querying of the criteria of excellence for muscles is also directed against the supposed *episteme* of muscles. This feature does not hold in the first example, of course, because what a thumbscrew is, and its defining role, is determined by purposes, in this case undesirable, of those who requisition them. In the second example the operation of the organism is something to be discovered.

Suppose we now marry this sort of position to the view on *episteme* and good that I have attributed to Plato. It will follow that all talk of good Xs commits one to a possible *episteme*. Conversely, any putative *episteme* will involve talk of good/bad Xs. (An objection based on Plato's talk of arithmetic and geometry as *epistemai* will be considered in a later chapter.) Waiving that, any supposed *episteme* will embody the assumption that it is a good thing that certain sorts of X exist. Unless that assumption can be substantiated it will remain in doubt whether it is a genuine or pseudo-*episteme*. Such substantiation will take the form of putting the subject-matter of the earlier *episteme* in a wider context and so getting a more synoptic view. The possibility of talk of good and bad situations in the wider context supposes the possibility of an *episteme* covering that topic and so on. Either it is possible at each stage of some progression to supply the necessary context, or else no *episteme* is possible. But clearly such a process must end somewhere, there must be a final context. So either we can reach that final context, or no *episteme* is possible. This does not, of course, mean that no knowledge would be possible, but that no *epistemai* would be available, for all putative *epistemai* would be shown to rest on either a false or unsubstantiated assumption. In neither case could they be justifiably called *epistemai*. This would not affect our certainty about our toothaches.

Such a view would suppose, of course, that it is always possible to find a wider context until such time as we clearly reached a universal context. The *episteme* of muscles is subject to medicine, but medicine supposes it is a good thing that bodies be healthy. This would require reference to some wider context for the operation of bodies. This could lead to some view of the balance of nature, or if human bodies are in question the aptness of healthy bodies for subserving the operations of human souls could supply a context. This in turn would raise the question of the excellence of souls, and why it is a good thing that there be wise, brave, sober, just people. The role of souls in the universe would need to be unfolded. In the end one would reach the stage where the whole universe was exhibited as an interconnected whole, the requirements of interconnection determining what constitutes the excellence of the parts. The fact that the system is of this particular interconnected sort is what makes it possible to speak correctly of *X*s as good and bad, and thus makes *epistemai* possible. The *epistemai*, on the other hand, can now be looked upon as parts of the *episteme* of the whole, just as the *episteme* of muscles is a part of the *episteme* of the body.

So much for the picture. It is now time to see how it relates to Plato. It might be as well to start by noting a set of discussions which may seem to bear on the issue and even tell against the interpretation offered, but are in fact, I think, not relevant. In the earlier dialogues there are several discussions of the suggestion that virtue is a form of knowledge. A number of these discussions are directed to the question what virtue is knowledge of, and what a branch of knowledge would have to cover to be a possible candidate. Characteristically these discussions contrast this form of knowledge with the familiar *technai* (cf. e.g. *Charmides* 173 seq., *Euthydemus* 288d seq., *Republic* Book I, 332 seq., *Laches* 195 seq., *Alcibiades* I 106 seq.). One or both of two points tend to be emphasised. First this proposed *techne* must be given some specifiable benefit distinct from those that define the other *technai*, and secondly, it will be its function to regulate the use of the other *technai* or the use of their products (cf. *Euthydemus* 288d seq. and compare *Politicus* 304 seq.). Now it seems to be part of this sort of argument to separate the governing *episteme/techne* from others which it is wise to subject to it. These others are, however, *epistemai* whether governed by it or not (see esp. *Charmides* 174b–c). It is not the function of this overriding *episteme* to embody the operations of the subject ones. So this set of passages suggests a measure of independence of *epistemai* incompatible with the interpretation offered.

While these passages illustrate Plato's tendency to associate *epistemai* with the discernment of good and bad conditions in a subject-matter, they in fact have no bearing on the question in hand. The interpretation offered purports to explain how Plato might have thought that there is a general account of goodness to be given which enables us to explain how the *epistemai* we have can correctly be said to be distinguishing between good and bad states of affairs. A person with knowledge of the good would not thereby be good at medicine, strategy and the rest, but he would know that these were or were not pseudo-*epistemai*. He would also know whether a proposed set of criteria for judging between good and bad states of man were correct, and so whether someone's claim to have the *episteme* needed for virtue or politics was justified. In short, the question we are concerned with is not whether there is a special moral skill that should govern others, but whether establishing that something is a genuine *episteme* consists in showing that it is right in supposing that the conditions it declares to be good are in fact so. Still, it may be that in the middle/late dialogues the *episteme* governing an individual life is subject to the *episteme* of the whole system.

It does, however, seem that this last question is one that comes to the fore in the middle dialogues, not the early ones. In the earlier ones there is more concern to bring out that the pretensions of teachers and politicians to advise on or direct our lives have no foundation, and that it is difficult to make clear what they would have to know for their claims to be well-grounded. The emphasis is first on the difference between the goodness of man and the goodness of other things, and second on the difference between being concerned to benefit and being concerned to please. In the *Phaedo* Socrates looks longingly at the possibility of seeing the excellence of particular things (including men) in the context of the best sort of arrangement (97c–99c). His hopes were raised by Anaxagoras' suggestion that the world was the work of intelligence. An intelligent agent would not arrange things badly. It would be a mark of his intelligence that he arranged them well. Socrates was led to expect therefore that Anaxagoras would explain how it was best for the sun and the moon and the stars to be and behave as they did.

> As he said things were arranged by some intelligence, I did not think he would have resort to any other explanation than one showing that it was best for them to be as they were. I expected him to explain each individually and all of them together by explaining what was best for each and what was the good for all together respectively (98a 6–b 3).

This passage expresses the aim of being able to give a comprehensive account of the good arrangement of the universe, and the sentences quoted indicate two aspects: the good of particular things and the general good. These are two aspects of showing it to be best, say, that the sun moves as it does. Anaxagoras is expected to indicate both how it is best for the sun so to move and best overall that it should do so. This suggests a close connection between the good of the parts and the good of the whole, which would fit the interpretation given earlier.

In the *Phaedo* we find something described as an ideal which Socrates would like to see fulfilled (97d 5–7, 99c 6–8), but in fact he follows another method. In the *Symposium* we find a view attributed, but clearly with respect, to Diotima (201d–212c). According to this view love is to be seen as directed to immortality (207a), a desire which leads to procreation. But some it leads to physical, others to spiritual procreation (208e–209a). The latter are led to try to produce their proper offspring of excellence and wisdom. The proper course for them is to be attracted to an individual for his physical beauty. They should then reflect on what makes a fine physical specimen, so that their appreciation develops beyond the individual to all fine bodies. He should be led to considering what makes a fine personality. This will make him think less of physical attributes, and prepare him for considering *epistemai*. After that he will reach the one *episteme* of *to kalon*.

The details of the passage are problematic, but certain things are clear: first, the progress has been, first, to greater generality within each field, and to an understanding of what constitutes fineness in that field; second, it is important not only to generalise over a field, but to move through the various later stages; third, these seem to be hierarchically ordered; fourth, the final term is a form of knowledge, and a knowledge of what is responsible for the fineness of the earlier stages. In other words, the progress is at least partly to more synoptic understanding. The hierarchy is probably a first sketch of the overall ordering. Bodies are subject to souls, the virtue of souls requires reasoning and knowledge – this is directed to ordering things, and the *kallos*, fineness, of knowledge is seen when we see the total order of which souls are a governing part.

By the *Republic* Socrates is claiming things in his own person, though he is still not spelling out the details of the programme, and indeed disclaims the capacity (506d–e). The claim, however, at 508e–509b, is that the form of goodness is responsible for truth and knowledge. While these last conform to the good they are not (the) good. The good is responsible for the being and essence of things known, but the good is not an essence, it is beyond essence. Sense can be made of this as follows: since there can only be *episteme* if it is possible to distinguish between good and bad ways for things to be, the fact that this can be done is responsible for *episteme*. As only a mind in good condition is capable of *episteme*, goodness will be responsible for anyone's knowing. The 'truth' covered by *epistemai* concerns such things as health and melody, and these are ways for arrangements to be good; but the arrangements are only good because they have a place in a harmonious system; so that system that explains the goodness of various arrangements thereby makes possible *episteme*.

If we consider the universe as such a system, then we shall be able to ask for an account of the nature of various parts, classifying them in terms of what they do. Giving their 'essence' will consist in giving their role (cf. *Phaedrus* 270c–d). Now the whole may consist of sub-systems. Thus, for instance, the operations of the parts of an organism are first explained in terms of the organism. But as this is a mere part of the whole, the question can be raised what *it* does, and in what its excellence consists. On the view attributed to Plato, however, this question could not be asked of the total system, for the question requires, for its answer, relation to a wider context. There is no wider context for the total system. The interconnectedness of the system makes it possible to give 'essences' of things in the system, but it is itself 'beyond' them. The parts of the system conform to the system (are in good-form), but are not (the) good; the system does not conform, but is what constitutes goodness. On the other hand, grasping the system is what gives understanding of the general ordering of the parts, and so underpins the various *epistemai* (cf. *Republic* 533b–c, 534c). This fits well with the imagery of the Good, and the sun, as the final terms in the search for knowledge and also the general synoptic picture of the philosopher. It yields an account both of what the claim that there is a single overall form of knowledge amounts to and of how the Good is responsible for knowledge. It also explains a remark at *Phaedrus* 270b–e. Socrates is claiming that to do the soul good we need to know the nature of the soul, and for that we need to know the nature of the whole (universe). Phaedrus agrees, citing Hippocrates making the same point about the body. What we have to do is enquire whether what we are examining has a single form or many. When we have a single form of thing we enquire what its role is and how it interacts with other things. Now it is not clear why, if we are to know about the mind, we have to know about moon-dust or shellfish that are confined to the ocean bed, at least, not if simple interaction is in question. But if what Plato has in mind is the kind of view I have attributed to him, then we must take in the whole of nature in trying to understand a part. For always we shall be having to understand the nature of the other terms of interaction, and seeing what it is their nature to do, but this in turn will involve understanding all their interactions, and at each stage a view about their nature is a view about the part they play in the total structure, and so is only established in the total context.

In the *Timaeus* the same basic picture is presented. The interest there is cosmological, but the theme is that the world is ordered by intelligence, that intelligence will order chaos, and order it for the best, and the general style of argument is to show how, granted the material available, the world is the best we could have, by showing the interlocking appropriateness of its parts, the main example being the human person. The same emphasis, on the possibility and desirability of a comprehensive understanding of the universe and a belief in its interrelatedness, is still present in the *Epinomis* (976 seq.). In short, the interpretation offered fits Plato's remark about the Good in relation to knowledge very well and makes it intelligible not only that he should have held it, but that he should have been both excited and diffident about success.

All this discussion of knowledge and goodness has been entered into with a view to discovering what sort of desire the reasoning part of a person is. There are objections to this interpretation that I shall consider in a later chapter. For the moment I shall suppose it to be right and return to the earlier question. In respect to that, it might now seem that man's reasoning capacity is a desire for understanding, but for understanding as construed by Plato, and it would only count as that if it were understanding of how it is best that things be as they are. This might be a desire so great as to dominate a person's life so that he dedicates it to the acquisition of this understanding. Plato seems, indeed, to say things of this sort. In the *Symposium* we do not merely find a desire for truth alongside others, but a desire that will lead a man to spend his life in the contemplation of *to kalon* (211c–212a). This is the picture one gets of the philosopher in the *Republic*. Indeed, it seems so much part of Plato's thinking that he can surprise the modern reader. In the *Philebus* (55 seq.) we have a discussion of various forms of knowledge which are distinguished in virtue of their precision and clarity. At 58 there is a digression to make it clear that it is the form of knowledge with most claim to truth, not influence, that we are seeking. Quite suddenly at 58d 4 seq., Socrates glosses this as wondering whether we are capable of loving the truth and doing everything for its sake. The fact is that Plato seems to think of reason as an urge to understand which can dominate someone, and when it reaches the peak of philosophical interest it has reached that strength. The *Philebus* gloss would seem to him not a digression but natural.

This still, however, leaves us with the possibility of academic obsession. The language of *Symposium* 211d suggests a life given over to contemplation of *to kalon*. The education of philosophers in *Republic* Book VII suggests a progress away from practical affairs to ever more rarefied academic heights, from which a philosopher has to be dragged down to take part in running the state. A similar removal-from-the-world ideal seems implied by the *Phaedo* (e.g. 63b–64b, 65d–67b, 79c–d). Indeed, the earlier dialogues suggest a certain antipathy between philosophy and public life. It is claimed that philosophers would be best equipped to run the state, but that it is hardly something they would willingly do (cf. e.g. *Republic* Book I, 347b–c).

At the same time there is a contrasting theme. The role of intelligence is constantly given as one of ruling, governing, caring, planning. When in *Republic* Book I Socrates determines the characteristic operation of the soul he does not give knowledge or understanding as the answer, but caring, ruling, counselling and everything of that sort (353d). This is how the reason is looked on in Book IV 442c seq., and this is the role assigned to the soul in the *Phaedo* (e.g. 79e–80a, 94b–e). Also, the sort of *episteme* envisaged in dialogues such as the *Gorgias*, the *Charmides,* the *Euthydemus* is of great practical benefit, and its exercise is directive in form (cf. also *Republic* Book IV 428 seq.). In these earlier dialogues the issue is primarily how we are to live, and what form of knowledge is required. The requisite knowledge is concerned with right ordering and the nature of its subject-matter. The view is, however, vulnerable to the interpretation that the intellect is there to serve man's other desires, and in so far as it constitutes a distinguishable desire it is directed to the complete and ordered satisfaction of other desires. In the *Phaedo* and *Symposium*, especially the former, a stronger contrast between intellect and 'physical' factors, such as perception and desire, is developed, with a consequent suggestion of a rival interest for the mind, although its organising role is preserved. This tension is still present in the *Republic* between the intellect as a desire to contemplate the truth, free of physical distractions, and the intellect as concerned to organise and see to the satisfaction of the various aspects of the personality. These could, of course, be reconciled in the framework of the *Phaedo* in that the organisation of life could be seen as geared to the needs of philosophy and ensuring lack of distraction and domination by desires and emotions. In the *Republic* the desirability of philosophers entering public life is developed, and we find, in Book I (347b–c) an attempt to extend the argument. Even entering public life might be necessary in the interests of intellectual development, as matters might be much worse with a fool in charge. In the context of the ideal city, however, this is a less potent argument, since any individual philosopher might have reason to believe that he could escape the necessity while being sure that the alternative would be the acceptable one of being ruled over by philosophers. The appeal rests, as we have seen, on justice. But then it should be possible to show that it is best to be just.

It is interesting that after the *Republic* (granted that the *Phaedrus* is later), there is a development of view about the role of intelligence. It is not simply that it is appropriate for it to rule, it is, quite generally, the function of souls to have care of the inanimate, the more perfect having the more extensive area of operation (*Phaedrus* 246b–c). This line of thought is developed in the *Timaeus,* where the role of various intelligences is to preserve and further the good order of the universe. This is used in an ethical context in the *Philebus* (27–30). The issue there is the relative roles of pleasure and intelligence in the good life. All that is strictly needed for the argument is the identification of intelligence with the cause of the good life. In fact, we get inserted a passage claiming first that our bodies are to be seen as microcosms of the universe as a whole, reflecting in meagre form the combination of elements found more impressively in the universe at large. It is argued that we should similarly see our intelligences as deriving from the life-giving intelligence of the universe. The importance of this for present purposes is that it seems to be attributing to our intellects a function of assistants to the world – soul/intelligence, a function whose importance is not confined to the interests of the agent but includes contributing to the total ordering of the universe. Our intelligence might be expected to share the Demiurge's repugnance for disorder described in the *Timaeus* (29e–30b). A philosopher, then, will be expected to share the Demiurge's desire for an ordered universe, and see disorder as something calling for removal. The desire for understanding and the function of directing and ruling thus get blended. Understanding the general order is an essential part of understanding and performing this function. The blending would also ease the problem of the *Republic*'s philosopher-kings. For they might now be expected to see that their feeling that it is right to take part in public life is justified, for this is taking part in the divine work. A person who has come to live well, therefore, has come to understand what good ordering is and to want to see it imposed. The result is that in the end, at least, Plato can avoid egoism if, first, the statement that we want the best out of life is interpreted not as about the motivation of each action but about what we should acknowledge as our ideal; second, it is granted that what is the best life is open to demonstration; third, it consists in a life where reason plays the dominant role; and fourth, that role is one of sharing in the general good ordering of the universe. When I say 'role' this has to be read as not simply indicating its proper part, but also what it comes to want as it grows in understanding.

Before turning, in the next chapter, to draw together the threads of the discussion so far, I shall return to a difficulty brought earlier against the suggestion that 'reason' in the *Republic* is an academic desire for knowledge. The objection was that such a desire seems a poor candidate for running a state, and yields no clear sense to the notion of reason being used but distorted in degenerate types of person. The *faculty* of reason could, of course, be looked upon as 'fitted' for academic pursuits, and distorted elsewhere, but the *desire* seems simply to be non-operative in these cases. If, however, 'reason' is related to *episteme*, and this is to be interpreted as suggested above, the position is different. For all the degenerate types of person have their views on what is best – to obtain pleasure, to be able to do as one wants, to be rich, to have honour. It is now possible, in the manner of the early dialogues, to query each of these candidates, thus showing at the same time that their advocates' understanding of what is best (their *episteme*) is incomplete and that they have not yet got clear what they want. The very use of the terms 'good' and 'bad' by a sybarite is a sign of a desire for *episteme*, and of some apprehension, however dim, of the truth that the world is an ordered system. On the other hand reason does not emerge as an independent desire, for *Republic* Book IV purposes, until a person has become critical of his objectives, and wonders whether it is always best to satisfy one's thirst, or a good thing to be just. This critical interest in what is best, which can lead to the proper development of a man's role in the universe, usually comes late, if at all. This view does not, of course, remove the verbal inconsistencies of the *Republic*, but it does, I think, go some way towards rendering them innocuous.

V

The Defence of
Traditional Morality

In chapter I, I began trying to expound the form of Plato's defences against a position that threatened to erode traditional morality. It is now time to review the situation and see in what sense a defence has been offered. For this it is worth recalling that in *Republic* Book I (348), Thrasymachus' challenge is taken as having three prongs. 'Injustice' is preferable to 'justice' because it is more intelligent, because it gives one power to do as one wants and because it is generally good, while 'justice' is stupidity, an abandonment of the power to do as one wants and bad. Each of these points is countered, and they are treated as interconnected. 'The power to do as one wants' is interpreted as 'the power to do/get what satisfies one's desires'. It is argued that this is a complex matter, and it emerges as clearly requiring intelligence. If being 'unjust' is a good state to be in, then it will constitute the correct functioning of the *psyche* and so of the ordering, intellectual functions. If we study the requirements of *episteme* we realise that on Thrasymachus' sort of view there is no possibility of constructing an *episteme* that can be held to cover what is good for man. At best one could become adept at ensuring the satisfaction of the dominant desire of the moment, but that is a far cry from being *epistemon* about human life.

It is important in this connection to be clear on a lack of parallel between Plato and many present-day philosophers. In the first chapter I suggested that Plato and his opponents shared the assumption that a person only had a reason for adopting a course of action or way of life if it answered to some desire or desires. This should not, however, be taken to reflect Plato's way of describing the matter. The various Greek words that in varying degrees fail to correspond to the English 'reason', 'reasonable', 'rational', 'intelligent', and so on, are not used in this context. Thus Plato does not argue that it is *alogon* or *aphron* to do what one does not want. Nor does he have any interest in a special form of practical reason following a different pattern from theoretical reasoning. Similarly there is no axiom that it is irrational not to want what is good. Rather, it is a fact that we all want what is good. Intelligence comes in because it is also true that good is what *episteme* is concerned with. It is this that enables Plato to reject the opposition claim to intelligence in that what they advocate does not have the main features necessary to justify a claim to *episteme*. Traditional moral norms are nearer to what is required. Thus the analysis of desires characteristic of the human person shows 'justice' (a proper discipline) to meet all of men's desires; analysis of the characteristic operations of the soul shows it to constitute the excellence of the soul; as the soul has an excellence there must be an *episteme* of it, and intelligence in the conduct of one's life will require the exercise of that *episteme*; the exercise of it will produce a good, and thereby just, life.

In discussing the rejection of the view that only a life free of discipline is one where one does as one wants, I tried to bring various main points out. First, the dispute is primarily about patterns of life. Second, it is about what men's ideal is. Therefore, in so far as it can be described as about what men really want, this has to be interpreted as what they would choose if they had the power and intelligence. Third, the Thrasymachean position is that the ideal is to be in a position to do as one wants and to be able to succeed in getting what one wants. The first suggests that one should be unhindered in one's pursuits, the second that one be able to achieve the goals one sets oneself. Plato's answer takes the form of claiming that every man has three types of desire, whether he likes it or not, and only in a certain pattern of life will he be able to achieve what he wants. But 'able to achieve what he wants' does not now mean 'able to achieve the goals he sets himself', for a man may just not try to satisfy these proposed desires, and the enquiry about what he wants is not an enquiry about what he pursues. In so far as this answer is going to tell against Thrasymachus, therefore, it must be shown that his goal only sounds worthwhile when it is not understood. Fourth, Plato meets this point by casting physical desire in a disordering role, and arguing that choices about education and conduct should be made in the realisation that the only sure alternative to the tyrannical-type personality is a philosophic one. In this way he might hope to persuade people that they would prefer, if they could, to be fully 'just', i.e. philosophic.

In chapter II, I turned to the reply to the claim that lack of discipline was better than discipline. Plato's argument here relies upon a number of theses. First, it has to be accepted that men really want the good, and second, that for any substitution for X in '. . . is a good X' it has to be possible to answer the question 'what is the function of X?' This last has to be possible in a way that yields, at least in the human case, the same characteristics as constituting the excellence of every X. Third, it has to be assumed that saying that men really want the good, or the best out of life, is not just a formal point. That is to say, it is not simply that one way of interpreting 'A really wants life X' is 'A thinks that X is the best life to lead'. Rather it means 'A wants most (will give preference to) what measures up to the requirements of an excellent human life', and as the last are open to demonstration, it can be shown of a particular pattern of life that it is what he wants, whatever he may think. Fourth, Plato seems to shift between a version of 'everyone wants the good' as a comment on what men would acknowledge, on reflection, that they want and as a claim about the object of every desire. In the latter part of the chapter I turned to the question of whether Plato was committed to an egoistic view that everyone wants his own good. While it may well be an egoistic interpretation that makes plausible the ready acceptance of the thesis that everyone wants the good, or the best life possible, I argued in the last two chapters that in Plato's developed view a person living the best life will not be governing his conduct by reference to his own welfare, but will be concerned for the welfare of the universe at large and to fulfil his part in it.

Granted all this it is possible to see how Plato might marry the two apparently disparate approaches, that through man's desire structure and that through the soul's function. There are, of course, many unanswered questions about Plato's view of the universe, especially at higher levels. Thus, it is not clear why the Demiurge should want embodied souls, nor why such souls should start life benighted and have to struggle for understanding. But granted there have to be such souls, and they have to start this way, it might seem reasonable that the resultant beings have an interest in the things conducive to their physical welfare, and so be equipped with physical desire. But if physical desire is as Plato portrays it, then if there is to be any prospect of developing an interest in understanding things there will have to be an inhibitor on desire. Men need, in fact, their admiration for manliness, with its contempt for luxury and any growing tendency to pursue physical comforts, as this ensures that physical desire does not have everything its own way. Further, such admiration involves having views about how a man should be and about noble (*kalon*) ways of behaving, which form the subject-matter of reasoning and *episteme*. Even a fully developed philosopher will need the protection against insistent desire provided by his respect for the right ideal. In short, a full understanding of the counselling, deliberating, caring function of the soul makes it clear that that functioning, which is itself the operation of a desire, requires both for its development and safe continuance a desire to be manly. The whole also requires, during life in this world, some interest in physical needs. So a good life might be thought to require the operation of them all, and a life where each desire was met would be one where a person was functioning well. It is, however, the reasoning function that determines the requirements of the whole. There are, of course, great gaps in this sketch, and it remains a question whether it is more than a contingent fact that a properly functioning and fully satisfied life will always coincide. But Plato probably thought it safe to allow the question of what life is good to be answered by reference to the question of what answers to our desires because, on his view of the soul's operation, the answer would coincide with that reached by the other route.

In all this the so-called spirited element has an important part to play together with the development of the view of the human person as having three types of desire. Its importance will become clearer if we review the development of Plato's position. First, however, it is necessary to argue that there is a development in this matter, as both A. E. Taylor (1926) and J. Burnet (1911) find the tripartite division before the *Republic*. Taylor (p. 120) notes that in the *Gorgias* (493a–b) Socrates refers several times to that part of the soul where desires reside, and infers that Plato was already familiar with the doctrine. If so, he had certainly not seen its potentialities, for he makes no move to turn the tables on Callicles in the way I have suggested that he tries to on Thrasymachus in the *Republic*. In fact all one can safely infer from the *Gorgias* is that Plato has come across the view that a whole range of desires can be looked upon as opposed to (in a different part of the soul from) reason. There is no sign of the 'spirited' element. It is true that in the *Gorgias*, like the *Republic* (cf. 577–9) Plato opposes the view that people in power can do what they want, but the argument is significantly different. There Socrates argues that a man wants (466 seq.) the purpose of his actions and generally the good. But the good is very different from what tyrants think. So in fact they fail to do what they want. This puts no reliance on an analysis of varying desires and is in fact based on the premiss that everyone wants the good. The *Republic* relies on the assumption that a man does what he wants only if all his wants are met. Further, in the *Gorgias* there is no development of the view that desire for the good is reason, nor is this passage brought into relation with that where Socrates talks of the desiring part of the soul. The *Gorgias* has many of the seeds of the later position, but a seed is not a plant.

Burnet, in his commentary on the *Phaedo*, sees the doctrine of a tripartite division in such passages as 68c, 82c. In these passages we certainly have a reference to the philotimos and philochrematos and their corresponding lives. As they are contrasted with the philosopher this can safely be taken as a reference to a traditional division of lives. Further, no development of divisions of the soul is required in the *Phaedo*, so lack of development is not an objection, although it might be taken as significant that physical desires are there described as a function of the body, rather than of a part of the soul. Even waiving this, however, it is hardly safe to infer from the fact that a man mentions a distinction between three kinds of life which later are correlated with three parts of the personality, that therefore he has already developed the further division and the correlation. For a person could well distinguish the types of life while denying any corresponding tendencies in each person. He could simply postulate differences of temperament. Even if he thought everyone capable of appreciating the attraction of each life, he would not have to suppose three ever-present desires in the way developed by Plato. He could well believe that the attractions are absorbing of interest, so that a person giving himself to philosophy has no interest in honour or food, although potentially he could have. This would deny the presence of other desires making themselves felt. In fact, arguing for a tripartite division of the personality of the sort Plato requires is a considerable step beyond a belief in three types of life. Further, the amount of trouble Plato goes to to argue for it, suggests that he realised it. Nor will the mention of anger and fear at *Phaedo* 94 support the view that he already had the special concept of *thymos*. Fear is not a function of *thymos* and the occurrence of a mention of anger is quite insufficient, especially in a passage which portrays internal conflict simply as one between soul and body.

The facts are, then, that Plato does not make *use* of a tripartite division of the soul before the *Republic*; he goes out of his way to argue for it in that work; it is used in a table-turning argument against Thrasymachus which would have been useful against Callicles in the *Gorgias* and seems more persuasive than the actual line taken there on the ideal of doing what we want. The simplest supposition therefore is that he did not have the division available for use earlier, and that its introduction marks a new stage in his counter to the attacks of men like Callicles and Thrasymachus.

The novelty in the tripartite division is partly its insistence on different and conflicting desires, partly the presence of all three in all men, but also, of course, the introduction of the 'spirited' element. While there had previously been a contrast between intellectual and worldly interests, the development of the argument that only a disciplined life meets all desires comes with the introduction of this new 'spirited' factor.

In order to bring out more clearly what seems to me a development in Plato's position, and the nature of his defence of traditional morality, I want to dwell on two points about the spirited element that loom large in its first introduction: the form of its education and its connection with manliness (*andreia*). It is a sad fact that many discussions of the spirited element tend to concentrate on the section of *Republic* Book IV, with an uneasy glance at the developments of Books VIII and IX. The fact that the major parts of Books II and III are devoted to the education of this part of a man therefore tends to drop out of sight. Yet this is very important because the account of education offered there closely parallels traditional curricula (cf. Aristophanes, *Clouds* 960 seq., Plato, *Laws* 811 seq.). In fact these Books are a criticism of the content of these curricula in that they tend to encourage the influence of bad models. The implication is that they would be influencing and miseducating the *thymos*. We consequently have Plato's view as to what this traditional education is educating. It is interesting therefore that even in ideal conditions the most we can achieve in this area is correct opinion, firm adherence to the norms in which we are instructed, manly behaviour. Inevitably we stop short of an ability to justify our opinions and give adequate defence of them under criticism. If this is the aspect of our personality developed by the traditional education in games, literature and the arts, it is hardly surprising that the average Greek traditional moral man, lacking the advantages of the education outlined in Books VI and VII, should show the inability to defend his views so characteristic of such people in the early dialogues. Nor is it surprising that the children of people like Pericles should not be like him in virtue. If Pericles was himself such a person he could only rely on a form of education that supplied no protection against the corrosion of the new inquisitiveness and questioning of the sophists.

The second point is the connection with *andreia*. This word is better translated 'manliness' than 'courage'. For though courage is a conspicuous element in *andreia*, the word conceals the connection with the word for 'man', and it is clear from a number of passages (cf. *Gorgias* 491–2, 512e, *Republic* 359b, 544–50) that it covers a wider range than 'courage'. Further Plato uses *'anandros'* (unmanly) as well as *'deilos'* (cowardly) as the opposite of *'andreios'*, and in contexts that clearly involve a general appeal to lack of prowess. In fact commonly *'andreia'* connotes the characteristics of the admirable, successful man usually connoted by *'arete'* (excellence) prior to Plato, and often by Socrates' interlocutors in the dialogues. For a detailed discussion of the value system involved, I must refer the reader to Professor Adkins' admirable *Merit and Responsibility*. It must suffice at present to draw attention to the frequency with which *andreia* is discussed in the earlier dialogues. It is the main topic of the *Laches,* an important maverick excellence in the *Protagoras,* is appealed to by Callicles in the *Gorgias* to support his ideal. It becomes clear in these examples that 'manliness' catches, as 'self-control' does not, an admired ideal. Self-control is prima facie objectionable, but *lack* of manliness is obviously objectionable. If some action or way of life can be portrayed as manly, then its worth is established. So Socrates tries to snatch the term from Callicles in the *Gorgias,* his attitude to death in the *Phaedo* is portrayed in terms matching this description, not that of the philosopher's critics, and Alcibiades' description of Socrates in the *Symposium* brings his self-control within the ambience of manliness. If we put these facts together with the connection of 'spirit' with *andreia,* and remember the relationship of 'spirit' to a particular form of education, it becomes tempting to suggest the following picture. Plato was impressed by Socrates' intelligence, his unbiased pursuit of the truth, and also by the fact that he stood out for and manifested the traditional virtues. At the same time Socrates' questioning reveals the difficulty of defending the worth of these virtues. The inability of ordinary worthy citizens to produce any such defence is repeatedly portrayed in the earlier dialogues. Also, however, Socrates' defence in the *Gorgias* is not particularly satisfying. It is largely a matter of arguing for inadequacies in the opposition and then claiming that the original contender therefore holds the field. This makes an assumption about where the onus of proof lies. It also leaves unexplained the connection, if any, between pursuit of the truth and virtues like temperance and courage. It is interesting, however, that Callicles does not simply attack Socrates' ideals as non-proven, he clearly despises them, and considers the resultant style of life unmanly. The same is true of Thrasymachus in the *Republic*. His view of the man who does not submit to discipline is meant to win assent to the manliness of such a man in contrast with the meek submission of the 'just' man. If one remembers the common connotations of the word for excellence, '*arete*', its connection with success and prowess, military and political, one can see how Thrasymachus can readily consent to Socrates' suggestion (Book I 348–9) that he considers *adikia* to be *arete*. Plato's whole treatment of 'good' and 'excellence' is an attempt to wrest them away from such connotations, or at least to loosen the connection. Plato commonly tries in his turn to win our recognition of Socrates' manliness. See, for instance, his attitude to death as portrayed in the *Phaedo* (in particular compare 58–9, 68–9, 114d *ad fin.*), and Alcibiades' account of Socrates in the *Symposium* (cf. 215–22). The use of '*aner*' (man) in *Republic* VIII 550a, *Laches* 188c, to appeal to a sense of what is manly, should be compared with the references to *andreia* in the passages referred to in the *Phaedo*.

In all this, however, the relation of the traditional virtues to the pursuit of philosophy is unclarified. We have, instead, a battle of appeals, with a persuasive attempt on Plato's part to redraw the picture of manliness in Socrates' favour. The general inability of the worthy citizen to defend his case is recognised, as also the claim of Socrates as to the value of the traditional virtues, but for the rest there is uncertainty. Against this background the *Republic* looks like a conscious attempt to clear up some of these problems. To begin with there is the elaborate analysis of the main divisions of motive in the human character, one of which is an aspect of our nature that aspires to manliness. The notion of manliness is close to that of *arete* as it occurs both before Plato and among his contemporaries. The development of this side of the personality is achieved by a touched up version of a part of traditional Greek education in the arts, and it is made clear that the danger of not accepting the proposed modifications is that one acquires bad models and bad norms, and might allow the lower elements of one's character to take over. Since the ordinary Greek education was an unbowdlerised analogue of Plato's, it follows that it would train, but mistrain this aspect of a person. The result would be a slightly misdirected notion of manliness. Plato's course is so clearly an adaptation of what was usual that it is hard to credit that he was not intending this critique of the product of the standard education. Even in ideal circumstances the most we can hope for from this side of ourselves is attachment to a correct ideal. Education at this stage is a form of training rather than instruction, and cannot result in an ability to defend the norms instilled. That would require a development of a man's reasoning capacities. It is therefore hardly surprising that the average worthy Greek shows himself at sea in face of intellectual criticism. We have, in fact, the fruits of considerable thought on the possibilities of traditional education and the sort of motivation it develops, which provides an answer to the puzzle why, if virtue is teachable, Pericles did not teach his sons. Pericles only had a 'spirited' grasp of virtue, and could at best hope to produce a similar product. But any such product is a ready prey to critical undermining. It remains, however, that this 'spirited' element of the personality has an important role, even in the best of us, and that the view of manliness embodied in traditional morality is not in general far from the truth.

The result is that the defence of traditional morality is something less than whole-hearted. No doubt, in keeping with the order of degeneration in Books VIII and IX of the *Republic*, one is less far removed from the ideal if one lives up to the traditional norms than if one has thrown them over, but one is further removed than one who has had the privilege of being educated in Plato's state. What Plato defends is not the content of traditional morality so much as the type of motive that it develops. This type of motive is vital as a safeguard against domination by physical desire. A person who is guided by this motive, however, is not being guided by reason. If I see someone being maltreated and in indignation go to his assistance, it is not that I have reasoned that it is best to help him. Rather I have recognised his treatment as contravening the norms on which I have been brought up. Plato in fact is far from trying to reveal any implicit principles which, when revealed, bring coherence into the mêlée of moral discussion. He thinks the confusion that is so obvious a feature of ordinary moral thought to be endemic to it and a direct result of the sort of motive expressed in that thought. If a person has been ideally trained, however, and has achieved the full development of reason, then his reason will be able to establish two things: first, that it is a good thing to have an admiration for the ideal of manliness, and second, that the ideal he has is the right one. This will not supplant the operation of that motive, but establish its operation as an important feature of a good man's life, and ensure that it is directed to the right ideal. The ideal is not confined to courage, but embraces disciplined behaviour. It thus includes self-control and being law-abiding. A person in whom a proper ideal of manliness dominates will in fact subject his lower desires, and so be self-controlled, and will be dyed in the law and so law-abiding. In this way the traditional tie between excellence and success or prowess is reconciled with advocacy of self-control and obedience to law. The correct view of manliness (*arete, andreia*) is shown to bring in its train what Adkins calls the quieter values.

At the same time it is clear that the high point of development of the motive on which traditional norms of excellence rely is thought by Plato to fall short of the ideal. It is not simply that such a man is felt to be in an insecure position. Plato wishes to hold up another interest as a higher and more noble one. What was traditionally thought to constitute human excellence is only a part, and a minor part, of the ideal. This is done by seizing on *sophia*. Most people would admit that stupidity was incompatible with excellence, and that ideally a man should show *sophia*. But this would amount simply to the cunning of Odysseus, or the kind of shrewdness required to stay on top in politics or war. Plato supplies a new content for this excellence, and one which would seem close to an impractical other-worldliness inviting the average man's contempt. Plato shows a constant sensitiveness to this point (cf. *Gorgias* 485-6, *Republic* 487 seq., 517-18, *Phaedo* 64b) and is intent to underline the practical value of *sophia*. Increasingly, also, this excellence is allied to godliness, and his religious views, closely bound up with what *episteme* can attain to, come to underline the contention that the fully admirable and successful life is one dominated by *sophia*. This constitutes a new ideal in sharp contrast to the traditional ones. It is also one whose attainment is clearly difficult and whose attainment by more than a few per millennium would require a complete restructuring of society. This accounts both for Plato's pessimism and his concern for politics.

In short, Plato is not concerned to defend the traditional ideals of *arete* – he wishes to substitute another. Nor is he trying to exhibit the form of traditional moral reasoning, for he thinks there is nothing there to deserve the name reasoning. Nor does he unearth an underlying principle of traditional morality, for again he thinks there is no such principle. He is, however, prepared to argue that the motive of admiration for manliness that is the mainstay of traditional morality is one that has a part to play. But the traditional ideal needs correcting. Moreover, that motive needs underpinning by reason if there is to be any security. Even in an ideal state there is no final certainty of perseverance for those who have to rely on this motive. In any actual fourth-century state the chances of survival are not great, especially as most of those concerned will have been educated in a way which, even if not plutocratic, will still involve some distortion of this motive through distortion of the ideal of manliness. The likelihood is that such ideals will progressively lose their hold. The correct ideal is one that in fact satisfies all our wants, on a special interpretation of that requirement, is in fact best, on a special view of how to determine excellence, and is the only ideal that embodies a full understanding of what is advocated.

There are, of course, numerous other points to be pursued in connection with Plato's moral views. The ideal of doing what one wants often becomes mingled with some form of hedonism; his view of human excellence raises the question of whether there is any sense in talking of various virtues; it also raises questions on the sense in which moral norms can be said to be natural or conventional, and one could continue the list. I propose simply to take one further topic, the famous paradox that no one willingly does wrong, because it is very closely bound up with the ways of meeting the criticisms of men like Callicles and Thrasymachus that have been discussed in the previous chapters, and also discussion of it helps to underline some of the differences between Platonic and modern approaches. That will complete the account of those parts of Plato's ethical views to the criticism of which I shall turn in chapter XIII. Before that it will be necessary to get a clearer picture of certain features of his position on knowledge which in turn affect his views on morality.

VI

Freedom and Virtue

As was pointed out in chapter I, in the *Republic* Plato aims to show that a really undisciplined man least of all does what he wants. This claim takes two forms, first that he is dominated by a subset of his desires, so that not all his desires are satisfied, and second, that like all men he wants the best out of life, but lacking adequate knowledge pursues something else. Already in the *Protagoras* (352–8) Socrates has argued that no one willingly does anything but what he thinks to be best, and so no one willingly does wrong. Some such doctrine runs through later dialogues too (e.g. *Philebus* 22b, *Laws* 731 seq., 859 seq.). In the argument with Thrasymachus one of the points at issue is who is free, and the fact that the philosopher does what he wants, the indisciplined man not, is used to argue that the former is free, the latter not.

All this looks like a familiar determinist accommodation of freedom: a man's free acts are determined, but are differentiated from non-free acts either because caused by our desires, or by certain desires. To this can be added Plato's way of treating virtue as health of the personality, vice as a form of disease (*Gorgias* 464 seq., *Republic* 444–5), and speaking of ideal rulers as doctors of the soul (e.g. *Gorgias* 462–6, *Phaedrus* 269–70). This suggests a determination to treat wrong-doing as a form of illness, for which the patient might be pitied and treated but hardly held responsible. And this seems to fill out the slogan that no one willingly or knowingly does wrong. Granted certain conditions of knowledge and psychic balance a man will, if he can, do what is right. In any other conditions there is something the matter with him.

In order to get clear how much, if any, of this picture is right I propose first to consider certain possible uses of the notion of vice as disease, and then see how Plato's use fits. Then I shall consider interpretations of 'no one willingly/knowingly does what is wrong' and then see how Plato's account fits, and how it is related to his notion of freedom (*eleutheria*). This will, I hope, make it easier to bring out how Plato's position lies askew much modern discussion of freedom of the will, and how most attempts at matching lead to distortion.

To start, then, with his tendency to speak of vice as disease. Clearly someone who talks this way may be proposing or hoping for some diagnostic account of vice to explain our wrongdoing, rather in the way that a high temperature might explain the failure of man or animal to walk steadily. Thus suppose there are clear criteria for diagnosing depressive states, it might be possible to show that certain forms of deviant behaviour, say failure of punctuality, lack of consideration, were only, or usually, the result of such a state, and the exceptions the result of some other diagnosable state. A man free of such states, it might be, is always punctual, considerate or whatever it may be. This would make it possible to speak intelligibly of any tendency to wrongdoing as one or other of a number of specifiable illnesses. But what follows? It is not at all clear that as yet we have a case for saying that no one can help being unpunctual or inconsiderate. It might, indeed, be that such a view would make us more sympathetic to shortcomings, since presumably the 'illness' makes difficult of performance what is usually easy. But there is no reason to suppose the situation for these purposes different from that of a man with a high temperature. It is more difficult for him to walk steadily, but not impossible. Similarly, while it would always be sensible to try to cure the illness and for the long term more constructive, the appeal to illness need only win sympathy, not exculpation.

For this latter something more dramatic is needed. Suppose for instance, that we can set up a category of mania whereby anyone suffering from any mania is incapacitated from deliberating calmly and cannot keep his mind off whatever his mania covers. Let us also suppose kleptomania and dypsomania to be of this sort. A person suffering from them cannot, in certain situations, keep his mind off pilfering or alcohol, and is rendered incapable of choosing any other course. By this time we no doubt have a case of temporarily or permanently diminished responsibility. If we can now portray all vice as some form of mania, we shall clearly be able to exculpate the wicked, and see them as simply subjects for treatment. Of course, to produce this conclusion, as in the previous case we should need sufficiently clear criteria for the various illnesses and it would be an empirical question whether every vice could be brought under some mania, even supposing there are no *a priori* objections to such a generalisation. I shall not go into these questions, and will merely remark that without additional support to be suggested later, such a position has no prima facie plausibility. If one thinks of the sorts of conditions normally required to establish diminished responsibility, in particular such psychological disorders as would be clearly acceptable, it would seem that they are sufficiently extravagant to be safely deemed exceptional. Yet it is only extravagant examples that would in any clear way suggest that the wicked were not responsible.

These two ways, which could of course, unless one were wanting complete exculpation of wrong-doing, be held together, both involve some programme for the diagnosis of disease. But clearly someone might well want to talk of vices in terms of disease for purposes not of exculpation but of denigration. Indeed, if one described someone who plotted disappointments for others as diseased, the remark would more likely be abusive than diagnostic. It would be an unfavourable comment on the personality rather than a claim about the compulsions leading to the behaviour. Interest would be in distance from the preferred norm, not in causal mechanism. Such a use would be as consistent as the other with a view of the norm as a state of proper proportion between various elements of the personality. I can believe an inordinate interest in book-learning to be unhealthy without thinking it caused by a disease.

There are doubtless other possible ways of looking on vice as disease, according to the model of disease one takes or the number one wishes to combine. In general, however, failing the addition of an *a priori* argument to be discussed later, the position would seem to be that it will be necessary to give a proper clinical account of the illnesses and show their correlation with what is usually deemed vicious behaviour, and if one wants to conclude that every wrong-doer can be exculpated one has to be sure to choose forms of illness that are in some way incapacitating. This, of course, is only what one should do. A given philosopher may fail to satisfy this condition while nevertheless clearly wanting to hold that vice was illness and therefore a wicked man could not be held responsible. His failure to meet the above conditions would be a criticism of the philosopher concerned, but would hardly show that he did not hold the view. This last might become clear in the way he describes his thesis. Thus, if Plato does tend to describe vice in terms of mania and mania as producing behaviour for which the subject is not responsible, or if he talks predominantly in terms of treatment and sympathy when dealing with vice, assuming the subject's inability to help himself, then it might be true that he is wanting some diagnosable account of psychological illnesses, even if he fails to expound their pathology.

One thing that is quite clear about Plato is that he is fond of comparing legislators with doctors, and the desired state of the person with physical health (cf. e.g. *Gorgias* 462–6, 505, *Republic* 444–5, *Politicus* 293, 299–300, *Laws* 720). Granted, however, an account of health in terms of balance of elements, and a view of men as possessing various capacities and inclinations, it is only natural for someone who wishes to talk of a balanced life being a matter of skill to turn to the analogy of medicine. For these purposes there is no need to develop any views on mental pathology, and indeed, the analogy allows for the possibility of a self-curing mental physician, very much in control of matters. We need something stronger to yield the kind of result we are looking for, and we might hope for this in three types of discussion, first where Plato treats of punishment, second a passage in the *Timaeus* where he seems to account at least for some vices as diseases, and third where he is inclined to use the term '*mania*' ('mania') when talking of vice. I shall now take these in order.

In the *Gorgias* (476–9) Socrates argues that while the best thing of all is to do no wrong, the worst is not, as Polus thinks, to be punished, but to do wrong and go scot-free. Proper punishment aims at the improvement of the criminal, and so it is better to be corrected than to escape correction. So far we have no more than the familiar analogy with medicine. Later, however, in the myth (525) we get a further account of punishment, this time allotted after death. With every proper punishment either the person punished should be improved, or at least others should be benefited by the example. It is recognised that not all are curable of their vices, and the only benefit from their punishment is to those who learn from their example. The description of incorrigible wrong-doers as incurable is clearly using a medical analogy, and if we press it it at least allows for the characterisation of some states of vice as incurable. One could presumably infer not simply that no one else can do anything about them, but also that the subjects themselves are impotent to effect a change. So these wrong-doers are unable to be anything but wrong-doers. It does not follow, of course, that each individual act is somehow compelled, but only that the main trend of their lives cannot be changed. But what of the others? After all, they are said to be curable. Can we infer that the diseases are incapacitating? Certainly they have in some sense to be treated, but the *Gorgias* only suggests that a cure confers a benefit, not that it releases one from some incapacitation. The most one could claim is that there are clearly in-curable states and possibly curable ones are looked on as at only slightly higher points on a slippery slope. They may consequently be looked upon as states where the free exercise of judgment is impeded. But not even this clearly follows. In fact the attempt to read into the *Gorgias* any view to the effect that criminals are really subjects for treatment seems to be a misconstruction. What Plato is trying to do, rather, is get us to see punishment as aimed at beneficial consequences, usually for the person punished, instead of looking on it simply as an infliction of evil, as Polus and Callicles do. Granted that it is bad to be wicked, someone who escapes punishment is likely to pat himself on the back and continue as before, thus leaving his character in a worse state. A dose of punishment, on the other hand (note the naturalness of the medical term 'dose'), may well divert him from his evil ways. All this is in keeping with the deterrent view outlined and does not require the supposition that Plato is suggesting the substitution of curative techniques for penal ones. Rather he is saying that well-selected punishments can be beneficial, and so described as curative. Indeed, the assumption is that the 'treatment' will be penal.

The *Timaeus* comes much closer to providing what we are looking for. At 86 after discussing various forms of physical illness, Timaeus proceeds to discuss illnesses of the soul that have a physical source. Sexual intemperance and generally uncontrolled pursuit of pleasure is put down as a form of madness induced by physical conditions, and such behaviour is said to be involuntary and not to deserve blame (86d). A little later we are told that certain physical states are responsible for various forms of irritability and depression, rashness and cowardice, forgetfulness and stupidity (87a). We seem, then, to have a situation where a number of defects, some of them familiar vices, are put down as illnesses. They are clearly psychic illnesses (86b 2–4) though of physical origin, and are said at 86b 7–c 3 to incapacitate a person from the proper exercise of various faculties. Although the description leads one to expect something dramatic, we are told that it fits people commonly held to be deliberately wicked (86d 1–e 3). It looks, in fact, as though vices are being said to be forms of incapacitating madness that exculpate the vicious. This might well be thought to commit Plato to a pathology of vice that frees one of responsibility for one's wrong-doing.

The matter is not, however, so clear as this would make it sound. To begin with, we are only told that some cases of vice are caused by physical conditions, and it is not clear that all even of these count as *mania*. Further, while forgetfulness and unwillingness to learn can be caused by one's physical condition (87a), two points need noting: first, that education, too, can result in bad states of personality (86e, 87b), and second, that while the argument suggests some lack of responsibility for one's character it is not clear what follows with regard to individual acts. At least everyone is urged to take steps to avoid evil and choose good (87b). It would be possible for Plato to hold the following: some undesirable states of intemperance, cowardice and folly are physiologically caused states of *mania*, and those suffering from them in specifiable conditions could claim diminished responsibility for their acts. On the other hand there are milder forms of undesirable state that are physiologically caused, and others that result from education, where diminished responsibility on particular occasions could not be claimed, although responsibility for the state of character could be avoided, and this might lead to some mitigation of blame. Indeed, at 87b 4–6 Timaeus says that educators have more blame than those they bring up. If this is taken seriously then it allows that those who underwent a form of education may nevertheless be partly to blame, and asserts that the educators certainly are. This last implies that the educators can be blamed for educating badly, which is presumably a series of bad acts. It would be difficult, however, to be certain on the evidence of the *Timaeus* where Plato stands. It might still be that he thought all vices were forms of *mania*, or that for some other reason people were not to be blamed for them or for resultant vicious acts. The remarks at 87b may turn out as so out of line as to be discounted. Even as they stand it is said only that educators should be blamed *rather than* those educated, which might be interpreted as a slap at those who, while responsible for education, yet administer the law, rather than a committed assertion about who is responsible.

Still confining the discussion to what can be derived from Plato's talk of vice as disease, is it possible to find any extension of the *Timaeus* doctrine? There is certainly evidence that Plato tends to think of vice as madness elsewhere, and if this is general for all vices, then the case would be made. Thus, for instance, in *Republic* Book IX we get a description of the development of the tyrant-type personality which by 573 is naturally collecting descriptions in terms of *mania*, and this type of personality is surely a paradigm of vice. Further, at least in many places, the attribution of *mania* relieves the agent of responsibility for his acts. We have seen this suggested in the *Timaeus*. Earlier, in the *Ion*, Socrates argues that rhapsodes do not have anything that can be called a skill. If they interpret the minds of poets this must be through divine inspiration. It is a god, not the man, who speaks (*Ion* 533–6). The language is that of enthusiasm and possession and is spoken of at 536d as *mania*. As the whole argument is directed to robbing Ion of the credit for such truths as he pronounces, it seems safe to infer that the attribution of *mania* is thought sufficient to produce this result. But later, at least, Plato is prepared to describe love of the truth as mania (cf. *Symposium* 218b, *Phaedrus* 244 seq., esp. 252c–253c). This would be compatible with the project of depriving good as well as bad men of responsibility, but is hardly consistent with the thesis that the good only are responsible for their actions, so that they can be praised while the wicked can only be pitied. Alternatively, of course, some forms of *mania* are not incapacitating, but enabling, and this seems to be the case of the special examples reinterpreted as *mania* in the *Symposium* and *Phaedrus*. When it comes to vices, the word does seem to be used in contexts that strongly suggest diminished responsibility, but it also only seems to be used of extravagant cases. In *Republic* Book IX we have a description of a man, dominated by one or more of his lower desires, and these are pictured true to form as analogous in operation to drunkenness and lunacy (cf. also *Phaedrus* 237c–238c and 254). Gluttony, drunkenness, lechery may perhaps be plausibly portrayed in these terms. So, too, timorous forms of cowardice. The picture is less plausible as applied to the vices of men further from the tyrant-type. The neglect of duties and idleness of a democratic-type man, or the dishonesty and injustice of the plutocratic-type do not invite, and nor do they get, this sort of description. It is, in fact, reserved for the condition of a man under the influence of 'physical' desire and pleasure, the sort described in the *Philebus* (45e) as driving men mad (cf. also *Laws* 783).

If, then, we confine ourselves to Plato's talk of vice as disease, it seems that while he speaks of all vices as ailments of the personality, this does not carry with it any clear connotations of incapacity. There is, however, a set of vices, consisting in complete domination by some physical desire, which get spoken of as *mania*, and in a way that suggests that those subject to them suffer from diminished responsibility and are to be pitied. Often these conditions have physiological causes. This account does not cover all vices, and it is not clear whether it is meant to cover all incurable ones. The incurables mentioned in the *Gorgias* (525d–e) are known bad tyrants of cities, and while there is some suggestion in Plato that such men are dominated by their lower desires, it is certainly not obvious that they were quivering gluttons or drunkards nor certain that Plato thought so. Nor does anything necessarily follow from the fact that (e.g. *Laws* 731b–d) Plato sometimes quite generally declares evil-doers to be pitiable. For it is not only those who cannot help themselves who deserve our pity, but also those who labour under difficulties or ignorance, or simply fail to achieve some good.

Although nothing conclusive emerges from Plato's treatment of vice as psychic illness, it may be that this inconclusiveness derives from the fact that I have so far kept right out of the discussion the famous paradox(es) that no one knowingly/willingly does wrong. So although the views on psychic disease that have been considered might be consistent with a view that commonly a man may be responsible for acting wickedly, it may nevertheless be that Plato in fact thinks he is not, and this he shows by his acceptance of the paradox(es). It is therefore time to consider what these sayings amount to.

I have, above, put 'paradox(es)', because although Plato does not distinguish a number, he does talk in a number of ways, and ways which suggest that he may have a number of possibilities in mind that are not separated. Thus in the *Protagoras* he objects to the view that knowledge (*episteme*) can be dragged around like a slave (352a–b and cf. Aristotle *Nicomachean Ethics* 1145b 20 seq.), and also that anyone will knowingly do anything but what he thinks best (358b 6–c 1), or willingly (*hekon*) pursue evil. In the *Timaeus* (86d–e) we are told that no one is willingly evil, where this seems to refer to a state, and somewhat similarly in the *Laws* that no one is willingly 'unjust' (731c) or intemperate (733b). In the *Republic* Glaucon's challenge is that no one is willingly just, and this is supposedly countered by Socrates by a complete turning of the tables to the effect that no one is willingly unjust. In principle, therefore, we have two main forms of paradox: that no one willingly does wrong, but only right, and that no one knowingly does wrong, but only right, and it may be significant that Aristotle treats them separately, the first in Book III, the second in Book VII of the *Nicomachean Ethics*. Each could subdivide into a thesis about states of character or a thesis about each individual act. If in either or both cases it takes the latter form then it might look as though Plato wishes to exculpate evil-doers for every wrong action. In this case it will be worth asking, with Aristotle (*Nicomachean Ethics* Book III c. v), whether this can be done in such a way as to preserve credit for the virtuous man. One might, for instance, argue that all good and bad acts alike are caused by the agent's desires and character. In neither case is the agent responsible for the cause. If so, then the good man can take no more credit for his virtue than the bad responsibility for his wickedness. So far as their ability to help doing what they do is concerned they will be in the same straits. 'Disease' will not now be distinguishable from 'health' in terms of incapacitation. Either the word will simply indicate that the state denoted is not desirable, or the distinction will be between conditions that allow of a wide variety of reaction under varying stimuli and those that allow of a relatively limited range of reaction. Even in the latter case the use of the word 'disease' will presumably do no more than indicate the, for some reason, undesirable nature of limited response conditions. Similarly, 'voluntary', 'responsible' and other similar words will serve to indicate that a particular (sort of) cause has been operative, not that the agent could have done anything but what he did. If Jones runs Smith down willingly, then the cause is his will, not a slippery road. This is the sort of *a priori* argument that I mentioned earlier which, if accepted, would make all mental illness exculpatory in some sense although, notoriously, by breaking down the barrier between normal and sick cases so far as the agent's ability to act otherwise is concerned. To exculpate someone via mental illness is, on this view, to declare them not suitable for one sort of treatment but only for another.

The question, then, is: does Plato expound his view that no one knowingly/willingly does wrong in a way to suggest acceptance of this *a priori* determinist view? I call it an *a priori* view because it is noticeably different from ones that claim that all behaviour is physiologically determined, or that all behaviour is determined by psychological factors other than those immediately supposed by the agent, or that all wrongdoing is caused by some incapacitating malfunction. In all these cases there is empirical work to be done. The present argument relies on an analysis of such expressions as 'of his own free will', 'deliberately', 'voluntarily', and claims that always they are attributing a cause of some behaviour, and consequently the only difference between free and unfree behaviour is in the type of cause operative. Now Plato is clearly a good deal of the time at least appealing to the ordinary use of the Greek word '*hekon*' and its relatives, and hoping that his reader will acknowledge that strictly wrong-doing should not be described as done *hekon*. Thus in the *Laws* (733–4) we have an argument to the effect that a restrained man's life is pleasanter than an unrestrained one's. From the added premiss that an unrestrained man wants as much pleasure as possible it follows that no one is unrestrained *hekon*. It is assumed that anyone who admits the premisses must acknowledge the justice of the characterisation in the conclusion. He only needs to understand '*hekon*' and admit the truth of the premisses. The question is therefore not whether Plato's is an *a priori* view, but whether it is the same one as that familiar from present-day literature on free-will; while Plato seems not to distinguish the thesis that no one knowingly does wrong from that that no one willingly does wrong. I shall treat them in that order. The wording is not only different but different in a way that seems to rely on slightly different considerations to give the position plausibility.

To start, then, with 'no one knowingly does wrong'. This thesis is stated in the *Protagoras* at 352 following and used in combination with the premiss that pleasure is the good to refute the view that anyone can be overcome by pleasure so as to do wrong. Socrates is portrayed as quite clear that the common view is that a man may often have *episteme* but be ruled by pleasure, fear or some other emotion. By contrast he wishes to hold that *episteme* is suited to govern a man's actions and that if a man is knowledgeable about good and bad nothing is strong enough to make him do anything else.

To some extent this position is bolstered by the assumption that everyone wants what is best, and the equation of good and pleasure is then used to produce the absurdity that 'being overcome by pleasure' must mean 'being overcome by good'. As it stands, however, this is a weak position. The commonsense view seems far more attractive. Even if we accept the equation of good and pleasure it seems possible, not to say necessary, to allow for occasions when, while knowing perfectly well the long-term pleasure advantages of resisting, we are overcome by the short-term attractions. Faced with such examples one might either identify the person with his decisions and deny that a person always does what he thinks best, or identify him with his reflective views on what is best and describe him as overwhelmed by passion. Both these descriptions preserve his knowledge of what is best. They are not strong enough to yield Plato's conclusion that the man lacks *episteme*. This could be achieved in one of two ways. First, one could stand by the position that a person always wants what is best and identify the person with the taker of all actual decisions, i.e. refuse to speak of 'him' being overcome by his desires. In that case, one would have to suppose that he did not really know/believe that what he was doing was not for the best. This has the obvious weakness that on some ordinary interpretations of 'know' I may well know that the long-term effects of my behaviour are undesirable. The second way would be to rely on a use of 'know' which was felt to be preferable and in terms of which the natural conclusion in cases of being overcome by pleasure was to attribute lack of 'knowledge'. This is, I think, what Plato is doing. He is aware that it is slightly unusual to speak of knowledge as 'ruling' or 'governing'. On the other hand, if what I said in chapter IV is right, he was wanting to draw attention and give importance to *epistemai*, and to look upon knowing how to conduct one's life as an *episteme*. Suppose we take a typical *episteme*, medicine. If a man's child is ill he may be expected to want it to recover. His resultant behaviour, however, if he recognises his ignorance, will be undirected, since he simply will not know what to do. By contrast the behaviour of an actual or self-styled doctor will be governed by his actual or supposed skill. Further there will be obvious types of situation that a person will be expected to be able to manage if he has a given skill. Thus a surgeon will have to be able to keep a steady hand and cope with the sight of blood. Failure here will damage his claim to proficiency. Now Plato wants to suggest that knowing how to organise one's life is a form of *techne*, which may govern one's behaviour and determine what is best to do. Such a person's knowledge will not be confined to, although it will include, apprehension at a theoretical level. It will also involve ability to cope with certain sorts of situation. In the context of the *Protagoras* argument such a man is taken to be an expert at pleasure. Fairly clearly he has no claim to such a title if he can be toppled by short-term delights with large long-term distress effects.

If this is right, then Plato, in claiming that no one knowingly does wrong, is at least in part claiming that since doing right is a matter of skill, and everyone wants what is best, then the man who fails shows a lack of *episteme*. This will be true whether the person is identified with what a man thinks best or with what he decides. If the latter, and a man always wants what is best, then wrong acts are failed attempts and so show lack of competence or ignorance of fact. If the former, then a person who is overcome by passion and acts against his better judgment shows an inability to cope with some of the material covered by his skill, and so a failure of *episteme*. Consequently, with the interpretation of *episteme* that he espouses Plato, when faced with a man overcome by passion, or calmly but deliberately doing wrong, will naturally attribute this failing to lack of *episteme* and feel no great inclination to drop either of the other premisses.

I said above that this is at least part of Plato's position. But although it does something to explain the notion of knowledge governing behaviour, and Plato's readiness to resort to ignorance as the explanation of wrong-doing, it is clearly not the whole story. For Plato also, in passages arguing that no one knowingly does wrong, makes it clear that he thinks it impossible for anyone to do wrong believing it to be wrong. This thesis does demand a choice: *either* when a person is overcome by passion 'he' does not act, but is carried away *or* he does act, and it is by reference to his act, not any words or calm behaviour of his, that what he believes is determined. As I argued in chapter II Plato shows signs of vacillating on this point in his uncertainty about the thesis that everyone wants what is best. In English 'no one knowingly does what is wrong' would quite naturally be interpreted as claiming 'no one does what is wrong thinking it to be wrong', and it may be that this possibility in the Greek encourages Plato to feel that what supports the one thesis supports the other. They are, however, distinct, and sometimes, as in the *Protagoras*, the view that no one does wrong believing it to be wrong is used to support the apparently further conclusion that if anyone does what is in fact wrong, then he must be ignorant. It may well be that despite this Plato does not distinguish them. Both wrong-doing through passion and through mistake can be accommodated as failure of *episteme*; the choice that would have made clear a possible parting of the ways between the theses does not seem to have occurred to Plato, or at least he was unwilling to face it.

A further cause of lack of discrimination may have been that 'no one knowingly does wrong' and 'no one willingly does wrong' are treated as equivalent. The words translated 'willingly', 'unwillingly' (*hekon, akon*) require slightly more elaborate treatment. After all, if I am arrested and carried off by the police just as I am about to be accosted by an unwelcome neighbour, then if I am sure of my innocence I may go willingly enough. But as I am taken willy-nilly this hardly counts as *hekon*. For me to do X *hekon*, X must be what I want to do, but also be done because I want to do it. For it to be done *akon* it must be done without benefit of my wanting to or not, and contrary to my desire at least to the extent that the result displeases me. Obviously there are cases that do not readily fit either. Thus Aristotle's sea-captain jettisoning his cargo (*Nicomachean Ethics* 1110a 8–14) might well catch one uncertain what to say. The suggestion that it was what he wanted to do and that is why he did it seems to impute irresponsibility, unless, with Aristotle, one qualifies and says that it was not what in general he wanted, but only in the special circumstances of the storm. For the moment the important point is that X must be what I want to do if I am to do it *hekon*. Clearly this condition opens wide the way to querying whether I *really* want to do X. If it is already acknowledged that everyone wants what is best, then any proof that what is pursued or done is not what is best will show that what is done is not really wanted, and so not, strictly, done *hekon*. If we suppose that everyone is always after what is best then failure will be due either to force (or accident) or error. No doubt this is too simplified – it is not clear where carelessness or clumsiness fit – but the model whereby we all in some sense have only one goal at least invites one to take force and ignorance as the predominant explanations of failure. In Plato's case the preference for ignorance is reinforced by his view of *episteme*. The fact remains that the force possibility receives scant attention, especially in the earlier dialogues (though cf. *Philebus* 22b, *Laws* 864c). This is probably due to the fact that he is opposing people who want, like Thrasymachus, to make out that it is stupid to be 'just', the clever thing is to be above morality and the law. By contrast Plato wants to argue that wickedness shows incompetence. It also shows a person's failure to get what he wants, so that he deserves our pity rather than our admiration.

If we now ask how Plato stands on the free-will controversy the answer is, I think, complicated, and possibly the best answer is 'nowhere'. If one looks at discussions on freedom of the will by English-speaking philosophers over, say, the last fifty to a hundred years, it becomes clear that 'I could not help it', 'I could not do anything else' have been seized upon as excuses that exculpate and rule out the charge that I did it of my own free will. Consequently attention is concentrated on the moment of decision. Granted that a man could have done something else if he had chosen or if he had wanted, could he have chosen or wanted anything else? If, as seems plausible, the choice is always explicable by reference to some want, and wants are not themselves chosen, then it seems that all our actions are predetermined. We cannot help any of them in any strict sense. We can interpret 'he did it of his own free will' as 'his action was determined by such and such desires without interference of other influences', but in no serious sense could he have done other than he did. Consequently no one can, in the way men used to suppose, be blamed or held responsible for wrong-doing. If we imagine philosophers seizing on 'I did not mean to' as the paradigm excuse the situation would doubtless have been different. There is no similar temptation to develop a thesis that we never mean to do anything we do. Nor is it at all clear that because I did not mean to do X this shows anything as to whether or not I could have done otherwise. Suppose a man invites to supper two friends whom he believes to be engaged to each other. Unfortunately the engagement has just been bitterly broken off and each party assumes the man to know. When each finds the other invited both are extremely upset. The host can claim that he did not mean to upset anyone – quite the contrary. But this carries no suggestion that he could not help inviting them. For that special extra arguments would be needed. 'I did not mean to' is not a plea of incapacity, and in many situations, such as thoughtlessness, may not exculpate. But it does ward off a charge of malice. It is consequently usually effective in meeting the most serious charge in personal relationships, securing forgiveness or at least preserving friendship. Someone who started from this area taking this as the predominant excuse would have a different account of praise and blame.

Plato certainly shows a notable lack of interest in the question of whether a person could have chosen to do something other than what he did, or in the mechanics of explaining particular choices. The English word 'choice' strongly suggests alternatives between which a choice is made and so invites a query as to what makes us go one way rather than the other. Plato, in discussing the present question, typically uses terms for 'want' or 'pursue' or, in the *Laws*, a word for 'take'. None of these words so readily suggests possible vacillation between alternatives. This may be part explanation of the difference. But at the linguistic level far more important is that '*hekon*' and '*akon*' are the two terms selected, because of current practice, for discussing the question of blame and wrong-doing. For each of these terms indicates the agent's success or failure in doing what he wants to do. Thus although it is sufficient generally (although cf. Aristotle, *Nicomachean Ethics* III 1110b 18 seq.) to prove an act was done *akon* to show it was done under compulsion, it is also true that mistake together with agent's displeasure at the outcome will suffice. Further, Plato's development of the paradox relies on these last. Consequently his position is nearer to 'no one intentionally does wrong' than to 'no one can help his wrong-doing'. The reasons for pitying rather than blaming a wrong-doer will be similar to those operative with the man who unwittingly entertained the parted lovers: he has unwittingly done something that goes against his aims. On the other hand no sympathy is needed for the person who succeeds.

In all this no detailed attention is required to the mechanics of choice. Indeed, the familiar move that free acts can be characterised as those done by a certain motive is not open to Plato as an account of those acts that are done *hekon*. For the only candidate is desire for what is best, and on any account that motive is often, when the agent is mistaken, responsible for wrong acts. But however free these may be they are ones that Plato clearly wishes to say are done *akon*. This is not to deny that Plato has an interest in a person's ability to do otherwise. In the *Laws*, where we get the strongest defence of the paradox we also get strong statements to the effect that the agent is responsible on various occasions and should be encouraged to pursue courses that will bring improvement (*Laws* 727, 732, cf. also *Timaeus* 87). But even here Plato is not interested in whether the agent concerned *could* have done other than he did at the time, but in whether he *can* do anything about his liability to do such things again. It is in fact not true of common English practice even that the question whether the agent could have done something else is always crucial for determining blame. For instance, when someone is learning to drive a car he is liable to crash the gears. He will be reprimanded by his instructor and told to co-ordinate the depression of the clutch and the movement of the gear lever. It is obscure in what sense the learner could have chosen to do anything else, or could have done anything else at the time. More to the point is the cry 'I can't help it' – but the obvious response is 'of course you can help it – you must practise.' If it is true that he cannot do anything about it, then he must be unteachable, which is usually not the case. Similar points hold when, say, someone is being corrected for flying off the handle too quickly, or not being sufficiently considerate. The reproach is made on the assumption not that the agent could have acted otherwise but that he can do something about acting otherwise.

It might seem an objection to this contrast-building that Plato does in fact reserve not only the term '*hekon*' but the term 'free' for virtuous philosophers. This suggests that some factor in the explanation of philosophic behaviour is what makes it free in contrast with that of others. It may be that Plato does not achieve his end by picking on a desire as the one whose operation determines that the behaviour is free, but could it not be that he thinks that behaviour done from *episteme* is free behaviour? But once again, one has to be careful of Plato's terminology. The word translated 'free' is '*eleutheros*', and there is no doubt that Plato considers the philosopher *eleutheros* and Thrasymachus' ideal man a slave type. But this characterisation relies heavily on common views about freemen and slaves, free cities and despotisms. Slaves were people always at someone else's beck and call, not allowed to decide for themselves (cf. e.g. *Lysis* 207–8), and there were many menial tasks, unworthy of a free man, that were reserved for slaves. Part of Plato's purpose in, say, the *Republic* is to portray the sybarite as always at the beck and call of ignoble pleasures. By contrast the philosopher is in full control of his life, using his own judgment in its conduct. The point is not that in every action the sybarite has no choice, but that he (his reasoning faculties) is at the beck and call of unworthy elements whose thrall he cannot shake off or at least has not shaken off. In the comparison with free states as against despotisms the point again is not that the sybarite is incapable of choice, but that his varied desires do not get free and fair play. In neither case is the concern with freedom of the will or the power to choose between alternatives.

95

To draw the threads together, the picture is as follows: everyone wants the best out of life. Anyone who is unjust is failing to achieve what he wants and deserves pity. He lacks the expertise necessary to achieve his goal. But usually he can do something about it, and if so should be encouraged or, if in need of some sharp stimulus, punished. In so far as he fails he is pursuing a life unworthy of him; if he succeeds his life will be spent in occupations worthy of a free man; if he fails completely he will, like a slave, be given over to ignoble occupations. He will also, in this last case, be analogous to a despotism, not giving his various inclinations and capacities free play. There is no tendency to suppose that our blaming or punishing practices should be abandoned and have some form of psychiatric treatment substituted, nor that people cannot help themselves. Where Plato innovates is that first he wishes to view punishment as a constructive practice whose infliction should be looked upon as beneficial rather than disgraceful (though, cf. *Protagoras*, some such position was familiar with intellectuals); and, second, as he looks on the ideal community as one of reasoned agreement he considers that punishment should only be resorted to if necessary. In the ideal situation a person will be responsive to instruction, and the presumption must be that wrong-doing is a mistake that the person will rectify when it is pointed out to him. In the *Laws* this is carried to the lengths of requiring a reasoned preface to every law. On the other hand if a person turns out to be incurable, so that neither we nor he can do anything to change him, then he is a canker in the community that must be excised (cf. *Laws* 862d–e). We may still pity him, but the question of pity is quite independent of deserving punishment. The point of insisting on pity is to bring about a constructive view of punishment and the possibility of looking on wrong-doers as failures. In none of this is Plato developing either a determinist picture or a reconciliation of libertarianism and determinism of the general type attempted by Hume. He has simply not faced the possible difficulties of setting limits on the excuse 'I could not help it'. '*Hekon*' and '*akon*' are not in that family.

Plato's concern in developing the Socratic paradox is not with the conditions under which someone may be considered morally responsible or liable to just punishment. His views on willing wrong-doing are part of a general offensive to the effect that the ideal man flourishes in the context of law, and his production is the legislator's aim. The exercise of proper authority is therefore for the subjects' good (*Gorgias* 504, *Republic* 341 seq., 428, *Laws* 628 seq.), not for their disgrace, to help them, not stunt them and so on. Wrong-doing shows ignorance, not cleverness, slavery, not freedom and so on. At the same time the position would seem bizarre to the average Greek, and seem to have the conclusion that criminals should not be punished. This context and conclusion are clearly envisaged at *Laws* 859 seq., where Plato insists on the point that no one is a willing wrong-doer, and examines the conse-quences for punishment. This is done (862 seq.) by distinguishing between doing wrong and harming. The first is a matter of the character of the agent. If an act is done by a 'just' agent, then it is 'just' even if not quite right; if done by an 'unjust' agent it is 'unjust' even if right. If punishment were only appropriate to 'unjust' acts, this would clearly involve radical revision of actual practice, but Plato distinguishes between two activities of a legislator (862b, c). He has to consider both the question of wrong-doing and that of harm or damage. The first has to be cured, and for the second amends must be made to restore good will. Consequently, while he will have to take note in general of bad characters, irrespective of particular good results, he will also have an eye to damage caused and ensure that proper amends are made. So a good deal of customary legal practice will continue. It is clear, how-ever, that the prime concern is the production of good characters and a consequently harmonious society. The questions of intention and degree of deliberation are therefore of considerable moment as indica-tive of the kind of character, which determines the form of treatment appropriate.

There are complexities about the details of this position which I propose to leave aside. For present purposes it is enough to note that Plato thinks that the appropriate method for getting a 'just' character to change his ways is not bullying but reason. The result of successful persuasion will be a person who acts rightly not from fear but because he wants to. The legislator's concern to produce such characters is partly of course a wish to produce fully developed people. But also such people will have an intelligent and effective desire for the welfare of their fellow citizens. In other words they will have an attitude of true friendship towards the other members of the state. A properly ordered state, in fact, is one united by the bonds of friendship which is the ideal of relationships between men. It is the ideal because it results in a smooth-running, united and therefore more efficient state.

This general picture of Plato's position on 'willing' wrong-doing is open, however, to two objections. The first is that Plato quite clearly says that no one will do anything but what he believes to be best. Consequently if a man believes it is the best thing possible to be a head-master and believes that the only way to become one is to take a course in education, then he will inevitably, unless prevented, take a course in education. So Plato is after all committed to a determinist picture of deliberate action, as of all action, and so to the *a priori* thesis that would entail that no one is responsible for wrong-doing.

To this the first point to make is that this is not what he is saying when he says that no one does wrong *hekon*. For this point holds, if at all, of all deliberate acts, but Plato argues in a way that implies that some people, e.g. a philosopher, might act *hekon*. Second, he makes no deterministic noises in conclusion from this point. It might be, nevertheless, that Plato is strictly committed to some form of determinist thesis. Whether he is, and if so to what form, would depend in part on general arguments about determinism. The fact remains that Plato's approach does not draw his attention to these questions, and we cannot tell what option he would take if faced with them. There is, however, some suggestion of uncertainty. As I have already pointed out in chapter II, it is not clear whether the dictum that everyone wants what is best is to be taken as saying that everyone, in reflective mood, will acknowledge the priority of what is best, or more roughly as saying that every desire of every man can be expressed as his believing that what he desires is best. This second formulation has determinist possibilities, but the first would require some further doctrine about always doing what one wants most, together with criteria for strongest desires. Not only does Plato not work out any such view, but it would conflict anyway with the idea that a person always does what he thinks best. For the thesis that a man always does what he wants most is expressly introduced, to give a determinist account of the result of conflict where 'wants' is not confined to reflective consideration of what is best.

The vacillation on how we are to take 'everyone wants what is best' makes its mark elsewhere, too. Thus, the tripartite division of the personality as a combination of conflicting desires may suggest to the modern reader a view of the person as a combination of forces, whose movement could be calculated on some analogue of the parallelogram of forces. But while Plato is interested in the fact of conflict, and in what part *ought* to lead, he gives no account of the mechanics of victory on particular occasions. Once again, it is change of character not determination of choice that interests him. In general the conflict between one's higher and lower self, or one's reason and one's physical urges, or however he is at the moment portraying it, is a conflict it is open to one to win. One can, like Socrates, be captain of one's soul. In fact a view of desires in general as forces would be foreign to Plato. His tendency is to contrast blind force with reason, and reason is at least one of the desires. In his terminology, a man whose behaviour was determined by some quasi-force would be determined despite reason. Thus the Demiurge in the *Timaeus* is limited by necessity (48), that is the recalcitrant nature of matter. He could not be necessitated by reason. Similarly an individual might conceivably be necessitated by blind passion, but not by his reasoning faculty. Plato's terminology militates against the development of a determinist thesis. It is not even clear what he thinks about a person dominated by his lower desires. He seems both to want the *mania* picture – which would suggest incapacitation – and at the same time to accommodate a person who deliberately and skilfully pursues his financial ambitions. The first invites talk of a person being overwhelmed, the second of his being misguided.

All this suggests that Plato is not clear quite what he wants to say on a number of related topics. It is consequently not clear which possibility he would choose to follow up if faced with the supposed consequences of the view that a person always wants what he thinks best. There is at least as much anti- as pro-determinist language. In general, however, the question is one asking for the most futile speculation. There is some indication that Plato thinks that some states of character stem from physiological disorders and amount to incapacitating forms of *mania*, and also that he considers that a person has less responsibility for his character than his educators and his physiology. For the rest it has to be recognised that Plato is not interested in modern problems. His central terms *'hekon'* and *'akon'*, *'eleutheros'* and the term for 'necessary' invite a different approach. Further, they are operating in a different context. Plato thinks we all want *arete*, and that it can only be achieved with difficulty in a well-devised political setting. Everything is geared to enabling men to get what they want. Attention is focused not on whether they could have done otherwise, but on whether they can improve, not on whether they are sincere but on whether they are thinking efficiently. In general, the whole approach is very much what one would expect from someone developing the views outlined in the first five chapters.

VII

Mathematics and Goodness

In the previous chapters I have tried to develop a picture of Plato's attempts to counter a rejection of traditional morality, a rejection based on a rival ideal of the man who is above rules and conventions and able to do as he wants. It does not purport to be a complete account of Plato's treatment of moral questions, but only of a set that clearly seemed to him to be of considerable importance. In connection with his defence of morality he developed a view that somehow virtue was a matter of exercising knowledge. In chapter IV, I offered an account of what that claim amounts to, but that account is open to a number of objections to which I shall now turn as meeting them will make clearer its implications. In the present chapter I shall consider one based on Plato's approach to mathematics. This will lead to considering other objections from his reaction to Heracleiteanism and his dictum that knowledge is of what is, that will involve a more extended consideration of his views on *episteme* and their ramifications.

Briefly, the view advocated in chapter IV was that Plato's statements on the relation of knowledge and goodness are more readily understood if one reflects that the plural '*epistemai*' naturally covers a set of accomplishments such as medicine, music, navigation, building and such like. It is plausible to consider these as concerned with distinguishing good from bad. It is also possible to suggest a route that might have led Plato to think that there is an overall knowledge to be developed of how it is in fact best that things should be as individual branches of knowledge claim it is good they should be.

The objection that I wish to consider might start from the observation that one important set of *technai* often cited by Plato is that consisting of the various branches of mathematics. In the *Gorgias* (501a) it is assumed that anyone possessing a *techne* will need arithmetic, and later (*Republic* 522c, *Philebus* 55e, *Epinomis* 977d–e) it is belligerently stated that anything worth the name of *techne* or *episteme* must involve the use of numbers. Arithmetic, geometry and the rest therefore clearly emerge as the paradigm *technai*, and this seems to be an increasingly dominant view. Yet in no obvious sense is arithmetic concerned with good and bad. In Plato's view (e.g. *Gorgias* 451b) it is knowledge of the odd and the even. This no doubt involves knowing the interrelationships between numbers and a capacity to deal with arithmetical problems, but there seems to be no analogue to the medical notion of health to yield the good that arithmetic deals with. One might hope to claim that Plato's point about mathematics is that any *techne* such as medicine only develops fully in so far as it involves some branch of mathematics, so that it is mathematicised *technai* that are the paradigms. But this seems barely tenable in face of *Republic* Book VII (525-6, 532-4). It seems all too clear that rulers are to be encouraged to get away from practical pursuits such as medicine, strategy and the rest, however mathematically sophisticated, and simply study arithmetic and geometry. These are the important, high-powered *technai* contrasted with more mundane ones at 533b, and they seem clearly to have no relation to vulgar notions of value embodied in concepts like 'health'. In fact it seems more plausible to hold a quite different picture of Plato's development as follows: he started with Socratic questions roughly about definitions and a dissatisfaction with an understanding of phenomena limited to observation of correlations between observable events. The influence of the Pythagoreans and their success in giving a mathematical account of the relationships between notes on a scale led him to look for a different model of explanation that preserved the universal unchanging truth of Socratic definitions without abandoning the explanation of phenomena as sought by the Heracleiteans. The kind of mathematical picture presented in music might be generally extended, revealing that the universe at large can be described as constructed according to certain mathematically expressible relationships. Such relationships are fully intelligible, free of the muddy uncertainties that attach to sense-observations. They are expoundable with complete clarity and rigour, and are just what we should expect a rational constructor of the universe to work with. Knowledge is of the good in that all knowledge is a grasp of intelligible principles, and understanding of the universe consists in knowing that it is as a whole constructed on such principles and in grasping the principles concerned. Being rational ourselves we appreciate such construction and recognise its value, i.e. its rationality. The view espoused in chapter IV has underrated the mathematician in Plato, and so fails to appreciate that mathematical order for him is tantamount to goodness (cf. e.g. *Philebus* 25-6), and disorder is simply equivalent to being resistant to description in accordance with such principles.

Some such view seems to be espoused by I. M. Crombie (1962) and certainly seems to fit a growing insistence on the importance of mathematics from dialogues like the *Gorgias* or *Protagoras,* through the *Republic* and *Timaeus* to the *Epinomis.* The objection could be made stronger if one further adopted the sort of interpretation of the *Republic*'s philosophical ideal given by Robinson (1953) or Wedberg (1955) and rejected by Crombie. According to this view Plato's objection to contemporary mathematicians was that they started from unproved assumptions. His model of proof was deductive, and his hope that philosophers would be able to deduce from some self-evident first principle the at present assumed starting points of mathematics. The self-evident first principle about which Plato is understandably less than clear is the Form of the Good. The procedure is to make a hypothesis from which one can deduce what was previously a hypothesis, and then repeat the move on this second hypothesis until one reaches the non-hypothetical starting-point. From there one should be able rigorously to deduce what was first in question. Now this is a somewhat different picture from that suggested by chapter IV, and presents Plato as holding a more familiar view on the requirements for knowledge. It is one that does not invite the sort of explanation of the relation of knowledge and goodness that I have suggested, but instead gives us a Plato attracted, like Descartes, to the view that what is known is either self-evident or deducible from what is self-evident. The ideal is a system manifesting mathematical rigour, and perhaps itself consisting of axioms and derivations in mathematical form.

On one point I should be prepared to agree with this objection, in that Plato does seem to think that every branch of knowledge worth the name in some way involves mathematics, and so at least arithmetic or geometry. It is sometimes suggested that there are or should be moral analogues of the mathematical hypotheses of the *Republic,* and that it is only because mathematics obviously can be studied abstractly that it is chosen for the propaedeutic and its hypotheses spoken of as jumping-off boards for philosophy. In principle we should be able to find examples of moral thought that manifest a similar condition to mathematics, starting from certain unproved assumptions and then deriving moral conclusions. This assumption is the more attractive in that presumably such moral hypotheses would contain value words, and so it would be easy to envisage a progress to the Form of the Good. While it is stated that the study of mathematics will be a good starting-point for that journey (Book VI 511b), it is baffling to see how. This problem is eased if we suppose that Plato thought (i) that there were moral analogues but (ii) that they did not constitute readily recognisable branches of study, while (iii) mathematics did already exist as an abstract pursuit which illustrated the general type of study he was advocating.

For in that case he has simply assumed what he might expect his readers to gather, that there are moral hypotheses, analogous to mathematical ones, and the progress from them to the Form of the Good will be more obvious.

This seems, however, to underrate a number of Plato's statements, quite apart from any oddity in his omitting to make any explicit statements in this direction. To begin with, the philosophers need *episteme* for running the state, and the knowledge of 'moral' matters is the knowledge required. The same is true of the ruler in the *Politicus*, and the rulers in the *Laws*. Yet *all epistemai* worth the name are said to involve mathematics. Consequently, however bizarre it may strike us, it seems that Plato thinks that a proper understanding of the human psyche would involve the use of mathematical techniques. This whole line of thought seems also to pervade the *Philebus*, where number and proportion are responsible for all good conditions, including virtue (cf. 26), and knowledge of them is necessary for the producer of a good life. Similarly the Demiurge of the *Timaeus* seems to rely heavily on his mathematical knowledge. Consequently ethics properly pursued will be a mathematically expressible discipline analogous to, if not part of, music and astronomy. This suggests that any ethical hypotheses would in fact be mathematical ones. The whole trend is to assimilate value concepts to mathematical ones of measure and proportion. The statements that all *epistemai* involve mathematics taken alone could be a not uncharacteristic Platonic exaggeration. The use of notions of number, measure and proportion in ethical contexts, suggests it is to be taken seriously.

If that line of escape, then, is closed, what is to be made of the objection? This I shall tackle in two stages, first considering more closely Plato's statements about the value of mathematics, and then considering the proposed account of his use of mathematics as a model for philosophical demonstration. With regard to the first, some repetition of earlier remarks on some development in Plato's thought will be in order. I pointed out that in the *Gorgias* (cf. e.g. 501–7) we find Plato arguing for a connection between *techne* and number and order. Further, he wants to say that everything has its own proper order that constitutes its excellence. Now obviously, anyone who wishes to hold that mathematically expressible relationships somehow give a thing's excellence is open to the question whether for any given thing there are certain relationships that express it, or whether the simple fact that a relationship is so expressible is enough. This is a question that notoriously arises in the *Philebus* (23 seq.). There Plato seems to talk as though the mere introduction of specific quantities *ipso facto* produces good results. This just seems absurd, but in the *Gorgias*, at least, while there is the concession that each thing has its own proper order, which seems to tell against the absurd position just mentioned, there is no indication of how we judge propriety. In the *Phaedo*, *Symposium* and *Republic* there is a growing emphasis on the ideal of explanation taking the form of showing that it is best that things be thus and so, and in the *Republic* especially we get elaborated some account of how to tell what the proper ordering of a thing will be. This account is functional, not mathematical. Yet also in the *Republic* greater emphasis is found than previously on the importance of mathematics. This suggests two things: first, that Plato does not think that the simple fact of a relationship's being mathematically expressible is sufficient to show it to be desirable, and second, that the precise expression of notions of proper ordering will require mathematical techniques.

Next, it is worth noting an awkwardness in the mathematical programme of Book VII. The first two branches that are mentioned, arithmetic and geometry, while it is clear that they are considered useful as a help towards the Form of the Good (cf. 526d–e), are not themselves concerned with good or bad proportions, quantities or whatever. We are firmly in the non-evaluative world of Euclid. By contrast astronomy and 'harmony' as Plato wishes them to be studied, seem to involve notions of proper speeds and arrangements. This is particularly clear with music (cf. 531c), but the implication is that the same holds for astronomy. So these two are concerned with good and bad proportions and arrangements. Further, at 531c–d it becomes clear that even in their abstract form there is a useful and a useless pursuit of these disciplines. To be useful they have to be seen in relation to one another, in their mutual kinship and appropriateness. We have already been told at 530d that astronomy and music are closely related studies, presumably because of some relation between what are proper proportions in each (cf. *Epinomis* 990–1). But no doubt also Plato is thinking that, for instance, the points on the scale can be represented as points on a line, a representation that comes from another branch of mathematics. At any rate this all indicates that the first two branches of mathematics are to be considered and recommended in connection with the others, and they, at least, are concerned with good and bad situations.

In the *Republic* no attention is drawn to any distinction of the sort that in fact seems to hold between arithmetic and geometry on the one hand, and astronomy and music on the other. In the *Politicus* (283 seq.) the distinction is declared to be vital. Those *technai* that simply deal with quantitative relations are distinguished from those that measure the extent to which measures exceed or fall below what is proper, and the *episteme* of kingship falls into the latter class. It seems as near clear as anything can be where the *Philebus* is concerned, that the notions of measure and the rest used there are to be taken as used of this second form of measurement. The stress on the distinction in the *Politicus* suggests that Plato had become clearer on the significance of the difference, and also as to the sort of measurement he valued. By the *Philebus* he can take it for granted that this is meant (cf. also *Epinomis* 978). Clearly for this sort of measuring, more than just arithmetic or geometry is needed. In the *Philebus* it seems that the introduction of number by someone who discovers a *techne* is the discovery of a *metrion* or proper arrangement or proportion. This is used as a measure of excess and defect, in fact determining what are to count as such. Introducing, or discovering equality, is again introducing or discovering precise points on continua that can allow both of giving exact relationships to other chosen points and determining what is simply too much or too little. Thus the discovery of the musical scales is the discovery of related points on the continuum of high and low; their relationships can be expressed mathematically as ratios between integers; the notes also constitute a measure in the second *Politicus* sense in that they and the rules of melody determine excess and defect. As they are points on a continuum there remains an indefinite possibility of further divisions of high and low that lie outside musical skill. Indeed, the continuum is in the last resort never completely reducible by one's skill. However far one sub-divided the intervals there would be further possibilities of sub-division not covered, giving an area where one is not skilled. In this sense there is always an indeterminate beyond the 'number' discovered by the musician, and the indeterminate always spells lack of knowledge (*Philebus* 17e). Because each skill has its own measure in this sense, the introduction of measure always produces good and beautiful arrangements.

All this suggests that Plato did not think that the Demiurge simply needed arithmetic and geometry. His form of measurement would be the other, needing no doubt the skills of dealing with relative magnitudes, but also an understanding of the proper proportions in different areas. If he were human, he might be capable of the measuring concerned without knowing whether what he takes to be good arrangements are really so. Further, Plato was clearly aware of the two forms of measurement, or ways of using numbers, and they are both considered as forms of measuring. It looks, therefore, as though the insistence on mathematics and the importance given to it is not at odds with the interpretation of chapter IV. Rather, the line of thought suggested there seems to have influenced Plato's way of talking of mathematics so that subjects that embody notions of propriety not only count as branches of it, but receive preferential treatment. This last remark is not based simply on the *Politicus* passage. All the talk of the limit, or determinant, in the *Philebus*, a clearly 'numerical' notion, locates it in the context of the second form of measurement, and the knowledge exercised by both the wise man and the world soul is of this form. Further, the Pytha-

gorean assimilation of astronomy and music is approved in the
Republic. If one considers the reasons for selecting the proper sort of
music offered in *Republic* Books II–III, it is clear that Plato thought that
the better modes were related to the proper ordering of the soul (cf.
400–2). Astronomy, on the other hand, studies the working of the
whole universe. Increasingly, through the *Timaeus* and *Philebus* the
universe is thought of as a living thing of which our minds are microcosms. Consequently one would expect a close relationship between
astronomy and music. It would be no surprise if their study were vital
for any rulers or their 'measures' held the key to the structure of the
universe (cf. *Laws* Book X, Book XII 966 *ad fin. Epinomis* 990–1).

It might be objected that this blurs the contrast Plato makes between
technai such as medicine on the one hand and those like astronomy on
the other. For he clearly does contrast them, and not only in the
Republic. But the last few paragraphs have in fact been bringing them
closer and closer together. It is worth asking therefore what the
contrast is. The first and most obvious point about the vulgar *technai*
in the *Republic* is that they are geared to supplying human needs. A
doctor or a builder has his attention on the production of particular
changes (533b). A proper astronomer or musician has not, and the
former at least is both studying what is beyond his power to change
in any sense, and is starting to think of the structure of the universe as a
whole, and not just of human needs. Second, music or astronomy
practised in the wrong way fail to develop a mathematical account with
precisely expressed relationships. Their practitioners instead concentrate on audible similarities and contrasts or relationships between
visually observed phenomena. Either falls short of a clear exposition of
the demarcation between proper and improper arrangements. There
would, of course, on this view be nothing in principle to prevent there
being a proper way of doing medicine, and this is, I think, true. But
music and astronomy have the advantage of already being concerned
with the most important subject-matters. Study of the body, even in a
proper way, would be starting at the lower end, and so would anyway
be a less immediately appropriate pro-paideutic for dialectic.

It seems, then, that a survey of the dialogues suggests that Plato
thought arithmetic and geometry vital as being abstract studies and
having a part to play in the preferred form of measurement. The
'honourable' forms of mathematics, however, are music and astronomy,
and generally the preferred sort of measurement. The very distinction
between the two forms of measurement suggests that Plato was aware
of the need to be able to determine propriety of combinations, and this
was not a matter of arithmetical or geometrical expertise. Those who
do music and astronomy as recommended by Plato learn to represent
certain proper relationships mathematically, but do not thereby learn to

establish the assumption that what they are representing are good arrangements. It is of some interest that the preferred branches of mathematics are not pure mathematics as we should today use that term. The distinction between doing mathematics properly and improperly is between doing it as part of some practical pursuit and as part of a study of the nature of melody, the soul, the heavenly bodies or whatever it may be. The latter will be a detached, and if adequately done synoptic enquiry.

It remains, then, to see how matters stand with regard to mathematics being somehow the model for philosophical demonstration, and this will involve some consideration of the so-called hypothetical method. I have no wish to get involved in disputes as to whether the method proposed in the *Meno* (86 seq.) is the same as that at *Phaedo* (99 seq.). I shall concentrate instead on the latter as it is commonly supposed close to the *Republic*. The argument is briefly as follows: in the *Phaedo* Socrates holds (97–8) that the proper form of explanation of a thesis would be to show that it is best that things be as the thesis declares them to be. Failing progress with this form of explanation he turned to another method. This consisted in looking for a hypothesis from which to derive the thesis in question. The first step was then to examine the consequences of the hypothesis. Granted no objections arose there one might turn to the defence of the hypothesis. This would take the form of finding a further hypothesis and proceeding as before on the original thesis. In choosing a hypothesis one looks for something satisfactory, presumably to oneself and interlocutors. The details of exposition need not delay us. The main point is that this procedure has one obvious weakness, that however long one pursues it one is left with an unproved hypothesis. The most one can hope for is one that is acceptable to the present disputants. In the *Republic* mathematics, even correctly pursued, is portrayed as establishing conclusions (510b), but not starting-points. In other words, the subject satisfies the conditions of the first steps of the *Phaedo*, but it fails to defend its hypotheses. In this according to *Republic* 511a–d it contrasts with dialectic, which proceeds up to a beginning from which everything below can be derived. Indeed, as a result of this process the hypotheses of mathematics themselves become known (511d). It looks, then, as though the *Republic* is advocating the procedure of the *Phaedo* with one important difference: in the *Republic*, in some way unrevealed, Plato thinks that as we progress up the hypotheses we shall reach the stage where we achieve an intuitive, and presumably self-guaranteeing, grasp of the Form of the Good, from which all else follows. This last leap is mysterious, but Plato makes it clear that he cannot be clear, but can only talk in imagery, so that is not a point against the interpretation. Indeed, the visual imagery used, together with the Seventh Letter (342 seq.) might be taken to support the idea that Plato considered that all depended on some final intuitive vision.

This question of the weight to be attached to visual imagery I shall turn to in a later chapter. At present I want to see how the argument stands without resort to that. The first point here is that one might at least as well expect a different view of philosophical method in the *Republic* from that in *Phaedo* as expect basically the same. After all, the second best of *Phaedo* 99c–d is explicitly said to be an alternative to the preferred route of showing how it is best that things be so. In the *Republic*, by contrast, one would expect that Plato is advocating, though hardly describing, the route shied away from in the *Phaedo*. It all turns, therefore, on what is to be made of the talk of hypotheses in the *Republic* and the burden of Plato's complaint.

There are certain conditions which, it seems to me, any answer to these questions must satisfy:

(i) Plato must be considering a possible, correct way of doing mathematics that nevertheless is open to his objections. It is true that in some sense or another mathematics is 'less true' than dialectic, but also it is clear that 'with a beginning' mathematical hypotheses are graspable by dialectical understanding (511d), which they could hardly be if false. Further, if Plato was offering a radical critique of contemporary mathematics by suggesting that its foundations were false it is surprising that so dramatic a charge caused no ripple. We nowhere hear any mention of or reaction to these charges.

(ii) In some sense the hypotheses of mathematics can be established and will be by a philosopher.

(iii) Plato must have some conception of at least the first steps the dialectician takes. It may be that the end product disappears into the clouds, but it is surely incredible that Plato should have levelled all his complaints and elaborated his imagery of ascent without any idea of what the first rung of the philosophical ladder was like. It should, therefore, be an objection against a view that it makes it quite baffling what the first philosophical move could be.

I shall assume in what follows that Robinson is right in saying that a philosopher will not show the hypotheses of mathematics to be wrong, but will remove their hypothetical nature. The first question to ask, therefore, is what these hypotheses might be. Suppose we take statements like 'an even number is divisible into two equal whole numbers', and a similar statement for odd numbers, or 'a triangle is a three sided rectilinear figure'. These might do for 'hypothesising the odd and the even, the figures' and so on of 510c. But what is our dialectician to do with them? On the view under discussion he has to discover a hypothesis from which he could derive these as conclusions. As they are definitions it is impossible to see where he would start. At first sight there might seem to be two possibilities. First, Plato might think of mathematicians as assuming the definitions of 'odd', 'even' and assuming also that these are worthwhile definitions that reveal or answer to the nature of number. If we stick to the original version of the hypothesis, however, the sense of 'derive' has shifted. That an even number is divisible into two equal whole numbers has not been derived in the sense of 'deduced'. If a philosopher is concerned to show the worth of mathematical definitions he is engaged in a different activity from what we were led to expect. Also, he still seems to be doing mathematics. The second possibility therefore, is that we alter the example of a hypothesis to meet the difficulty. Perhaps hypothesising the odd and the even, the figures, and so on, is hypothesising that numbers are either odd or even, that there are so many kinds of figure, angle and so on. Granting that Plato is not questioning these suppositions, how does he envisage establishing them? On the view under consideration *reductio ad absurdum* arguments are not in order, we need a 'higher' hypothesis from which to derive these views. Once again even what the first faltering step would be is obscure. This is quite apart from the uncomfortable question, how many sorts of figure do mathematicians hypothesise?

It might be felt that one obvious possibility has been ignored. At 510d–e, we are told that geometers are really concerned with the Form of Square, and so on, and in other places the mathematician is described as apprehending the truth in a dream-like way (533b). Plato might think that mathematicians fail to realise that these statements are definitions. 'An even number is divisible into two equal whole numbers' is seen as an obvious general truth, whereas in fact it is true because of what it is to be even. So the nature of evenness or the Form of the Even is in fact seen in a glass darkly by mathematicians. The dialectician will establish these basic truths, and do so by understanding them more clearly.

The difficulty with this is twofold. First, the 'hypotheses' are hardly derived from a higher hypothesis as, on the view under discussion, they would have to be; they are, rather, said to be in fact definitions. Second, if this is how Plato thought of the first rung on the ladder the question arises: how could he have thought that *that* could have been established? In other words, how did he fail to see that the vision of an upward ladder was doomed?

Suppose, then, that we cast the hypothesis in a different form. Plato was said by Aristotle to have postulated not only Forms, that existed independently of things, but also intermediate mathematical objects. He might have thought, then, that mathematicians took for granted the existence of mathematical objects, of squares other than their diagrams, about which they could prove theorems. But it is not the function of mathematics to establish the existence of such objects. That is for a dialectician. One could now envisage further hypotheses. For instance:

what can be thought of exists, each form is unique, particulars are in a process of change, units can be thought of; units are not in process; units are not unique. These have not been put in special order, but together they make towards providing a proof that mathematicals exist. Each would then need proving, and it might be hoped that at some stage reference to the general value of things being so might be in point, even if it is not quite clear how or at what point.

In some ways this sounds more hopeful, but if true then Plato must be taken, in the *Republic*, as making the existence of intermediate mathematical objects a major point. Mathematics presupposes their existence, and dialectic can and will prove it. The complaint against mathematicians is that they proceed without having any proof of the existence of mathematicals. In that case it is odd, as Wedberg brings out, that Plato is so cagey about the objects of the 'state of mind' of mathematicians. At 510–11 we get apparently clear classes of objects for the two lowest frames of mind, and it seems clear that Forms are what the philosopher is concerned with. Mathematics, on the other hand is characterised entirely in terms of method. At 532 b–c, where it seems that a stage of progress from the cave is matched to the state of the mathematicians, they are looking at reflections, and though these reflect the reality more accurately than do the images of the previous stage, they are relatively insubstantial. None of this suggests a polemic for the existence of intermediate mathematical objects. Further, whatever is said to be hypothesised at 510c, is also said to be considered by the mathematicians to be obvious to everyone. It is hardly credible that this means that typical Greek mathematicians thought it obvious that there existed mathematical objects over and above their diagrams. The most that could be claimed is that this is what their procedures commit them to, but in that case it is not what they consider obvious. They do, no doubt, consider it obvious that their theorems are not about the diagrams, but that is not the same as thinking it self-evident that there are further quasi-substances, the mathematicals.

This last interpretation does, however, have one advantage: it recognises that Plato says the mathematicians hypothesise 'the odd and the even, the figures, three kinds of angle and such like'. In other words Plato's words do not suggest any recognisable axioms or postulates. Further, in other places where the verb for 'hypothesise' is used taking a simple direct object, it seems right to insert the verb 'to be' to make a proposition (cf. C. C. W. Taylor). Suppose now that we take it that at 510d–e Plato has in mind the way geometers might talk. If someone started complaining that the figure drawn was not quite square, a geometer might complain that he is not interested in the figure, but in .... At this point we get a form of words often used by Plato to refer to Forms. But Plato used such expressions ('the square itself') because the

'itself' idiom was the obvious one for anyone wishing to reject particulars as what he was talking about. It would be an equally natural
idiom for a geometer facing a complaint about his figures. Pythagoras'
theorem concerns the relation of *the* square of *the* hypotenuse of *the*
right-angle triangle to *the* squares of *the* other two sides. It is not
concerned with this figure on the board. What with then? The square
itself. This terminology runs all through mathematical discourse, and
indeed, if it is dis-allowed the whole possibility of mathematics collapses. Arithmetic is the study of *the* odd and *the* even; there are theorems
and problems concerning *the* doubling of *the* square, the relations of *the*
angles of *the* equilateral triangle and so on. The definite article may not
always be natural in English but would be normal in Greek, and would
serve, sometimes with the help of the 'in itself' idiom, to indicate that it
is not these perceptible diagrams that the proof is about.

It is, however, noticeable that mathematicians are not concerned to
explain or justify this talk of 'the square'. This, too, simply fits observation. When they are said to consider these things 'obvious to everyone',
this is not a belief that everybody in fact obviously realises what they
are talking about. Rather, if asked to explain, all they can do is go
through a theorem with a diagram. Failure to follow what he is doing
must be a sign of stupidity, it is just obvious what he means by 'the
square'. But it is not a square you can see, you have to think. Now this
is a non-answer to the questions 'what is the square?' or 'what square?'
At best it tells us how not (and embryonically how) to get to know. The
same inability to answer is portrayed at 525d–526b, where those who
are clever at mathematics are said to talk about units that are absolutely
equal. But when asked what sort of units these are they can again only
say that they can only be thought. The point in that passage is to
indicate that this way of doing arithmetic involves intellect rather than
practical experience, but the picture of the mathematician fits what we
should expect from 510–11. In short, the mathematician is unable to
'give an account' of his subject-matter, and yet if he is to be justified in
talking of *the* square and the rest, he ought to be able to say what he is
talking about.

If we are to keep this example of 'hypothesise' with a direct object in
line with others, we might gloss it as 'hypothesising that there is such a
thing as the odd and the even . . .'. For this way of putting it allows the
mathematicians to be supposing, and supposing as obvious, that one
can intelligibly talk of the odd and the even in the way in which they
do, and must. This seems a very plausible assumption to make about
mathematicians. It would also, as seems right, leave Plato uncommitted
on the existence of mathematicals in the *Republic*, while allowing that he
might have believed in them. For it might be that a part of what was
needed to make the mathematicians' talk intelligible was to show that

there is an intermediate class of mathematical objects. But that is not the defect that is seized upon in the *Republic*, which is simply the mathematicians' inability to justify the way they talk.

Supposing this to be right, however, the question remains: what is a plausible first hypothesis from which a philosopher might hope to deduce that 'there is such a thing as the square'? Not only is it hard to see how Plato thought one was to start, but also, as the 'hypothesis' is a claim that a certain way of talking is intelligible, one would not immediately envisage the making of hypotheses as the obvious procedure, but some enquiry as to what a mathematician is saying. Explication rather than demonstration seems to be what is required. This in turn raises a query about the whole deductive picture of philosophical method attributed to the *Republic*. This query may be reinforced by the consideration that the predominant terms to indicate epistemological progress or lack of it are not ones that suggest a worry about proof, but about clarity. They appear in Book V 478c, to indicate the superiority of *episteme* and run through the Sun, Line and Cave. Now it is a common early dialogue complaint that someone has failed to say anything clear or clear enough, and it is usually a complaint about the person's clarity on a subject, such as courage, or piety. Typically in these dialogues there is no attempt to derive an account of courage from some 'higher' hypothesis. A person is unclear, not if he has failed to prove *p*, but if he does not know what to say in face of objections. This takes two forms: if he wavers, or if he accepts that something false follows. Either will show him to be unclear about whatever it is. A person who was clear about, say, the nature of courage would be able to cope with all objections.

There still seems to be some of this in the *Republic*. In Book V, certain people are said not to have *episteme*. They are putative experts on what is fine and just, but whatever it is they say to be fine or just (which is open to dispute), is demonstrably quite as much poor or unjust. Consequently they show themselves not able to cope with the counter-example. Now it seems that they would want to claim that it is impossible to cope with the counter cases, but Plato's point is that this shows at least that they do not know what justice *is*, and the rest. Further, this is sufficient to show lack of clarity. It is inability to cope with objection, not inability to derive that is at issue. Similarly, it seems that the mathematician is unable to explain why an objection is ill-founded, and that this, rather than an inability to derive his basic propositions, is Plato's complaint. So very probably 'clarity' bears the same general sense as in earlier dialogues, and this fits the account offered of what the mathematicians hypotheses are, and why they are dubbed 'hypotheses'.

The question remains: what are the philosopher's first steps? Here it is worth recalling the contrast mentioned earlier between arithmetic and geometry on the one hand and music and astronomy on the other. These last two are not mentioned in the passage about hypotheses. They only come into their own when the philosopher's education is outlined. The only hypotheses mentioned are arithmetical or geometrical. There is no reason why there should not be hypotheses in the others (the dominant, the octave, the ellipse) but in fact Plato does not mention any. Ones that occur to one, especially in music, but also presumably in Platonic astronomy, would presumably embody assumptions about certain arrangements being good and so would readily encourage the right sort of question. But what of arithmetic and geometry? what sort of thinking on the intelligibility of talking of *the* odd and *the* even, leads to upward paths?

Here there seem to be two possibilities. First, one might consider these disciplines in isolation. To take arithmetic, one expects Plato's philosopher to put to the mathematician the question put to him at 526a. The problem is that units commonly (i.e. physical units) seem all too divisible, and rarely does one buy five tomatoes that do not manifest clear difference of size. The mathematician's requirement that units be indivisible and mutually equal immediately raises a question. Now in the *Parmenides* (129) Plato shows himself aware that whether X counts as a unit or a plurality depends on what we are counting. If we are counting men, Socrates is a unit, if limbs he is a plurality. If we think of the mathematician's units we might reflect that what he says about units is true of anything considered as a unit, but characteristically considering something a unit is considering it as one F. 'F' will determine what we are counting and where we stop dividing. If we have a group of men, 'man' would encourage us to stop at Socrates, but 'limb' to continue beyond him. It is now apparent that there could be no counting (no answering 'how many?') unless we had concepts determining what we were counting. But also, not everything can be counted together. If we have two men and their four legs there is nothing of which we have six, and while it is possible to have a set consisting of Fido, Bertrand Russell's third joke and the square root of two it has commonly been felt that these do not constitute a class properly speaking. One can say how many members the set has, but there is no defining property of the set in terms of which to give what is being counted and determine the 'units' of the set. One can only list the members. The men and their legs suggest that counting presupposes a way of determining the units to be counted. The oddity of the set of three and the difficulty of saying what it is that we have three of might suggest that there are proper and improper ways of grouping things. This is to start questions on how things should be grouped, or how reality should be divided, which smell of Forms. One might even expect knowledge of the Form of the Good to show that there are proper ways of grouping and what they are. It would then emerge that the mathematicians were expressing, but dimly, something that emerges as an important truth about counting. Similarly geometers, in their talk of *the* square and so on, will be dealing with figures with unusual properties: having surfaces without depth, starting at unextended points and so on. It is a good question what these 'bodiless surfaces' and unextended points might be. It will strike a geometer as obviously unobjectionable to talk this way, but will lead a philosopher to reflect on what it is to treat something as a point (the start of a line), or a surface, and whether it is arbitrary what is selected as a point, or delimited as the surface. Thus the geometer's points and surfaces may reflect a truth about measuring and demarcating, that to treat something as a point is to treat it as not to be measured but as where measuring starts, to treat something as having a surface is to treat something as having definite limits, the points at which it is demarcated from other things. But all this should raise the question of the arbitrariness of demarcation, and so lead to Form-type questions.

A second possibility is that Plato's philosopher does not start from arithmetic or geometry in isolation, but only viewed as intimately bound up with the other disciplines in accordance with 531c–d. In that case his reflection on talk of the odd and the even and the three kinds of angle will be coloured by his knowledge of their value in music and astronomy. Whereas the familiar arithmetician or geometer seems simply to be talking in the void of mysterious units, the philosopher will be able to exhibit the role of these disciplines in astronomy and music. If he can then show that what these assume to be good conditions are so, then he can show the activities of arithmeticians and geometers to be concerned with theorems that have an important part to play in an overall understanding of the universe. They themselves do not realise the significance of their subjects and so cannot explain what the value of arithmetic is, but the philosopher can.

On either of these views the hypotheses of mathematics, *the* odd and *the* even and so on or the assumption that there is such a thing as *the* odd and *the* even, are made by the philosopher genuine starting-points (511b). That is, from reflecting on them he is led to genuine *episteme*, an enquiry of how it is best that the world be structured as it is. It is, of course, a matter of speculation whether Plato conceived of the philosopher's journey in either of these ways. The point of the speculation is to decide not what Plato did hold, but whether, on a given view of mathematical hypotheses and his objection to them there is an intelligible account possible of the philosopher's first move. If not, that would count against an interpretation. If so, then that interpretation remains possible.

The argument, then, is that the attempt to father a deductive model of philosophy on Plato gets into difficulties. The alternative offered is compatible with the thesis of chapter IV. To establish this more clearly, I shall now first try to lessen an objection, and then try to illustrate that the problem of how we know that we have reached the unhypothesised starting-point is eased on this interpretation.

The objection is that Plato talks not only of clarity but also of truth as what the philosopher achieves. Indeed, at 510a–b the proportions of the line seem to be of relative truth or lack of it. Now Plato quite commonly speaks in terms of degrees of truth. In the *Philebus*, for instance (55b seq.), *epistemai* are graded according to their degree of truth, and it looks as though the point is that the results of some cannot be said without qualification to be certain. 'True' tends to be applied in the first instance to *epistemai*, and degrees of it to be degrees of certainty of results. If we have the deductive model, together with a view that universal 'definitional' truths are more certain than empirical ones, then we can give a perfectly good account of this talk, and the Form of the Good is only required in its proper mysterious role at the final stage.

At this stage I shall only try to lessen this objection. There is a considerable problem or set of problems surrounding Plato's talk of truth, which I shall treat more fully in a later chapter. For the present I shall be content with a few defensive observations. First, the point needs emphasising that when Plato talks of degrees of truth he is almost invariably considering the adequacy of a discipline to produce adequate answers. He is not primarily concerned with the truth or falsity of particular propositions. Thus he is not concerned with 'the cat is on the mat' and wondering how true it is. Rather he is concerned with building, medicine, geometry, dialectic and wondering about the extent to which they can yield reliable and accurate results. Consequently it will be important to know what sorts of result he thinks such disciplines yield. If they typically give information about good and bad states of affairs, then it is their capacity to give the truth about those that will be in question. In other words, goodness will be in from the start. Again, if the argument of chapter II is right, then Plato wishes to interpret enquiries into the nature of things in a functional way. But talking of nature and talking of being tend often to be equivalent, and similarly talk of being and truth. So talking of something's being will be talking of its function or good state. In many places it looks as though when Plato says knowledge is of being one has to interpret 'being' in the more restricted sense of 'essence', and this in turn has to be interpreted in a functional way so that knowing the essence of X is knowing the good way for X to be. This is particularly true of the *Republic*. Consequently it might well be that Plato conceives of the difference in truth as a difference of capacity to show what is best in a given area. If so, one would expect dialectic to follow the best method for this purpose, and the deductive model no longer looks so obvious a candidate.

The method that most naturally suggests itself is derived from a functional model. If one comes across a machine, then trying to understand it will consist in assigning a supposed function to the machine and its various parts. No doubt this will be a matter of two-way corrections. An assumption about general function will create expectations about the function of parts, and study of the actual capacities of parts will modify one's view of the general function. The challenge is to produce a set of proposed functions of parts that can be seen to interrelate in a general function and show them on the whole to 'explain' the behaviour of the machine. 'On the whole' because some exceptions could be accommodated as misfunctions. The procedure could, of course, be described as making hypotheses, but the relationship between thesis and hypotheses is generally looser than entailment or presupposition. Thus the assumption that the machine is a clock would entail that it had some mechanism or other apt for keeping time, but entail nothing about the form of mechanism, nor about the degree of accuracy required for it to count as 'apt for keeping time'. So the 'hypothesis' would not entail specific functions of specific parts, nor would their operation entail the interpretation of it as a clock. On the other hand, certain facts about the mechanism, e.g. that it is brown, would be compatible with its being a clock, but quite irrelevant. Others, as, e.g. that there are uniform motions through measures that more or less matched the revolutions of the sun would 'fit the hypothesis very well'. The metaphor of 'being in or out of tune with' would be very apt, and also the description of dialectic as discovering a melody (*nomos*) (*Republic* 531d, 532d–e). The aim is to exhibit the whole as constituting a unified system, and if we apply the model to the world at large it is easy to see how such an exhibiting would be a late stage. The deductive model is simply not helpful here.

The philosopher who has started enquiring into whether what are assumed to be good states really are is engaged in the task of exhibiting the universe as constituting the sort of system that talk of good and bad states of its parts supposes it to be. The model is not a mathematical deductive one. On the other hand, if I am right that Plato thinks that the use of the concept of health presupposes that it is good that bodies be in that condition, and also that that has to be established by reference to a wider context, then it perhaps becomes intelligible that he thought you could know when the end had been reached. For the normal Greek view was that the universe constituted a fairly manageable system, and, by definition, there was no wider one to appeal to. So once we have reached the universe at large we know we have reached the last stage. All previous assignments of 'good' and 'bad' have been provisional on the possibility of an exhibition of general order (the *kosmos*). That is not provisional on further contexts. At this point a philosopher has to defend his account of what is best against all objections and show its power to make sense of things (534b–c). Of course, even here it is in principle possible that someone should at any time come up with an unforeseen difficulty, but the capacity of a philosopher's account to cope with a wide range of circumstances would count as confirmation of his claims, and if he has wide success it would be plausible to suppose that any objections yet to come would result in modification rather than abandonment. In short, knowledge of the Form of the Good is not an intuition of an unsubstantiated first premiss. It is rather an account of a system in terms of interrelated functions which is substantiated by its ability to 'make sense' of the universe. There does, indeed, remain a problem of how Plato would rule out the possibility of two alternative accounts between which it is impossible to decide. What his answer would be it would be pure speculation to try to determine. It is quite possible that he never thought of it as a problem. At the level of arte- facts and organisms he seems to have assumed one dominant function and, anyway, at the level of the universe at large it may be hard to distinguish between having two alternative accounts and having one, more complex, account of a system of multi-functional parts. I shall pursue this in more detail in chapter XVII.

It is perhaps as well to end with a reminder of the role of mathe- matics. The exposition of the philosopher's task might suggest that mathematics has become unimportant again. After all, the required leap could surely be taken straight from the practical disciplines of medicine and the like. Why insert the extra stage of mathematics? To this there are two points to be made, one psychological and one *episteme*ological. The psychological one is as follows: Plato's outline of a progress of knowledge is also an outline of someone being weaned from some interests to others. A man in the lower conditions of *eikasia* and *pistis* is not only relatively unable to give an account of himself, he is also possessed of ability at best geared to satisfying human needs and desires. The *technai* so described at 533, and distinguished from mathematics properly pursued, are presumably practical pursuits that come in the lower half of the line. One important fact about becoming a proper mathematician is that one acquires an interest in the square and so on, as distinct from an interest in producing particular architectural results. Similarly a proper musician will acquire an interest in the principles of composition, instead of just in producing a piece for a festival. The acquisition of this more theoretical interest is important for the philosopher who has to be interested in discovering the structural principles of the universe as a whole, taking his mind off the immediate pursuit of his own or his fellows' needs. When we add that the mathematician is trained in astronomy and music, and the inter-relations of the various disciplines, it may well seem a prerequisite.

Second, one of Plato's demands on *episteme* is precision (*akribeia*). Now any of us, reflecting on a notion of health as physical balance can appreciate the possibility that various sorts of healthy body might turn out to have a part in an elaborate economy of nature. So the general picture of a system that nature more or less but not quite manifests is not too hard to grasp. But unless we can give a precise account of the balance supposedly needed in each case, and its relationship to others, then we cannot expound the system or show clearly where we have deviations from it. For this the precision supplied by mathematics is needed, and the 'this' is the important task of showing the universe in fact to be rationally constructed for the best. If we suppose or are forced to the conclusion that no such exposition is possible we are forced to suppose that the Demiurge had no clear idea what he was about and the universe is not intelligible. But if it is not, then in Plato's view we have no pretensions to any *episteme* at all.

To sum up: Plato does not have an ideal of arithmetical or geo-metrical proof for philosophy, nor do those two disciplines somehow determine rationality or goodness. Mathematics is important partly as starting an interest that is not, in elaborate form, in the satisfaction of ordinary desires, and partly as supplying the tools of precision necessary to exhibit the system on which the universe is constructed. Preference however is given to that form of measurement that is concerned with what is suitable or proper, and so some branches of mathematics as conceived by Plato are already handling notions of 'correct' number. Thus music properly pursued counts as a branch of mathematics, but is concerned with correct proportions and measures. Plato is prepared to use the terms for 'number' and 'measuring' in a way quite foreign to us, to cover proper quantity as determined by some subject-matter and the procedure of matching to those quantities. The philosopher's upward path involves working out the interrelations of the functions taken as good by particular disciplines until finally he can exhibit them as a unified system. The vision of how everything fits is the vision of the Form of the Good, a grasp of the breath-taking magnificence and ingenuity of the plan which inspires the philosopher with a sense of the nobility of his part in the divine work. Once the total context of the universe is reached he knows there is no further upward step, and his work now is to demonstrate the explanatory power of his proposal.

All this is intended to show the possibility of at least accommodating Plato's statements on mathematics to the view of *episteme* proposed. The difficulty is that the present objection together with those to be discussed in the following chapters are at many points connected. It would be unreasonable to expect anyone to accept the above exposition just like that, as very likely he might hold that this would all be possible if it were not that clearly Plato is more concerned with particular propositions or more taken with a visual analogy for knowing than this account allows of. It will be enough, however, if the above suggests that the proposed view of *episteme* is possible if only these other hurdles can be surmounted. Granted that, it is worth noting one final point. Plato's mathematics were essentially static. They were suitable for expressing unchanging configurations and relationships, and finding a number or measure would involve just this. Even the proper speeds of the planets would be expressed as fixed relationships between the speeds. There was no way of treating change and rates of change mathematically. Someone who prized the possibility of mathematical expression, therefore, would consider change disreputable because unamenable to treatment, intelligible only in so far as it could be seen as an approximation to a static pattern. This, as we shall see, has important effects on his moral views.

VIII

Knowledge as Vision

The view that in the *Republic* Plato is advocating a philosophical method consisting in an upward progress of hypotheses includes the claim that the first unhypothesised beginning is grasped intuitively. Such a position might receive reinforcement from the view that Plato predominantly seems to think of knowing as a sort of intellectual seeing. Argument, objections, and dialectic generally do not in the last resort establish conclusions. One of their main functions is to bring about that intellectual perception of the relevant Form that constitutes knowledge. Some people (e.g. Runciman, 1962) take it for granted that at any rate up to and including his middle period, Plato had a view of knowledge as a kind of intellectual perception. To know something was to be aware of it. For there to be an it to know, there must be something not in a process of change. Nothing in the perceptible world meets this condition. So knowledge could only be acquaintance with unchanging intelligible entities. No doubt Plato also wanted to say other things about knowledge, but this perceptual model can be shown to be operative in causing certain difficulties. Thus if one has this model it is natural to think that just as we get a better view of an object if we can see it in isolation and clearly separated from other objects, so if we wish to get a clear mental view of justice we must see it in isolation from equality, goodness and so on. We must see it in its pure simple form by itself. This is just how Plato tends to talk (e.g. *Phaedo* 78–9, *Symposium* 210–11, *Republic* 532–4), and it of course gives rise to difficulties. For Plato also conceives of knowledge as supplying the answer to 'what is X?' and so being expressible in terms of 'X is F and G'. This seems to be not just a shortcoming of language, but reflects the necessary fact that various forms are inextricably interrelated. In the earlier to middle dialogues the concern is to isolate items such as courage, excellence, equality as candidates for apprehension in abstraction from particular items that manifest them. The emphasis is therefore on these isolable units in contrast with the multifarious particulars which manifest a host of properties in a confusing jumble. The requirement that these units should be definable, however, leads to a sense that they were not so isolable but themselves constituted an interrelated set. This produced difficulties for the perceptual view of knowledge and a gradual progress to seeing knowledge as propositional. This development can be seen starting in the *Theaetetus* and coming to fruition in the *Sophist* where we finally get both a view of dialectic as discerning eternal interrelationships rather than viewing separate objects and a view of propositions as again combinatory of elements rather than complex names or pictures.

The direct evidence that Plato had this view of knowledge is varied. To begin with there is a wealth of perceptual imagery in talking of knowledge. Then there are passages where he seems to draw an expository parallel between knowing and perceiving. There is the common use of the term '*gnosis*' which is said to suggest recognition and so come close to seeing. There is the doctrine of reminiscence which again seems to presuppose an earlier vision, of which we are now reminded. There is the use in the *Meno* and in the *Theaetetus* of direct acquaintance examples to illustrate the contrast between knowledge and true belief. There are passages in the *Republic* where knowledge is spoken of as a faculty. There is the apparent concentration in the *Theaetetus*, especially in the argument that judgment is needed for knowledge, and in the discussion of falsity, on visual models for knowledge, models that are clearly largely responsible for Plato's failure to deal adequately with falsity problems in that dialogue. All these can be elaborated into a compelling thesis, and one that suggests a rather different account of Plato from that which I have advocated. I have suggested that Plato is from early on tending to think of forms or branches of knowledge rather than items, and the notion of acquaintance seems less happy here. Further, Plato must to some extent be aware of innovating. First, because in the *Protagoras* (352) and again in the *Philebus* (58d) he implies that his view of *episteme* as ruling, or as a desire, might seem novel. Second, because (cf. e.g. *Philebus* 55–8) he is well aware of studies that do not meet his demands although they would normally be considered to yield *episteme*. In this case the failure is that those in question are doing straight causal cosmology. In choosing the *epistemai* he does to illustrate his general thesis Plato might be partly governed by naturalness of language, but he is also partly wanting to recommend a particular method of approach and an ideal as to the final goal. All this might be compatible with a view that he was also attracted by some visual model for knowledge which resulted in obscurities and complications, but it is not so readily compatible with holding that the predominant influence was such a view.

I have spoken of 'such a view', but it is not altogether clear what attributing a visual model to Plato amounts to. It might simply be supposing that he thought it a necessary condition of someone's having knowledge on certain topics that they be acquainted with certain objects. Thus it is a necessary condition of the truth of one form of the claim that I know the Himalayas that I should have seen the Himalayas, though a good deal more is also required. So Plato might think it a necessary condition of my knowing about bridles that I be acquainted with the Form of Bridle, without thinking it sufficient. Alternatively, the analogy with vision might be intended to do more work than this. Plato might think that knowing simply is having an object before the mind's eye, so that knowing justice is a matter of viewing Justice with intellectual vision. Perhaps if he had started life tempted to think that perception is knowledge, but realised as a result of Socrates' enquiries that some imperceptibles are known, he would naturally have considered the knowledge of them as a non-sensory analogue of perception. But any view that considers knowing just to consist in the mental seeing creates considerable difficulties. For the subject must be able to recognise the object as Beauty or Justice if knowledge is to do the work required. But clearly in that case he must have some means of 'knowing what beauty is' that is not just 'seeing', but is a vital element in knowing. It is presumably this last sort of view that is being attributed to Plato as it is this that gives rise to the sorts of difficulty Plato is said to find himself in. The other view is not so obviously at odds with that which I have proposed, nor does it generate any opposition between acquaintance and propositional models. In trying to get clear what the truth is in all this, I shall divide the considerations into ones based on the language used in relation to knowledge and ones based on the supposed presuppositions or even intended conclusions of various particular arguments.

There seem to be three main sources in Plato's language. First, he has a tendency to use visual imagery (e.g. the Sun and the Cave in *Republic* Books VI and VII) to illustrate the mind's progress in knowledge, and especially to describe the final attainment of knowledge in terms of clear vision (e.g. also *Symposium*). Second, he tends to talk of the person with knowledge looking at/to (*blepein*) the Forms. Third, in crucial passages (e.g. *Republic* Book V, 477) he tends to use the word '*gnosis*' and its cognates, a term with overtones of recognition and acquaintance.

As to the first, it is difficult to know how much weight to put on these undoubted facts. Certainly by themselves they seem to indicate nothing. Greek is not the only language in which perception verbs are used to describe thorough understanding and complete explication. 'Clear', 'illuminating', 'see', 'grasp', 'look', 'get hold of', 'obscure', 'expose', are all familiar terms in describing intellectual success, failure or procedure, and philosophers can use them without being committed to an analysis of the nature of knowledge. They might even hazard describing the understanding of a solution in terms of the light dawning, or it being like coming into the light of day after stumbling through a dark tunnel. True, Plato does more than this. He builds elaborate images and has a climb of progress to ever brighter regions. But then, he also thought that there are various stages of knowledge, which had to be distinguished in the imagery, and he was perhaps more convinced than some of philosophy's powers of illumination. It is difficult to say that the imagery suggests a philosophical analysis rather than extreme enthusiasm about the possibilities of philosophical analysis.

Even if we take the imagery seriously, it is a moot point what follows. For, first, it equally fits the final or progressive grasp of a set of interrelations. Indeed in both the *Symposium* and the *Republic* this is what the language tends to suggest. In both the final stage is grasped as a result of ever wider synoptic considerations, in the *Symposium* (210d) of 'the vast ocean of the beautiful', in the *Republic* of the solar system of the Forms. The vision is of the explanation of why all the beautiful things are to be called beautiful, in the *Republic* of what makes all goods good. This is a common enough use of the 'seeing' metaphor in English as well. After much labour one 'sees' how the various parts of an argument hang together, or the intricate structure of a literary work. It suddenly comes to one in a flash, illuminating what had previously been obscure and so on. This use would fit the interpretation in chapter IV perfectly. Second, the imagery does not itself suggest more than that having some quasi-vision is a necessary condition of understanding, if it suggests so much. Of course, much weight cannot be put on this. In the *Theaetetus* Plato has clearly seen the need, at least with sense-perception, to distinguish between saying that someone has seen a red object and saying that he has seen that it is red. It does not follow that even by then he has realised that a similar point would have to be made if one took seriously the notion of intellectual vision, still less that at the time of the *Republic* he had understood the point.

The second source is from contexts where Plato talks of a person who is knowledgeable about something looking to the relevant Form. Thus the carpenter looks to the Forms of Bed or Table at *Republic* Book X 596b or the Form of Shuttle at *Cratylus* 389b. Similarly at *Timaeus* 28 seq. the Demiurge fashions the universe with his eye on the Forms, using them as paradigms in the execution of his work. This use of the seeing metaphor is no doubt related to the other, in that human beings, at least, would presumably only be able to 'look at the Form' in any strong sense if they had had the illuminating upward journey and final vision. The use of the metaphor does come in a slightly different context, however. It is not used to describe the acquisition of knowledge, but its use. It will be a necessary condition of someone's knowing about man that he be able to refer to the paradigm, but the whole metaphor suggests more than just perceiving, it suggests intelligent comparison. It does not seem to be illustrating a view that knowing just is a kind of mental viewing.

The third source is the use of the words '*gnosis*', '*gignoskein*'. These are sometimes supposed to be words out of the 'be aware of', 'recognise', 'be acquainted with' family, and so to be chosen by Plato in important contexts (e.g. *Republic* Book V 476e seq.) to indicate the mode of apprehension involved. This shows him to have an acquaintance model of knowledge.

There are several objections to this view. First, it pays to be careful about the notion of acquaintance. This has a technical philosophical usage deriving from particular epistemological requirements. If one is searching for something of which one can be certain, it is natural to retreat from propositions like 'all crows have two wings', which go well beyond our checked experience, to ones like 'this is a crow' which is confined to something here before us. The latter can, surely, be established by sense observation. But such establishing would involve further observations, and that would mean relying on memory for the earlier ones. Any ordinary empirical verification of such a statement is therefore again relying on judgments that go beyond experience at the time of declaring the proposition verified. To escape the uncertainties of memory we need to confine ourselves to the object of direct acquaintance here and now. Indeed, if we are to be free even of memory about the concepts by which we identify the objects of acquaintance, we have to make our knowledge consist in the acquaintance which also gives sense to any terms. Any such sense of 'acquaintance' is very specialised, and one notable fact about Plato is that there is no sign of the kind of philosophical obsession that leads to its introduction. As will emerge when we turn to a closer consideration of the *Theaetetus*, in the place where we might expect the development of some such argument we in fact find a very different brand. So Plato shows no signs of familiar philosophical motivation for such a sense.

Second, if we consider the day-to-day sense of 'being acquainted with' it does not have the close connection with perception that the specialised one does. To be acquainted with Socrates I have perhaps to have met him, and know something about him; but I do not have to be seeing him, nor is it enough to have seen him. There is more to meeting someone than seeing him, and even meeting is not enough. 'Aware of . . .', 'recognise' might do better, but the third objection concerns the supposed equivalence of '*gignoskein*' to some or other of these verbs. In some contexts where the verb takes a personal object it may be translatable by one of these terms, but even when taking a personal object it is frequently less restricted than the collocation of these terms suggests. The proverb 'know thyself' which uses the verb, is clearly an encouragement to know about oneself, and when at *Symposium* 216c–d Alcibiades says that none of those present *gignoskei* Socrates, he supplies their lack with a description in depth of his character. The matter is worse when instead of personal nouns we have expressions like 'the healthy' (e.g. *Charmides* 170a–c). It becomes clear that 'to know the healthy' either means 'to know the sort of thing a doctor should do' or 'to know how to distinguish healthy from sick bodies' (cf. *Ion* 540a–e). When we find the word used with *to on* (being ? truth ?) as its object one would therefore not expect it naturally to suggest to Plato a sort of viewing, but an ability to distinguish or tell about something. It is perhaps significant that in *Republic* Book V, where *to on* does appear as the object, there is also a that – or how – clause (477b 10–11, 478a 6) – but of that more later. For an extended discussion of the verb in Plato, and many relevant passages, I would refer the reader to J. Lyons (1966), pp. 187 seq. The result of that work is, I think, to dampen enthusiasm for the suggestion that the use of *gignoskein* in connection with forms indicates any attachment to a perception model of knowing, and indeed there is some suggestion that Plato is trying to establish connections between attributions of *gnosis* and attributions of *techne*.

So far I have been concerned simply to examine what might follow from certain facts about Plato's linguistic habits, his choice of certain metaphors and images and certain verbs. Of course it is highly unlikely that anyone would be foolish enough to rest a case on these facts. They are at best corroborative and the main burden of the argument must rest with particular passages of philosophical analysis. What I hope to have done is, first, to show that the visual imagery used to describe the acquisition of understanding is, as it stands, at least as apt for describing the final stages according to my interpretation as for portraying knowledge as consisting in intellectual intuition. Second, that talk of looking at paradigms is non-suggestive in the way required; and third that the use of '*gnosis*' and its cognates would not either suggest preference for a perceptual model of knowing.

It is time now to turn to passages of philosophical argument where Plato might seem either directly to argue for the proposed analysis, or to argue in a way that presupposes it. First, there are the passages where he argues that what we call learning is in many cases recollection. This is 'proved' in the *Meno* (82–5) by posing a problem to a slave boy. It is established that the boy does not know the answer to start with because at first he gets it wrong. Supposedly Socrates 'gives' him no new information but by questioning elicits the right answer. Presumably his ability to recognise where he has gone wrong and that a different move is better shows that he already has a grasp of all the concepts needed to establish the conclusion, but what he is said to 'recall' is in fact the conclusion, not the concepts. At the beginning of the passage Socrates says that the soul being immortal, and having lived many lives has seen the things of this world and the next, and so has learned everything at some time or another. But this is the only place where a 'seeing' notion is used, and nothing in what follows seems to require one. The argument is certainly for previous knowledge that is being recalled, but there is nothing to entail that that previous knowledge must have consisted in, or even relied on, some sort of mental perception.

The matter looks more hopeful in the *Phaedo* (73–6). There we are told what it is that we are reminded of – the Equal, the Beautiful, the Just and so on. We are reminded of them by things that we observe that resemble them but which we note to fall short of the original. If we refer back from the things to the original we can see that they aspire hopelessly to be like the original. In none of this is the metaphor of 'seeing' used for our apprehension of the Equal. It would, indeed, have been infelicitous. For the account of recollection contrasts sense-perception with being put in mind of what we recollect. The use of further perception verbs in metaphorical senses would have been confusing. But the whole argument supposes not simply previous knowledge but previous knowledge of something of which we are reminded by our sense-observations, and reminded because of a similarity. Further we can apparently compare image with original and confirm the fact that the former falls short of the latter. This at least invites the supposition of some sort of seeing with the mind's eye, which is knowing the equal, and comparing it with what is seen with the body's eye. That Plato is thinking this way is indicated once he leaves the particular argument about recollection and uses its result to contend that what is recollected in this case is eternal and known by the mind, which must be more like it than like perceptible things. For then he happily talks of the soul 'seeing' these eternal objects (83b). There are doubtless problems about the combined apprehension of both Form and sense-object, but that would of course be Plato's problem. The point is that this whole argument for learning being a matter of recollection seems to require more than just that we possessed certain concepts prior to birth. The conclusion seems to be that we were acquainted with certain objects with which we can compare what we now observe. 'Acquainted' here seems to involve some quasi-perception, and this is surely what constitutes 'knowing the equal'. This is further suggested by the *Phaedrus* imagery, where (e.g. 247d–e) the soul is portrayed as looking at various Forms in the course of its travel through the heavens.

The referring or comparing is something that happens when we, in our present life, notice resemblances, and *ex hypothesi* would not occur in the earlier existence when one apprehended the Equal and the Just and the Beautiful in isolation. That knowledge would surely consist simply in the 'seeing' of them. It looks, in fact, as though Plato is wanting to speak of knowing Forms as being simply some intellectual perception of forms, and has not yet realised that that 'perception' will require both experience and judgment, the latter being resistant to description as yet another perception.

A final assessment of this argument will have to wait until after a more thorough examination of the theory of Forms and its function. For the moment it can be conceded that there are possible interpretations of those points which would bolster the above argument. At the same time certain other facts have to be borne in mind. To begin with, the passage on recollection does not aim primarily to describe the nature of 'real' knowledge, but to claim that some knowledge does not come through sense observation. It is hardly licit, therefore, to suppose we have a treatment of knowledge, whose implications commit Plato. We have too little on that side. Second, even in the *Phaedo*, and even more in the *Symposium* and *Republic* 'real' knowledge involves more than just gazing at an intellectual object – one must be able to see the interconnections between a number. Even if this is some sort of looking and perceiving, it is not one that runs counter to my earlier interpretation. Even if one does think of this seeing of connections as a mental 'seeing' it is less natural to think of it simply as a form of perception, because the sort of seeing that is a model for it is a very inquisitive investigatory sort of seeing. If I see the pattern in a construction or composition my eye tends to run over it, not just see one item. In short, in passages that more directly purport to describe knowledge the visual imagery invites a somewhat different interpretation, which is found in the same dialogues in which the reminiscence arguments are found, and in others of about the same period.

The position might be strengthened, however, if we look at two places, one on either side of these central dialogues, where Plato argues for the distinction between knowledge and true belief. In the *Meno* (97) Socrates argues that while true belief is not knowledge, it is just as good for practical purposes. The illustration is that someone who knows the road to Larissa is no better a guide than someone who has a correct opinion on how to get there. It is said to be a condition of knowing the road that one should have travelled the route oneself. In other words, it is the person who has had direct experience of the road who knows rather than someone who guesses or has it at second hand. In the *Theaetetus* (201a–c), again, the distinction is made by contrasting a juror who might be persuaded to believe correctly that so-and-so committed a robbery, with an eye-witness, who alone could know. In both cases examples are chosen where direct acquaintance is needed for knowledge. Plato could have chosen other examples. For instance, in another place in the *Theaetetus* (207–8) he argues that correct opinion with a certain sort of account is not knowledge, for one might chance to write the word 'Theaetetus' correctly, believing that to be the spelling, but still not count as knowing how to spell it, for which more regular competence with the letters might be required. This example is used to show the inadequacy of one version of 'with an account'. It is not used to show what would constitute knowing, which indeed we are not told though it is fairly clear that capacity is going to be more important than acquaintance. When he gives examples of knowing they are always first-hand acquaintance ones. Further, this sort of example seems to be behind *Republic* Book V 476b–d. There Plato is contrasting philosophers with some others who have pretensions to knowledgeability about what is fine. The latter cannot claim knowledge since they have no first-hand acquaintance with the Fine, and indeed only believe in (let their thoughts run on?) what participates in it.

Once again it is important to be clear whether one is arguing that some sort of acquaintance with the object of knowledge is, according to Plato, a necessary condition of having knowledge about it, or that such acquaintance, conceived of as an intellectual perception, constitutes the knowing. For the first does not rule out other factors from being necessary as well. It is only the latter that leads to difficulties in accommodating propositional or judgmental elements. Now the example about the road to Larissa does not suggest the second, stronger view. One would not naturally assume that having walked to Larissa, even with one's eyes open, was sufficient for knowing the way, or that that was what constituted knowing the way. In this case, as with the eye-witness of the *Theaetetus,* previous experience is a condition of present knowledge. Also, in this case the previous experience is of going over a route in an order, not simply seeing something. Even in the *Republic* passage, nothing is made of simply 'seeing' the Form. It is the man who can follow a route to the *gnosis* of it, and distinguish it from other things, who knows. This is not to deny that these passages are suggestive as to what Plato thought to be a necessary condition for knowing, but even here the suggestion is confusing. The road to Larissa example indicates that only the man who has been over the ground has knowledge. This could be applied to proofs, to be saying that only the man who has been over the proof himself knows that the sum of the angles of a triangle is equal to that of two right angles. Taken with the talk of carpenters looking to the Form of Shuttle and the Demiurge looking to the paradigms it suggests someone, say, having to be acquainted with the plans, before he can know how to build a house. The former fits with the insistence that the philosopher must be able to give an account of his views, the second with the idea that *episteme* is of the structure of the universe and the universe is structured to a plan. In either case, the flavour is different from that of the later dialogue models of letters and syllables, weaving and so on and the knowledge of how to blend what with what. But while some shift from earlier dialogues to late may be indicated here, the examples do not carry any precise implications about the nature of knowledge, and certainly nothing strong enough to show Plato in the proposed perceptual-model difficulties.

For this we have to turn to apparently more direct statements. Thus in *Republic* Book V (476e–478) we seem to have an argument to the effect that *episteme* and *doxa* are two distinct faculties, like sight and hearing, each with distinct objects. What can be known cannot be believed (conjectured?), and what can be believed cannot be known. Knowledge and belief, and later the further sub-divisions, are distinguished by virtue of the objects they comprehend. Just as sight differs from hearing in being the perception of colour not of sound, so knowledge differs from belief in being the perception of Forms rather than phenomena. In Book VII (518–9) we find intelligence spoken of as the eye of the soul, making it clear that Plato thinks of the intellect as a quasi-organ directed to its own objects which are available to no other organ. Knowing simply is the intellectual vision of Forms. These direct statements on Plato's part make it quite clear how he is thinking of knowledge. While the texts previously considered would not of themselves show anything, these passages make it clear how those others should be taken and how we are to interpret all the visual imagery.

As a great deal of the previous argument has been to the effect that the passages considered do not prove the desired conclusion, it must be admitted that if the above interpretation of the *Republic* passages is right, then they would tilt the balance on the rest, and Plato would seem to be enmeshed in the sort of view of knowledge that produces just the difficulties from which it is claimed that he gradually extricated himself in the later dialogues. I have tried elsewhere (1960 and 1968) to argue against this interpretation of Book V. Here I shall simply adduce what seem to be the major arguments.

At the end of Book V (471 *ad fin.*) the question is raised whether the political structure outlined could ever be put into practice. Socrates claims that it could only if the rulers were philosophers. Philosophers are people who have a love of all knowledge. There are, however, others who might seem to fit this description, who must be clearly distinguished from philosophers. Now in the account of the ideal city it has become clear that the rulers must be knowledgeable about what is fine, just and good and their opposites, so it is in their pretensions to knowledge of these topics that the charlatans are contrasted with philosophers. To start with, they are contrasted on Platonic assumptions. There are Forms and what partakes in Forms. Clearly knowledge of what is fine requires apprehension of the Fine. The charlatans do not believe in any such thing and are incapable of comprehending it. Philosophers, on the other hand do. Consequently, philosophers have knowledge, the charlatans only opinion or conjecture.

This distinction is based on the admission of the existence of Forms, and the distinction is between those who admit and understand the distinction and those who are incapable of understanding it and do not admit it. At this point (476d) it is recognised that the charlatans might take umbrage, and another argument is produced to convince them. We need another argument because, of course, they are by definition incapable of following the previous one, and could not understand or accept its premises. Consequently in the argument that follows (476e–478e) there *ought not* to be any reliance on the theory of Forms. So when it is readily acknowledged at 477a that what absolutely is is absolutely knowable it would show amazing incompetence on Plato's part if this had to be interpreted as an admission that the Forms are knowable. At this stage we need a premiss readily acceptable to someone rejecting any dichotomy of the Form/particulars sort. One would expect, therefore, resistance to a distinction of two sorts of object for knowledge and belief, even of an unexplained kind. The most obvious way to take it is as an admission that knowledge is of what is the case, and that what is absolutely, or without qualification, the case is absolutely or without qualification knowable.

At 477b we get the sudden question: 'Is it [*doxa*] the same *dynamis* as *episteme*, or a different one?' '*Dynamis*' is the word which, for the view under consideration has either to be translated 'faculty', or shown to be treated in a way that in context makes it amount to the same. The suggestion that the word typically means 'faculty' for Plato would be too implausible, so I shall take the second possibility. Certainly, after the first talk of it, he considers it necessary at 477b 11 to start a further clarification of what he means by it. Up till then, we simply have this word used, together with an expression often translated as 'object'. This is a translation tailored to the translation of '*dynamis*' as faculty. Thus 477a 9–10 might be translated 'so knowledge has being [or reality] for its object, ignorance non-being . . .'. Equally, however, it might go 'So knowledge covers what is the case, ignorance what is not the case . . .'. Accordingly, '*dynamis*' might at 477b 5 be translated: 'Is it [*doxa*] the same faculty as *episteme* or a different one?' But equally it might run 'Is it [*doxa*] the same ability (capacity) as *episteme*, or a different one?'

Now the 'faculty'/'objects' translations immediately make the passage look like a piece of Platonic dishonesty. It is fathering on the opposition a dualism of objects which is neither obviously acceptable at first blush, nor likely to seem acceptable to people recently portrayed as believing in only one set of objects of study. On the other hand knowledge might naturally be thought of as a different ability from conjecture, and one that covers the truth. Perhaps, then, Plato is relying on that at this point, and only makes clear the faculty point later, when he expounds further on *dynamis*. For there, surely, at 477c 4–5 he compares *episteme* and *doxa* to sight and hearing. The argument may be dishonest, but the conclusion is clear.

In fact, however, Plato does not there do anything that could be called comparing knowledge to sight and hearing except in an irresponsibly loose sense of 'compare'. What he does is first give a very general account of *dynamis* whereby whatever anything can do it does by some *dynamis*, and then gives sight and hearing as examples of *dynamis*. Since seeing and hearing are things we can do, this is perfectly in order, but hardly amounts to assimilating knowledge to perceptual faculties. Nor is anything elaborated about objects of perceptual faculties. Anything we are to infer on that point has to be read back from what we are told about knowledge. It might be argued that nevertheless Plato had clear ideas on the objects of the different senses. For instance, in the *Theaetetus* (184d–185a) he clearly makes the point that sight and hearing have different objects, and what one sees one cannot hear, and so on. The different faculties are there described by the word '*dynamis*', and although the *Republic* expression for talking about the object of a faculty does not occur, the doctrine is clearly that of the *Republic*.

To this it needs saying, first, that the *Theaetetus* does not occur in the *Republic*, that the argument there is of a different sort in a different context, produced at a different time. One could as well argue the opposite way by reference to *Protagoras* 330a–b. There Socrates is arguing that, according to Protagoras, the virtues are distinct. In that case they must have different *dynameis*. Now here the word cannot mean 'faculties' but must mean 'powers', 'abilities' or 'capacities'. Nevertheless Socrates illustrates his point by reference to parts of the face, choosing eyes and ears for his examples. Their *dynameis* are presumably seeing and hearing. So Plato is quite capable of taking sight and hearing as examples of *dynamis* in a context where the word cannot mean 'faculties' and where the faculty implications are irrelevant. Considering the difference of context and date of composition it would be silly to argue from this to what is being said in the *Republic* – but no more silly than an argument from the *Theaetetus*. One has, in fact, to take the *Republic* passage as it stands, with its complete lack of elaboration of any analogy and its extremely broad definition of '*dynamis*'.

Can any weight, then, be put on the expression used to insinuate the notion of object? If it had a technical use in Plato, then maybe it could. But this does not seem to be the case. It is certainly not *de rigueur* in describing perception. It is quite absent from the *Theaetetus* passage where it would have been very much in order. We find the expression at *Republic* Book I 353a. 'You would manage to cut a vine branch with a dagger or a carving knife and a number of other tools?' 'Of course'. 'But surely with no other tool so well as with a pruning knife made *for this*.' The words in italic translate the preposition with its object which in the context of Book V people would want to translate 'with this as its object'. Yet in the present passage it means 'for this work'. Transferring this sense to Book V would make Plato distinguish one *dynamis* from another by the work it performs. In the *Philebus* (37e) we find the expression used in a different way to introduce that about which someone is pleased. This differs both from *Republic* Book I and Book V. There is no suggestion of tasks, nor of 'objects' being special to one operation. In fact it seems to emerge that one may well be pleased and have a belief about the same object. The use of the expression at *Republic* Book VI 511d–e is not usually mentioned in this connection, probably because the most natural translation is 'corresponding to', and the word '*dynamis*' does not appear.

In short, it does not seem that one can get outside help either from the use of '*dynamis*' or of '*epi*' with the dative to support the faculty interpretation. Further, at two places (477b 10–11, 478a, b) the statement that knowledge covers being is glossed 'to know that what is the case is the case'. In other words, we are given an operation covered by *episteme*, as we might expect on the Book I use of the expression. In fact, in Book V no distinction seems to be made between asking for the 'object' of a *dynamis* and asking what it does. If we start with a translation committing us to objects we shall expect two criteria for individuating a *dynamis*, its object and its operation, but in 477d the text suggests there is but one criterion, and the expression 'what it performs' is glossing, not giving an alternative criterion to 'what it is *epi*'. In fact a *dynamis* is distinguished by what it is a *dynamis* to do, and that is all. Knowledge is an ability to tell what is the case, whereas *doxa* can be mistaken, so a person with one has a different ability from a person with the other. All this might seem perfectly acceptable to someone who rejected the theory of Forms and had no faculty view of knowledge. As it is possible to interpret '*dynamis*' here in a way that has no suggestion of a faculty analogy, and as such an interpretation would better fit both the wording of the passage and its express purpose of being convincing to non-Platonists then such an interpretation seems clearly preferable.

It might be objected that this overlooks the passage mentioned in Book VII, where intelligence is called the eye of the soul. Certainly we have not dealt with that yet, but it is not a passage that can support the faculty-interpretation of Book V. For on that interpretation it is clear that one cannot have belief about the Forms or knowledge about phenomena, simply on the grounds that the faculties are distinguished by their exclusive operation on different objects. But at 518 the *dynamis* that is the eye of the soul is said to start by viewing phenomena and have to be turned from this dark and shadowy experience to look upon what is bright and clear. Knowledge, now, is not distinguished from *doxa* as a special faculty with objects peculiar to it, but as the operation of the same faculty on objects more appropriate to it. Yet the assimilation of intelligence to a sense-faculty is far stronger here than in Book V.

Still, it may be that we can abandon Book V and rely on the passage at 518? Not really. For while that passage makes it clear that the same intelligence that operates on phenomena operates on Forms, it is all part of the simile of the Cave, so that precisely what we can make of it will depend on what is entailed by the fact that such an image is used. What we are in need of, however, just is some argument to help settle that very question.

So far then, it seems that, after all, the *Republic* contains no argument that knowledge is a form of intellectual vision, and that nothing sufficiently strong follows from the widespread use of perceptual imagery. There is, however, the possibility that Plato's way of arguing that learning is recollection, together with other points, might show him to be taking it, at least at times, that knowledge is simply intellectual seeing.

Finally, do the arguments in the *Theaetetus* indicate that Plato was caught in the alleged snare? The first passage for consideration here is 184–7. In that passage Socrates argues that we do not see and hear with our eyes and ears but through them. In short, perception is a psychic function. But we are also capable of distinguishing sound and colour, noting that there is such a thing as each of them, that they differ from or resemble each other and so on. Sight and hearing are limited to special ranges of objects and cannot trespass on each other's territory. At 185c–e Socrates asks with what organ these facts are observed, and extracts the answer that they are viewed by the soul without the help of an organ. The seeing verbs (*episkopein* and *skopeisthai*) occur at 185e 2, e 7, 186a 10, and a word for grasping appears at 186d 4, so this might suggest as Runciman (1962) takes it, that Plato is thinking of 'knowing similarity' etc as a non-sensory perception.

Let us suppose that the two seeing-verbs used normally mean something like 'view', 'look at' or 'contemplate'. The context is one of considering standard perceptions and organs and asking which of them perceives similarity and difference (185c–d). The main point is to say that by none of the forms of sense perception can we perceive them. It is natural to put this point by saying that they are perceived not by the senses but by the mind. The word 'perceived' is used not because of any special theory of mental intuition, but because it is the verb used when talking of the senses and we wish to deny the senses power to perceive these properties. In fact, the verbs are not such heavy perceptual terms as, say, *horan*. The first commonly means 'to be concerned with' and the second, which is in the middle voice, more commonly, in that voice, means 'consider' rather than having a literal 'look'/'see' sense, which is more common with the active. So while the choice of those verbs may be due to the fact that they have perceptual connections, which, as I have said, would be natural, they are not heavy-weight perception words, and could hardly be supposed without more ado to carry substantial doctrine. Any terms that describe the function of the intellect in these matters in 186a–c suggest comparison and reasoning, not viewing. So this passage yields nothing, except a use of metaphor.

The second *Theaetetus* passage is 188d–189b. Socrates has established that judgment is needed for knowledge, and Theaetetus has just hazarded the definition of knowledge as true judgment when Socrates suggests that they return to the question of judgment, as he has often been puzzled as to how it can be false. At first a problem is set up on the supposition that a person making a judgment that *A* is *B* must know *A* and *B*. Then at 188d another problem is introduced. Anyone who sees, sees something, some one thing and therefore something that is. Similarly a person who judges must judge some one thing, and something that is. Judging what is not (=what is false) is making no judgment. It is agreed therefore that false judgment cannot be judging what is not, but must be misjudging – presumably what is, and the next section, to be discussed later, seems to suppose that anyone who judges that *A* is *B* is in fact asserting the identity of two objects grasped by the mind. The way in which this difficulty is introduced, and the way in which the result is developed, clearly suppose that judging is to be treated on exact analogy with seeing and hearing. If Plato thinks that it is an intellectual intuition, then a reminder of the position with sight and hearing will serve to bring home the difficulty. Otherwise one has only to reject the assimilation, and one is left with mere word-play from 'judges what is not' to 'judges nothing'. It is the analogy with the senses that determines the interpretation of the apparent word-play.

With most of this I think I agree, except the assumption that we are being given a Platonic problem. We may be, of course, but as I shall argue in considering the next passage, it is more likely that these problems arise from a consideration of judgment as so far discussed in the dialogue. In the dialogue so far Plato clearly wishes to distinguish and to claim Protagoras has failed to distinguish between seeing something red and judging that what one sees is red. The latter, as I shall bring out in the next chapter, necessitates abandoning the relativising interactionist view of Protagoras. But the argument for claiming that the senses are inadequate for supplying observation of distinctions between the sense objects or for comparing perceptions to form concepts, does not widen the sphere of judgement beyond perception. That is to say, what we notice is facts about sense-objects, and what we devise concepts for are sensible phenomena. We have not established a different world apprehended by different perceptions, but only that making judgments about what is perceived is not perceiving. We have no warrant to depart so far from Protagoras as to suppose there are judgments that we can make that are not about perceptions, and nothing has been done to show what we are to make of the difficulties about experts and the future. Theaetetus/Protagoras could still hold that perception is a necessary condition of judgment, as being its object. This would be enough to make the reference to sight and the rest in the present passage timely, and certainly there would be resultant problems about false judgements.

This brings us to the third *Theaetetus* passage, which is in fact the main falsity discussion. The argument about this goes as follows: in the *Theaetetus* (188–200) Plato faces certain problems about the possibility of false judgments. He offers a model for accounting for a limited range of false judgments, and quite fails to account for others. Those that he does account for constitute a limited subset of perceptual errors, those that consist in mistaking one object for another. Even this account seems in fact not too successful, and breaks Socrates' own rules, but the interesting point is that the problem is set up with an example of false perceptual judgments about the identity of individuals. It is stated that if I *see* two people only, then I shall not take one for the other. If that were all that knowing them amounted to, there would be no mistakes. But I may know Theaetetus in the sense that I have seen him and have a mental image of him. If I now see Theodorus in the distance he may resemble my image of Theaetetus so that I am led erroneously to identify him as Theaetetus. The first thing to note is that the problem is very much one that would puzzle a man who tended to think of 'know' as taking individuals as its object, and therefore knowing X as knowing the object for which 'X' stands. If I am to know that X is F I have to know two objects (188a), and the natural way to interpret 'is', with this perceptual way of taking 'know', is as the 'is' of identity. So a false judgment comes out as judging that A, which I know, is B, which I know, when A and B are different (188b). Of various possible escapes the one taken is to distinguish senses of 'know', or perhaps distinguish 'knowing Theaetetus' from 'perceiving Theaetetus'. This brings us to the second point to note: that knowing Theaetetus is described as in turn a sort of mental perception, of an image derived from perception. This gives the following: we are introduced to the name 'Theaetetus' in perceiving Theaetetus. That leaves an image, which is associated with the name (is its meaning?), and which is inspected when we want to know whether the man before us is Theaetetus. But no 'names for different things' can have the same image, and it is inconceivable that a person who knew Theaetetus and Theodorus should just by himself judge the one to be the other. For that is repeating the original difficulty of supposing someone with two people in front of him and judging the one on the right to be the one on the left.

This, however, leads to the next problem, because we clearly do make mistakes of a conceptual sort. This would be particularly important for Plato since in his view most people are in error on most important topics and falsely judge the good to be pleasure or 'injustice' or whatever it may be. Yet he again fails. He introduces an image of the mind as an aviary, with the birds as pieces of knowledge. He rightly distinguishes between knowing X in the senses of having learnt X and of recalling one's knowledge of X, but instead of accounting for mistakes in statements such as $6 + 5 = 12$ as made by using items known but not recalled, he uses the image differently. It simply accounts for the fact that I may know things when asleep. The answering of questions is always a matter of hunting up one's knowledge, but knowing is always a matter of having within view. It does not matter (and is quite unclear) whether the birds in the aviary are, say, particular numbers, or whether they are sums. If they are numbers then anyone who hunted for the number called $6 + 5$ would, if he found it, find the number whose name was 11 (204b–c), and no mistake would be possible. If they are sums, then for a mistake to occur there would have to be a $6 + 5 = 12$ bird, which would be a piece of non-knowledge. What has gone wrong (or one thing that has gone wrong) is that Plato is insisting that what is known is objects, and knowing consists in viewing the objects. At best propositions amount to declaring objects to be the same, at worst they are themselves names of complex objects, which, like names can only be understood in the context of acquaintance with what is named.

This view of propositions as complex names seems to bedevil the *Cratylus*. From 430 onwards we find Socrates trying to persuade Cratylus that false statements are possible. From 428 Cratylus has accepted the thesis that names are like what they name in a sense that commits him to holding that what are commonly called names are in fact descriptions that must be right. All through there is no distinction of any importance between names and statements. Indeed, Socrates' way out of the difficulty still involves looking on a proposition as a picture, and seems to be limited to explaining false statements (pictures) that are near enough the truth to count as statements about (pictures of) a given situation. Knowing Cratylus is seeing what 'Cratylus' stands for. Knowing 'Cratylus is a man' is seeing what that stands for. Even when it is allowed that understanding the proposition is not knowing its truth, still it is natural to suppose that knowing its truth is seeing the original for which the name/picture stands.

It seems, therefore, that at the time of writing the *Cratylus*, Plato has a complex-name view of propositions which would make it natural to think of knowing anything as being acquainted with the nominee. By the *Theaetetus* he is breaking up the name a little, but is still dominated by his perceptual view of knowledge. The result is that his whole account of error is conducted within the confines of examples of taking one perceived or quasi-perceived object for another, and interpreting misjudgments as mis-identifications. Only in the *Sophist* does he shake himself free from this complex of mistakes. There he sees statements as more than strings of names or complex names, as not all being identity statements, and knowledge not as vision but as competence at proper construction.

I shall consider the interpretation of the *Cratylus* and the *Sophist* in more detail later when I turn to Plato's treatment of error. For the moment I would merely remark that some care is needed in declaring certain difficulties to be Plato's. There is no doubt that the *Theaetetus* discussion of false judgment is curiously limited. We do not get the kind of mistake mentioned at *Cratylus* 430c or *Philebus* 38, nor the bent stick in water and other illusions mentioned in *Republic* 602c–d. So even in the context of perceptual mistakes familiar to Plato we are strangely straitened. When it comes to 'intellectual' mistakes, we are limited to arithmetic, where the perceptual account is least plausible, and there is no mention of definitional errors like those perpetrated by Theaetetus earlier in the dialogue. The question is, what can we infer from this? After all, the digression on falsity in the *Theaetetus* is something of a problem anyway. A sudden detour to discuss a basic problem through some difficulties whose relation to the basic problem is only with difficulty discerned is a strange operation at best. The limitation to examples which are as nearly as possible perceptual is in fact characteristic of the whole dialogue. Even when talking of true opinion 'with an account (*logos*)' towards the end, Plato surprisingly produces examples of a wagon and its parts, and the sun, as ones of which an account is given by giving its (perceptible) parts, or (perceptible) distinguishing mark. It seems simplest to suppose that the refutation of Protagoras does not introduce a radical broadening of the discussion. It has been shown that Protagoras' perception needs the addition of judgment, so that 'knowledge is perception' must mean 'we can know judgments on our present perception but that is all we can know'. But what makes them knowledge? If we stick as closely as possible to the original position, it is hard to think what better account we could give of *logos* than those discussed at the end. Similarly, the refutation of Protagoras involves the assertion of the possibility of error. This is not simply a formal point, that if what I judge is not *ipso facto* true, then it may be false. The argument frequently appealed to the relative liability to error of ordinary people as against experts, and the oddity for Protagoras if he does not consider others in error. So one would expect error to be possible. At the same time, all that is really driven home is that perception without judgment is not knowledge. The argument from 184 to 186 which brings out the necessity for the operation of the soul concentrates a good deal on the generation of perception-concepts. Even the discussion of being and similarity is confined to the point that we judge colours to be similar or dissimilar, or judge that this is red, that is blue, or this is what hardness is. There is no introduction of the Forms of Similarity and Being, only reference to common forms of judgment and their presupposition of more than perception. But since judgement is needed, then knowledge cannot just be perception, and since judgment can be false, it cannot just be judgment, even if we confine ourselves to judgments of perception. So why not try 'true judgment'? Which is precisely what Theaetetus does. But in the context it would be natural to take this not as a wild departure but as a modification of Protagoras. We acknowledge the element of judgment, but preserve the limitation to perceptual judgment. In the previous discussion this has not simply been a limitation on what is to count as knowledge, but also at times on what is to count as judgment (167a), and the final section, against Heracleitus, returned to that limitation. It is now a good question how we are going on such a view to allow for error. This is why, at 187c, Socrates does not introduce the discussion of error as a digression, but as going back again to the subject of *doxa*. The discussion that follows starts with modified Protagorean *doxa* and raises the question how it can be false, or how we can have error if we are confined to such judgments. Now some of the familiar errors, like the stick looking bent in water, might be met by saying that something *is* bent – the image I see – and my judgment is really about that. But this is a less tempting move when we consider 'that is Theaetetus', just because 'Theaetetus' is not a description that might be reapplied to an image. Still, with a little man-handling the account of *doxa* can, by means of the Wax Tablet image, seem to accommodate some errors. The Wax Tablet machinery, however, depends on the distinction between perception and memory image. A mistake is a mismatch of these. It clearly cannot cope, and is not devised to cope, with mistakes where sense-perception is not involved. This is presumably why Socrates confidently declares impossible mistakes of image when the person or object is not perceived. It is not that error is here in general inconceivable, but that it cannot be accommodated on the model of the Wax Tablet. A wide range of common mistakes, ones that mark off the novice from the expert, such as mistakes of addition and multiplication, can thus not be catered for. The move to the Aviary model, however, is not one away from images. All that is dropped is actual sense-perception. For the rest we are left with quasi-vision, and the point of the aviary is to introduce the distinction between having in hand and having in a cage (having in hand potentially). There is nothing to suggest that the knowledge we have is not thought to be images of whatever we know, as Protagoras would presumably hold, and the strongly visual suggestion of the passage makes it all too likely. So the section on falsity brings out the limitations of even a modified Protagorean view when it comes to coping with familiar facts about error, and the possibility of error has been forced on Protagoras.

If this is right, then the limitations on the problem of falsity are set by the opposition, and are not necessarily Plato's own. It is they, not he, who cannot cope. Similarly with the *Cratylus*, as I shall argue later, the naming/picturing analogies derive from Cratylus' position, and cannot be concluded to be Plato's own. It could, of course, be that Plato did suffer from the difficulties alleged and saw that the problems of these dialogues were ones for his own view of knowledge as intellectual perception. But that is no longer to argue that the dialogues do show him to be in a difficulty, but that they would if they were different dialogues. Plato's unwritten dialogues are not the topic of this book.

Of course, it is not possible either, on the basis of the *Theaetetus* and *Cratylus*, to argue what Plato's view on these matters was, at least in that one does not find his views argued there on the relevant points. The main point, however, is that the dialogues are polemical, and show Plato's view of his opponents' difficulties, not his own.

To sum up, I hope to have shown that there is as yet no reason to suppose that Plato thought that knowledge consisted of some sort of intellectual perception. It is not simply that none of the points considered shows it. The imagery used is quite inconclusive. Of the passages that might seem to imply or directly assert such a view, there seem to be no reasons for supposing that in the *Republic* passages Plato is asserting anything of the sort, and some reason for supposing he is not. The *Theaetetus* on falsity can only be used if we suppose that the difficulties there are Plato's own, whereas it seems more plausible to suppose that they are those of the opposition. That leaves us with the implications of the recollection argument in the *Phaedo*, which will be more easily assessed later.

IX

Knowledge and Perception

In the last chapter I considered the view that Plato thought that 'know' always does or should take a direct object, and knowing consists in the intellectual perception of that object. I noted that the recollection argument in the *Phaedo* might suppose this view, especially if it could be supported by other arguments on related topics. The argument that learning is recollecting is itself tied up with some view about the senses' inadequacy to yield knowledge on certain topics, and about the objects of sense observation not properly exemplifying the properties of Forms. In other words, the argument about recollection seems to form a part of Plato's polemic against sense-perception and the physical world, in contrast with the unchanging perfect-paradigm world of intellection. It is somehow related to his wish to introduce a special term 'participate' to gloss the 'is' of 'X is F' wherever 'X' denotes a particular physical object. This brings in the welter of problems about Plato's attempt to distinguish between sensible and intellectual objects, the criteria suggested and resultant difficulties with the verb 'to be', the theory of Forms and so on. The problem here is to bring the subject-matter into manageable form. After all, the theory of Forms, the term 'participates' and the rest were not introduced in face of one single clearly apprehended problem. As is usual with technical ideas in philosophy, they are put to work on what might have seemed similar or related tasks, with resultant strains and uncertainties. Consequently someone looking back on the various uses they are put to is at a loss to discover a single coherent set of views. The matter is worse if one adds in the hypothesis of development on Plato's part. What follows, therefore, will involve some distortion as I shall try to deal to some extent separately with a number of different strands in Plato's reactions. To begin with I shall take his reaction to Heracleiteanism. According to Aristotle (*Metaphysics* A 987a 29 seq.) Plato was attracted to the

Heracleitean view that everything is in a state of flux, at least so far as the sensible world is concerned. At the same time, Socrates' persistent pursuit of definitions led him to postulate Forms as the subject-matter of definitions and of true knowledge. This suggests an obvious picture of his development: for clearly, when Socrates asked 'what is courage?' he was not examining individual actions in the field, nor could his questions be settled by pointing to examples. At the same time, he and his answerer seemed to be able to recognise when answers were inadequate which indicated that in some way they already were acquainted with what they hoped to define. So there must be non-sensible objects of study. Further, definitions seem to be timelessly true, and so the objects of them must be unchangingly as they are. So besides the world of constantly changing particulars there is a world of unchanging meanings, or definables, which can be grasped once and for all by the mind. A circle is, eternally, a figure, all points on whose circumference are an equal distance from its centre. But this saucer may change its shape, along with other properties. Thus we can see how the theory of Forms is born of Socrates out of Heracleitus. The Forms are the objects of Socratic definition, and true knowledge is their apprehension. Dialectic sharpens that apprehension, but also that apprehension governs dialectic. The process of putting up definitions and finding them wanting leads to sharper and more accurate definition, but our knowledge of what is inadequate, what better, shows prior grasp of what is to be defined. The end term is to see clearly the objects to be defined, and by reference to them judge the title of particulars to be described by the term standing for the relevant Form.

So much for the picture. The question is now what in the original corresponds to it? There are, first, two major sources in Plato where he seems specifically to be working out where he stands on Heracleitus, the *Theaetetus* and the *Cratylus*. Second, there are in various places indications of how the inadequacy of the senses requires the postulation of Forms (e.g. *Phaedo* 73 seq., *Republic* Books V–VII). So we have to ask what Plato's complaints against Heracleitus and against sense-perception seem to be.

It is sometimes suggested that the doctrine that everything is in flux does not, in Plato's eyes, allow of sufficient stability for conceptualisation to get a grip. It postulates a formless world (and thereby a Formless world?), too fleeting to admit of description. The truly Heracleitean world would be that primeval amorphous wish-wash described in the *Timaeus*, place unstructured by conformity to the Forms. It may indeed be that this is how Plato took it, but first I want to ask what sort of view would be vulnerable to that objection. After all, if we take it that the view concerns the observable world, there is no obvious reason why the fact that it is in constant flux should render it indescribable. Let us suppose that every object consists of minute particles in constant motion, and that the whole is constantly moving backwards and forwards a minute amount. At the same time, for any colour it seems to have it is in fact true that it is ceasing to have it. The wall we have just painted is a brilliant white. In a year or two it will be a dingy off-white or creamy yellow. The changes have been imperceptible but constant, and there is no reason to suppose they are not in process from the start. So the wall is already in process of ceasing to be white from the moment we paint it. Similarly, seeds are on the way to becoming plants, men are declining into corpses, buildings are decaying. In short, it may well be that the world is in flux. But it is still describable.

One might, then, try to strengthen the position by claiming that this could hold of some changes, but not all. After all, I have chosen fairly specific concepts and confined the change within their range. But that 'range' supposes an area of no change. The wall that is changing from white to cream is remaining coloured. If the flux is total it should also be ceasing to be coloured, but also, of course to be tangible, or a wall, or existent. But this strengthening only strengthens the thesis if it is filled out in one of two ways. First, it might be that Plato is requiring that if the wall is changing then the wall has already changed to a different colour on the spectrum, into a different object, etc., or second, he might be wanting to claim that it cannot be true for all F, that everything that is F is also ceasing to be F. For instance, 'being in flux' must be an exception, as also perhaps, 'being different from something'. In this case it is his purpose to press the point until certain general concepts are reached such that it is clear that even on the Flux thesis at least one applies to everything.

The first possibility requires one to take 'change' very strongly, so that the wall is in flux only if the moment after our dubbing it a wall it has ceased to be white, a wall, the same shape, coloured. Certainly, in this case, the supposed world would be a very bewildering place, and arguably one where anything resembling our standard concepts would be useless. But it is worth noting that for this result we have to add in a condition that the constant change be not merely constant, but very rapid, and very radical. Otherwise we have, probably, the world we have, and with which we are perfectly able to cope.

The second possibility requires one to concentrate on certain predicates in particular. Having got there one could draw out the incoherence of the thesis, in that while according to it all predicates are always ceasing to hold of their subjects, there is at least one predicate that never ceases to hold of any subject. Alternatively, if it is true that everything is in flux, and also true that 'is in flux' is ceasing to hold, then it must be going to be true of everything that it is free of flux. In other words, the thesis only holds fleetingly, and is, on its own terms, false as a general thesis of the nature of things.

So far I have limited the Heracleitean thesis so that it only applies to observable objects, but I have extended the notion of flux so that in accordance with *Theaetetus* 181c–d, it includes both motion in one place and from place to place on the one hand, and qualitative change on the other. I have not as yet made the thesis cover concepts, meanings or Forms. The reason for this is as follows: although some (e.g. Cornford, 1935) assume that the views in the *Theaetetus* and the *Cratylus* are the same, it is arguable that while in the *Cratylus* Plato is saying that if you allow flux even in the area of Forms knowledge is impossible, in the *Theaetetus* the range of the Flux theory is more limited. It is in fact not easy to be sure quite how the argument is supposed to go in the *Theaetetus*. We have had, early on, a proposed definition of knowledge as perception and an accompanying account of perception that portrays it as a ceaseless interaction of movements. The first objections are to the view's relativisation of knowledge to subjects. At 179d Socrates turns to the constant flux element in the Protagorean position. That is a thesis that there is constant flux of percipients and percepts and consequently of qualities, but nothing explicit is said about concepts or meanings, nor even souls. The conclusion drawn at 183c is that the view that knowledge is perception is false at least according to the Flux theory. Now if the Flux theory is to cover concepts and meanings as well as things, and if in that form it is as incoherent as Cornford claims, then nothing is anything. In other words, the result is to show the Flux theory to be untenable, not to show the thesis that knowledge is perception to be false. The proper deployment of such an argument would be against the Flux theory, not against the position that knowledge is perception. The way in which Plato talks, however, suggests that we have a choice, to retain flux and drop Theaetetus' definition, or retain the latter and drop the former. Now flux comes into the argument because the position that knowledge is perception is taken as equating knowledge with perception as analysed at 156 seq., and that analysis does two things. First, it postulates constant motions both 'on a spot' and between points, and second, qualities are individuated temporally by the interaction of terms of an interrelation. Consequently, the constant motion results in constant qualitative change. But all this motion and change is postulated as part of the account of perception. So the thesis that knowledge is perception already, through the account of perception, includes the view that everything is in flux. The Heracleitean argument is therefore bringing out a strain within the original account of knowledge and claiming that to be incoherent. Consequently, while we do not have to suppose that Plato believed the Flux theory and relied on it to reject the other, at least he must have wanted to leave it as possibly coherent for the purposes of his argument. For if he showed it to be incoherent the view that knowledge is perception would be unscathed. All that would suffer would be the position that knowledge is perception granted that that account of perception is right. But if it was the view of perception that entailed the Flux theory, then the consequence of finding the Flux theory incoherent would be that the account of perception was also incoherent. So the conclusion would be simply that that account of perception is wrong. But then knowledge might well be perception according to a correct account. Yet the general style of account offered, according to which perception is a function of constant interaction between changing object and changing organ is at least plausible. It would be more natural to suppose that the account of perception and theory of Flux were being treated as coherent, but incompatible with the view that knowledge is perception. One is now left with a choice of dropping one or the other – the choice Plato seems to leave us with. Indeed, it might well be that Plato thought the style of account of perception, with its Heracleitean consequences, basically right, and so a convincing starting-point for a refutation of Theaetetus' definition. At any rate, he *ought* not, from the way the argument is laid out, to be claiming that the Flux theory is simply incoherent.

What ought to be does not, however, always happen, so it will now be necessary to examine the argument a little more closely to see how it does go. First, it will help to go back to the beginning. When Theaetetus defines knowledge as perception Socrates (152) rapidly takes him to be putting forward a Protagorean view that man is the measure of all things and what seems to me is to me (i.e. what a man deems to be true is true – for that man). It is somewhat puzzling why this is thought to be equatable with 'knowledge is perception'. This last, after all, seems to express the view that a man knows all but only what he perceives. It seems quite distinct from the wilder view that all a man's judgments are true. In fact this latter seems a tiresome red herring. If we dropped it out we should have quite a nice development. The skirmishes against Protagoras would largely be devoted to bringing out the implications of taking seriously the dictum that knowledge is perception. Now someone who said that could be holding that only statements based on sense-observations could be known, where he was commonsensically allowing corroborative evidence from the observations of others. But in that case it is being assumed that one knows there is a set of objects open to common observation, a fact not open to observation. So one might retreat to saying that only what is established by the agent's observation can be known, but allowing for general propositions about himself. But this assumes that he knows that two observations are observations by the same subject, and that supposed fact is not open to sense-observation. So finally he might end up with the position that only the current perception of a subject is known to that subject, which is itself relative to that perception. There are doubtless intermediate possibilities, but the main progress is one towards taking increasingly seriously the view that knowledge is perception, until finally we reach a position of equivalence between 'A knows that p' and 'A perceives the fact asserted in "p"'. This would not be a progress determined by repeated failure to answer the challenge 'how do you know?', but rather by the requirement that, according to the definition, knowledge is to be perception. So we find Socrates trying to find examples such as knowing a foreign language (163), being mistaken about flavours (159), remembering past events (163–4), which are supposedly examples that break the equivalence one way or the other. Protagoras' ripostes serve to draw sharply the lines of the thesis strictly taken. We could then see Plato's objections as pushing one away from the strict thesis at least as far as (but apparently no further than) the position that we have to assume a persistent subject capable of memory and of reviewing various perceptions if we are to have knowledge at all. So that is the strongest tenable version of the knowledge-is-perception thesis.

This picture unfortunately is confused by the intrusion of 'what seems to me is to me'. The reason for this intrusion must lie with the Protagorean arguments for the position. As I have remarked, there are no signs of any Cartesian style arguments driving one to limit one's knowledge to what is at any moment before the mind. There seem only to be two lines of argument. First, the one mentioned, from taking the definition strictly, and secondly one based on the premiss that knowledge is of the truth (of what is). This one at least is probably derived from Protagoras himself, whose work was, after all, entitled *Truth* (*aletheia*, not the disputable *to on*). To say that knowledge is of what is is a summing-up description for the unlimited set consisting of knowing that the sky is blue, that water is wet and so on. In each case knowledge is of what X is. With regard to a whole range of perceptual predicates, however, it seems that, first, X is only F to A, or B or . . . and second, to say 'it is F to A' means 'A sees, hears, . . . it as Γ.' There is no such thing as an object being F in itself. Thus the wind may be warm to Socrates and cold to Theaetetus. In the absence of all percipients it is neither warm nor cold, and there is no sense in trying to settle the question whether it is 'really' one or the other. But on the question of whether it is warm to Socrates, Socrates and only Socrates is judge. It is not difficult to generate an analogous position for colours, and perceptual predicates generally. Strictly speaking, the relativisation of sensory qualities to percipients only produces the result that the percipient if anyone is an authority. But Protagoras, like many after him, seems to have drawn the further conclusion that the percipient will always be right about the description of his experience. In other words, he does not distinguish the truth-values of 'Red is the correct description of how it looks to me.' and 'I think it looks red', and considers the last not open to mistake.

So far we have a thesis about a limited range of propositions, those containing perceptual predicates. Someone who wished to claim that only these propositions could be known would, of course, have to abandon the possibility of experts in various fields counting as knowledgeable (161–2), and also the possibility of knowing his own thesis (170–1). But the objections to Protagoras in those respects are not, or not primarily, based on the fact that only what is perceived can be known, but on the supposition that what everyone judges is right for him. Why, then, does Plato think one should move in that direction? Some light may be thrown on this if we refer back to the equation of the truth values of 'Red is the correct description of how it looks to me' and 'I think it looks red.' The first is already a reinterpretation of 'X is red.' In fact we have the following moves: 'X is red' really means 'X strikes me as red', which is equivalent to 'I think X is red.' Now 'I think X is red' may serve either (a) to give my verdict on X's colour, or (b) to say what my belief is about the description of X's colour. I may be mistaken as to whether I do really believe it, but it is natural to think I will normally know. On the other hand it is hard to know what to make of the idea of being wrong about my verdict, as distinct from my verdict's being wrong. For my verdict is given in the judgment. We have, then, the following: 'X is red' is interpreted as saying how X looks to the speaker, and so as equivalent to 'X looks red to me.' It is possible, though for various reasons not common, that the speaker should come to acknowledge himself mistaken and withdraw his description. Second, 'X looks red to me' might be seen as giving the speaker's judgment on X's colour, and while the judgment may be mistaken, the speaker cannot be mistaken as to its being his judgment. That is to say, 'he is wrong' entails that X does not look red, not that it is not his judgment that it does. Third, 'X looks red to me' might be taken as a statement about the speaker's belief as to how X looks to him. Here again there is a general presumption that a person will know what he believes, and it is easy, though wrong, to think that he cannot be mistaken. The second and third points can reinforce the feeling that 'X looks red to me' must be true if sincerely uttered, a feeling that is fairly natural to anyone who recognises that a range of kinds of mistake are not possible here, and who has encountered the difficulty of devising a plausible example of error. Consequently, it is easy to think error is impossible with 'I think it looks red.' Consequently error will be impossible with 'X strikes me as red.' This can now be extended to cover aesthetic and moral judgments (157d, 167c,

146

172a), where the position can again be bolstered by appealing to the absurdity of trying to show that something really is beautiful or just/ legal in general. Though the range is now fairly broad there are left many judgments which it does not seem absurd to claim are true independent of individuals' judgments. On the other hand, if we have in the other cases absorbed the position that all judgments in effect say how the matter strikes the speaker and so give his verdict, it is easy to see that the same holds of these others too. If I say 'there is going to be a war', then I am telling you how matters strike me, and that that is my judgment. But I cannot be mistaken about that. In other words, the natural gloss 'in my opinion' gets incorporated into the judgment, so that 'in my opinion there will be a war' does not express the judgment 'there will be a war' but the judgment 'I believe there will be a war.' In the starting examples from perception this may be relatively harmless and the difficulties are less obvious. The passage from 'I can hear a screech' to 'I think I can hear a screech' is mediated by the ambiguous 'that sounded like a screech', and can also be helped by being put in the first person. The conflation is nevertheless there, so that the truth-values of 'X is F' and 'I think X is F' are equated. This same equation, generalised to all judgments, produces the Protagorean 'what seems to me is to me'. Whatever may have gone on in Protagoras' work it seems that Plato is wanting to draw out the consequences of accepting this conflation and failing to distinguish judgment from what is judged about. Consequently it is not the point that we only know what we perceive that is worked on, but that we can only judge about what is to us, what affects us (167a). From this, too, it follows that experts are impossible and Protagoras' thesis unproveable. But these difficulties are adduced against the position that what seems to me is to me, which in turn generalises the conflation made in the elaboration of 'knowledge is perception.' So while it is true that we gradually move away from limitation to perception to the development of a critique of 'what seems to me is to me', this second thesis is not unconnected with the first in fact, nor, in all probability, in Plato's mind.

At least it is clear that Plato thinks they are prima facie different. For at 179c, after the critique of 'what seems to me is to me' Socrates allows that it may be that our perceptual judgments are always true and so perception is always knowledge. In the following section dealing with the Heracleiteans we hear no more of 'what seems to me is to me' but are strictly confined to the thesis that knowledge is perception. The refutation of this necessitates recalling the earlier account of perception (182a–b). This is wedded to the view that everything is in flux (182c–d) to prove something about perception, i.e. that it is as much not perception as perception, and so conclude that if knowledge is perception it is as much not knowledge as knowledge (182e–183a).

At 181c–e two kinds of 'motion' are distinguished, movement and qualitative change. But it seems clear from 182a–b that Plato is not getting his opponents to admit, say, that tables are constantly rotating and moving from place to place, but rather that the two sorts of movement mentioned at 156–7 are always taking place, and also that their interaction is always resulting in qualitative change (cf. 156a, 159e–160a). This latter point is insisted on at 182c–d, where it is pointed out that if the interacting movements took place without qualitative change we should be able to describe the interactions as of such and such a quality. The recalling of the theory of perception and the insistence that qualities are individuated as functions of interactions of numerically distinct movements is vital for the argument that follows. For one result will be that if 'white' names a quality, then it names the result of the interaction of movements M_n and M'_n. The result of interaction of M_{n+1} and M'_{n+1} must be another quality, and if the experience is visual, another colour. Now according to the theory of vision (156–7), the result of interaction is not only, say, a coloured object, but a seeing eye, and just as the 'white' is relative to *this* seeing, so the seeing is relative to this white. As the colour quality is different from moment to moment, so is the perception. This point may lie behind a curious apparent overstatement by Socrates. At 182e he seems to argue that as vision must be in process it must be as right to call it 'not seeing' as 'seeing'. This involves translating 182e 3 as 'In fact something should not be called "seeing" rather than "not seeing". . . .' But it seems more natural to take the object of 'call' from the earlier sentence: *Socrates:* 'What shall we say of perception of any sort, say seeing or hearing? that it persists in that seeing and hearing?' *Theodorus:* 'We must not say that, if everything is in flux.' *Socrates:* 'In fact it should not be called seeing something rather than not seeing something. . . .' In that case Socrates is remembering that a seeing is always seeing X, and so the 'something' is object of 'see'; but as X is always moving on, so, for any X, is seeing X. So for any seeing – seeing Q_1 – since everything is in flux it is as right to call it not seeing Q_1 as seeing Q_1. It will not do, with Cornford (1935), to complain that *at the moment* it is clearly seeing Q_1 and therefore knowing it, for on this view talk of moments must be talk of stretches of process *at* which nothing happens but *during* which there is as much a no longer seeing Q_1 as a seeing it. One must not make the mistake in exposition of halting the process (183a 6–7). Further, it is not possible on this thesis to say – 'but seeing Q_1 and Q_2 are still seeing, so that continues', for according to this view there is no 'that'. There is not something, seeing, that persists, there is at best seeing Q_2 that succeeds, but is quite different from, seeing Q_1; the products of distinct interactions are not reducible to the same description. But if this holds of seeing, it holds of all perception (182e 3–5); and so if knowledge is perception it must hold of knowledge (182e 7–11). That is to say, any knowing, being a perceiving, is always and only knowing Q_1 or Q_2. But on the Flux theory that must mean that anything is as correctly called 'not knowing Q_1' as 'knowing Q_1'. This conclusion is then generalised to all assertions.

Now this argument does not use the premiss that all meanings are in flux. The Flux theory is limited to the account of perception. It is not even used to yield the *conclusion* that all meanings must be in flux, but only that if the Flux theory is combined with the thesis that knowledge is perception, no terms could have application because there could be no way of distinguishing the conditions under which they were applicable from those under which they were not. A further point worth noticing is that the Flux theory as considered here is not either the one I declared harmless earlier in this chapter. That was the view that every object was, (i) in local motion, and (ii) in process of qualitative change in a familiar sense of those terms. The position Plato is considering holds first, not that objects are in constant local motion, but that there are perpetual interacting motions as claimed in the theory of vision, and second, not that there is qualitative change in a familiar sense, but in a very peculiar sense of 'quality'. For one thing Plato is drawing attention to is how strange that view of 'quality' is. The familiar notion of quality has a role in the activity of comparison, and so allows the same quality to be manifested by different things. But the view in question cannot allow comparison nor, therefore, any such notion of quality. According to it qualities are distinguished and individuated by reference to the interaction of movements that are themselves quality-less and individuated only temporally. The statement of the theory includes talk of X being F to Y and X' being F to Y' as though there were a quality common to the two percepts, but its purpose is to show that there is no truth to the assertion that they are both white or even whitish. Indeed, it is logically impossible that it should be true, and so the claim would be senseless. The same goes for two percepts of the 'same' subject. This amounts to abandoning talk of qualities, though the retention of quality-words in the exposition can disguise the fact even from the expounder.

What then does the argument show? As the Flux theory is part of the account of perception and the exposition of Protagoras' thesis (cf. e.g. 168b) the options seem to be to deny the equation of knowledge and perception or deny that account of perception. Plato does not in fact canvass the second. He develops the first (184–6) by developing the point that we can compare and think about and distinguish perceptions, and that if we are to grasp what hardness and softness are, this requires more than feeling hard and soft things; it requires comparison and thought about such perceptions. This in effect does two things. First, it distinguishes between feeling something hard and judging that what one feels is hard (e.g. 187a), and second, the capacity to judge is seen as requiring property-notions whose possession in turn presupposes the comparison of perceptions and so the manifestation of the same quality by two percepts. It seems, then, that Plato is opting for a use of 'perceive' ('see', 'hear', etc.) whereby animals may perceive as well as men (186b 11–c2), and contrasting it with the power of judging which requires concepts. It is a moot point whether Plato conflates talking of perception simply as a physical process and speaking of it as the experience of seeing, etc., resultant on such a process. The talk of the various sorts of motion in the theory of vision might certainly seem like a physical account. It should be noted, however, that to be taken that way we have to interpret the 'slow motions' as motions of particles in objects, the fast ones as motions of particles or rays between objects. This would mean speaking of certain things being movements of unperceived objects. This is incompatible with the perception-relative conclusion of the theory, and it also runs counter to certain direct statements. For at 159c the percipient and thing perceived are distinguished as passive and active terms of the interaction relation, a point confirmed at 182a where it is clear that these correspond to the slow movements of 156d–e, which generate the quick movements whose meeting results in a seeing eye and a white object. Yet both at 157a and again at 182b it is said that the active and passive elements are only such in interaction and action and passion are not just any action and passion: the terms are technical ones in a description of perception and are confined to their role in that description. Active and passive elements are not to be thought of as doing anything unperceived. The theory ought, then, not to be a physical account of perception, but a representation of certain facets of perceptual experience, perhaps the apparent relative stability of some parts of the perceptual field together with rapid slight changes corresponding to changes, say, of perspective. This would suggest that Plato is at least not primarily interested in the physical mechanisms, but in the perceptions on which judgments are made, which can reach the soul through the body from birth (186b 11–c2). If 'perception' is used in this way, and physical interactions constitute perception, if but only if they 'get through to the soul', then indeed a pig is as good as Protagoras (161c). If it is not, then perception is not open to the kind of interaction analysis offered in the theory of vision and in effect turns out to mean 'a judgment of perception'.

It might be thought that there is one possibility that Plato overlooks, although he mentions it at 182c–d. For surely it would be possible for everything to be in motion except qualitatively? In that case one could talk of seeing the same white over a period and it would not be as much not seeing it as seeing it. But Plato is not here envisaging a possibility but underlining a feature of the opposed position. To talk of qualitative stability would be to allow of comparison of percepts and would entail abandoning the relativisation of qualities to moments of perception. That would mean allowing knowledge to stray beyond perception. So while it would allow for characterisation of the flux it can do so only by letting in what the opposition thesis is devised to exclude.

In all this Protagoras is being kept to a view of perception that straddles perception of men and animals, and the stultifying results are being brought out. It is Protagoras' need to take 'perception' both this way and to cover judgments on one's perception that Plato considers important. By taking 'perception' in the first sense he can show that for the second more is needed. As the Flux theory and theory of perception are themselves caught up in the confusion Plato cannot simply either accept or reject them. One might be able to produce a revised version holding of perception proper which Plato would accept. Consequently, he does not argue that a Flux theory of perception is incoherent. The main point is that by no stretch of the imagination can perception proper constitute knowledge.

In the course of this argument it has in fact been established that implicit in all supposed knowledge is the claim of a persistent intelligent perceiver. It is not shown that we do not know the correct descriptions of our perceptions, nor even that they do not constitute our knowledge of the material world, together with those memories necessary for the acquisition of property-concepts. Further, the judgments of similarity and distinction that we hear of all concern colours, sounds and sensible objects generally. Similarly we judge that there is such a thing as sound; and that judgment is more than hearing, it is a function of the mind, which reviews perceptions. The claim is not that knowledge is concerned with other things than sense objects, but that knowledge of sense objects involves judgments on what they are, what they resemble and so on, and these are not perceptions.

In short, Heracleiteanism as treated in the *Theaetetus* seems a very special thesis, and that dialogue leaves it possible that first, we do have knowledge of the sensible world, and second that knowledge of the sensible world constitutes the bulk of our knowledge. There may be in the argument of 182c–d an implicit rejection of the first form of strong version of the view that everything is in constant change mentioned on p. 142, but there is no sign of the second. In fact, it is still possible to hold that the objects of perception are in a state of constant change, and that this is well described as a state of constant interaction of percipient and perceived. One would have to drop the peculiar means of individuating qualities espoused by Protagoras, but that is simply part of accepting the distinction between perception and judgment. With a normal notion of property one could allow of constant change so long as one can also keep it not too fast and have the mind able to review various perceptions. It is difficult to see, however, how as yet we generate an argument for separable intelligible objects, requiring in the *Phaedo–Republic* manner a 'turning away' from the sensible world if we are to apprehend them. According to the *Theaetetus* concepts are acquired by close attention to perceptions. What is more, it is doubtful whether they would clearly measure up even to early dialogue Socratic requirements. For it would still be possible to preserve the general Protagorean insistence on process language, which in the *Timaeus* (49–50c; cf. 37d–38a) is said to be appropriate to the description of the physical world but not of Forms. There is no reason why concepts such as 'hard', 'man' and so on should not be seen as covering more or less extended and complex stretches of change. Indeed, with a concept like 'man' it seems distinctly plausible. Lack of change over a period of, say, sixty years would normally be sufficient to prove lack of identity or lack of humanity, just because the concept covers a particular mode of change from infancy to senescence. So it would be perhaps possible to give an account of the meanings of the terms from which it was clear that in saying 'this is a man', we are really saying 'this develops somewhere in the range of process covered by "man".' Any search for an answer to 'what is man?' that yielded characteristics that all men would share would be doomed to failure, unless 'is part of such and such a process of change' were to count as a characteristic, which would seem not to be so for Socrates. So nothing in the *Theaetetus* suggests that Plato thought that a combination of constant local motion and constant qualitative change in any ordinary sense would make concepts and language impossible, so that we need Forms. Possibly a certain stability, i.e. lack of extreme rapidity of change, is needed for concepts to be possible, but the resulting possibility does not look very Form-like. It might be, of course, that Plato thought that the sorts of concept yielded were in fact inadequate for the generation of *epistemai*, for which something more than slicing up stretches of change is required. I shall return to this possibility later, but for the moment it is enough to remark that it is a different objection to Heracleiteanism, and not one that suggests an equation of Form with meanings.

If we turn now to the *Cratylus* we find a different use of the Flux doctrine. Cratylus had been holding a view of language whereby words represent the nature of things, and the nature of the representation is 'natural'. In effect, this means that words represent things by resembling them, and so revealing their nature. It would follow from this that the world could as well be studied by examining words as by examining the things they stand for. Socrates rejects this on the grounds that words from different languages and even dialects give incompatible representations, some suggesting fluidity others a constancy in nature. It is important to get behind words to the reality, and in particular to settle the question of fluidity as against constancy. For if everything, including Forms, were in flux it would seem that no knowledge would be possible.

Now this looks very different from the *Theaetetus*, and not only in the near-total lack of argument. The Flux theory is here envisaged as being applied to Forms, and is taken without any additional premisses to yield lack of knowledge. It is not quite so easy to see what attributing flux to Forms amounts to, but at 439c–d Socrates first wins the concession that there is such a thing as Beautiful and Good, and then declares that in discussing flux he is not concerned with whether beautiful faces are in constant flux (the point of interest in the *Theaetetus*), but with whether the Beautiful itself is. The points that follow (439d–e) would hold of anything in flux – that one cannot fix it with a demonstrative, or say it *is* of such a sort – but are obviously unacceptable of anything unchanging. At 440a–c we are told that whatever it is would be unknowable (*gnosis*), and so if everything is in flux, knowledge would be impossible, as there would first be nothing knowable, and second knowledge would be changing to non-knowledge. All this follows from the supposition that the Beautiful, Knowledge and so on are in flux, irrespective of what is true of the material world, and the matter is left as a possible subject of dispute between Socrates and Cratylus.

Now this is fairly clearly claiming that if there is knowledge there must be unchanging Forms, so that if there is knowledge not everything can be in flux. Further, of course, it seems that there cannot be knowledge of anything that is in flux. The ground for this seems to be the necessity for knowledge being expressible in non-flux terms – terms that would necessarily be inapplicable to objects in flux. We have therefore indication of considerations that lead Plato to posit Forms if there is to be knowledge at all, and also lead him to conclude that in some sense there is not knowledge of the material world. 'Indication' is, however, the right word, and we must now try to see what it amounts to.

According to Cornford (1935, p. 99) Plato's conclusion is 'unless we recognise some class of knowable entities exempt from the Heracleitean flux and so capable of standing as the fixed meanings of words, no definition of knowledge can be any more true than its contradictory.' This is said to be the conclusion we are meant to draw from both the *Theaetetus* and the *Cratylus* discussions. The point presumably is either that unless 'knowledge' has a fixed sense it cannot be defined, for if 'knowledge' is constantly shifting its meaning 'knowledge is F' is no more true than 'knowledge is not F', or that unless there is an object or set of objects that is unchanging then there is nothing that can be defined, and in particular if there is no such thing as knowledge for 'knowledge' to mean, then no definition of knowledge is any more true than its contradictory. Yet all this is somewhat baffling. Of course, if the word 'knowledge' has already changed its sense by the time the definiens has been enunciated, then the definiens, supposing it to be right for the earlier sense, would no longer hold. Further, as the terms of the definiens are ex hypothesi also constantly shifting it would seem there is never a possibility of giving sense to its 'being right'. So on this hypothesis, knowledge would not be expressible in our language, and the meanings of words would not be among the items knowable. It does not follow without more ado either that there are no knowables, or that we cannot know them. It is no objection, of course, that the hypothesis is fantastical. Perhaps it was Plato's point to indicate where the flux doctrine would reach fantasy. It may also be that he erroneously thought the conclusion followed, although this might be surprising if, as often supposed, he thought knowledge was a form of wordless intuition. The real objection is that throughout he makes no mention of words at all, but only of Forms. So the passage could only be about changing meanings if, in Socrates' view, all meanings are forms. But this position is not open to Socrates. For at 434d–438 he has first argued that what a noise means is a matter of convention, showing this by the fact that we readily understand words although they contravene Cratylus' similarity rule and so should not be intelligible. Second, he argued that words might well have been ill-devised. But the danger of an ill-devised word is not that it is senseless, but that it is misleading. So there can be, in theory, meaningful areas of language which are nevertheless likely to lead us astray. Yet if they always in virtue of being meaningful isolated Forms which constituted their meaning, they could not be misleading. The whole point of the discussion is in fact to suggest that if we reflected on the realities (Forms?) we might need a thorough revision of our language, and this could only be done by showing that our words in their present sense were inadequate to express the true nature of reality. This does not allow talk of a flux of Forms to be equated with flux of meaning. Although Plato might admit that in the extravagant circumstances outlined, communication would be impossible, he could not allow that meanings of words were incapable of changing.

On the other hand, granted that not all meanings are Forms, and that for some possible language situations it could be that no Forms were meanings, why should one hold the other alternative, that unless there is an object or set of objects that is unchanging then there is nothing that can be defined? One reason might be that any definition has to express a timeless truth. It cannot be a timeless truth about the noise 'good', say. It can only be a timeless truth about such and such a sense of 'good', in other words, the possibility of definition supposes the existence of actual or possible senses of actual or possible words. Between such senses there are everlasting relationships. The supposition of a flux in this region, if it means anything, must mean loss of intelligibility and so of knowledge.

The difficulty here is that the actual senses that words do have must count among the eternal objects, together with the possible senses of terms in even more misleading possible languages. Either they are all, because definable, Forms, or there is some special reason why a flux of Forms is more disastrous than a flux of meanings. The first seems utterly un-Platonic. What of the latter? Here it would seem that a flux of Forms might make knowledge impossible, but not because it introduced any flux of 'senses'. Suppose Plato considers that the language we have reflects an imperfect grasp of reality, but also thinks that there is a structure to reality to be grasped, that it is not just a haphazard purposeless succession (cf. *Philebus* 28d). The claim that there can be *episteme* will be a claim that some questions can be answered in the form '*X* is *F*' (where 'is' can be taken 'eternally'), and these answers do not simply give definitions but reveal the structure according to which the sensible universe is formed. An answer to the question 'what is the Beautiful?' will require more than an account of how the word is used. It will be necessary also to be able to show what makes things beautiful, and how to judge the actual phenomena by relation to the ideal. If none of this could be discovered, then there would be no *episteme*. So there are three conditions to be satisfied: the 'is' in the answer must be timelessly true, the concept analysed must correctly reflect the nature of reality, and the analysis must make clear the application of the concept to the reality. The first two conditions are fairly clearly in the *Cratylus*, the first in the rejection of the possibility of knowledge of what is in flux, the second in the warning that words may be ill-devised. The third is also implicit in this last for it is clear that the dialectician does not simply have words that are adequate to the reality, but also understands how they are so.

If this sketch is right, then the Forms are required for the intelligibility not of language, but of the world. A flux of Forms would not make language impossible, but knowledge. Again, it would not make knowledge in any day-to-day sense impossible, but 'true' knowledge. This becomes impossible because no timeless 'is' propositions would be true that had any role in the account of the universe. It looks, in fact, as though Plato is taking the truism that *episteme* is of what is (the case), and then tightening the screws so that 'is' excludes any change.

This question of changelessness will come up again later. For the present it is worth noting one point that came up in discussing the *Theaetetus*. It was there pointed out that Plato might have objected to a form of Heracleiteanism on the ground that there must be some F such that the sensible world is always F. Thus, for example 'in flux' must always hold. Now this point looks as though it might be turned against Plato's denial that there can be knowledge of the sensible world. For that denial seems to be based on the premiss that there is no F that can at any point be attached by an 'is' to any sensible thing. Yet surely 'in flux' must be an exception? In fact Plato will need some distinction between kinds of predicate. Certainly 'in flux' is a predicate that pre-supposes other predicates 'between which' changes take place. So being in flux and its opposite might be thought of as in some way second-order properties. Further, neither is a property that can be cited in answer to 'what is X?' For 'in flux' in effect says that there is no first-order F that X *is*, and 'not in flux' simply says that there is such an F without saying what it is. So Plato could hold that some predicates do not stand for properties that constitute the nature of their subjects so that they can be properly cited in answer to 'what is X?' Alternatively, he might distinguish between predicates that attribute modes of change in contrast with ones that do not. Thus, 'running', 'learning' and so on attribute a mode of change, so as to cancel the strict implications of any 'is', while 'square', 'good' do not. These last may be attached to their subjects in ways implying process, but do not themselves come in conflict with the strict implications of 'is'. 'In flux' would presumably fall in the first category. Whichever way he does it, Plato will need some means of classifying predicates into those which can feature in timeless 'is' answers to 'what is X?' and those which cannot.

So far as the *Theaetetus* and *Cratylus* are concerned, then, we get the following picture of Plato's reaction to Heracleitus: the doctrine of flux can be treated as confined to the sensible world or as also applying to Forms. In the *Theaetetus* it is taken the first way, and in that dialogue we get no indication of its creating any difficulty except in conjunction with a thesis that knowledge is perception which confuses perceptual judgment with perception proper. There is no suggestion of any need for Forms, although when one considers what concepts that dialogue might leave one with, one might suspect what Plato would consider lacking. This suspicion is borne out if one turns back to the *Cratylus*, where clearly Socrates is committed to confining knowledge to eternal truths, where these are more than definitions. Socrates is not against evolution of meaning, but he is against unlimited evolution in the universe. If that held, then *episteme* would not strictly be possible, for while the truths, if dated, would be eternally true, they would not if undated. Plato wants 'X is F' to carry no time-reference, and '"X is F" is true' similarly to carry no time-reference. The result of a flux of Forms, which is envisaged in the *Cratylus*, would not be a world with which we could not cope, for which no concepts could be devised. It would only be a 'senseless' world and one of which there were no universal truths expressing its unchanging structure. Therefore there would be no *episteme* of it. Similarly, we are left in the *Theaetetus* with the possibility that that is how the world is, one which we could certainly describe but only in terms of process-concepts. No *episteme* of it would be possible, according to the *Cratylus*. The simple fact that the world is in constant change does not lead to postulation of Forms. Nor that fact together with the fact that we can describe it, nor in conjunction with the fact that we can define terms. It is special conditions put on what is to count as *episteme* that ensure that there is no knowledge of sensible phenomena, so that if there is knowledge we must postulate more than phenomena.

In all this I have been working backwards, partly because these two dialogues are the main sources for explicit statements on Heracleiteanism, and the *Theaetetus* passage is the most extended, and partly because they supply fairly good reason for doubting that Forms are meanings or that the possibility of defining a term is sufficient to generate a theory of Forms. If we look at earlier dialogues (at least earlier than the *Theaetetus*) we find already some dissatisfaction with the senses, in part at least due to the fact that their objects are in flux (e.g. *Phaedo* 78–9, *Symposium* 210–11, *Republic* 507–8), and a similar stance is taken in the *Timaeus* (51–2). It is now time to see whether we get some hint of why Forms should be postulated, and whether what is said there is consistent with what has been inferred from the *Theaetetus* and *Cratylus*. If it is not, then we shall have to see whether that disproves the interpretation of those dialogues or shows Plato to have changed his mind or failed to see implications of what he said.

X

Complaints about the Senses

In the *Phaedo* we get a number of remarks which seem either to contrast the objects of sense-observation with Forms, or to contrast the possibilities of enquiry with the aid of the senses with that pursued by reason alone. These contrasts are not distinguished in the dialogue. Thus at 65d we are told that there are such things as Just itself and Good, but that no one has ever perceived any of them with any of the senses. They are best studied by the intellect, and by it alone, without 'help' of the senses. But this is part of a passage where it is also said that the senses 'contain no truth', which is the preserve of reason. The objects that cannot be seen are objects of reason, and the objects of sense-observation do not yield truth and are not proper subjects of reason's interest. Now it is not obvious why these contrasts should go together, nor quite what they are. Thus, it might seem that I cannot see Just itself in that the definition of 'just' is not a visible object, but then, why cannot I discover the truth about empirical facts, or at least use reason on them? Of course, seeing is not reasoning, nor are men what it is to be a man, but there is no obvious reason for pairing off the first members of each pair and second members of each pair. One explanation could be, of course, that Plato is thinking of reason as a form of non-sensory perception which therefore must have exclusive possession of certain objects. In that case he might naturally suppose that it must have a non-sensory object, and then, having found some non-sensory objects that are the subject of definition and argument, he would accept the pairing without more ado. Before just accepting this, however, it would be necessary to go through the various *Phaedo* passages in order.

At 64–7 Socrates is explaining why a philosopher will try to free himself from bodily influences. As the poets say, there is little truth in the senses, as they lack precision and clarity. As 'having the body as companion in one's enquiries' means using the senses, it is therefore as well to be as free of it as possible in any investigation. Now there is such a thing as Just itself which is not perceptible, and the truth about which is best acquired by isolating it in thought, so that the soul may by itself examine these things themselves. For this purpose it is best to liberate oneself from physical desires and the use of the senses. From the point of view of the average man's approach to life, this can look like giving up life early.

In this passage the 'body' is down-graded for two reasons, first because it is the seat of a number of desires that distract one from the pursuit of the truth, and second because its sole equipment for discovering the truth is imprecise and deceptive. Further, this equipment is simply not able to observe Just, Large, Health and such like, the truth about which is apparently of interest to the philosopher. There is no real argument in the passage, and the existence of Forms is appealed to as a familiar fact. Certain things are worth noting, however. To begin with, we have some special strict notion of truth. Not even favoured particular statements such as 'this looks red to me now' count as obviously true. The senses in general lack clarity and precision. We are not told more of what the complaint is, but it obviously might be the one met in discussing the *Theaetetus* and *Cratylus* that what we observe is in process, and so one cannot give precise reference to one's 'this', nor strictly use 'is'. So it is not strictly true that the senses ever tell us anything of the form 'this is F'. But as the truth is always what *is* the case, they never strictly give us the truth. Second, certain topics are selected as ones in which a philosopher will be interested and the senses inept. These are billed as concerned with 'the being, what everything happens to be'. This emphasis on the verb 'to be' suggests again the strict notion of truth, but it leaves a question as to the range of things in which a philosopher is interested. The general description given in the barbarous translation 'the being, what everything happens to be' might allow 'what it is to be red', but then the list does not in fact contain such an example, and might be intended to exclude it. It all depends how we are supposed to judge whether or not something can be perceived. The point might be that while I can be asked whether this tomato is red and use my eyes to get the answer, I have to know what it is to be red (what the word 'red' means) in order to do this, and my eyes cannot tell me that (I cannot see the meaning of 'red'). On the other hand the point might be that I can be taught what it is to be red by being shown red objects, and I can see their redness. By contrast, I cannot be taught what it is to be just or healthy simply by being shown examples, nor can I see their justice or health. I should have in these cases to have it explained to me why this description of society or act was a just one, or why this condition of body was healthy, and the explanation would not collapse into 'well, ones that look, feel, smell etc., like this one just are'. So we have none of us seen or smelled justice or health, in contrast with redness or sweetness. We have to get at what they are through reason.

Taken the first way, the point resembles that made in the *Theaetetus*, that seeing is not the same as a judgment of perception. The latter requires concepts, knowledge of what it is to be *F*. Taken the second way, the point is like that made at *Politicus* 285d–286a. There we are told that many fail to realise that many similarities are perceptible, and there is no difficulty in satisfying an enquirer without resort to reasoning; but there are others on which an enquirer cannot be properly satisfied by reference to perceptibles; these are 'bodiless' and require reasoning – they are also noblest. This may be the point also at *Parmenides* (130d) where we are told that the young Socrates rejected the idea that there are Forms of things like hair because 'they are what we see them to be'. This presumably means that what makes them hair or whatever is the fact that they have the properties we see, without further explanation. The first way ties Forms to questions of meaning, the second to a subset of universals.

A little later in the *Phaedo* (73–6) we get a further discussion of the contrast between Forms and reason on the one side and physical objects and the senses on the other. Socrates is arguing that a person must have existed before birth. First he outlines the conditions for being reminded of *A* by *B*, and then argues that these are satisfied in the case of our seeing equal objects. For, first, we admit there is such a thing as the Equal itself over and above equal sticks and stones, second, we admit that it is quite different from these things, third, we could only have got to know of the Equal from sense experience. Since equals resemble the Equal, although being quite distinct, and we always refer back to it, noting their comparative inadequacy, it emerges as a clear case of recollection.

I do not wish to consider the worth of this argument, but the implications of it. First, it seems from 75c–d that the specimen list of Forms is much the same as at 65. Each list contains members the other lacks, but not only is there important overlap, but they also both omit the members whose inclusion would settle the issue of interpretation left in discussing the last passage. Second (73a–b), it seems that we are not merely concerned with what philosophers might be concerned with, but with anything that might properly be called knowledge. In other words, Forms are being tied to *episteme* proper, and this latter is without exception a matter of recollection. This means that it must be concerned with those concepts for which the recollection argument holds. Third, for that argument to work we have to recognise that the things that are *F* are different from the *F* although aspiring to be like it. We refer them back to the *F*. Fourth, once again, the *F* is not something we perceive with the senses.

It is in the second and third points that we find a difference from the earlier passage, or rather some addition to it. It is a pity, therefore, that on these points the passage contains apparently irresoluble ambiguities. Before examining them, however, it may be worth seeing how the two interpretations of the previous passage fare. If we accept the first, then Plato must be saying that for any concept, or perhaps for any predicate-concept according to some intuitively acceptable notion of predicate, we must realise, when we apply it to things, that the things are not what F is, though they resemble it. To say they resemble it is at least to say that they qualify for the relevant description. But if Plato thinks that the word 'just' must mean what is just, then he might have thought that Forms, or what the words really or strictly mean, have pre-eminently the property meant. In that case the notion of resemblance might be stronger. At the same time it has to be recognised that as a view about all predicates this would have results that should have struck Plato as peculiar. If we take 'red' for instance, it is hard to see in what sense the Form of Red could be red without that being a perceptible property of it. And yet the Forms are said implicitly here and explicitly at 78–9 to be imperceptible (and cf. *Phaedrus* 247c). Plato does not in fact mention any Forms of perceptible properties like red, and granted that unacceptable consequences are less obvious in other cases it might have escaped his attention. But in that case it starts looking as though it may be significant that he concentrates on certain concepts, and that might suggest that it is not just the importance of concepts in general that he is interested in. Alternatively one might keep to a weak sense of 'resemble'. In that case presumably the talk of actual sticks being inferior in their equality will refer to their lack of sure grip on their being what they are, in this case equal.

If we take the second interpretation, then Plato is holding that with regard to certain special predicates, to which *episteme* is especially related, we recognise that particulars to which we are tempted to apply these predicates in some way fall short of what these predicates stand for. Whereas we can just see what colour things are, when we call them equal or just we are always referring to some standard, and in some way we recognise the distinction, not to say gap, between the standard and the sticks. The apprehension of the standard, which requires some use of the intellect, and also the reference to it, are needed in the application of the predicates to particulars. The actual use of these concepts, though not of others, to describe particulars, involves reference to something other than the particulars.

Clearly, a good deal hinges on what is meant by the declaration that particulars aspire to be like the original but fail. If that was clear we might be able to tell how Plato is thinking either of concepts in general or these special ones. It is, of course, just here that the passage's ambiguities come into play. To begin with there is the notion of similarity. When Socrates is elaborating the conditions that establish recollection in general, he lays down that if A is to be reminded of B by C then (i) A must previously have known B (ii) knowing B is not knowing C and conversely (iii) the perception of C puts A in mind of B. There is then a special condition (74a) for cases where B and C are alike, where one is reminded of B because of a resemblance. This is (iv) that one should notice whether or not it falls short at all in its resemblance to that of which one is reminded. The verb translated 'notice' can mean something milder such as 'think of', 'have in mind', as perhaps at 73c 8, but it can also have the stronger sense, as at 74e–75b. Nothing can be made of the condition at 74a on the weaker translation. What is more, to make anything plausible of it one has to suppose two further things. First, that 'noticing whether or not' means 'noticing that in fact'. This is what we have to notice when the point is applied at 74d following. Second, we have to suppose that to fall short in similarity is to lack some feature of the original. In other words, any portrait, however good, falls short in similarity to its original if the original is three-dimensional and the portrait two-dimensional. This is precisely the way Plato uses the idea in the *Cratylus* at 432 following, so it cannot be said to be un-Platonic. What is more it yields something that might sound a plausible necessary condition for being reminded. For unless a man notices that a painted Simmias lacks some feature of Simmias he has not yet realised that it is not Simmias. He may be ready to mistake the picture for Simmias, but not to be reminded of him by it. So failure in similarity is failure to have at least one feature possessed by the original, and this must be how equal sticks fall short of the Equal. We have, then, a choice of possible respects in which equal sticks fail to resemble the Equal. Now at 74b–c the distinction between equal things and the Equal is 'established', so we might hope there for some illumination. But one ambiguous sentence is enough to deny it us.

The troublesome sentence is 74b 7–9. Socrates asks: 'Surely equal stones and sticks while remaining the same sometimes . . .' and after the 'sometimes' comes either 'seem to one man equal, to another not', or 'seem equal to one thing and not to another' or 'are clearly equal to one thing and not to another'. If we take the first translation, then the difference between equal sticks and the Equal is that there can be disagreement about the equality of the first, but not about the second. In that case it looks as though Plato is wanting to distinguish between particular objects, which can conceivably have either of two incompatible properties, and Forms, which cannot conceivably have the opposite property to that of which they are the Form. This would be a first attempt at a distinction between necessary and contingent truths, hampered by a belief in the existence of certain objects that are either necessary possessors of some properties or necessary possessors of all the properties they possess. So instead of distinguishing between truths like 'dogs eat rabbit', whose opposite 'dogs do not eat rabbit' is false but not self-contradictory, and truths like 'dogs are animals', whose opposite 'dogs are not animals' is necessarily false, Plato distinguishes between physical objects, that may have either of two incompatible properties and Forms that may not. Certainly this seems to be a view that Plato canvassed. At 102 Socrates distinguishes between himself, who may, while remaining who he is (compare the 'remaining the same' of the present passage), change from being large to being small, and the Large, either in us or in general, which cannot. The point there is a stronger one, that a particular can change from having one property to having its opposite, but at least if that is possible it must be conceivable that it should have either.

On this translation, either the point about particulars falling short of the original is unconnected with the way in which they are clearly different, which should not be the case; or they fall short in that they have a contingent relationship to equality, while the Equal is necessarily and eternally equal. That Plato did think that this lack of resemblance could be significant is suggested by the *Timaeus* (37c seq.). There the Demiurge is trying to fashion the world on the model of the Form of Living thing, and it is not enough to give it life, he also tries to make it an image of eternity. This is not wholly possible, but he gets it as near as he can. What seems clear is that the respect in which the world will fall short of its original is not in the character of which the original is the Form, but in unchangeability, which is a general character of all Forms. It may well be, therefore, that in the *Phaedo* too, the way in which equal sticks fall short of their original is not in equality but in unchangeableness of equality.

I have so far taken this translation as making a point about the equal possibility of believing A is F or A is not F, where A is a particular, in contrast with where A is a Form. There is, however, another possibility. The reason why sticks may seem to one man equal, to another not, may be nothing to do with contingency, but rather with the fact that physical objects are thought not to be strictly measurable. Any stick is a material continuum, and for any measure, say in inches, it is always in principle possible to produce a more refined measure, say in half inches and so on ad infinitum. It will therefore sometimes happen, as this passage claims, that sticks that seem equal to one man will seem unequal to another, because the latter will be using a more refined measure. But just because there is an indefinite possibility of more refined measurement there is in many cases no answer to the question whether even agreed equals are really equal, however many refinements they have success-fully survived. This should be distinguished from a different point. The claim is not that they are really and forever unequal. It is not strictly true either that they are or are not simply because no sense can be given strictly to the idea of the precise length of a stick. Consequently it cannot strictly be said that the lengths of two 'equal' sticks have such and such a relationship to each other either of equality or inequality, and this is a general feature of 'equal' objects. They remind one of equality and aspire after it, but of their nature lack the precise measurability needed.

If we take the translation that the equal sticks are clearly equal to one thing, unequal to another, the point is quite different. Particulars are now viewed as capable of possessing apparently contradictory properties. The equal sticks are now not pairs, but individual sticks of any one of which one might say 'this is equal (to A)'. Yet any one is also clearly unequal (to some B). Their equality (and inequality, for that matter) is always a qualified equality. If we suppose the limitation to equality in length, the qualification is by reference to something to which A is equal. Without the limitation the qualification will always add 'in length', 'in weight' or whatever it may be. When we perceive sticks that we wish to call equal, we are 'reminded' of the procedure of relating measures. This procedure, however, demands familiarity with notions of measure, to whose applicability one is committed in calling them equal, and this is an intellectual not a perceptual matter.

There is a problem on this interpretation as to quite what is meant by the contrast between particulars and the Form. The complaint about particulars is that while equal in some respects to certain other particulars they are unequal in others to others. This suggests a contrast with something that is just equal, and this is a notoriously puzzling idea. Either it means it is equal, but not to anything, or it is equal, but its equality is not limited as 'in this respect' or 'to this'. It is a moot point which is more objectionable. And yet Plato does seem prepared to talk this way. For instance, in the *Symposium* (211) the Form of Beautiful is contrasted with beautiful bodies and characters in that it is not, as they presumably are, beautiful in one respect not another, to some people not others, and so on. Now in that particular case, a person who has grasped the Form of Beautiful has come to understand why the various beautiful things and characters are beautiful and to appreciate the beauty of the total system. He might understandably be described as having passed beyond what is beautiful as a such and such, or just in this respect. In the case of equality it would also be possible to think of passing beyond an interest in being equal in particular respects to the whole procedure of matching measures, but there is no similar temptation to call the end product 'equal'. This is, of course, part of the wider problem as to what Plato means by holding that Forms have the character of which they are Forms, and I shall return to that later. For the present it should be noted as a problem.

There is one slight pointer in favour of the first translation, and that is that the rogue sentence is followed by the question 'did the equals themselves ever seem unequal to you, or equality inequality?' The 'to you' in the dative, suggests that one take the dative in the previous sentence as also governed by 'seem' (instead of by 'equal'), in which case it must go 'seem equal to one man, not to another'. The point is hardly so weighty as to be decisive, however, and even if one accepts it, it remains uncertain what Plato's point is. On the other hand, the way in which he talks of particulars falling short and thereby being inferior (74d seq.) suggests more than that particulars are not concepts. They fail to be equal in the perfect manner of the Equal. This, as we have seen, is probably not a matter of being less equal, but of lacking some property possessed by the Equal. This might be lacking eternal equality, or lacking unqualified equality, or lacking, in the last resort, precise measurability. In the first case, the argument would only suggest that we are reminded of eternal by emphemeral being; on the last two, we are reminded of equality proper by equal things.

It is not possible to settle, at least from within the passage, which of these translations is correct. There are, however, certain things that emerge from the passage quite independently of that issue. To begin with, the concepts that are of interest at least for the purposes of this argument have certain special features. First, they are ones that we are inclined to apply to sensible objects, that is, actually observed objects. Concepts such as 'unicorn' are not of interest. Second, they are ones whose application typically embodies a claim to *episteme* which again would rule out 'unicorn'. Third, their application involves some reference to some standard to which observables are compared, or by which they are judged. If we consider the examples listed at 75c–d together with those at 65d–e, the suggestion is not, I think, of a contrast between having concepts and perceiving, but rather between judgments made on the basis of sense-observation using concepts such as 'equal', 'good', 'large', and some understanding implicit in the use of those concepts which cannot be yielded by the senses. Some of these terms are quantitative ones ('equal', 'large'), and others ('good', 'healthy', 'fine') are either specific to some skill or general to all. If we bear in mind Plato's insistence that all *epistemai* involve the use of mathematics it begins to look as though the point is that if we consider common *epistemai* it becomes clear that they employ concepts whose use implies reference to something outside the sphere of perception. It does not follow that for ordinary purposes of communication we need a clear understanding of this reference, nor that all concepts involve it. It is rather that all so-called knowledge employs concepts implying such reference. The complaint about the senses is not that they yield perception only and not judgment. The point is that certain judgments made about sensible objects certainly cannot be verified by the senses because the concepts used are ones whose applicability can only be judged by reason. Judgments of equality, for instance, require the use of mathematical techniques, and judgments about health require reference to a theory of proper physiological balance.Further, in some sense none of these concepts is strictly applicable to sensible phenomena. So far as this passage is concerned, of course, there might well be Forms of red, unicorn and so on, and it may be that Forms serve the function of safe-guarding the meaningfulness of all areas of language. All that is argued, however, is that certain terms that we tend to apply to the world, and whose use embodies a claim to *episteme*, imply a reference to Forms, and that to learn these terms a person has to acquire something more than an ability to identify by perception the things to which they apply and to apply them accordingly.

The point made in the earlier passage, that the senses cannot yield the truth is not made here, although it is implied that they cannot yield the truth on certain topics, and those ones essential to *episteme*. Later, at 78 seq. we find the point insisted on that the Forms are unchanging, particular objects rarely the same as themselves or each other. This is a distinction between types of object rather than methods of enquiry, but the distinction is made not simply in terms of changeableness and its opposite, but also in terms of the changeable being perceptible and the unchangeable not. Further, we are told at 79d that the grasp of un-changing objects is wisdom. It seems therefore that we have the same position as at 65 seq. that a contrast of capacity to reach the truth is tied to a contrast of object investigated. Also, the objects that do not yield the truth are now characterised as in constant, or near-constant change. In other words they are not susceptible of application of predicates taking a strict 'is'. So this would fit the view that in that earlier passage Plato has in mind this objection to the objects of observation, that they never strictly *are* anything, and consequently to judgments about observables that they are never properly to be construed as in the form 'X is F'. As this is the form for true judgments, they are never strictly true. So far, then, the objection to the senses is that judgments based on them about their objects can never strictly be true, and that they are incapable of yielding information about certain topics vital to *epistemai*, topics which demand the use of reason.

If we move on to 96 following, more is added to this picture. Socrates there recounts his dissatisfaction with accounts of the generation, destruction and existence of things offered by other philosophers. Study of these accounts left him confused. We are not told precisely how, but the result was that whereas he used to think that food turned into flesh and bone, and the addition of flesh and bone explained people's growth, he was now unsure of that explanation. The reason seems to have been a general uncertainty of the proper answer to 'why is A larger than B?' It would be natural to cite the additional material by which it exceeds B, but if one does that and says 'because of an extra head of height' or, in straight numbers, 'because it has two more', there is a dual peculiarity. First, we are assuming that the explanation of increase in quantity is addition, whereas division looks like being on occasion an equally good explanation. Second (cf. 101a–b), the head or the two units cited as explaining why A is larger than B can equally well, indeed do equally, explain why B is smaller than A. In other words we have the paradoxical situation where the proposed explanandum is explained equally by F and by the opposite of F, and where the proposed explanans will do equally well to explain F or the opposite of F. Socrates understandably feels that so accommodating an explanatory system is too generous by half, and must be incomplete. The shift from accounts of the generation of the universe to more mathematical examples presumably occurs because the 'cosmologies' are supposed to explain the changes in the universe, including growth and diminution. These latter changes will all naturally be explained using notions of addition or division, and the explanations will equally answer why A is now larger than B or B now smaller than A.

Socrates looks longingly at a mode of explanation suggested by the work of Anaxagoras, but which he has failed to develop, and from 99d onwards sketches an alternative way of explaining changes which will both avoid these paradoxes and help to prove the immortality of the soul. The beauty of things is to be explained by reference to the Beautiful, and things become large not by addition of units but by the acquisition of largeness. A thing's being large is never explained by its smallness, nor does its largeness ever explain its being small. So the explanans is limited in what it will explain, and the explanandum in what will explain it. This makes the explanation more acceptable than those considered earlier, and apparently also (cf. 100d) preferable to explaining a thing's being or becoming beautiful by referring to its gay colour or its shape. The inadequacy of these latter is not spelled out. It might be simply that they are at least different (but hardly opposed) explanations of the same feature, but he may also have in mind the point developed at *Hippias Major* (290), and possibly *Republic* Book V (479), that gay colour or a given shape which might seem on occasion to explain a thing's beauty might just as well explain why something else is ugly. In that case the situation will be similar to that with the other examples.

In all this nothing is made of any inadequacy of the senses. In the passage where Socrates hankers after Anaxagoras there is criticism of explaining happenings in terms of the physical conditions necessary for their occurrence, but while one may suspect that Plato thought this was a general absurdity, it is only developed as one for a person who claims that intelligence governs the universe. If one takes it, however, that Plato himself believes this, then he will be committed to the position that no amount of citing prior physical conditions will explain anything's coming to be as it is, or ceasing to be such. As physical things are all the senses observe, sense-observation will similarly be impotent to supply any adequate explanation of these matters. The rest of the passage insists on the superiority over other explanations of one referring to the Forms. The role assigned to the Forms here is not that of supplying meaning, but of accounting for the acquisition and possession of properties and the justification and rebuttal of the attribution of predicates. Not indeed all properties, but non-perceptible ones, and so not all predicates, but predicates whose application cannot be justified or refuted by observation alone but only at least in part by reasoning. Once again, the point is not any distinction between perception and judgment, but between an explanation offered in certain terms and one offered in others. The main complaint, however, is not in any obvious way against the senses. Indeed, the explanation of ten's outstripping of eight, that it is because of the two additional units, is one based on simple arithmetical considerations quite independently of observation. In the *Republic* also Plato was inclined to lump such examples together with ones more easily accommodated to sense-observation, and we have already noted that in the *Phaedo* he cites giving a gay colour as a possible example of the sort of explanation he deplores. This is certainly one likely to be based on observing what properties tend in certain circumstances to go with judgments of beauty. So it is quite likely that Plato does think that when it comes to questions of beauty, largeness and the rest the sort of answer to 'why is $X F$?' supplied by sense observation typically has the kind of unsatisfactoriness found in the examples given.

It has to be remembered in this context, that Plato does not start with any clearly worked out view of different styles of explanation. He does not even have the Aristotelian distinctions between formal, final, material and efficient causes. Consequently, when he asks 'why is $X F$?' or 'what is the explanation of X's being F?' he is likely to treat as possible candidates any answers that a person might give. We therefore find specimens that are likely to strike us as obviously not really explaining the matter at all, and many of which show considerable mutual differences. We do, however, habitually accept in various contexts a fair rag-bag of 'explanations'. Suppose someone wants to know why Jones' daffodils are larger than Smith's. He might be told that they are older, that they had more water last season, that they were larger bulbs, that they are a taller kind of daffodil, that they have longer stalks and so on. The last might seem futile, but after all it may be important that while Smith's daffodils are larger because they have bigger flowers, Jones' are larger because they have longer stalks, and on the settling of the dispute may hang a prize. Certainly such variety was played on in Plato's day. Plato's reaction was not, in the first instance, to distinguish kinds of explanation, but to insist that explanations should satisfy certain conditions of adequacy. To us it might seem that answering 'why has Sam more marbles?' by 'he has just got an extra twelve' is very different from answering 'why is Rachel beautiful?' by 'she has a clear complexion'. Plato is interested not in their differences, but in their shared inadequacy, their equal suitability in context for explaining someone's ending up with fewer marbles, or something's being ugly. Again, it might well strike us that when Plato complains that the explanans equally well explains opposite circumstances he is making an elementary mistake. The head of height or the gay colour may explain smallness or ugliness, but not of the subjects whose largeness or beauty they explain. Yet this is very likely Plato's point: that we only really understand the explanation if we also understand how and why these factors enter in in different contexts to explain some subject's deserving the opposite predicate. It is in fact an important feature of the predicates concerned that they are incomplete. No object can be just fine without being a fine such and such, nor equal without being equal to A or B. At first sight these examples still seem fairly dissimilar. The first suggests reference to a kind of thing so that substantiating the attribution of fineness would need knowledge of the kind of thing in question, and granted Plato's views on the principles on which classification should take place this knowledge is not to be acquired simply by sense-observation. At first sight nothing of this sort seems to hold with 'equal' or 'large' as it appears in the examples in the *Phaedo*. The only implied reference is to forms of measurement. If we remember, however, what was said in chapter IX on kinds of measurement, it may well be that Plato was not aware of the extent of the gap. Before the *Politicus* distinction between comparing relative quantities and discerning 'proper' quantities is made sharply the contrast would not be glaring. In that case Plato probably tended to think of measuring as primarily concerned with 'proper' measurement. So while questions of largeness would include *Phaedo* questions of relative size they would also be felt to involve questions of right size. This would be helped by the fact that not only could the Greek positives for 'large', 'small', 'fat', 'thin', like their English counterparts, carry connotations of excess and defect: the comparatives could mean 'too large' as well as 'larger', and similarly with the rest. Once these implications of excess intrude we have once more the situation where the relevant judgments require for their substantiation reference to the kind of thing that is being said to be large or whatever it may be.

Plato, then, shows interest in the *Phaedo* in explanation of the possession, loss and acquisition of certain properties. The sort of explanation one comes up with if one concentrates on observing what 'brings about' the changes fails in certain important cases to be a clearly complete explanation. This is where the change or possession in question is of one of a certain range of properties, the terms for which all show a form of incompleteness. The failure of the standard explanations is not in pin-pointing the physical conditions that produced the change, but in showing why the change produced should be described in the way proposed. This is not, however, Plato's way of describing the difference. He does not have any clear conception of different types of answer or different types of question. The answer sought is the complete answer to the original query, and indeed it seems from 104e following that the Forms do something like operating on the particulars, and thereby justifying our applying the relevant predicates to particulars.

So far this passage has been primarily concerned with differences of method and the adequacy of answer provided. The implicit objection to the senses has not been to their inability to yield any or certain concepts, but to the impossibility, by following certain methods relying on their use, of adequately explaining certain changes. There is also, however, a corresponding contrast of object. Thus at 102–3 particulars such as Simmias and Socrates are contrasted with Forms like large. The latter always is what it is, large, and will never admit of its opposite, small, while Socrates can, while remaining the same Socrates, admit of smallness (102e). In general, things are capable of receiving opposed attributes, and this is a necessary condition of changeability. The opposites themselves, on the other hand, do not have this capacity and cannot change (103b). Once again the stress seems to be on what can and what cannot properly be the subject of an eternal 'is', and it is propositions that contain such 'is'-es that are the mark of *episteme*. Quite what this difference of 'is'-es amounts to will be examined more fully in a later chapter. For the present it may be worth noting a peculiarity of the position as we have it in the *Phaedo*. It looks as though Plato wants to make it a mark of particulars that they do not possess eternally at least those attributes of which there are Forms. Within limits this might seem all right with Socrates and largeness. But what about 'man'? It sounds bizarre to suggest that Socrates can, while remaining the same (same what?), cease to be a man. Nor will it do to claim that after all Plato is not interested simply in particulars, but in physical particulars, and Socrates is a soul. To begin with, Socrates is Plato's own example, and second the objection holds equally well of, say, a particular hawthorn tree. Plato will have to do one of two things. He might say that the proper subject of propositions about physical objects is Place (or space). Even kind-nouns have to be interpreted as characterising space. The proposition 'this hawthorn tree is green' has to be read as 'space hawthorns greenly here'. Space, as the receptacle of (most) properties of which there are Forms, does, just by definition, have the required characteristic of being able, while remaining space, to acquire and lose the relevant properties. For thoughts along these lines, see *Timaeus* 49. It will, of course, be necessary to put restrictions on the range of terms to which there are corresponding Forms, but we have already seen reason to suppose that Plato already accepts limitations there. Alternatively, Plato might hold that his point is true only for certain of the properties for which there are Forms viz. those of which there are opposites, such as largeness. It does not work for ones like man. To this there are two objections. First, we should not in that case have any general difference between Forms and at least *physical* particulars of the sort that the passage seems to suggest – although it is true that opposites are the only examples given. Second, even if we restrict ourselves to opposites, the point could only hold within a fairly limited range of changes. Socrates may be smaller than Simmias without ceasing to be what he is, but he could hardly be or become smaller than a mosquito while preserving identity. At least, this could only be done with any plausibility by leaning heavily on identifying Socrates with his soul and claiming that that can readily inhabit a mosquito body. This saves the point, however, only by introducing obscurity elsewhere. For it is difficult to see how the predicates 'large' or 'small' apply at all, by participation or otherwise, to souls, and souls could not solve the difficulty with hawthorns.

I am not wanting to suggest by all this that Plato was clearly wanting to make a contrast in a specifiable way and was wrong. Quite the contrary. The point is that Plato does, in the *Phaedo* as elsewhere, want to contrast the Forms and physical particulars in terms of being and becoming, and this is related to capacity or incapacity for taking on opposed characters. But he is not clear how to do it and if one presses his statements difficulties quickly arise. Even within the present argument for immortality in the *Phaedo* some obscurity is caused by the example of fire. For this is said to be related to heat in such a way that it will not admit of cold without either being destroyed or retiring before it, and snow has a similar relation to cold and heat. It is hard not to take fire and snow as physical particulars, and yet they at least cannot admit of certain attributes while remaining the same sort of thing. Of course, the point of these examples is to enable us to understand what is being said about the soul, which is not a physical particular. It may therefore be that Plato would explain them away, if pressed. The fact remains that he does not do so, and it is quite possible that he did not clearly see how to.

If we now look back over the whole of the *Phaedo*, the following emerges: There are two dichotomies. First there is a dichotomy of objects of investigation. On the one hand there are visible (generally perceptible) physical objects, which are capable of receiving opposing attributes without changing their nature, and are in fact in a constant process of change; there is no F such that any of these strictly *is* F. On the other side there are Forms, which cannot be perceived by the senses, but only by thought and reason, which never receive the attributes opposed to them, which do not change but always are whatever it is they are. The second dichotomy is one of means of investigation. Here we have on the one hand the senses which are characteristically deceptive and go with an interest in the satisfaction of physical needs; these do not yield any finally satisfactory explanation of the situations and changes of the sort the early philosophers were interested in. On the other hand there is reason which can achieve the truth and an adequate explanation of what is to be explained. These two dichotomies are thought of as a single one. The capacity to receive opposing attributes is associated not only with the possibility but the actuality of change. There will therefore be a range of values for F such that no particular ever strictly *is* F, leaving other values of F which cover modes of becoming, so that once again the 'is' joining them to any subject is not to be taken seriously. If knowledge yields the truth and true propositions are of the form 'X is F', where the 'is' is to be interpreted strictly, then no form of investigation that either produces conclusions about changing objects, or conclusions expressed in predicates denoting modes of change, will constitute knowledge. Enquiries using sense-observation are all concerned with changing objects and the modes of their change. The requirement about truth similarly severely limits one both as to the possible subjects and predicates usable in expressing knowledge. Even within the domain of perceptibles any explanation of the changes observed by reference to observable antecedents will be demonstrably inadequate when the change is in respect of an attribute of which there is a Form. Any adequate explanation will require reference to something not subject to change. Forms consequently emerge as the only possible subjects of strictly knowable propositions, and as required for the explanation of certain changes even in the phenomenal world. Further, the use of certain predicates to describe phenomenal objects is never strictly justifiable, quite apart from the fact that the 'is' cannot be taken strictly and supposes some relation between the object and a Form, so that our use of these predicates of physical things, if correct, implies some acquaintance with Forms. The 'if correct' is important, for it is always possible that there is no knowledge properly so called, that our use of these terms is in no way justified and the world is not intelligible or explicable. So far as the *Phaedo* is concerned Forms are needed not to make language possible – for all it tells us, that might be possible without them – but to make *episteme* possible. *Episteme* is not a matter simply of, or perhaps even at all of, knowing the definitions of terms but of justifying their application. Further, it does not seem to be all terms that are in question, but ones whose application cannot be justified simply by looking to see how matters stand. We may judge that a horse is a fine horse just by looking at it, and appeal to visible features to justify our judgment but it is always assumed that the visible features are signs of a horse being in good condition – they do not constitute its good condition. Thus in the last resort the judgment's justification relies on appeal beyond simple correlation of observable phenomena. The complaint against the senses is that enquiry confined to sense-observation cannot supply knowledge on a given range of questions, and a range to which alone the answers deserve the name of knowledge. Such enquiry is at best useful for seeing to the satisfaction of the body's needs, to which Plato seems to think it will be typically directed. 'The senses' in fact, in this context, does not refer to the mere fact of perception, but to a whole range of intelligent enquiry that in Plato's view necessarily fails to produce answers of timeless validity, or even adequate explanations of the phenomena investigated.

A similar situation seems to hold in the *Republic*. There again the senses are associated with an inferior state of knowledge, which deals only with changeable and perceptible objects (cf. 508–9). This inferior grade of knowledge, however, does not consist just of seeing or hearing. At 533b–c the condition of the man who does mathematics proper is marked off from inferior states, which can only be forms of *doxa* concerned with the perceptible world. They include nevertheless skills directed to satisfying the opinions and desires of men, or concerned with development and construction or the care of living things and artefacts. This presumably covers accomplishments such as building, medicine, farming, generalship and those skills that at 525–6 are said to involve the use of mathematics but not in the way that Socrates is interested in. This is what one would expect from the first introduction of the distinction between *episteme* and *doxa* in Book V. Those only capable of *doxa* are certainly said to be mainly interested in sights and sounds (cf. 475d, 476b, 480a), but they are also men of practical interest with a love of competence (476a–b). There is no suggestion that people who have only reached the stage of *doxa* are not competent and do not, in the ordinary English sense, know how to (what will) produce the effects they pursue. In Book V the context is one of looking for someone who will know what is best for the state, be able to rule it justly and educate its citizens properly. It is here that the competent pretenders to influence are criticised, in that they cannot claim to have knowledge about what is fine and just and the rest. They fail because what they offer is as it stands just as good an answer to 'what is base?'

or 'what is unjust?' They are in no position to explain why their answer is even satisfactory up to a point. The people considered there are portrayed as making a virtue of this fact, but the argument from 476e to 479d is intended to rebut any possible claim on their part to *episteme* on certain important topics, and on the grounds, reminiscent of the *Phaedo*, that their answers just as well answer the opposed question. So once again the objection is to a method of enquiry as incapable of supplying adequate answers on a given range of questions. Once again, also, it seems clear that the inadequacy is not primarily to do with inability to give a definition of a term. This becomes clear in at least two ways. First, the knowledge of what is fine and just that it is hoped that philosophers will acquire is considered important not because they will now know what the words mean, but because they will now know what rules to lay down (484c–d) and how to tell real from apparent good (520–1). Second, it is apparent that there is an issue giving rise to some animus between those who say that there are many justs and beautifuls and those who claim there is just one, an animus that it is difficult to understand if the claim that there is a Form in each case is simply the claim that the terms can be defined. If, for instance, we defined 'good' as 'found likeable' no offence could be caused to the sophists of 493. Indeed, that seems to be the definition with which they are operating, and their experience might lead them to conclude that any (any sort of) thing found good will also be found bad, on the lines of 479a. So the simple fact of the term's definability cannot be objectionable to them. Yet they are portrayed at 479a as not being able to bear the suggestion that there is one Fine, and this suggestion is said at 493e–494a to arouse general hostility among non-philosophers. It seems fairly clear from the context there that asserting that there is just one Fine, Good and so on would involve rejecting the appeal to people's likes and dislikes practised by the sophists and politicians. In other words it would amount to saying that whether or not something is fine or good can in principle be established. To say that there is a Form of F is more than to say that 'F' has meaning and can be defined; it is to claim that statements of the form 'X is F' are either true or false, and their acceptability is to be judged objectively and not by reference to the tastes of individuals or groups. In short, the claim that there is a Form of F is tantamount to the claim that *episteme* is possible in a certain area. This brings out a further restriction on the use of 'is'. After all, if 'good' meant 'found likeable' Plato could have been satisfied to claim that his opponents could not have knowledge of goodness because their concern was solely with things in process. Instead the further point is made that if we are seriously to say that X is F, then 'F' must be an 'objective' predicate.

In this chapter I have been considering objections to the senses found in the *Phaedo* and the *Republic*. The purpose has been to see what light they throw on arguments in the *Theaetetus* and *Cratylus* and whether together with those they support a particular picture of Plato's reaction to the combined influences of Socrates and Heracleiteanism. I have not dealt with all the passages where Plato indicates his reasons for discounting the senses and the objects of perception (cf. e.g. *Timaeus* 28, 37–8, 49) because while they undoubtedly exist, I think they neither add to nor subtract from the account given. What emerges from the texts considered so far is that Plato shows no signs of objecting to a flux doctrine as applied to the physical world, and that his objection to it as applied to Forms is not to the idea of a flux of meanings but to a flux in the way the world is structured. Forms have to be posited if the universe is to be intelligible, not if language is to be possible. There could be language in a Formless universe. They are needed for an intelligible universe at least because the answers given by *episteme* must be expressible in strict 'is'-es. The Protagorean/Heracleitean claim is that no 'is'-es can be strict. If they are to be, this imposes conditions both on the subjects and predicates admissible. Plato is particularly interested in a subset of predicates whose application cannot be justified by reference to observable properties but which play an important role in the *epistemai*, and the conditions for learning which differ from those that obtain with terms for perceptible similarities. All this tells against the view that Forms are meanings or are posited to explain the possibility of general terms. At least it tells against that being their sole function, for of course it may be that they seemed to supply the answers to a number of problems which are in fact different and require different tools for their solution. Certainly there are remarks in the *Sophist* (259e) and *Parmenides* (135b–c) which suggest that no Forms would mean no language, and the earlier dialogues seem full of demands for definitions and often, especially as one gets into the middle dialogues, these occur where it is clear that what we are interested in is Forms. It may seem that, though Plato confused definitions with something else, he was at least interested in them, that Forms are at least sometimes supposed to be meanings, that part of the time anyway he felt that Heracleiteans left concepts out of account, and that he made this point by saying that they ignored the fact that there are Forms. To sort this question out it will be necessary first to discuss the search for definitions in the early to middle dialogues and then examine what Plato's difficulties about 'is' amount to in these contexts. This might help us get clearer as to just what his main problems were and trace some development in his treatment of them. It might also be helpful in deciding how many problems are being run together and whether the use of Forms commits Plato, in relation to any of them, to treating knowledge as a form of perception. Finally, it will bring out more clearly the importance for him of strict 'is'-es, a point that is open to considerable criticism.

XI

Being and Definition

It has, I hope, become clear that Plato's complaint about the senses and sensible objects does not stem from the view that if the world was in flux it would be indescribable so that we have to postulate stable meanings for general terms. The point is rather that such a world, while describable would not be one of which *episteme* was possible. It is not only that sensible objects are not possible subjects for strict 'is'-es; the predicates appropriate for their straight description cannot be tied by a strict 'is' to any subject. This is not to deny that they retain the same meanings but to assert that the accounts of their meanings will make it clear that they attribute modes of change. Since Parmenides it had become in many circles axiomatic that any true proposition must be expressible in the form 'X is F' and the 'is' be quite unqualified. Greek epistemological scepticism tended therefore to take the form of arguing that unqualified 'is-'es are impossible, either on the grounds that any X that is F is in some way also not-F, or on the grounds that the world is in constant process and all descriptions are attributions of process. The first tends to the conclusion that any X is only F in relation to something and there is never any general method of settling whether it is F. This can cover a multitude of positions. It might be the claim that nothing is ever good, but only good to Jones (i.e. in his opinion good) or good to Smith. Or it might be the claim that a transaction that is good for Jones is bad for Smith, and there is no question of whether it is good or bad *simpliciter* (cf. *Dialexeis*, Diels (1954), II, p. 405). The predicates in which Plato was particularly interested were very susceptible to this sort of treatment, and he was concerned to assert that they could not be subjectivised or relativised in these ways. The second line of attack, from process, claims that the world is such that there is nothing for the stabilising 'is' to apply to. Plato wants to hold that such an 'is' does have application. It is here that he seems closest to an interest in definition, for definitions certainly seem to contain the sort of timeless 'is' sought for. We have seen reason to suppose that it is not just anything that could count as a definition, however. The question remains whether it is right, with regard to the cases in which Plato is interested, to describe his interest as one in the definition of these terms, perhaps allied to a position that some terms are not, in some strict sense, definable.

If we look at the examples in the early to middle dialogues where Plato complains about the answers given by others to his questions and at his own illustrations of proper answers, it can certainly look as though he has some ideal of definition in mind. To take the complaints about answers first, many of these are of course criticisms of the actual answer, showing it to cover too many or too few cases. But some are of the style of answer. Thus in the *Laches* at 190e, Laches answers the question 'what is *andreia*?' by saying that a man who is prepared to fight off the enemy, keeping his place in the battle order and not running away, is brave. Socrates complains that in the cavalry fighting is some-times conducted by running away which is what courage consists of there, and that men in danger at sea or in political life can be brave. What he wants to know is what it is in all these cases that is picked out by the word '*andreia*'. To start with it looks as though the objection is going to be like those mentioned in discussing the *Phaedo*, that what Laches gives as making a man brave would in other contexts count against his being so. But it develops simply into the point that *andreia* can be manifested in many different contexts and we need some account of what is in common to them all. We are not interested in examples of people who are brave, but in the meaning of 'brave'. No doubt it is assumed that 'brave' is not a word like 'nice', that there is something in common to the things to which it is applied and not just to the circum-stances of its use. Still, the complaint seems to be that Laches is giving instances instead of giving a definition.

The complaint seems much the same at *Meno* 71d–73c. Meno has been asked to say what *arete* is and has answered that it differs according to whether you are a man, woman, child, slave and so on. Socrates replies that if he had asked Meno about the nature of bees, they would surely not differ in so far as they were bees, but only in respect of other properties. As I have already pointed out (p. 34), there are peculiarities about Socrates' objection, in that he is not concerned with the question 'what is excellence?' so much as the question 'what is human excel-lence?' It remains that with regard to this second question there is the demand for a common feature in all human excellence whose presence justifies our use of the expression of various human beings. Meno has cited examples of excellences which differ in some ways, but has made the mistake of giving things that are excellences instead of telling us what it is to be an excellence. The point is made even more clearly in the *Theaetetus* in criticism of Theaetetus' first 'definition' of knowledge, where he says (146c–d) that shoemaking and other skills are all and each precisely knowledge. Socrates points out that each of these skills is knowledge of some subject-matter, and the question was not 'what is there knowledge of?' nor 'how many branches of knowledge are there?' but 'what is it to be knowledge?'

These passages are samples of a common theme where Socrates tries to persuade his interlocutor to give not examples but a definition, and other complaints are the ones one would expect from someone looking for a definition, indicating that the answer is either too broad or too narrow to correspond to the term in question. This picture is further borne out if we turn to the illustrations of answers that would be satisfactory. At *Laches* 192a–b speed is defined as the ability of accomplishing a good deal in a short time; at *Meno* 75–6 figure is defined as what always accompanies colour or surface and as the limit of a solid; at *Theaetetus* 147a–c mud is defined as earth mixed with water. In all these cases we have what seem to be attempts at defining the terms concerned. Moreover, in the *Theaetetus* passage (147b) the point is explicitly made that no one can understand the word for X if he does not understand what X is. This seems to tie the operation to the understanding of ordinary words. Definition by species and genus, say, is not typically connected with elucidating the meanings of day to day words like 'cat' and 'dog', but rather with establishing satisfactory zoological classifications of cats and dogs. The *Theaetetus* remark sounds as though Plato is less concerned with the proper cutting up of reality and more with what is necessary for language to be possible viz. that words have meanings. In this it seems nearer to earlier definition seeking dialogues than middle/late specimens like the *Phaedrus, Sophist* or *Politicus*. So whatever may be true of later trends, it seems that the early hunt for something that is X is well described as a search for definitions. It is no doubt an unfortunate fact that Plato assumed that the terms concerned operated like proper names, so that he thought there was some object named of which the proposed definition was a complete or at least identifying description. The fact remains that within the range of terms in which Plato is interested any definition would count as an answer to 'what is X?', and any answer that seems acceptable at least looks like a good attempt at a definition. Consequently one might expect that Plato would recognise an adequate account of definition as meeting at any rate his major needs.

For all that, the picture is not so clear as this makes it look. To begin with, as has often been pointed out (e.g. Robinson 1953 ch. V), the sample definitions are typically informative definitions that might be expected to help one identify instances and settle doubtful cases. It is true that when in *Republic* Book I Thrasymachus tells Socrates not to give an answer of the form 'the just is what is fitting or what is beneficial', Socrates suggests that if that is the right answer then perhaps it should be given (336–7). But when Socrates actually addresses himself to the examination of 'justice' in Books II–IV he is clearly interested in a more informative answer, and the definition 'justice is each part performing its own task' sums up an elaborate account of the operation of 'justice' and the functions of the various parts of the soul/state. Indeed, Plato seems not at all interested in a verbal equivalence but rather in understanding the role of an identifiable phenomenon. Plato might, of course, have a realist view of the (primary) function of language, that its purpose is to reflect reality and so enable us to acquire and transmit the truth about the nature of the world (cf. *Cratylus* 388). In that case he might be inclined to concentrate on characterising terms, ignoring ones like 'and' or 'but' which obviously simply have the role of indicating connections between other terms or sentences. He might now tend to assume that nouns and adjectives stand for realities and that their definition will consist in itemising any simpler elements of which the reality for which they stand is composed. With such a view it would perhaps be understandable that he should conflate the questions 'what does "*dikaios*" mean?' and 'what constitutes a "*dikaios*" arrangement?' It might seem to us possible to distinguish the questions fairly sharply. Thus we might answer the first by saying that '*dikaios*' as applied to a city's or individual's life means 'correctly regulated'. But that rather obviously leaves open, not to say raises, the further question 'what sort of life counts as properly regulated?' That is a question that anyone who understood the definition of '*dikaios*' might well want to ask, but one whose answer is not given by the definition. If Plato holds the view of language attributed to him above he might be inclined to think that unless a person knows what sort of life is properly regulated then he does not know the reality for which the expression 'properly regulated' stands and so has no grasp of its definition/meaning. If this is true then not merely is Plato requiring 'descriptive definitions of evaluative terms' but also, more generally, fuzzing the distinction between understanding an expression and knowing what it is true of. Indeed, it seems to be a feature of many expressions such as 'large', 'above average', 'the conclusion of the premises . . .' that understanding them involves realising that they can be used in many contexts. While, if one understands them, one will have some idea of the way to go about checking the claim made one could never learn them if it was a condition of doing so that one had to know what substantiated it. Thus if a person is said to be above average in at least one respect, then we shall know that if this is true there must be some feature allowing of degrees in which he can be compared with other things and in respect of which he comes out as having a higher degree than the average – and we have some idea of how to determine averages. But this is a far cry from knowing what sort of feature he excels in or all the possible features that would constitute being above average. Even if we specify intelligence as the relevant feature, and granted we know how to measure it, understanding the expression is clearly only understanding the problem set, not knowing the answer to it.

This conflation would suggest that Plato's prime interest is in knowing what is just, fine, good and so on even if he mistakenly supposes that this will be achieved by better definition. It might be worth wondering whether the concentration on definition may not be misleading. As we have seen, the approach to the question 'what is "justice"?' in the *Republic* does not look at all like an attempt to define if this is taken to consist in elucidating the meaning of the term. In the *Theaetetus* again (147d–148d) Theaetetus suggests that his own discovery in mathematics is an example of what Socrates is after, and Socrates agrees. Now the details of that discovery need not delay us, but one thing at least is clear: Theaetetus was not concerned to give a clear account of some familiar term. Rather, he had discovered a way of distinguishing one set of numbers so as to make it possible to answer in a general way a question that Theodorus has had to tackle piecemeal. If Theaetetus' answer really is the sort that Socrates wants, then one would expect something more than a verbal equivalent as the requirement. An answer on the lines of 'knowledge is justified true belief' would be unhelpful just because it leaves open the question of when, if ever, true belief is justified. In fact, of course, many philosophers have been at least as concerned to answer this last question as the definitional one. If Theaetetus' solution is taken as a model of what Socrates wants, then one would expect him to be looking for an answer that would enable him to distinguish among putative *epistemai* between those whose claim to that status could be justified and those whose claim could not. Someone possessed of the answer would be able to tell the genuine from the false claimants and explain why each should be put in their respective categories. Someone pursuing this ambition will, of course, have some interest in definitional points, and definitional objections will be in order. His main interest, however, will not be in how to define '*episteme*' but in establishing which claimants to the title are genuine ones.

The suggestion is not that Plato had a clear grasp of the distinction between asking what '*episteme*' means and asking how we establish that a given discipline is an *episteme*. The question is rather which of these questions best reflects his predominant interest and the suggestion is that the second does so. It is not, therefore, that he is working out views on definition that get distorted by misguided requirements about meaning. His interest is in what constitutes a just life, what is genuine *episteme* and so on, but as he has not got a sharp distinction between this question and definitional ones, we get a mixture of examples. Many of the examples look like attempts at defining familiar terms, but Plato's interest in them is not that they are definitions but that they have the required completeness. Even so, it seems clear from the *Meno* that what is sought is some account that isolates the phenomenon in question rather than an account of the meaning of the term. If one takes medicine as an example, the suggestion is that Plato wants an answer to 'what is health?' In Greek this can be phrased as 'what is the healthy?' There is therefore a temptation to give a list of things that give health, or to talk of the health of men, the health of chickens and so on. Neither of these answers is satisfactory because neither tells us what constitutes health. An adequate answer, however, would not be of the form 'health is physical well-being' but would explain how to judge physical well-being in men and other animals. Medicine (here including veterinary medicine) would in his view need some theoretical account of health. This would not be a description of states of change but an account of a standard that enables us to judge actual conditions and the desirability or otherwise of various changes. The description of the norm of health would be in the desired strict 'is'-es, and there would be no room for counter-examples. On the other hand, for Plato to illustrate what he wanted by reference to an example like medicine would obviously be extremely cumbersome and open to all the *Meno* style of objections on the way. The quasi-definitional examples are briefer, clearer and not so vulnerable. At the same time the definition of 'figure' shows how the many can be brought under the one: the fact that there are three-sided and four-sided figures is no hindrance to saying what figure is. The quasi-definitional examples are valuable, not because Plato is interested in defining terms and these are cases in point, but because they are examples of strict 'is'-es that are readily appreciated, and ones that accommodate a variety of kinds in the way characteristically needed for the examples in which Plato is interested.

At the same time Plato does seem to have certain half-formed views about words that cause difficulties and become subject to development. In the earlier dialogues questions like 'what is courage?', 'what is temperance?' and so on are expected to receive answers that give a feature in common to all cases. With some words, like 'red', there is an observable common feature. With those in which Plato is interested, the notable point is that there is no observable common feature. On the contrary, if one looks at typical examples one is struck by the dissimilarity. It is assumed nevertheless that there must be a similarity to be found, even if it is one that has to be found by reason. This is a very natural assumption. If a general term in some vague sense describes, and applies unambiguously to a number of different things, then surely those things must have something in common? They must resemble each other at least in the respect covered by the description in question. No doubt the notion of similarity gets a little stretched: squares are not all that like circles. That is not simply the point that they do not look alike. The conditions for being the one are incompatible with those for being the other. Yet in so far as they are figures it must be possible to give the necessary and sufficient conditions for being a figure which are satisfied by all figures, and it is hardly an extreme move to call this a respect in which they resemble each other. This position seems to be implicit and sometimes explicit in the earlier to middle dialogues (cf. e.g. *Euthyphro* 5d, *Meno* 74d, *Republic* 435a–b). In cases like 'courage', 'human excellence' and so on, unless one has views about evaluative terms not being susceptible of descriptive definition, it might seem sensible to hope that one could find answers on the general lines of that for 'figure', so that one could have necessary and sufficient conditions for being an instance of courage that accommodated and even explained the other dissimilarities between instances. Further, one might hope that the properties common to all members of the class were such that knowing them would enable one to identify members of the class independently, and without knowing relationships between them. The position looks less attractive if one moves to examples like 'fine', 'good' and wishes to hold the synoptic type of position that Plato seems to want in the *Symposium* and *Republic*. At least the notion of similarity has to receive an even sharper stretch. Suppose we take an excellent rhubarb plant and an excellent human being. What is the common feature denoted by 'excellent'? We are not requiring sensible similarity, but it is hard to see what analogue of the illustration on figure is likely to be forthcoming. If Plato holds the sort of view attributed to him in chapter II, then the functions of rhubarb and men might be expected to be quite different, so that the characteristics that make for excellence in each case will be different. The sort of demand made in the case of human excellence in the *Meno* will therefore hardly be in order. One will be able to expect that each function can be shown to play a part in a more complex system, but, as the parts will be different, calling this fact a point of similarity is to use a very attenuated notion of similarity. If Plato does not hold that view, then presumably his answer to 'why are all good things justifiably called by the same name?' is 'because they all partake in the Form of the Good'. Once again, however, this contrasts with the figure example. For there we at least were given an answer that supplied conditions and did not amount to the uninformative 'they are all figures'. 'They all partake of the Form of the Good (or all resemble it)' seems at best, so far as the present point is concerned, to assert that there is a point of similarity. The only grounds for this assertion, however, would seem to be the assumption that there must be, since otherwise it would be unjustifiable to use the common term. In face of the apparent all round dissimilarity of goods, this looks like a move born of desperation. In either case the similarity demand is running into difficulties. In dialogues after the *Republic* Plato starts to show some awareness of these difficulties. Thus in the *Phaedrus* (265–70) we find a shift in methodological recommendation. It cannot be assumed that a term like '*mania*' denotes a point of similarity between *maniai*. It is important to distinguish and characterise the forms of *mania*. Any given form of *mania* does constitute a way in which certain *maniai* resemble each other, and isolating these resemblance groups is important for the furtherance of knowledge. The question 'what is *mania*?', however, can no longer be assumed to be answerable by giving the way in which *maniai* resemble each other. What form the justification of the use of the same term might take is left obscure, but it is made clear that if we are to understand about *mania* it is as important to examine the differences between different kinds of *maniai* as the similarities between members of subsets. This shows dissatisfaction with the assumption in the demands of dialogues like the *Meno*. At the same time the importance of discovering similarities is still there, as it is still in the *Politicus* (cf. 285). By the *Philebus* the similarity assumption comes in for explicit attack, and in terms and with examples that so closely recall the *Meno* (cf. *Philebus* 12c–13a, *Meno* 72–5 esp. 74c–d) as to suggest conscious change of mind. At *Philebus* 18b–d we get the example of Theuth discovering how to reduce the formation of speech to a manageable discipline by the invention of letters. The purpose of this and the preceding examples is to show how one name may not only not indicate a point of similarity, but even cover opposites and so perhaps give a respect in which things may be opposed. The various sounds for which letters are devised do not resemble each other. On the contrary, they are opposed to each other as pronounceable in isolation and unpronounceable in isolation. What justifies the use of the common description 'letter' is that they all form part of an interrelated set of elements which make it possible to expound the difference between properly and improperly combined sounds in the context of a given language. Apparently the important factors in the advancement of knowledge are to be able to establish a single set of elements and explicate the relationships between the elements. This is not hunting for any similarity, but, in Pythagorean fashion, finding ways of reconciling opposites. There is by now a complete abandonment of the earlier view that one is only justified in using a common term if one can give necessary and sufficient conditions whose satisfaction by instances can be independently tested, so as in some not too weak sense to count as a similarity.

Unfortunately, once the difficulties start the floodgates open. It is not clear that what looks well with terms like 'note' and 'letter' will look so good when it comes to '*mania*' or '*episteme*'. In all these cases, however, one might hope for some account of why the various instances receive the same name, however different in style the accounts might be. When it comes to terms such as 'is', 'other', 'same', 'similar' and so on the position seems quite different. It is difficult to say to what extent Plato recognised this. The examples of 'note' and 'letter' are supposedly illustrating a way out of a difficulty that has arisen in relation to pleasure and knowledge. That suggests that he thought of them all as susceptible of the same treatment. *Parmenides* 147c–148a might suggest that he had seen the absurdity of supposing that 'different' stands for a property, but it only in fact shows that he has seen that it does not stand for a respect in which things resemble each other. It does not exclude his thinking that there is some general account available to explain why things that are called different are justifiably so called, nor that that account takes the form of establishing an *episteme* of difference. *Sophist* 257c–d, indeed, suggests that he thought difference and knowledge basically alike. Perhaps, too, the sophistry denounced at *Philebus* 13d is the one used at *Parmenides* 147. But it is used to illustrate the results of applying Protarchus' principle indiscriminately so as to damp his enthusiasm for it as applied to pleasure. No doubt it would be or should be adequate for that, but for what it is worth there is no sign that Plato thinks there is any important difference between difference and similarity on the one hand and knowledge and pleasure on the other, simply that he thinks the unacceptable consequences of Protarchus' stand more obvious in the former case than in the latter. In fact from the *Sophist* it would appear that even at quite a late stage he was still in the wood. The three great kinds, Being, Sameness and Difference, are all-pervading. That is to say, for every X, X is something, is the same as itself and is different. But these kinds are like the vowels of reality (253), and true knowledge consists in knowing what vowels join what consonants, in knowing what everything is joined to by 'is' or separated from by 'different'. There is consequently a study of difference to be engaged in, and in this case it is explicitly said that difference like knowledge has parts. In other words not being beautiful and not being large are related to difference in the same way that geometry and astronomy are related to *episteme*. For all that some kinds, including difference, are likened to vowels in contrast with others that are like consonants, the point made by that seems merely to be one of greater degree of pervasiveness. This indicates a lack of sharp differentiation between the terms.

All in all, then, it looks as though Plato started with an assumption that any general term that could be true of some subject must stand for some identical nature that was shared by the subjects of which it was true, and constituted a point of similarity between them. As time went on this came to seem progressively unacceptable, but he never arrived at a satisfactory sorting of the different types of term involved. This failure is probably at least partly due to the fact that he is not primarily interested in the meanings of terms or differences of type of term, but, to put it crudely, in the nature of the universe. Interest in being and difference is consequently an interest in proper ways of classifying and differentiating, an interest in knowing the proper concepts to have and their interrelationships. It is of some significance that the awareness of difficulties comes immediately after the *Republic* group of dialogues. As I have already pointed out it is about that period that Plato becomer enamoured of the ideal of explanation in terms of how it is best for things to be. In so far as this goes with a tendency to ask for a thing's function no difficulty would arise. That would simply involve a tendency to show an interest in kind-concepts like 'man', 'bed' and 'shuttle'. Possibly knowing man's function would be important for determining what true manliness is, but one might hope for early dialogue style answers to 'what is man?' as well as to 'what is manliness?' If, however, as I have suggested, the shift goes with a desire for establishing the relationship of this function with others in a broader system, then it will no longer be possible to ask in *Meno* terms for a definition of excellence, confining it to human excellence. Once one starts asking on a broader front what excellence is, and why/if the supposed human excellences are good, then one will obviously start feeling dissatisfied with the early dialogue assumption.

What emerges so far then is the following. From the start Plato is primarily interested in knowing what justice, courage, temperance consist in, in the sort of way in which a doctor might be expected to know what health consisted in. He does, however, start with an expectation as to the form the answer will take which seems to stem from a general view as to what would justify using the same word of a number of subjects. This makes him hope for answers to 'what is X?' such that armed with them we could settle the question of whether or not any proposed candidate was an X independently of reference to other members of the class. This project becomes less attractive when it comes to terms like 'good', and then starts looking unattractive in many other cases as well. The old ambition to justify the inclusion of a variety of forms of X under a single heading by finding a more rarefied similarity begins to wane until by the *Philebus* it is claimed that advance in knowledge is only achieved by recognising that we should abandon the search for similarity and seek for ways of bringing dissimilars, not to say opposites, into interrelation in a single discipline. This certainly involves recognising in effect that terms like 'note', 'colour' and so on, differ from others such as 'red'. He is not, however, starting a Wittgensteinian line on family resemblances, or any view about the impossiblity of giving unified complete accounts of the meanings of ordinary terms. In fact in *Philebus* 16–18 vocal sound (*phone*) is something in which a unit can be found in at least two ways, in music and the devising of letters. Neither of these is giving an account of the meaning of '*phone*'. Each is the devising of a means of dealing with the phenomenon of *phone,* and each leads to the devising of its own technical vocabulary. It is true that the technical vocabulary does not meet the requirements of the early-dialogue prejudice, and that that point is considered important. But the procedure of discovering a unit has nothing to do with elucidating familiar terms, but with bringing an amorphous phenomenon under the management of a discipline. The interest is in how true science is to be advanced, not in how concepts are to be analysed.

Although, if this is true, Plato moved away from an interest in every-day words, and never had a general interest in ordinary language, it is nevertheless true that one of his starting-points is an area of ordinary language and its elucidation. As we have seen in discussing the *Phaedo,* Plato thinks that our use of some terms (e.g. 'equal', 'healthy', 'just', 'fine') commits us to some reference beyond the things to which we commonly apply them. These terms do not describe observable features of what they are used of. 'Equal' involves a claim about measures, 'healthy' a reference to a norm, and similarly with 'just' and 'fine'. Even calling something large or fat invites the question 'what is the proper size?' If I am right about Plato's approach to mathematics (cf. chapter VII) then a reference to measure will in the end be one to proper measure. There is, therefore, implicit in the use of these terms, if Plato is right about them, a view that the world is not just a succession of events, not even a regular succession, but consists of things constructed on a functional model. For of any X of which these terms can properly be used it must be possible to answer the question 'what does X do, what is its function?' The answer will not give the actual performances of actual men, or whatever X may be, but the man-function by reference to which actual men can be judged as good or bad. So the use of terms assessing merit presupposes a functional interpretation of the terms for the things assessed. This is thought to be a fact about language, and Plato is fairly confident that if his fellow Greeks call something good, etc., they will feel the appropriateness, when pressed just a little, of the demand for some account of the function of the thing called good. 'Good at what?', 'good for what?' are felt to be questions that will be taken as always relevant. This would mean that these classifications were done on the basis of functions. If people can further be got to recognise the paradox of talking of good Xes when Xes seem to be a bad sort of thing, then it will emerge that we betray, in the way we talk and think, that we assume a certain view of the universe. On the other hand, this is not a generally recognised assumption, and indeed after a little Socratic pressure it becomes clear that most of us are not at all clear what we are saying when we use these particular terms, although in some sense we must know what they mean in order to recognise the inadequacy of our answers. This is sometimes taken to be the familiar paradox of philosophy, that in some way philosphers already know the meanings of the terms whose meanings they seek. But Plato is not, at least primarily, interested in this. His point is not that we are possessed of words of which we cannot readily give adequate definitions but that we apply words of whose application we can give no ready justification. The words concerned are not abstruse ones, but very common. Yet to justify their application it is not enough to observe how things actually happen, one would have also to show that the way things are is interpretable as a functional system. This is well beyond the average man's capacity, and cannot be achieved simply by accumulating sense-observations. The average man's radical inability to justify his application of these terms might well have seemed to raise doubts not only about his ability to define them, but even about his really understanding them. It might therefore in these cases be tempting to slip in the converse, that really understanding them is knowing whether their use is justified or not. As *'episteme'* is a case in point, the remark in the *Theaetetus* is very likely a sign of this mistake, but also the mistake is probably not one that is made as part of a thesis about meaning in general, but as part of a thesis about a certain range of important terms and the possibility of justifying their application. To start with there seems to be little question that the classifications we have are pretty well right, though not commonly thoroughly understood. In theory, however, it could be that we are radically mistaken. This possibility seems clearly envisaged in the *Cratylus,* and the *Parmenides* (130d) may give us an example where Plato thinks reform is needed. The young Socrates is portrayed as being unsure as to whether there are Forms of mud and hair, as they just are what we see them to be. Parmenides tells him that as he progresses he will be less abashed by the possibility. Socrates' unwillingness to admit these Forms might well have sprung from the fact that the ordinary terms as commonly understood do not invite talk of good mud or hair. The terms are not defined in terms of any function. It would be uncritical acceptance of the language we start with to let matters rest there, and further investigation might well reveal previously unsuspected functions. So while ordinary language embodies an assumption, the assumption could be unjustified, or ordinary language might not carry it far enough. But of this more later.

The result of all this is that while, in accord with his objection to the senses, Plato is, in positing Forms and asking 'what *is X*?', looking for answers that contain strict 'is'-es, it is not definitions of familiar terms that he is interested in. This becomes clearer if we look more closely at his manœuvres with the verb 'to be'. Notoriously, Plato wants to gloss the 'is' in 'Helen is beautiful' and read it as 'Helen partakes in the Beautiful'. The introduction of a special term suggests that he thinks that 'is' is somewhat misleading. The Beautiful itself, on the other hand, does not partake of the Beautiful, but just is beautiful. Often some term for 'resembles' is used instead of 'participates', but in either case there is clearly a contrast intended between 'is' when used of Forms and 'is' when used to attribute the relevant property to physical particulars. One attractive account of what the distinction amounts to goes as follows: Parmenideans declared that change and multiplicity were impossible, because if they occurred it would follow of some things either that they while being ceased to be, or were and were not at the same time. By introducing his glosses Plato is giving an interpretation of 'is' whereby it is possible for Socrates, while remaining Socrates, to change from small to large. He could not, of course, cease to be Socrates, but he is not, in the sense in which he is Socrates, either large or small. He simply has these properties, and so may lose them. The gloss is a not wholly successful attempt to distinguish between identity and attribution. It is not wholly successful because it is done via a special model of attribution. The model is what might be called a portrait model. Faced with a number of pictures of Socrates one might well say 'there is Socrates, and there he is again'. In a sense one seems to have a number of Socrateses and yet none really is Socrates. Only Socrates is strictly Socrates. Taking this as a model, we might look on particular beautiful things as imitations or portraits, only being beautiful in the derivative way in which the portraits of Socrates are Socrates. But Socrates alone is without qualification Socratic, and similarly the Beautiful alone is without qualification beautiful. Socrates is, no doubt, paradigmatically Socratic just because he is Socrates, and similarly with the Beautiful. The result of the model, however, is not quite to catch the contrast between identity and attribution, because one consequence of it is that the attribute of beauty does attach to the Beautiful if to anything, and that is part of what is meant by claiming that the Beautiful *is* beautiful. Further, the cost of accounting for change this way is that one has to postulate a Form corresponding to every attribute. Now Plato might say things that commit him to this, and he might have thought that this sort of argument supported the same position that other considerations lead to, without at first or even at last realising that it lets in many more Forms than are required or even desired on other considerations. The fact remains that, as we have seen, Plato tends to concentrate on a special set of terms as requiring Forms, and to talk as though others do not raise similar problems.

Whatever we make of this last point, it seems certain that the proposed interpretation at least gives too clear a picture of what Plato is up to.

For the suggestion is that Plato is trying, although unsuccessfully, to isolate a sense of 'is' by which we can make sense of things having but being able to lose properties. Now the general point that the participation and resemblance metaphors are supposed to help with Parmenidean difficulties is doubtless right. But the notion of having a property as distinct from being it would not suffice for coping with these, even if Plato got it clear. The Parmenideans did not produce a difficulty or set of difficulties based on a clearly recognised interpretation of 'is'. That is the whole trouble. As remarked above, one objection was not to change, but plurality. This is the form of objection that the young Socrates is portrayed as facing in the *Parmenides*. Zeno there claims that there cannot be a plurality because if there were things would be alike and unalike. The argument is not spelled out, but must be one of the following.

1   There cannot be a variety of things, for, if there were, each thing would be like itself but unlike something else, and so like and unlike.
2   There cannot be a multiplicity of things, because if so each thing would be like itself but necessarily in some respect unlike everything else even if only in place. On either view the difficulty is that we should be committed to the supposed contradiction of saying of something that it is like and unlike. Now this contradiction is not eased by saying 'but they aren't those properties, they only have them'. If the properties are incompatible it is no easier for something to have them both than to be them both. The solution is a non-starter. But clearly participation is supposed to ease it. The obvious riposte is to say that 'like' and 'unlike' are not necessarily incompatible. Nothing is just like, it is always like X and in a certain respect. It may very well be unlike X in another respect. The metaphor of participation might have been felt appropriate because it suggests having a bit of likeness, being like in one way or to some extent. This is in fact the way Socrates talks at *Parmenides* 129a. If this is so, then one can see how the metaphor might have been thought to help as a gloss on 'is' in face of this sort of problem. But whereas we might want to say that 'like' is incomplete or a relation or a two place predicate, Plato wants to say that the subject *is* like in an incomplete way. The blame is put on the verb 'to be'. At the same time, it becomes clear that participation is getting at more than simply possession of properties. It is supposed to help both with talk of change and with the apparent contradiction in calling the same subject like and unlike, large and small and so on. These functions are not distinguished in the text, and only the notion of possession would be needed if Plato's concern was the general one of how to talk of things acquiring and losing properties. It seems to be a more limited one related to a special range of 'properties'.

There is in fact little reason to think that the introduction of Forms and the metaphors of participation and resemblance are connected with problems about attribution as distinct from identity, or that they constitute an attempt to give a general model for attribution. Any such attempt would presumably arise out of some puzzlement as to how it is that many subjects could be described by the same predicate, and the proposed model would be attractive if predicates were looked on by analogy with proper names. Now there is no clear sign of a theory of separable Forms to which particulars are related by the special relations of participation or resemblance before central dialogues such as the *Phaedo*, *Symposium* or *Republic*. Before that stage there is indeed a fair amount of concern with what could be called one-over-many problems. We have already noted Socrates' repeated complaints at being given instances of F rather than what F is. But this way of describing the matter can be misleading. While in the *Laches* and *Meno,* for instance, a plurality is contrasted with the unit desired, the plurality is one of forms, not of instances. 'Holding one's place in the battle line' does not point to an instantiation of courage, but gives the sort of act that is brave. White is a colour (*Meno* 74c), but not an instantiation of colour, which would be a particular white thing. The typical one-many problem is not that one thing has many instances but that it takes many forms, and often the forms seem mutually incompatible, like retreating and refusing to retreat, being circular and being square and so on. It will follow from this that two instances of courage, colour, figure could be opposed to each other in the respect in which they resembled each other, and it is this, not the simple fact that there are many instances that is the problem. It will in fact follow from this of course that any particular instance will be both like and unlike. When we come to the central dialogues this sort of point is made much of (cf. e.g. *Phaedo* 102 seq., *Republic* 523–5), there emerges a distinct interest in particulars and 'the many' now sometimes refers to the multiplicity of instances (cf. e.g. *Phaedo* 78d, *Republic* 596a–b). Indeed, the notions of participation and resemblance seem at first especially geared to pointing the distinction between Forms and particulars (though cf. *Republic* 476a). The points about particulars, however, that necessitate these technicalities are that they are in constant change, that they are capable, with regard to some properties, of having them and their opposites, and that attributing these properties to them involves, roughly, some comparison with a standard. As we have seen in relation to Zeno's argument in the *Parmenides* the point about the possession of incompatible properties is related to the multiformity of those properties – there are many bits of likeness and so on. So this feature of certain properties is still important. Further, it is often unclear, even when Plato refers to the multiplicity of particulars, whether it is this simply that is important. Thus at *Phaedo* 78d–e, when he refers to the many beautiful things he does not simply refer to the fact of multiplicity, but says 'such as men, horses, cloaks and such like'. In other words, he cites various sorts of beautiful thing with different styles of beauty. The interest in particular beautifuls is as much that they are multifarious as that they are multiple. The point is probably the same at *Republic* 476a, that by participation in particulars Forms appear varied. This I have argued elsewhere (cf. Gosling, 1960) and shall not go into here. If this is right, it seems that Plato is not interested in the simple fact of many things having the same property, but that even his interest in the multiplicity of particulars is due to the fact that that multiplicity seems to give rise to a multiformity of one property.

There are, so far as I can discover, only two places where Plato seems to betray an interest in the argument that if there are many instances of F, then there must be something, F, to which they are all related in a way that justifies the use of the common term. The first is *Republic* Book X, 596a–b. Here Socrates refers to a familiar procedure of postulating a single Form for each multiplicity covered by one name. This seems to take the fact of a number of things called by the same name as sufficient for postulating a Form, and so to show that even if the argument is not the whole story, it is at least playing its confusing part among various reasons for talking of Forms. The second place is the *Parmenides*. There (132) Parmenides attributes to the young Socrates the argument that if there are many larges (large things) then there must be a Large over and above them. But then if the Large is itself a large, then the process must proceed ad infinitum. The starting argument is accepted by Socrates, and the consequent difficulty appreciated. So it looks as though Socrates accepts the argument that if a common term is used of many subjects we have to postulate a Form to explain that fact. He might escape the regress by refusing to list the Large as a large along with the others, but that would not affect the original move. Nor can much be made of the fact that the term on which the argument is illustrated is 'large', one of the subset in which Plato is particularly interested. The argument is quite general in form, and even if Plato would like to confine its use to certain cases he has no protection against its wider use.

It is difficult to know how cogent these considerations are. So far as the *Republic* passage is concerned, two points could be made. First, it cannot be inferred from this passage with any safety what the reason for the procedure is. It could well be that it has usually or always been found that our common names do stand for things of which there are Forms, so that it is sensible practice to suppose that where there is a common name there will be a Form, though one might, as with 'barbarian' (cf. *Politicus* 262), on occasion find that there is not. Second, the word for 'postulate' is commonly provisional in sense. In other words, we posit a Form rather than declare that there must be one. So this passage may well contain no reference to a standard form of argument for Forms, but only to a common procedure.

The *Parmenides* is more difficult. It is not clear what, if any, significance should be attached to Socrates' youth. It can hardly be intended as an accurate report of an actual conversation. It could be that Plato wishes to acknowledge debts to Parmenides, in which case he could hardly do other than have Socrates young if he is making him part of the conversation. On the other hand it might be that we are being given a critique of either early arguments for the Forms, or arguments of neophytes, so that the portrayal of Socrates as a youthful beginner is felt to be appropriate. Consequently Plato might be criticising favoured arguments for Forms, dropping youthful ones or criticising inept ones current in the Academy. It is clear from Aristotle that there were many varied arguments supposedly all tending to the same conclusion that there are Forms, and there is no reason to think either that Plato only found the better ones attractive, or that he at least would never run together two that were in fact for different conclusions. It remains that there is room for doubt about his acceptance of this one, and it is clear that it is not the predominant argument in the dialogues and ill suits his restrictions on the predicates corresponding to which there are Forms.

One point that tempts one to accept that Plato is giving an account of attribution, is that one can, via the portrait model, get some understanding of why he thinks that a Form must have the attribute of which it is a Form. If one thinks that those considerations were of minor importance or none at all, that Plato has a view of the conditions necessary for the existence of *episteme* and Forms are seen as one of them, then the onus is of course on one to say why he thinks it so obvious that the Just is just, the Beautiful beautiful and so on. At the best of times, of course, this is puzzling. The portrait model is not difficult to interpret with terms like 'man', perhaps, but it looks pretty mad with terms like 'large' or 'small'. Still, something can at least be done with some terms. What, then if we abandon that model?

The first thing is to divest oneself of the prejudice that when Plato uses abstract nouns or the equivalent neuter adjectives with the definite article, he must be trying at least to talk of concepts and/or universals. The tendency to say such things as 'justice is just' can be found in dialogues that show no sign of a theory of separable Forms (cf. *Protagoras* 330c), and when it appears in a dialogue that does contain such a theory, the *Phaedo*, we find Beauty spoken of as making things beautiful just as heat or fire make them hot. This suggests that Plato may be relying on the possibility of talking of Helen losing her beauty and so ceasing to be beautiful, of someone recovering his health and so becoming healthy and so on. Even so far, it would not be unidiomatic to compare the beauty of Helen with the looks of some lesser mortal and declare the former to be really beautiful. This sort of possibility may make the 'safe' answer that Beauty makes beautiful things beautiful seem safe and also talk of Beauty being beautiful seem appropriate. But this will not get us very far if, once we have an account of justice or health spelled out, it becomes absurd to call it just or healthy. In the *Republic* we get some indication of the form the answer to 'what is justice?' might take, and what we get is an account of a condition of state and person where each element keeps to its own role. It seems here quite proper to assert also the converse, that the condition of each element keeping to its proper role is just. Similarly one would expect a Greek doctor to answer the question 'what is health/the healthy?' by giving an account of that proper balance of elements that constitutes health, and it will be perfectly proper to call that proper balance healthy. In general, saying what justice, health and the rest are is conceived of as saying what justice, health etc. consist in, and if being F consists in being A, B and C, then being A, B and C is F. This last 'is', of course, means 'constitutes being', not 'consists in being', but that is an ambiguity that Plato is not likely to have spotted. It is the introduction of an order that makes everything keep to its own role that makes a state 'just', of a proper balance of elements that makes a body healthy. If Plato is thinking of health and justice along these lines then it will be natural to think of them in connection with productive operations, and quite proper to attach the adjectives 'healthy' and 'just' to what is known to constitute health and justice. In short, if Plato's main position is that Forms are what a person with *episteme* has *episteme* of, then it might be expected that he will think of them as what an expert will want to embody in order to bring about a situation of a corresponding description, and at the same time think that they are to be characterised by that description, although they will not be in any straightforward way just or healthy individuals.

In all this I am not wanting to suggest that Plato had a clear and well-defined view, and well realised the difference between defining the word 'health' and saying what health consists in, and could spell out the distinction between these two and saying 'health is health'. The point is rather that talk of what health consists in better describes what meets Plato's requirements than does talk of definition and similarly with the rest. That Plato is not clear is one of the few things that is clear. Early on it looks as though he wants a strict contrast between things that are in process and things like health that just eternally are what they are. At the same time it seems that to give what health is is to give what just and only health is (cf. *Symposium* 210–11 on beauty). Some such talk one might expect if he is hunting for what health consists in. But such an account of the *ousia* of health will not exhaust the eternal truths about health. There will be things that health is 'of its nature', and other things that it eternally is that seem to have nothing to do with its nature. Thus, it is eternally true of health that it is not justice and is something that can be studied, but these facts do not tell us what it consists in. In the *Sophist* Plato is aware of this distinction, for he wants to claim both that Difference pervades everything, i.e. that everything is necessarily different, and at the same time that it is not 'of the nature of' change to be different (cf. 255e). Eternality in fact is not sufficient to isolate the sense of 'is' hankered after in the earlier period. This passage in the *Sophist* also betrays a tendency already remarked on to talk as though difference did have a nature, as though its function was peculiarly to differentiate and knowledge consists in part in knowing what the 'real' differentiations are. The change side of the contrast is not very much happier. To begin with, Plato seems to want to deny change of property altogether of the Forms (cf. e.g. *Phaedo* 78c). Now it may be all right to contrast health as unqualifiedly healthy with bodies which are sometimes healthy sometimes not, or healthy in some respects not in others; but there will have to be characteristics that health can acquire and lose, like being understood by Hippias, being partaken of by Socrates. This point, too, is noted in the *Sophist* (248–9) and is perhaps responsible for a growing interest in the notion of change. No doubt these are not changes in what it is to be health, but if one insists on this point one gets into difficulties with the other term of the contrast. For if one insists on the point with the *Phaedo* example of the human body, the results are very strange. For the point will have to be that only Forms are such that they have some properties that give what X consists in, that physical things do not. Now in the *Phaedo* (102 seq.) we find two contrasts. First, one between Socrates and Largeness, in that Socrates may, while remaining the same, acquire or lose largeness, while largeness cannot. We then get a daring advance to saying that there are further items which, while not *being* F always 'bring F with them'. The first example is Fire always being accompanied by heat, and the soul is said to be similarly bound up with life. These are examples of things that with regard to some properties cannot lose these properties while remaining the same. It then becomes clear that the body is not related to life in this way, and the second contrast is between the body which may acquire or lose life by acquiring or losing a soul and the soul which cannot. Now this seems a strange thing to say of the body. It is true that we talk of corpses as human bodies, but in so far as medicine is the study of the human body, corpses are not bodies. The examination of them may help, but they are not its subject-matter, which is rather how to postpone their occurrence. Someone who wished to explain what medicine studied could only do it by reference to corpses if he also explained about the 'norm' of living bodies. This is presumably why Aristotle holds that corpses are only human bodies in a secondary sense. In other words, it does not seem true that the human body, while remaining the same (thing, sort of thing) can acquire or lose life. Even if we waive this, a similiar point would have to arise later on, for there will be degrees of disintegration whereby whatever we have is not still a body and so not the same body. So it still will not be true that for all properties a body is capable of losing them without ceasing to be the same thing. This sort of position is in fact suggested by the use of the example of fire. Plato is therefore faced with a choice. He could say that the example of fire was given to make a point clear for the vulgar, but would not be one he would want to retain as genuine under examination. In that case he would have to hold that statements about the body changing should be analysed as statements about space receiving different properties, and space is a bastard entity, not having an *ousia* but 'being' a receptacle of characteristics. Alternatively, he could take the fire example seriously – and after all there is no sign that he does not – in which case more would have to be said to establish that only Forms have *ousiai*. This could no doubt be done by claiming that while, so long as a thing is a body it must be living, the thing concerned only 'is' a body and living in the sense that it is in a process of change interpretable in terms of those concepts, but from period to period of its existence there will be different facts that justify that interpretation.

Whichever alternative Plato takes he will have problems, if he wants to preserve the sharp contrast between Forms and physical particulars in terms of being and becoming. For on either alternative he has to clarify the concept of becoming that is involved. The term '*genesis*' was doubtless chosen as the obvious contrast with '*ousia*' (being), but it is not a happy one. For Plato does not want to interpret this as 'coming to be', in the way mentioned at *Philebus* 53–5. However perfectly a body manifests health, it will never come to *be* healthy in the required sense, nor will space come to be F but only to have F. We find Plato trying to clarify this notion of becoming in such a way that descriptions of the physical world must all be taken as covering stretches of time in contrast to Forms of which 'was' and 'will be' cannot be used, since time stretches do not come into the description of them (cf. *Timaeus* 37d–38b). The difficulty with the first part of this is that there are some changes where the notion of a time stretch seems inapplicable. The change from being at a standstill to moving is something that can be attributed to physical things, but takes no time at all. One can approximate to the point of change from the prior stretch of rest or the later stretch of motion, but while the point will always lie between it will never be within either stretch. That the whole concept(s) of change will need further examination for his purposes Plato may well have felt, as this range of problems clearly intrigues him (cf. *Parmenides* 156), but there is no exposition of an answer. The second part comes up against the objection already mentioned, that if the Forms are to be knowable and discoverable by men, then there must be some past and future tense propositions that hold of them. But this contrast seems to have a further consequence. If attributing change to the physical world involves thinking that all predicates that describe it give forms of process, then to preserve the absolute contrast we shall have to deny that any such predicates enter into saying what health is etc. Now if we suppose that there is a single account to be given of what constitutes health, one might expect that it would take the form of indicating the activities and processes of healthy living. So 'health consists in . . .' would be filled out with process verbs. But one could have a different picture, whereby all the activities of healthy living were thought of as the only means in a changing material of preserving the requisite balance of parts. Similarly someone asked to devise a dance portraying a rose would have to work out ways of combining the dancers' movements that resulted in a constant visual pattern. The movement would be an essential part of the dance, but the static pattern would give what the rose pattern consisted in. Now Plato certainly has a tendency to talk of health and justice as involving operations of parts, but he also seems to think that what they consist of can be expressed in terms of proportions or relationships between parts. These relationships do not involve reference to changes, though their preservation in an actual body or society would necessitate all sorts of processes. Plato seems to have a definite preference for such a static rather than a dynamic version of what constitutes virtue or health, which is probably partly the result of the strong contrast between being and becoming in terms of which he wants to distinguish between Forms and physical things. Now the static picture at least encourages a somewhat uniform view of health, and discourages a view whereby it might be easier to delimit circumstances where things had gone wrong without our being able to distinguish between various different conditions within those limits as more closely or equally closely related to health. Jones and Smith might both have nothing wrong with them, each be differently developed, equally healthy, but not equally close to or distant from some ideal. One might be a fit weight-lifter the other a fit cross-country runner, but it may be impossible to be perfectly fit in both ways. The static picture also, as we shall see, rules out certain possible views of virtue.

Many of these problems are ones into which Plato does get, and into which one would expect he might get if the account offered of his predominant interests is right. He agrees with the regular Greek truism that if there is to be *episteme* it must be of the truth, of what *is*. He agrees with the Heracleitean sceptical position that unqualified true propositions do not hold of the perceptible world. He sympathises with Socrates' determination to discover what justice, courage and so on consist in and is impressed by the rigour of his enquiries. But he approaches these enquiries with a view to seeing whether *episteme* is possible, and he comes to think that if so, then it will be possible to show that it is best that things be thus and so. This leads to a tendency to answer what things are in terms of their functions and thinking of establishing what these are in terms of showing that that function has a part in the total system – goodness is the explanation of being. The whole tendency is also to distort the concept of truth. Because this in Greek is often expressed as 'what is', the sceptical arguments that tend to deny that 'is' can be used of various subjects also show that no truths hold of them. Because of the way the arguments go the result is that even 'this body is in flux' is not a *truth*. In the central dialogues, at least, the expression 'what is' tends to get tied in Plato's writing to those cases where what X consists in is being given (cf. *Phaedo* 78), with a resultant tendency with the usual word for 'truth'. Plato is not interested in what makes language possible, and so not in problems of meaning or of universals. He is interested in discovering whether *episteme* is possible, and that in his view involves showing that the universe is a system of a certain sort. Assertions that the Forms are necessary for *logos* (cf. *Parmenides* 135b–c) see them as necessary for argument not speech. If we just had concepts like 'red' there would be no place for arguing and reasoning (cf. *Phaedrus* 263). He is not concerned about special objects only open to intellectual vision, but about a structure to which the visible universe approximates. This is only discoverable by reason, though we have an inkling of it from birth. Its discovery brings clarity and makes the *metaphor* of seeing appropriate.

Before turning to criticisms of this ambitious total project for understanding the universe and bringing knowledge of the best life within the scope of this understanding, I want to discuss one further strand in Plato, his concern with the problem of falsity. For the above exposition has taken it that Plato is not moving from an acquaintance view of knowledge to a propositional one. He does indeed think that ordinary Greek concepts involve an implicit theory about the universe, so that in applying them we are committed to referring the phenomena in question to some standard, but knowing that standard does not seem in any serious way to call for analogy with perception (as it might with the portrait model of attribution), although the metaphors of looking at and so on would be obvious ones to use. Knowing is 'of' what is good and bad, not objects or propositions, primarily, although it will involve knowing that X consists of A, B, C. But one popular style of account of his treatment of falsity succeeds in making sense of what he says by tracing in that treatment the desired progress from an acquaintance to a propositional view of knowledge. If that is the only way of making sense of what he says, then it would clearly be a powerful argument.

XII

Falsity in the *Cratylus*

So far we have to a large extent been concerned with arguments to show that *episteme* is impossible. These arguments have relied on the difficulty of producing areas where strict 'is'-es are applicable. Plato thinks that he can isolate such an area, though the result is to agree with the sceptic that on most topics on which people claim *episteme episteme* is not in fact possible, and that in fact very few people if any have knowledge in any strict sense. The concentration on 'is', however, makes it possible for someone to counter-attack from a quite different direction. For just as good Greek for 'believing the truth' is 'believing what is' so good Greek for 'believing what is false' is 'believing what is not'. One favourite sophistical argument was to claim that believing what is not is impossible, for it is equivalent to believing nothing which is just not believing at all. This verbal jugglery could be made to look more respectable as part of more elaborate positions, like that of Protagoras in the *Theaetetus* (cf. chapter IX), the outcome of which was to deny Plato's contention that knowledge, while possible, is only for the few, and substitute an epistemological egalitarianism. No one, so far as I know, thinks that Plato ever believed that false judgements or statements are impossible, but there is room for disagreement over whether or not he at any point held a position that would seem to lead to that. Thus one possible view is that he was inclined to think of statements as complex names (cf. Crombie, 1962). Signs of this view can be seen in the *Cratylus* (422 seq.), where naming something is treated as describing and so making a statement about the thing named, and no distinction is made between naming Cratylus 'Cratylus' and saying that Cratylus is bald. The latter simply names the complex fact of Cratylus' baldness. Part of Cratylus' difficulty in the dialogue is that he thinks that if there is no Cratylus then the name is an empty noise that names nothing, and similarly if there were no such thing as his baldness, 'Cratylus is bald' would be an empty noise too. In other words, all false statements would have to be names of non-facts, or of nothing. We have here a way of viewing statements whose attraction can be felt and which would make the arguments to the impossibility of false statements seem more than just verbal play. In the *Sophist* Plato begins to fight his way out of this difficulty by distinguishing between naming and stating. The function of naming is to fix the subject of a statement and falsity comes in in the misallying of the subject with a description. This only allows him to cater for a subset of false statements. It does not enable him to analyse the false 'unicorns exist'. But there is worse. Plato was tempted to interpret 'X is F' as 'X exists F-ly', and so to read 'X is not F' as 'X non-exists F-ly'. The subject/predicate distinction leaves this necessarily false or empty. If 'X' has successfully named something it is necessarily false, if 'X' has named nothing it is empty. Plato's escape is to read all such statements as 'X exists non-F-ly'. But now we get difficulties over the true 'unicorns are not believed in by scientists' which has to be read as 'unicorns exist in an unbelieved in by scientists way'. This either makes 'unicorn' successfully name something non-existent, or implies a special mode of existence for what are vulgarly held to be non-existent entities. All this results from attaching an importance to naming as an essential part of all statements that is hard to square with a review of a representative sample of statements, but is intelligible in someone who is struggling out of a position that statements and judgments are complex namings. Now the view that all words are names and propositions are complex names is one that goes well with a position that knowledge is a matter of being acquainted. Learning a name can plausibly, though erroneously, be represented as being introduced to the bearer of the name, and giving a name seems feasible only by someone acquainted with the nominee. To be acquainted with the nominee in a way sufficient for acquiring the name, one must be able to distinguish it from all other name-bearers, and then one has a grasp of this name as just and only the name for that nominee. This fits the way Plato talks early on about Forms: they have to be seen in pure isolation as just what they are, and then the reference of their names is understood in contrast to that of other names. This ambition is not compatible with the actual procedure of 'giving an account', which plainly involves non-isolation of Forms, and the *Sophist* shows Plato advancing to a propositional model of knowledge. The *Cratylus* and *Sophist* together mark this advance in his ability to cope with problems of falsity and negation. The *Cratylus* shows him in what is for him a real difficulty, and the *Sophist* shows the beginnings of escape partly by the distinction of subject and predicate and partly by important distinctions in the sense of 'is'.

This interpretation relies for its attraction to some extent on an over-all interpretation of Plato's epistemology, other parts of which have been criticised in previous chapters. Those criticisms, however, do require an alternative account of what is going on in these dialogues. In the present chapter I propose to examine the *Cratylus* more closely, and shall argue that so far as the paradoxes about falsity are concerned Plato's arguments are purely polemical and show nothing about his own difficulties. The positive contribution of the dialogue is to underline a basic distinction and to make a point about the corrigibility of language. In the following chapter I shall argue that the account of the *Sophist* needed for the above interpretation is quite untenable and mislocates the inadequacies of Plato's analysis.

The topic of falsity in the *Cratylus* will probably suggest to many the passage at 430 and following where names/statements are likened to pictures and false ones to inaccurate pictures. I shall be arguing, however, that the *Cratylus* as a whole is an attack on positions which hold that all statements must be true and that falsity is impossible. It is Plato's aim to show the incoherence of allowing that statements may be true while ruling falsity out of court *a priori,* and to point out that this would involve holding that language is beyond criticism, that one could not find fault with the distinctions embodied in it. It is considered important for making these points to establish that there is no natural relation determining that a given sound carry a given sense in a language. These three points are dealt with as part of a discussion of the question whether the correctness of names (*orthotes onomaton*) is determined naturally or by convention. This question is indeterminate as between (i) Is it a matter of convention that the name 'horse' is the right name for horses?, a question about noises (ii) is it a matter of convention, granted the sense of 'horse', that it is the right name to apply to this animal before us?, a question about truth (iii) is it a matter of convention what names we have (what we have names for)?, a question about the corrigibility of language. Plato plays on this indeterminacy to pass from discussion of one to another of these topics, though by the end of the dialogue, I think, we are expected to be clear enough.

Now it could well be that these points emerge for anyone trying to struggle his way out of the toils of the dialogue, but that does not mean that Plato had seen the points or had in mind the aims I have attributed to him. There is, however, I think, an interesting pattern in the dialogue, which suggests deliberation. I propose first to sketch this pattern, and then to argue that it holds in the particular passages. The dialogue consists of three main sections (i) the critique of the position of Hermogenes (383–91); (ii) an illustrated exposition of the view that names, when taken down to elements, turn out to be right (390–428); (iii) the critique of the position of Cratylus (428–38), followed by an epilogue. The critiques of Hermogenes and Cratylus follow an interestingly similar pattern. In both cases the thesis under discussion seems, to begin with, to be about what makes a given noise bear a certain sense, convention according to Hermogenes (384d), similarity according to Cratylus (cf. 428b for his acceptance). In both cases the theses are interpreted as committing their holders to the view that all names can only be correctly applied, i.e. only true statements are possible (cf. 385b and 429c), and this leads to an argument that we must be able to criticise statements, thus allowing the possibility of their being false (cf. 386–8 and 430–2). In both cases this leads into a further argument that the formation of a language demands knowledge and cannot be left to any Tom, Dick or Hermogenes (cf. 388–91 and 433–38). In other words, in both passages the dispute about the correctness of names is taken first as about what makes a noise the right one, then as about what makes a statement right, and then as about what ensures that our language has the right distinctions (though for reasons to be mentioned later the first of these comes twice in the Cratylus passage).

This seems to me a significant similarity, and there are, as will emerge later, cross-references which confirm the suspicion of deliberateness. There are also other points worth noting. Anyone who wishes to hold that only true statements are possible can only do so either by attributing incorrigibility to the maker of the statement, or by denying the title of statement to anything false. The first of these is the position attributed to Hermogenes, the second the one taken by Cratylus, so that the two critiques form a complete treatment of the possibilities, and together constitute an argument for the incoherence of any such position. Further, in the Hermogenes passage, all the argument is directed against the views (a) that whatever statement we make is *ipso facto* true and (b) that what distinctions it is right to make is determined simply by convention; the distinctions there are are just any we choose to make. It is argued that it is the facts (i.e. nature) that determine whether a statement is true, and the nature of the world that determines what words it is right to have. But the position that what noises we should have for our words is just a matter of convention remains untouched. This, surely Hermogenes' real position, is in fact defended by Socrates at 435 and is a main part of the refutation of Cratylus. For the time being, however, it is supposed at the end of the refutation of Hermogenes that we are committed to a natural determination of the senses of words. At first this is expounded as holding that the parts of names have senses which determine the sense of the whole name. But towards the end of this central section of the dialogue it is pointed out (421 seq.) that some account has to be given as to what determines the sense of the simple parts. If one is wanting to give a non-conventional account here it is difficult to see what else one could try but similarity. This could be made crudely convincing by reference to onomatopoeia: it would be wrong to attach the noises 'splash' and 'cuckoo' to anything but splashes and cuckoos. It could be made more sophisticated by arguing that while the letter 'l' does not *sound* as oil sounds when it moves, still the sound is like the *movement* of oil, and is a naturally proper part of the representation of what oil is like: it is of the nature of oil to ooze and liquid consonants suggest oozing. The importance of this view is (a) that it is, on reflection, the only really plausible version of the thesis that sounds naturally bear a certain sense (b) that if it can be held that a sound's meaning is naturally determined it is easier to confuse the sense of what is said and its truth, arguing for the unintelligibility of the sound in conditions which cannot give it a sense. Granted the earlier arguments against Hermogenes, the view that the sense a given word has is a matter of convention makes it clearly possible for the word to occur with that sense in inappropriate circumstances. Indeed, it is part of the view that sense should be determined independently of application. Further, it makes it clearer that language is something of man's devising, and so something we might devise badly. The view that names only *are* names if they resemble reality easily suggests, if supposed intelligible, that we cannot go wrong in making the distinctions we do. For we only make distinctions when we are right. If, on the other hand, the possibility is allowed that our distinctions may be misconceived then the statements we make in terms that embody misconceived distinctions will necessarily be inaccurate, however internally consistent (436). In short, those who hold that all statements must be true have to face the arguments first, that any interpretation of the thesis in fact leads to difficulties that can only be met by denying the thesis; and second, that language being a matter of man's devising might well be ill-devised, which constitutes an *a fortiori* argument against the thesis. The establishment of the conventionalist view on noises is important for establishing clearly the separation of sense and application, and lending plausibility to the view that language is corrigible.

It is now time to consider the details of this proposed pattern, and first to deal with the critique of Hermogenes. When Hermogenes states his position at 383a, and again at 384d and 385d, it seems fairly clear that it is a position on how the meanings of words are established; that different countries have different words for the same things, and that whether 'horse' or 'cheval' is the right word for horse cannot really be answered. The English have agreed to the noise 'horse' which makes it the right word in English, the French have agreed to 'cheval'. It is true that the statement at 384d unfortunately allows the individual and not just the community to determine the rightness of names, but still this reads naturally as allowing for Humpty-Dumpty. It comes as a shock to find Socrates from 385 a–d treating it as a thesis that whatever I say is true. The argument there starts from the admission that statements can be true or false; that they are so in virtue of being so down to their smallest parts; but their smallest parts are names; so if there are false statements there are false names; but Hermogenes is committed to saying that however many names I attach to something I am right. Now Hermogenes is bewildered by this, as he might well be. What is clear, however, is that Socrates is trying to argue that Hermogenes' view commits him to denying that there are false statements. For false statements must involve giving wrong names. This move is helped partly by the mention of individuals giving names in Hermogenes' statement at 384d, partly by the ambiguity of Socrates' statement at 385a, which hovers between two interpretations, and partly by the ambiguity of the expression 'the correctness of names' in terms of which the dispute is set up. None of this, however, changes the fact that the transition is abrupt and surprising. It is, I think, meant to be so, and Hermogenes is portrayed as finding it so; at 385d–e he just restates his original position in a way that makes it clear that he has not seen Socrates' point. The argument never returns to Hermogenes' thesis as most naturally understood. From 385e onwards the concern is still with the possibilities of saying what is false and of constructing an inaccurate language. While at 390e Socrates claims to have shown Cratylus right on the original dispute, the reader's feeling that that has not perhaps been settled is voiced by Hermogenes: 'I cannot refute you, but it is hard to be convinced all of a sudden. It might help if you would expound the natural correctness of names that you are asserting.' In other words, we are meant to feel that the original dispute has not been settled, and in fact it gets settled the other way at 435. Our attention is being drawn to different interpretations of 'the correctness of names': (i) a dispute about the correct noise (ii) a dispute about the correct application of words to things.

The argument from 385b–e is an attempt to interpret Hermogenes as not allowing the possibility of false statements; for 'a thing has, at the time anyone says it has them, as many names as he says it has' (385d 5); the 'at the time' which is slipped in here clearly indicates the interpretation; whenever X applies a set of names to Y (=makes a statement about Y) he applies them correctly (=makes a true statement). In 386 the argument apparently shifts, and Socrates asks whether Hermogenes agrees with Protagoras that what seems to someone to be the case is the case. In a way this is a shift, and might well seem to poor Hermogenes a quite new topic. But in fact there is a natural passage from Hermogenes' position *as interpreted by Socrates* to that of Protagoras as presented. For Hermogenes is interpreted as saying that when I (seriously) apply a name/description to an object I apply it correctly, that is: as I deem it to be/as it seems to me to be, so it is. So the passage to Protagoras is a continuation of the same subject. Hermogenes' failure quite to see this makes it easier to shift attention from the natural interpretation of the original thesis. If he had been portrayed as a little sharper Plato would have had to make Socrates draw attention to the shift too early for convenience. A dim interlocutor is a dialogue writer's godsend. The need to separate our opinion of the facts from the facts themselves, that emerges from the refutation of Protagoras, is then specifically applied to the activity of saying: it is not necessarily as we deem it. So it must be possible to assess saying as well or badly done.

One might alternatively take the Protagoras passage as starting a new argument. That is, Socrates first refutes Protagoras and then uses the resultant unwillingness to say that things are as we judge them to be in order to help the argument that our actions (including sayings) are not just as we judge them, but are determined as well or ill done by the relation to the facts and the appropriateness of the acts to the subject-matter. Whether this is right, or whether Plato felt that Hermogenes, as interpreted by Socrates, was anyway committed to Protagoreanism is, I think, an unsettlable issue. The important fact is that on either view what is being argued in this whole section is that what we say can be judged as correctly or incorrectly said by reference to the facts, and it is clear that anyone who wished to exempt sayings from the general thesis about actions would in fact be back in Protagoreanism. In short, it is an argument that the truth of a statement cannot be determined by the opinion of the maker of the statement, but must be determined by the facts, of which the speaker is not the determinant. In other words, Socrates is still pursuing the thesis that he attributes to Hermogenes in 385a–e. (It is interesting to note, in passing, the use of various parts of the verb 'to name' in 387e following. This word is ambiguous as between 'give a name to' (= christen) and 'use a name of', and the play on this ambiguity can make the present discussion *sound like* a discussion of Hermogenes' position.)

So far, then, I hope to have shown that 385a to 387 (inclusive) is taken up with refuting a position, attributed with every appearance of dishonesty to Hermogenes, that all statements are true and are made so by fiat of their maker. In 388 the analogy between saying and other skilled activities is developed, and the emphasis shifted to the idea of a name as a tool (cf. 388b 13: a name is a tool of instruction). There are various peculiarities in this passage, but the main development is clear. A weaver uses a tool that someone else has made. Similarly a teacher uses a tool which someone else has made (388d 6–e 1). In this case the tool-maker is the law-giver. But a toolmaker has to know the nature of the tool, and this is best judged by the expert user, in this case the dialectician (390c). It is not a task to give just anyone to make words (388e 7–390a 3). It is a skill, and so a task which could be badly done: it comes under the possibility of criticism (cf. 389c echoing 387d 6–8 at conclusion of the earlier passage).

What is being discussed in this passage is the devising of words, and the point is being made that it is a skilled work that could be badly done; that is to say, the words we have may be bad tools for teaching and discriminating how things are (cf. 388b 10), and so our instruction be ill-based. In starting the discussion about the maker of the tools we all use Socrates has openly moved from assessing a man's performance with the tool, which occupied 387, to assessing the construction of the tool; in other words from discussing the necessity of being able to assess for falsity if you can assess for truth, to discussing the possible corrigibility of language, of criticising the word-maker's products.

In the argument with Hermogenes, in fact, we start with what looks like a thesis on what determines that a given noise is the right one to convey a given meaning; there is then a shift to discussing whether nature or convention determines the correctness of a statement; finally there is a move to the question of whether nature or convention determines what distinctions are to be made. The first shift of topic is marked by the abrupt oddity of Socrates' moves and Hermogenes' marked bewilderment; the second by Socrates' open introduction of the point that the making of tools is open to criticism as one different from the point that the actual use of the tools is open to criticism. Thus it seems clear that the argument with Hermogenes has the three stages claimed for it.

As was remarked earlier, Hermogenes' thesis that convention determines what sounds are the right ones for a given sense is quite untouched by the argument that the truth or falsity of statements is determined by the facts. It would also seem to be untouched by the argument that to devise words well you have to know what words are for, *unless* it can be shown that different materials are best for the different jobs names do. If different sounds bear to the functions of words the sort of relations of appropriateness that different materials bear to the functions of various tools, then the expert who knows what is to be done might be expected to know that the nature of the task makes certain noises more appropriate for certain purposes than others. Without this we should be left with the meanings of words being laid down by the law-maker, which is on this point hardly different from Hermogenes. It could still be, of course, that the actual words in, say, English, were a result of convention, and that this made them the right English words, but it would be possible to argue that they never quite succeeded in conveying their supposed meaning, or always conveyed some inappropriate meaning, or something of this sort. In other words, sense could still be given to the claim that English had the wrong sounds for doing the tasks to be done, and this leaves the uncomfortable feeling that in some way they cannot *really* have any sense. Sense only attaches to well devised words: these are the only real words. Further, as emerges clearly in the elaboration of the view, the devising of a name is itself a description of the object, and so a real name is a true description. It is consequently easy on this view, since the establishing of a term *is* a statement, to confuse the two and suppose that what makes 'horse' a name for horses (similarity to horses), being what makes the statement involved in the naming true, yields a general account of statements: they are *all* cases, after all, of describing/naming. So if this view of what makes 'horse' the right noise to attach to horses is left alive, so is the possibility of reintroducing confusions about falsity. In the end, of course, Socrates argues for Hermogenes' original conventionalist thesis. For the moment Hermogenes, understandably unconvinced that Socrates' display of fireworks has refuted him, asks for an exposition of the view that it is nature that determines the correctness of names.

The long central section where Socrates does this is hard to take seriously, and the treatment is such that it is hard to believe that Plato took the view seriously either. Two pertinent points are, however, made in the course of it. First, Socrates points out that an anti-Hermogenes thesis will get nowhere if it is simply arguing that complex names can be shown appropriate or inappropriate by an analysis into elements where an element is constituted as an element by simplicity of sense. Not every name can be treated that way, and when we get to simple names Hermogenes will want to know what gives *that* name *that* sense. This point is reached at 421d–427, and makes it clear that the anti-conventionalist in question must hold a thesis about *sounds*. This is what Hermogenes could have done with seeing at the very beginning. Second, it cannot plausibly be a thesis that the sounds are perceptibly like what they signify; they must somehow imitate/represent the nature of what they signify. In other words, if it is to remain a plausible thesis the natural relation that holds must be unlike any familiar case of similarity. This point is brought out from 422d–6.

For the rest, the function of the central passage would seem to be partly to rest the mind, partly to bring home the unplausibility of a thesis which, if described but undeveloped, might seem to have some attraction.

The position that is reached just before Cratylus re-enters the discussion is that a person who properly understands the nature of things, such as the dialectician of 390c, will skilfully choose his letters to construct words which imitate the nature of what they signify. It would be perfectly possible to hold that while this man might produce bad noises for his words, still his function is relatively unimportant. The important thing is that (a) the right distinctions be made and (b) it be generally known which noises stand for what, whether the noise be fixed by dialectician's dictate or general agreement. The choice of appropriate sounds is a minor embellishing aspect of the word-maker's art. This point has not yet been brought out in the argument and it is one that Plato wants to bring out clearly. Otherwise the possibilities of confusion, mentioned in speaking of the central section, will still remain. For the moment, therefore, it remains unmade and Cratylus can consequently make the appropriateness of sound the important point without clearly missing a distinction already made. The impossibility of following Cratylus will make clear the necessity of making convention the important factor.

At the beginning of the discussion with Cratylus we are dealing with a thesis about how the sense of words is determined. Although there has been talk of skill in devising words, the necessary distinctions have not been made, and the previous talk has been as much about how various words get the sense they have. At 428e Socrates recalls the agreement with Hermogenes that good words indicate the nature of what they stand for and are for instruction (cf. 388b seq.). The earlier passage opens the discussion of the function of the law-giver as a word-maker.

As Plato now wants to scotch the view that ill-devised words (= inappropriate noises) are meaningless, Cratylus is made to reject the view that any name could be inappropriately laid down and remain the name of that thing. It is appropriateness to its nominee that makes it possible for a sound to stand for/be the name of, its nominee. From 428e to 429b (inclusive) Cratylus is clearly holding a thesis about what determines the sense to be attached to a sound. At 429c following we move from the setting-up of names to the use of names and making of statements. On the Cratylus position this is not a harsh move as the very construction of the name when you set it up is a description of the thing named, and so a statement about it. The fact remains that as in the argument with Hermogenes the discussion rapidly moves to the question of falsity. The details of this section I will deal with later. The burden of the discussion is much the same. Hermogenes was interpreted as denying the possibility of falsity by making the truth of a statement an automatic result of a person's making a statement. The purpose of the criticism of the position was to show that saying something is independent of the things spoken of in a way that makes it possible to measure the one against the other. Cratylus tries the alternative of holding that whether or not a statement has been made is determined by the facts, that is: that a statement has been made, rather than just a noise, is a result of its being true. Once again, the purpose of the criticism is to show the independence of what is said and the facts: it must be possible to know what is said without knowing whether it is true.

In the falsity section, then, Socrates aims to show that even on the anti-conventionalist thesis no cogent resistance can be given to the suggestion that falsity is possible. As with the Hermogenes argument, however, there is the possibility that a lot of the words we have do not in sound represent any reality, and so many of our utterances are meaningless. From 433c to 435d Socrates takes actual examples of different sounds for the same reality and extracts the admission from Cratylus that whether they are well-devised or not has no bearing on their being intelligible: for that, custom and convention of use are enough. In other words, what the names are names of is not determined by what they name, but by convention. If this is so it is clearly possible to know what is said, and to know that something intelligible is said, without knowing whether or not it is true.

All this argument shows is that it is not *necessary* that words should resemble things. From 435d following Socrates argues that it is not, either, plausible to hold that it is the case. This is run in conjunction with an argument that language is open to criticism. If Cratylus were right about actual language, that in fact all the words we have are good representations, then it would be possible by a study of language to study the world; but we should have no guarantee that words did reflect the world; Cratylus' suggestion of language's internal consistency is no good, since consistency does not guarantee truth (436c–d); but worse in fact our language must fail to represent reality in this way because of the similar sounds of words of contrary sense. So we have an argument from the consideration of actual language to show that it cannot be a general feature of actual words to represent reality by any form of similarity. Consequently (438a–d) we cannot study the world via names, but must be able to study it independently. The words we have reflect our conception of the world, and study of the world can be used as a critique of the distinctions our language makes.

In short, we have again the same three stages: first a thesis about how words get their sense, this evolves into a discussion of the possibility of statements being false; and we end up with an argument for the possibility of criticising language. Between the last two is sandwiched an argument in favour of Hermogenes' original conventionalist thesis. This serves two purposes. First, it frees us from any lingering uneasiness left by the argument with Hermogenes (see above) which might cast doubt on the arguments about falsity; second, it makes it quite clear that the skill needed to devise words has nothing to do with choosing good material, but is solely the important skill of discerning what distinctions can properly be made, or the joints at which reality is to be divided. As I remarked earlier, at the end of the Hermogenes argument the dialectician's skill clearly involves this, but it is still allowed that he might have to choose his material carefully. Now that is shown to be no part of his skill and the point about the corrigibility of language is consequently more sharply made. The same three stages recur, with a passage inserted to clear away possibilities left open in the Hermogenes argument. A reader returning to the Hermogenes argument

armed with the conclusion in favour of Hermogenes' convention-
alism will find a critique of Hermogenes' supposed denial of the
possibility of falsity that parallels the critique of Cratylus, followed by a
similar position on the skill required to devise a language (note that it is
this passage that introduces the notion of law-giver in connection with
devising a language, and this legal analogy is henceforth used in this
connection, e.g. in 429 and 438. Consequently the section at the end of
the Cratylus argument can rely on recalling the more detailed treatment
in the Hermogenes argument). The similarity of pattern seems too
close to be accidental.

Before the last section can be accepted it needs to be shown that the
point of the argument about falsity in the discussion with Cratylus is
what I have said it is, so I will now turn to it.

First, a brief sketch of the passage's development. To begin with,
Cratylus is unwilling to allow false statements. A man whose utterance
is what most people call false is simply making a noise and no more
(430a 4–5). Socrates gets him to admit that a name and its nominee are
two different things and suggests that one could put the wrong name to
something, just as one could allot someone the wrong picture. Cratylus
begins to waver, but then claims that with a name for instance, if you
alter the order of the letters it is not that you have miswritten the name:
you simply have not written it. Socrates then claims that whereas something of that sort holds with numbers (addition or subtraction changes
the number) with other things subtraction is possible without such
effects. Thus a representation may be of such and such despite various
subtractions, and a name and a statement may be well or ill-formed (so
long as it has some indication of its subject-matter), and still remain a
statement.

This is all very obscure, and there are various problems. First of all,
why does Socrates make such heavy weather of it? After all, Cratylus'
thesis is not so very attractive. Even with the picture analogy it seems
obvious that a picture of Cratylus cannot become a picture of Cratylus
only by being correctly *applied* to him. Perhaps it only becomes one by
being like him, but a person who knows Cratylus can identify a picture
of Cratylus, and so judge whether it has been rightly or wrongly allotted.
If names too are images the same situation will hold: names are not what
they are names of; 'Cratylus' can be discovered to be the image/name
of Cratylus, and so be seen to be misattached. Why is more needed?
Why, in particular, the elaboration to images that have some of the
appropriate elements but either lack others or add inappropriate ones?

To answer this we need first to note some curiosities of the picture
analogy. The first is that falsity comes in not simply in virtue of a
picture of Cratylus not being one of Hermogenes, but when someone
misattaches the picture. The second is that the cases given of misattach-

ment are not of fantastic misattachment, but of, say, attaching to a particular man the label 'woman'. Indeed it is assumed throughout the passage that follows that the misattached image will have some features of its original, and will be poor in so far as it adds inappropriate ones or lacks appropriate ones. In other words, Socrates is considering cases where a mistaken allotment is *understandable*. It is understandable that in some circumstances a man might be mistaken for a woman whereas it is quite beyond understanding that someone should allot a picture of a clothes peg to a polar-bear. The possible treatment of the Cratylus position suggested in the previous paragraph operates equally well for understandable or fantastic allotments. It is because we know the picture is the wrong picture that we can tell that the allotment is fantastic. The way in which Socrates sets up the picture analogy and develops it suggests that he has not clearly separated questions about what the picture is a picture of and attaching the picture.

The reason for this is one that explains why Cratylus' position might seem to Plato a strong rather than a silly one. Suppose we imagine someone saying something obviously false. Faced with a joint of beef, beautifully cooked, he says 'this is a clothes peg'. There is no clothes peg in sight. He is pointing at the beef. Just because what he says is so patently false it is impossible to take him as making an assertion. He is clearly babbling. If we now ask: was his assertion true? there is surely a question whether there was an assertion at all. The fact that the proposition 'this is a clothes-peg' is so obviously false makes it silly to take the expression of it as an assertion. If we now use the word 'statement' to combine the senses of 'proposition' and 'assertion' above, and ask: is the statement that this is a clothes peg true or false, we might be in a dilemma. On the one hand we want to say that of course it was false, on the other that no statement *can* have been made. Now Plato did not have to hand the distinction made above. The word '*logos*' embodies the elements distinguished. Consequently it would seem very *plausible* to say that a false statement is not really a statement except in cases, as for instance with misidentification of similars, where someone's seriously asserting what is in fact false is quite intelligible. This lack of a distinction between assertion of a proposition and a proposition is also influential in the Hermogenes argument. In expounding the connection between Hermogenes and Protagoras I said 'Hermogenes is interpreted as saying that when I (seriously) apply a name, I apply it correctly.' The 'seriously' has to be inserted or the 'apply' taken strongly. The possibility is simply not envisaged of a *logos* in any other sense than as an assertion of a proposition. In fact, the falsity dilemmas have far more bite if it is borne in mind that for Plato a *logos* is always part of an activity (cf. 386e following, where the problem is dealt with in terms of the activity of saying something, as well as the already mentioned features of the pictures passage). It is quite unconvincing to suggest that every proposition must be true. But if an important feature of *logos* is the assertion of a proposition then difficulties can get off the ground. If, on epistemological grounds, I am held to be incapable of making false judgement, then as a statement is simply putting my judgement into words, there will be no false *statements*. Even with lies, because I do not assent to the proposition, there is no genuine assertion, for a lie does not put my judgement into words. Unless true a putative statement is just a noise (430a 4).

This, then, explains, I think, some features of the treatment of falsity, and why Socrates does not make certain moves. There is another reason for the elaboration of the picture analogy. In its first form it amounts to no more than saying 'If words are images, why cannot they be misallotted as pictures can?' In its elaborated form it is intended to *force* Cratylus to choose: he can either allow that false statements are statements, or he must find another account of the correctness of names and abandon the view that a name is a showing forth of a thing. In the elaborated form Cratylus is faced with a dilemma.

There are various problems of detail about the presentation of the word/picture analogy, but the main intention is, I think, clear. Cratylus wants to say that words are the right words for a situation if they resemble/represent it, and he is tempted to say (431e 8 seq) that if you add or subtract you end up with no representation of that situation. Socrates thinks this is a mistake. It is true, for instance, with numbers: to add or subtract simply produces a different number (432). With representations, on the other hand, a representation of the Battle of Waterloo does not by just any addition or subtraction cease to be a representation of that battle. It is worth noting that in this passage Socrates takes Cratylus as saying that if any similarity is lacking, then a picture of X ceases to be that (cf. 432c 7–d2, d5–e3). But Cratylus never in so many words says this. The accusation comes after Cratylus' suggestion that any alteration in an image would make it no longer that image (i.e. an image of *that*). Cratylus says that to alter the letters of a word is to produce a different word or no word. This is true: 'car' is a different word from 'cat', i.e. a word for something different and as words are being treated as images it must be an image of something different. It is to meet this that the necessary lack of similarity in images is argued for. The point is that if you hold with images that *any* change makes it cease to be an image of the same thing you must be claiming that no addition would make it more like (a better image), and any subtraction would make it unlike, and so no longer an image of that thing. In other words, your claim is that an image of X must have exact similarity or nothing. If it turns out that every image, to be an image, must fail to resemble what it is an image of in some respects then it becomes clear that no general principle will hold that missing a point of resemblance to X on the part of A will lose it the status of image of X. But now it is clear that similarity alone cannot establish that A is an image of X, or dissimilarity that it is not. The notion of appropriate similarity has to be introduced, or of sufficient similarity to indicate the subject matter. But this means that it will be possible to establish that A is an image of X while leaving open the question whether it has inappropriate features as well. In other words, in the case of statements, what is said can be established independently of deciding whether it is appropriately said: the determination of what is said is within limits independent of the determination of its truth. I say 'within limits' because of the difficulties mentioned about obviously false utterances. So we reach the need to be able to distinguish what is said from the truth of what is said, making a parallel with the Hermogenes argument.

I hope now to have done enough at least to suggest strongly that the Hermogenes argument and the Cratylus argument follow a similar pattern in their development through three different ways of taking the theses that the correctness of names is determined by convention or by nature. There is a tidiness about this, as about the way in which possibilities left uncertain in the first argument are cleared up in the second, which suggests deliberateness. No doubt Plato had various purposes. So far as falsity is concerned, however, his purpose was polemical. He wished to show that any thesis that denied *a priori* the possibility of false judgements must be wrong because whatever form it took it would have to deny the distinction between knowing what is said and assessing what is said, and failure to make that distiction leads to absurdity. The positions that lead to that absurdity, however, are not Plato's positions, and that includes the view that naming is describing or describing is just naming at great length. Plato does try to do as much as possible towards allowing for falsity on such a view, but there are no grounds for inferring that it is his own, nor even one with which he is flirting. What does emerge is the distinction between knowing what is said (or with words, what a name is the name of) and knowing whether what is said is true (or with words, whether a name holds of this or that). Also, Plato does seem to have a further antipathy to the no-falsity thesis, that it would entail the incorrigibility of language. The final state of play on the dispute as to whether the correctness of names is determined by nature or convention is that so far as noises go it is convention, but so far as the application of names or their devising is concerned it is nature. The devising of names is a skill that is not concerned with choosing the right material for names, but with discovering the proper distinctions to make. I shall deal with the problems of this in a later chapter. For the moment it is enough to see the *Cratylus* as non-probative as to Plato's views on the relation of naming and stating.

XIII

The *Sophist*

While we cannot infer from the *Cratylus* that Plato is in fact in difficulties as a result of treating statements as complex names, it is of course perfectly possible that he is. It may still be that the only way of making sense of the *Sophist* is as an attempt to extricate himself from these difficulties. If he does think of statements as names, then it is likely that he has a bias towards interpreting any strict 'is' as one of identity (or perhaps of identification). It is the bearer of the name, Socrates, who *is* Socrates. At the same time this raises a problem about common statements if all terms are treated as names. For 'snub-nosed' and 'Socrates' now emerge as two names, and strictly only 'Socrates is Socrates' and 'snub-nosed is snub-nosed' ought to be allowable, with the further possibility, of course, of 'snub-nosed Socrates is snub-nosed Socrates'. 'Socrates is snub-nosed', by contrast, must be false, strictly taken. To escape this difficulty a clear distinction between the 'is' of identity and the copula is needed. If it is also true that he thought that it was only possible to name what exists and was inclined to interpret the copula as having existential import, then one would expect some motion towards distinguishing denials of existence from denials of attribution. This would involve at least a move towards isolating the existential use of '*esti*'. It has in fact become quite common to suppose that Plato makes some distinctions at least (cf. Ackrill, 1965, Crombie, 1962, Runciman, 1962, Moravcsik, 1962). Commentators vary in the number of distinctions they hold are made or intended, on the tools used to draw them and in their views on the degree of success. That he is making some distinctions is not in doubt. It seems to me a mistake to suppose that Plato succeeds or even intends to make any of these distinctions. He is neither so sophisticated in his problems nor so clear in his solutions as some of these interpretations suppose. To show this I shall consider and criticise the thesis that Plato succeeds in distinguishing between the

213

existential, identity and attributive use of 'esti', and hope to emerge with a clearer view of what he does and does not succeed in doing.

In the *Sophist* Plato picks on five so-called great kinds, Being, Sameness, Difference, Change and Stability. The first three are all-pervasive and their intermingling is in some way vital to resolving the Sophist's objection that false statements are imposssible because they involve saying what is is not. If Plato either intends or succeeds in distinguishing the existential use of 'esti' then he must do it via the isolation of the first great kind, Being. That he does so can be argued as follows: in the last section of the passage intended to show our uncertainty about Being (248–51), Being is treated as equivalent to Existence. At 254d, at the beginning of the serious passage about the great kinds, a start is made with those kinds discussed in the previous section. So one would expect the first, Being, to stand for Existence. This is borne out when the Stranger proceeds to say that Being, Change and Stability must be three kinds, since the last two cannot intermingle, but both share in Being in that they are. This last must mean in that each exists. This is clear again at 255e where we are told that Change is not Stability, but nevertheless is (exists), and this time the word is given a special philosopher's gloss, 'because it participates in Being' (cf. also 256d 8–9, e3). It looks therefore as though Plato is offering us a rendering of 'esti', in circumstances where the translation 'exists' would be required, as 'participates in Being', thus making it clear that in distinguishing the kind Being he is showing awareness of the existential use of 'esti' as distinct from others.

One of the other kinds distinguished is Sameness. At 256a–b Plato considers the paradox that Change is the same in some sense and yet not the same. He goes on to say that when we say it is the same and yet not the same we are not speaking in the same way. In other words there is an ambiguity, and once it is recognised, the apparent contradiction is resolved. The 'is' of 'Change is not the same' is the 'is' of identity, since the truth asserted is that they are not identical. If the 'is' of 'Change is the same' were also that of identity there would be a contradiction, but in fact it is the 'is' of participation, and so no contradiction arises. Further, Plato seems very careful in his use of 'participates' in the crucial passage 254d–260a where the important distinctions are being made (cf. Ackrill, 1965), in a way that suggests that he is using it to isolate the copula.

If this is admitted it would follow that Plato is making a clear tripartite distinction. First he distinguishes Being (Existence) from the other kinds, including Sameness. Then he goes out of his way to use '... participates in ...' as a gloss for the copula, and invites us to interpret 'Change exists' as 'Change is (copula) an existent' and all identity statements as 'X participates in the Same with respect to ...'.

Finally, two considerations of relevance to the argument may be adduced. First, Parmenides' dictum seemed to embody a horror of the opposite of Being. It seems plausible to suppose that what is unthinkable and unknowable and without number and the rest is the empty void of non-existence (cf. 237–9). Plato seems to share Parmenides' misgivings (258e), and so clearly needs to isolate the notion of existence in order to show that the non-being with which he is dealing is not its opposite. Second, it looks as though those referred to at 251 following, who reject the mingling of kinds – the late learners – hold that all statements are identity statements and that therefore, since any statement is of the form '. . . is . . .', it must have the same filling in each space. This is what is meant by denying that kinds intermingle. In order to lay this spectre Plato needs not merely to show that it cannot be right, but also to offer an alternative interpretation of 'is' that nullifies the pull of the paradox. For this he needs to distinguish the 'is' of identity from the copula. Consequently two considerations of relevance to the general argument would lead us to expect the threefold distinction that more detailed considerations suggest that Plato can be found making.

I have been somewhat rushed over the favourable points. If they are not already familiar they can be readily found in the literature cited. I shall now develop some objections. Since some of these can be found in authors who doubt the threefold distinction or a particular account of how it is achieved I shall not spend an undue amount of time elaborating them. To begin with the thesis that Plato isolates the existential use of '*esti*', as I have said, if he does this it must be by means of the distinction of Being from the other great kinds and the glossing of '*esti*' in its existential uses by 'partakes of Being'. There are at least four passages that individually throw doubt on this and jointly refute it. I omit 255c–d, since the correct interpretation is a highly complex and disputed question (cf. Michael Frede, 1970, for an extended discussion).

The first passage is 256d 11–e 6. Here we are told that difference makes each thing not be by distinguishing it from what is, and that all things can therefore rightly be said not to be while, nevertheless, because of their participation in Being, being rightly said to be and be beings. We have here both a reference to Being, the great kind, and a use of the gloss 'participate in Being'. The Stranger's next sentence sums the point up as follows: 'In fact with each Form that which is is considerable, that which is not of indefinite amount.' It is hard to see what could be meant by saying that with regard to each Form 'that which exists is considerable'. It seems clear that what must be meant is that of each many positive assertions hold and numberless negative ones. Here, in fact, to partake of Being is to be some F (attributive 'is'), not to exist, and Being has to be interpreted accordingly. This suggests that Plato is at least less than successful in his isolation of the existential use.

The second passage is 259a 4–b 1. This is a minor reinforcing passage summing up what we have just found. We are told that 'On the one hand Difference, by partaking of Being, is, in virtue of this participation'. If the sentence ended there we could translate by 'Difference, by partaking in Existence, exists in virtue of that participation'. But the sentence goes on ' . . . not that of which it partakes, but different'. In other words the 'is' is either that of identity, or also that of attribution (Is – not that of which it partakes (a denial of identity), but different (either asserting identity or attribution)). Here again we have the supposed philosopher's gloss on 'exists' used in a way which makes it clearly not a gloss on 'exists'. The point is that you can say 'Difference is' but this is not because Difference is Being but because it is different.

The third passage is 259b 5-6. Here we have a repetition of the point of the first passage, that all things are in many respects, in many are not. Once again, the point must be that there are many affirmations and many denials that hold of everything. While the denials would seem to be of identity, the affirmations are clearly attributions. A thing is only identical with itself, so there will not be many things that it is the same as.

The final passage is 263b. This bears out that the above interpretations of the first and third passages are what Plato intended. It occurs in the discussion of falsity. The Stranger has just said that a false statement says something other than what is, in fact puts forward what is not as what is, in short some things that are other than those that 'are' of Theaetetus. 'For as we said, there are many things that are of each thing, many that are not.' The 'as we said' must refer back to 256e or 259b or both, thus confirming the interpretation of at least one of those passages. For at 263 the things that are are the attributions that hold.

We have, then, a number of passages where Plato refers to Being, the great kind, and uses the expression 'partakes in Being', where what he has in mind is not existence but positive attribution, and one passage referring back to such an occasion where again it is attribution of properties, not assertions of existence that is in mind. If, then, he is trying to isolate the existential use of '*esti*' he certainly fails to do it with any clarity and shows considerable signs of being in the confusions he is supposed to be removing.

If Plato does not succeed in isolating the existential use of '*esti*', does he fare any better with the separation of the identity sense from that of the copula? The argument here certainly looks stronger. Even so it starts to wobble on examination. To begin with, the distinction is supposed to be made at 256, and it is made to remove an apparent contradiction in saying that Change is the same and not the same. In order to succeed in doing this it must rely on our realising that 'Change is not the same' is a denial of identity, not a denial of

[handwritten marginalia: So all he proves is "that which is not" only exists in the non-attributive sense]

attribution, which it would have to be to contradict 'Change is the same'. Consequently, Plato could not have made the distinction this way without being clear on the distinction between denials of identity and denials of attribution. Indeed, one would expect this distinction to be important to him as a means of making the distinction on the positive side. It is extraordinary, therefore, that the analysis of not being in terms of difference covers denials of identity and attribution indifferently. The first introduction of the analysis at 256a–b is to release us from the apparent contradiction that Change is and is not the same. The sense in which it is not the same is that it partakes in difference – and so is not identical with the Same. It is still non-identity that is interpreted as participation in Difference a few lines later for explicating 'Change is not different' and later again for 'Change is not (a) being'. This holds down to 256e and into 257a. So far only non-identity is catered for. On this analysis of 'is not', granted that 'man' and 'two-footed' are not the same, then 'man is not two-footed' is a truth, and one has as yet no analysis for catering for the interpretation of it as a (normal) falsehood. By 257b there is a hint of change. We are asked whether, when we call something not large, we are not rather indicating that it is the same size (of medium size) or small. But however large an elephant may be it is, on the analysis to date, not large, and that has not indicated that it is either middle-sized or small, for on this analysis it is not these either. So there has been a shift, without notice, from proposing 'different' as the analysis of ' "man" is not the same as "two-footed" ' to taking it as the analysis of 'man is not two-footed'. The Greek unfortunately operates like the English, where the general description 'a negative statement says that the subject is something other than what follows the "not" ' would cover denials of identity or attribution equally well. So far, then, we have two possible interpretations of 'is not' that are not distinguished. Accordingly 'man is not two-footed' either is plainly true or asserts falsely that man has some number of feet other than two. Similarly, 'angels are not bald' must either be plainly true, or assert that they have some hair. There is no indication of the possibility of making the 'not' operate on the proposition as a whole.

While there is no overt mention of a distinction, still there is a clear break between the passages where the examples are of non-identity and the ones where they are of denials of attribution. If in what followed the two were kept clearly separate it might be possible to suggest that Plato was aware of the difference. In what follows, however, the two interpretations are run together, though on the whole it is 'is' and 'Being' that are collecting attribution, 'is not' and 'Non-Being' denials of identity (cf. 259b). But when at 263b 11–12 we are told that 'Theaetetus flies' says 'things that are other than the things that are about you, for as we said, many things are about you and many are not', the 'things that are not' must include the attributions that do not hold. As I pointed out earlier, the only places to which the 'as we said' can refer are 256e or 259b, in both of which it is hard not to take 'is not' as covering non-identity, and in all the 'is not' is to be rendered in terms of participating in difference. This is all very strange in someone supposedly clear about, and insistent on, the difference between denials of identity and denials of attribution. It would be surprising enough in someone who had straightforwardly distinguished between assertions of identity and attributions.

It might nevertheless be possible, I suppose, that Plato has made the distinction on the positive side, but got into difficulties on the negative side. He cannot make the obvious move of contrasting 'X partakes of otherness with regard to Y' and 'X does not partake of Y', because the latter makes use of the negative which is precisely what he wants to analyse. It is perhaps understandable that the cumbersome 'partakes of difference . . .' vaguely seemed to cover everything and did not receive further examination in the general excitement of finding a way of rendering the negative harmless. All depends, then, on the positive evidence. The main prop here is 256a–b and its context. On examination it emerges that there is no need to suppose a distinction between identity and attribution, and that distinction has no part to play in the argument.

The context is the sophistic argument about Non-being, which claims that the expression could apply to nothing and nothing could be said of that which is not. In general, everything of the form 'that which is is not', 'that which is not is' or 'X is and is not' is forbidden. After distinguishing the five great kinds and their capacity for interrelation, the Stranger starts in 255e establishing and neutralising certain apparent contradictions. First, that Change is and is not the same, then that it is and is not different. These are cases of being and not being in a way, but they lead up to 256d where Change is said really to be a not-being and a being. This is baldly and extravagantly to do what Parmenides forbids. In each of these cases the important point for resolving the paradox is to realise that the negative half of the pair should be interpreted in terms of partaking of difference. This is illustrated first on the *relatively* uncontentious examples so that finally even the bald one is seen to be innocuous.

The supposed contradiction could be resolved in one of two ways. The first is that already suggested, the distinction between identity and attribution. The other would be to fix on the expression 'the same' and point out that when we say that 'Change is the same' we mean the same as itself, whereas when we say it is not the same it is something else it is not the same as. This last point has, of course, to be put in terms of difference, for the reasons given earlier. So we have to say that when we say it is not the same it is because of participation in difference which separates it from something else. Once again the apparent contradiction vanishes, only this time the blame is put on 'the same'. It is in favour of this interpretation that the Stranger's words are 'For when we call it the same and not the same we do not speak in the same way'. There is no occurrence here of the verb 'to be', and the rest of the paragraph fits this rendering well.

Still, while the other interpretation is less likely, it is possible, and may become mandatory if that distinction is required for the general argument. This might be made out as follows: those who at 251 following deny the interrelation of kinds are failing to distinguish the 'is' of identity from the copula. They are supposing that only statements of the form 'man is man' are allowable, presumably on the assumption that 'is' is always and only to be interpreted as an identity sign. In that case 'man is white' is necessarily false. Anyone who is going to reject that position must hold that there is some other interpretation of 'is', and also realise that its establishment and distinction from the 'is' of identity will be needed for the routing of the opposition. The assertion of the intercommunion of kinds must involve a recognition of other interpretations and the use of 'participate' as a non-symmetrical version of 'mingle' strongly suggests a fairly, if not perfectly, clear grasp of the copula.

This is admittedly very persuasive, but it relies on the assumption that the 'late learners' are interpreting 'is' as the 'is' of identity. It seems to me that Moravcsik has shown this to be wrong. As described, they are doing nothing of the sort. They are, rather, peddling the view that no two terms of distinct sense can be applied to the same subject. 'Man' applies to man, 'good' to good. To use 'good' of a man is simply wrong, though if good is also present in a complex situation of which man is a part, no doubt it will be applicable to that part of the situation. But on such a view to say 'man is man' is also wrong, because 'is', *however interpreted*, is being used of man. It is no help to expand the 'is' to 'is the same as'. It is significant that these men are not portrayed as only allowing us to say 'man is man', 'good is good', but rather as only allowing us to call man man, good good (cf. 251c 1–2). In other words, a term can only be used of what it is true of, and is only true of what it alone is true of. This is tantamount to the view that every word is a proper name in a world where no two things have the same name. This is why Plato's objection is relevant. Anyone holding such a view has stymied himself. A man holding that all true statements are identity statements might hope to make his point by repetition of correctly formed statements and use of the words 'yes' and 'no' or head-nodding equivalents. Certainly it could not be flung in his face that he used the word 'is' (cf. 252c 2). More particular indication of the limits of his

Procrustean bed would be needed. Plato's opponent is not in bed at all.

If this is right, then the distinction between the 'is' of identity and the copula is simply not relevant to the difficulty. What we need to escape from is the view that neither the identity 'is' nor the copula can be used of anything but identity or copulation. The assertion that kinds can mingle must at least be the claim that many 'names' are applicable to one and the same subject. In fact Plato wants to put forward a view that makes a statement not just a stringing together of names, but a complex that has to satisfy certain composition requirements before it succeeds in saying anything. An account of false statements as saying something other than what is of a subject supposes the possibility of saying something that is of it. It cannot get off the ground if using two names of the same thing is anyway impossible, and in the terminology of 251 following, 'Theaetetus sits' would be doing just that. In short, distinct senses of 'is' are of no help with the late learners, and so one cannot argue that the context leads one to expect that distinction.

To draw together some of the threads so far: I have argued that Plato does not seem with any clarity to have isolated the copula by his use of the metaphor of participation, nor the existential use of '*esti*' by the great kind, Being. Indeed, sometimes at least 'X partakes in Being' seems to mean not 'X exists' but 'For some F, X is F', and sometimes to be excluding instances of not being F. I have also argued that the distinction between the copula and the 'is' of identity is not brought out. Plato fails to distinguish between the denials of these two, there would be no point to his making the distinction for the purposes of the argument, and the passage where he might seem to be making it in fact shows him to be making a different one.

All this may seem to leave the metaphor of participation somewhat unexplained. There is no doubt, I think, that Ackrill is right to say that this, as distinct from 'mingle', is a non-symmetrical relation. But what 'participates' indicates, within the confines of the Great Kinds passage and often elsewhere, is that the term for what follows it is applicable to what the term that precedes it stands for. Thus at 259a we get the statement that through participation in Being, the different is, not Being, but different. The different partakes in Being in that 'is' is applicable to it, and it does not matter in what sense. But it is not automatically true that if 'F' can be applied to something the converse is also true, even allowing for Plato's lack of distinction between mentioning 'F' and using 'F'. The important point, however, is that uses of the copula are themselves instances of the attribution of 'is'-ing and so of participation in Being. Now any attribution of a property is thereby an attribution of 'is'-ing, for it is the claim that for some F the subject is F. As everything must have some property, Being is all-pervasive. On the other hand 'is the same' and 'is different' also hold of everything, and so 'same' and 'different' too. Spelled out, doubtless, everything at least partakes of that part of being that is being different (or some part of being which is a part of being different) and similarly with sameness, and so at one stroke 'is' and 'different' are applicable. But 'participate' does not isolate the copula: it is needed to indicate the applicability of the copula.

If this is right, however, surely one is committed to holding that Plato does after all isolate the copula by means of the notion of Being and the resultant great kind? For it now looks as though all the occurrences of 'is' in '. . . is red', '. . . is the same as' are distinguished from what follows. The 'is' manifests Being, 'the same as' identity and so on. The argument has only shown that 'participate' is not the tool of isolation.

It would be nice to be able to say this, but I fear it will not do. To begin with, it is not just obvious that the passages usually cited in favour of saying that 'participates in Being' means 'exists' do not tell in that direction. On the face of it at least it seems that 'change and stability both are' means 'change and stability both exist'. There is, however, a problem. For this cannot be taken in the normal way the English sentence would be taken, to assert that there are instances of change and stability in the world. 'Change' and 'stability' are the names of kinds or Forms. Now it seems that commonly in the dialogues the claim that there is such a thing as change or justice or whatever amounts to no more than that it is possible to say what constitutes it. Thus someone might admit that there is such a thing as justice while going on to deny that there is any really just man or state. This suggests that to say that X is is to say that there is such a thing as X, and that in turn is to say that there is an account to be given of what constitutes being X. To be a being is to be something of which it is possible to answer the question 'what is it?' In that case we should have to admit unicorns as beings, since it is possible to answer the question 'what constitutes being a unicorn?' In earlier dialogues, while there is no discussion of unicorns, it seems clear that they would not count as 'beings' (i.e. Unicorn would not count as a being), because Forms always play a role in explaining why the universe is as it is, and Unicorn has no such role. It is only sufficient for establishing that there is such a thing as justice or health that there is an answer to 'what is it?' because one has already restricted the range of possible values for X in 'what constitutes being X?' to ones that have a part in this explanatory system. Unicorns do not even appear on the horizon.

In the *Sophist* it remains uncertain where Plato stands. We get no mention of mythical beasts – though Plato of all people must be held to be familiar with myths – yet if he is using 'Being' in such a way that it is intended to be sufficient for something's qualifying that it be possible to say what constitutes being it, then in the light of previous restrictions one would expect a special point to be made of the change. The obvious way would be via non-existent things. At the same time, if we consider the presentation of the sophistic paradox at 237–9 it often has more immediate bite if we suppose that 'that which is not' is taken not as 'that which does not exist' but 'that which for all F is not F'. For instance, the statement that that which is not cannot have number, if 'that which is not' means 'that which does not exist' is not just obvious. If I mention unicorns and centaurs I seem to have mentioned two things that do not exist, and if individuals are required, the man in the moon and Minerva will do. No doubt there are difficulties about 'how many unicorns do not exist?' that do not attach to 'how many African elephants exist?', and if 'that which does not exist' is taken as standing for the empty void of nothingness one may feel that numbering is out of place there too. It remains that to bring home the inappositeness of numbering what is not, on this interpretation, it would need some elaboration. It would hardly seem obvious in the way the exposition expects. On the other hand if 'that which is not' means 'that which for all F is not F' then it will seem very clear that number predicates will be excluded along with the rest. Also, the contradiction referred to at 238d following consists in the fact that in declaring 'that which is not to be unspeakable and "without account", we have said what it is'. Once again, if it is that which for all F is not F, then how comes it that some F (unspeakable and so on) hold of it? The appearance of contradiction is immediate.

There is then room for doubt about taking the Form of Being as the Form for 'being F', and if the doubt is justified then there will be many occurrences of the copula that do not give cases of 'is'-ing (e.g. 'being a unicorn is being single-horned', 'centaurs are dreamed of by drunken Greeks'). Further doubts arise when we consider the failure to distinguish between the 'is' of identity and the copula, especially as manifested on the negative side, and the erratic tendency to confine Being to positive attributions of properties (cf. 256e, 259b), while at the same time wanting to say that not being is itself being something (258b–c). Between them these produce, as we shall see, obscurity into Plato's whole project.

The conclusion, then, must be that Plato certainly does not succeed in making any of the distinctions proposed in any of the ways proposed. So gross is the failure that one would need very strong reason for supposing the intention. It is quite possible for us to see that in various passages different translations are needed to bring out the point made, but Plato gives no indication of noticing the differences. It will not do to say that of course he left it to the reader to work it out for himself. There can, no doubt, be special circumstances where this would be justified – odd hints, facts about the structure of the work and so on – but the *Sophist* notably lacks these. Any general acceptance of this principle would make all philosophers immune to criticism except perhaps on grounds of explicit contradiction. For the rest, if they are great, the apparent confusions are being left for the reader to pick up; only if they are not great are they confused. Which is which we shall never know.

I said earlier that I would end with some suggestions as to what Plato is doing and some comments on his success or otherwise. The problem from which the Stranger starts at about 236d is about the usability of the expression 'that which is not' (cf. 237c 1.) The position expounded is that 'that which is not' must apply to something of which it alone is true. If anything else were true of it, it would be true that it is something (is some F). If 'that which is not' holds of anything, then it must be true of it simply that it is not anything. The Stranger proceeds to produce difficulties about 'that which is'. To begin with they simply illustrate a general condition of disarray, for all that important points are made in passing. By 249–50, however, he produces a conclusion to match that on 'that which is not'. That of which 'that which is' is to be used must simply *be* something without there being anything else that it is. Since everything is either changing or stable, 'that which is' cannot apply to anything. Consequently, not only is it impossible to use 'that which is' and 'that which is not' of each other's applicanda, but in fact neither can be applied to anything at all. At 250d–e the Stranger draws attention to this equality in non-application between 'that which is' and 'that which is not', which suggests that we are supposed to notice the point. We have, in fact, two problems about falsity. First, to describe a statement as false is to say that it is saying that what is is not or the converse (cf. 240e), which seems contradictory. Second, it seems that 'that which is not' is an empty expression, or at least without application, so there cannot be false statements since they, in Greek, would be things that are not. This last difficulty supposes that 'that which is' does have application. The point of raising a similar difficulty about this expression is presumably to draw attention to a mistake. Further, it is one that must be removed before the question of resolving any contradiction can be dealt with. For the contradiction only arises if the two terms can be applied in some sense to the same subject. Both the sophistic argument and the Stranger's riposte on 'that which is' argue that the expression in question can hold of nothing, and each argument proceeds on the assumption that the expression, if it applies to anything, must apply to something to which it alone applies. In these particular cases it will be impossible to apply many names to one thing, but the argument assumes that it will always be impossible.

If this is right, it is obviously relevant to raise the general question of how it is ever possible to apply many names to one thing. Of the possibilities rejected on the intermingling of kinds, the only one that receives any extended treatment is the one that rejects the possibility of intermingling. As we have seen, this is precisely the view that each name can be used only of that of which it alone is the name. From this view it will follow directly that if 'that which is' and 'that which is not' are different names they will not both apply to the same subject. Even when this is rejected, it might still be that these expressions are contradictories, but that can only be dealt with when the more radical assumption is out of the way. The assumption does not cover just that uncertain range that later philosophers have gathered under the heading 'predicate', but all expressions. The consequence is that what we call a '*logos*' is in fact a collection of names each only applicable to some part of a situation, no two applicable to the same part. Since 'is', 'same', 'different' and so on count as names here, 'man is not a vegetable' cannot hold of *man*, but 'man' of man, 'is' of is and so on down to 'vegetable'. At this point it is important to note the expressions to whose use the Stranger appeals to reject the view, as this indicates how Plato takes the view he is rejecting. If the opposition were thought of as interested in, say, empirical concepts like 'man' and 'white', and holding of these that they only applied respectively to man and white, i.e. to different elements in a complex situation stated by 'man is white', there would be nothing to stop them saying 'only man is man' or 'only white is white'. For they could hold that words such as 'only', 'is' and so on are not terms for describing the world but for indicating how we are to take those that do. So Plato's objection would not apply and his rudeness about the worth of those peddling the view would not be so obviously justified.

The assertion of the intermingling of kinds, then, is to the effect that different terms must be co-applicable to the same subject, in rejection of this view. This is a precondition of the possibility of speech (cf. 259e). Unless we reject it we cannot even say the true 'Theaetetus sits', since 'sits' could only hold of sitting, not of Theaetetus, let alone the false 'Theaetetus flies'. When spelled out the view looks absurd, and Plato plainly thought it was. A position may, however, rest on an unnoticed absurd assumption while not itself seeming absurd simply because the assumption has gone unnoticed. This is presumably Plato's diagnosis of the falsity paradox.

The assumption does not require any distinctions of senses of 'is' for its puncturing, but its rejection does call for an alternative account of the applicability of expressions which insists that it must be the rule for a variety of expressions to hold of the same subject. Once this is allowed it becomes a possibility for any two expressions such as 'is' and 'is not' to co-apply. In this case, however, there is the further obstacle that they seem to be mutually incompatible. At this stage (256 seq.) we get the introduction of the analysis of 'is not' in terms of difference. It thereby emerges not merely that Being and Difference are always co-applicable to every subject, but Being and Non-being. These might be better rendered 'is'-ing and 'is-not'-ing. Not only are they always co-applicable, but their ubiquitous co-applicability is essential for discourse. This, as the Stranger points out (cf. 258c seq.) is quite the other extreme from Parmenides, and so satisfyingly provocative. It would, of course, have been enough to show that their intermingling is sometimes possible. It is more exciting to show that it is at all points essential to *logos* and therefore, *a fortiori*, to true *logos* (cf. Parmenides' poem).

In all this, Plato sees the main thrust of the falsity paradox as coming first from the assumption that no two expressions can be applied to the same subject, and second that 'that which is not', and in its train 'is not', function as general contradictories of 'is', denying, for any F, that the subject is F. The intermingling of kinds removes the first difficulty, the analysis of negation in term of difference the second. When it comes to falsity Plato is extremely brief. There is no very detailed account of what a *logos* is, only a few examples of very simple ones. There is no indication of how, if at all, the name/verb analysis is supposed to apply to quantified propositions, for instance. Plato's interest does not seem to be in an account of propositions, nor in an account of true ones, but in indicating how one can describe false ones as saying what is not, using the analysis in terms of difference. The main work is plainly making 'is not' acceptable, not expounding the possibility of falsity, and this is understandable as the objection to falsity has rested on the unacceptability of the expression 'is not' in general.

Once again, there are no grounds for supposing that in the *Sophist* we see Plato struggling out of difficulties of his own. As it was part of his position that most people's opinions on important topics were false, he would have to tackle various arguments current to the effect that false opinions or statements are impossible. There is no reason to suppose that before the *Sophist* he thought he knew just where the mistakes lay. But it is possible to be baffled by arguments that do not even begin to tempt one, and learning how to meet them can be very illuminating. That is not the same as seeing one's way through one's own bad arguments. There are, it is true, signs in the *Sophist* that all stating is naming, but Plato is rude about the holders of such views in a way that does not suggest that he thinks of it as the sort of position a sensible man (like himself) might misguidedly hold. Neither the *Sophist* alone nor it and the *Cratylus* together, therefore, supply any reason for supposing that Plato started life thinking of statements as names and so, in so far as that might lend support to the view that he is moving from an acquaintance to a propositional view of knowledge, they supply no reason for believing that either.

It remains to ask how successful Plato was in the task he set himself. This means asking whether he has an account of 'is not' which satisfactorily enables him to describe false statements. The answer is that he has not, and the reasons are partly because of his analysis of negation, partly because of the uncertainties we have noticed about 'is'. To take the first first. We have already seen that Plato wants to gloss 'is not' generally as 'partakes in difference from', and while sometimes his examples are of non-identity and sometimes of non-attribution (and occasionally, in discussing the latter, he adds to the analysis in terms of simple difference), he nevertheless treats both indifferently as partaking in difference. When his examples are clearly of denials of attribution at 257b following we get limitations on the simple account in terms of difference. They are not heralded as that, nor are we led to expect a change of analysis. At 257b there is, indeed, a change of direction. We have just been persuaded that a thing can be and not be, and it is now to be explained how 'is not' is not the *opposite* of 'is'. The illustration is with large. When we say 'not large' this does not denote the opposite of large, small, in preference to middle-sized. In short, not-*F* simply signifies something other than *F*. But this is clearly not enough. 'Red' is other than large, but hardly signified by 'not large'. So we get told that there are parts of difference that stand over against beings (257d–e). So when we talk of what is not beautiful we are talking of what is different from nothing other than the nature of beauty. This confines the range of 'not-*F*' to properties that rule out *F*. If the example of 'not large' is taken as serious, Plato seems to have in mind sets of properties, such as the colours or the animal species. Saying that something is not red is saying it is some colour other than red, if it is not a pig it is some animal other than a pig. As it stands the account is confused, because Plato says that 'not' simply introduces something antithetical to what follows. This is fair enough with 'not large', but is no help with 'not being'. What he needs to say is that 'not being' is the name of the set of negations of properties, whose members are not large, not red and so on. These do not signify the opposite of being, but being something incompatible with (not being) but what follows the not. This account would not of course apply to the 'not' in the name 'not being' itself. But Plato does not say this. The idea of a range of incompatible predicates, the disjunction of all but one of which is signified by the negation of any is needed because otherwise it would follow, from the vaguer account, that if someone is hairy, then as being hairy is being something other than nice, he is not nice. This might seem simply eccentric, but it would also follow of anything that had two distinct properties, say round and white, that it was round and not round, which has a less acceptable air. Yet the resultant account of 'not *F*' is too limited. Plato gets at it through that of an opposite. His use of the word for 'opposite' could do with examination, but usually he seems to have in mind cases where there are degrees of opposition. Thus if we take hot and cold, cool and lukewarm come in between. They too are opposed to each other, though less so. Neither is the real opposite of cold, though they fall in a range of opposition in places incompatible with it. This way of thinking does not encourage one to think of the possibility of a property incompatible with the whole range and what its relation is to being cold. Suppose we take an argument that Plato might be expected to accept: if the soul were cubic, it would be extended, and if extended, perceptible by some sense. Plato might accept the validity of the argument, but would want to object that the soul is not cubic. For all that the *Sophist* tells us he would be saying that it is some other shape. Plato's account does not allow for taking 'the soul is not cubic' simply as 'it is not the case that the soul is cubic'. This results in one type of false statement which cannot be accounted for on the proposed analysis of negation in terms of difference.

If we turn to the uncertainties about 'is' there are further difficulties. If Plato was consciously concerned about the existential implications of '*esti*' then he would presumably have been aware of the limitations of his account. For then the point of the naming function is to attach the proposition to something that exists. Consequently, statements about Minerva or unicorns are unaccounted for. Neither 'Minerva is a Greek goddess' nor 'Minerva is spoken of by Homer' can be accounted false, since they are as yet unpermissible. Further, true denials of existence are not allowed. So 'unicorns do not exist' is forbidden, and the false 'unicorns do exist' therefore cannot be denied. If the offending notion of non-being is not non-existence, but being something of which it is not possible to answer the question 'what is it?', some of these difficulties will ease. As we can answer the question 'what is a unicorn?' or 'who is Minerva?' it will be possible to make statements about them. Even 'unicorns do not exist' could be rendered as 'everything partakes in difference from unicorn', perhaps, though that might need some expansion of the name/verb distinction. If, as I have suggested, Plato is not consciously concerned about existential implications, but is inclined to allow the possibility of answering 'what is F?' only to be sufficient for establishing that there is such a thing as F when 'F' is a term needed as part of the general explanation of the universe, then the matter is more complicated. This restriction only clearly applies to general terms, so we should not know what to do about Minerva (but cf. 262d–e). It is not, as with the present queen of France, impossible to answer the question 'who is she?' With general terms, statements about unicorns would be in difficulties, but not denials of existence generally. If horses were exterminated that would not show there was no Form of horse, only that the world was to an extent defective, so that 'everything fails to participate in Horse' might render 'horses do not exist'.

Plato is coming near to saying that for any statement there has to be an answer to the questions 'what is the topic?' and 'what is said about it?' If there is no answer, nothing is said. If both are answerable, then either what is said holds of the topic or it does not. The topic is often determined by a name, but names cannot be grammatically identified; for these purposes, whether or not a word is a name depends on whether or not it is being used in a given context to perform this function. But while names will perform this function, it is not true that they alone do it. But Plato has a notion of name whereby they can be listed irrespective of context, and seems to suppose that they are always needed to fix the topic. Also, he has not clearly got the idea of a topic. The description of the dialectician in 253–4 suggests someone who is examining reality at least as much as tracing connections between concepts, so that while some of the things he says about Being invite the interpretation that X is a being if and only if there is an answer to the question 'what is it?', other things suggest that it is also necessary, if 'X' is a term like 'man' or 'unicorn' that 'X' be a member of the set of concepts needed for the explanation of a properly constructed universe or at least one that has application, and if 'X' stands for an individual, that it be a real individual (cf. 262d–e). The whole project is further hampered by an inadequate analysis of negation.

In the *Sophist*, then, Plato does not succeed in producing a clear explanation of the possibility of false statements, nor is he at last abandoning an early view that statements are either complex names, lists of names or assertions of identity. Indeed, Plato never held the view that many predicates cannot be applied to the same subject – the doctrine of participation is incompatible with it – nor, as we have seen, is he led to postulate Forms, primarily at least, by any view that general terms are really proper names. At the same time, his rejection of other accounts of what constitutes health, justice and so on, and what explains their occurrence, leads him to require that what constitutes justice should be without qualification and unambiguously just. That 'unambiguously' can be expressed, ambiguously, by saying that it must be simply just and nothing else. This has a distinct isolationist ring. As we have seen the tendency of the later dialogues is to insist on interrelation rather than isolation, and it is quite likely that in dealing with the falsity paradoxes Plato learned more clearly the necessity for insisting on interrelation, but that is only to say that analysing other people's mistakes can sometimes help with one's own different ones.

XIV

The Conditions for
Determining Excellence

It is now time to recapitulate the central Platonic position that I wish to discuss. The position goes roughly as follows: all men desire what is best. They show this in desiring what is best for themselves, for if it is really the best for them, then it is because it is best in general. As being an excellent human being is being as it is best for a human being to be, this will involve wanting to be an excellent man. Being able to achieve excellence is only possible if one knows what it is, and this means if one reaches the heights of intellectual development. For to understand is always to understand how it is best that things be done one way rather than any other, so a full understanding of things would be a full understanding of how it is best for things to be. The development of such understanding goes with the growth of a revulsion against disorder and things being done badly, so that the initial desire for what is best takes the form of a desire to have things done properly. Traditional moral norms and standards are seen in this context to be desirable and what any reasonable/knowledgeable man would advocate (at least with some modifications), and the type of motivation underlying it is something that is essential to any fully developed man. What makes the world intelligible and what all men desire, goodness, are thus identical, and it shows traditional morality to be desirable, although something less than its advocates seem to suppose.

I now want to select certain aspects of this view for more detailed discussion. A good deal hinges on what can be said as to the conditions that have to be satisfied if it is to be possible to speak of good and bad Xes, and the consequent conditions for determining excellence. This in turn raises questions about the move from saying that this is a good X to saying that X is a good thing, and about the connection between either and what men really want.

All this is concerned with the possibility of one of Plato's main projects, that of showing the question of what is the best sort of life to live to be a matter of proof. As I pointed out in chapter I, it would be quite possible for someone to hold that it is impossible to give any criteria for distinguishing between good and bad arguments on that general topic, but to believe that it is possible to give an account of what morality is concerned with, and so of what distinguishes relevant from morally irrelevant considerations – though that leaves open the question whether it is a good thing to be moral. Plato has a view on 'what common morality is about', and this is the second aspect of Plato's position that I shall discuss. The position also has an epistemological side in that Plato is committed to considerable restrictions on what is to count as knowledge and what is to count as an explanation. This will form the third item for discussion and the fourth will be the related view that our ordinary language carries a theoretical assumption and is in principle open to correction.

In chapter II I argued that Plato's procedure for determining what a thing's excellence is assumed that it only makes sense to talk of a good X if it is possible to say what X's function is, and its goodness is a matter of its effective performance of that function. A wide range of terms already serve to classify things by function ('eye', 'typewriter', 'detective'), and in these cases it obviously makes sense to talk of good or bad specimens. In other cases it becomes somewhat baffling what is meant. Thus if someone tells us he has a good bit of dust, as 'bit of dust' does not classify anything in terms of function we are at a loss to know how it is being assessed. The situation can be retrieved if he adds 'I mean, it is good as an itching powder'. Now Plato, of course, would want to say that while things can be assessed from many angles, for their performance of many functions, there is one that is the thing's real function, so that speaking of its excellence is speaking of its performance of its real function. For the present I shall leave that complication aside. In that case, the point about function can be put as saying that to assess the excellence of X is always to assess its excellence as a Y (where 'X' may, but need not, be the substitution for 'Y'), and 'Y' must always be a word that gives, either generically or specifically, a function. Plato may want to add more, but this much at least he seems committed to. So one strand in Plato's procedure for determining excellence is that all such assessments are assessments of the performance of a function.

Another strand is that already referred to, that for anything there is one function that is its real function, so that to determine the excellence of X is not simply to satisfy oneself about its performance of some function or other, but of some special function that can be said to be *its* function. So long as one confines oneself to examples of words that already classify by function this can seem a very acceptable point. One can consider the merits of a typewriter as a doorstop, but the situation is different from that with the bit of dust being considered as itching powder. There it would be linguistically acceptable to distinguish between good and bad bits of dust. But in the case of the typewriter, which is in other ways analogous, the function is so firmly built into our notion of a typewriter that there would be widespread resistance to labelling typewriters as good or bad ones by reference to their success or failure as doorstops. After all *the* function of typewriters is to type, and their capacity to perform other functions is incidental. So some things have their own real functions, and can seriously be said to be good or bad such and suches, while others do not have a special function, and one cannot strictly speak of better or worse bits of dust and the rest.

This move becomes very much less persuasive if one takes a wider selection of examples. Suppose, to start with, that we confine ourselves to examples where the functional story seems plausible. To begin with a mild point: some terms suggest a functional interpretation, but in an indeterminate way. Is it the function of an argument to persuade or to prove, of the tongue to taste, help speak or help swallow? Here one might opt for a multi-function answer and determine excellence by reference to performance in the combination, but it at least opens the door for a more complicated picture. Again, take the account of human excellence. As I pointed out in chapter IV it would be quite possible for someone to view this from the point of view of the species, decide that this demands a community form of life which in turn requires the performance of a variety of functions. It would still be possible to define the species in terms of a role in the economy of nature, but that function would not necessarily enable us to judge the excellence of individual members. For it might be a function performed by the community *en bloc* or by one section of it, while the community's existence requires the performance of functions by members who never individually perform the community function. It would be a bad member of the species that performed no function required by the species, but there would be no function that was the one whose performance constituted the excellence or otherwise of every member or even of any member. Plato's failure to see this possibility has important results for his treatment of virtue, as we shall see later. While the tripartite division of the personality/state allows for a variety of functions, it is treated as a set of functions of which one is the dominant one, and all three of which should be performed. The predominant one is the one that determines what human excellence really is. If one now asks how Plato would go about selecting the function that is the thing's 'real' function, or the function of a thing the term for which does not readily suggest any function, the answer is not far to seek. One has to see what part that thing plays in the total system, and if it does several things then the most important one is selected and allowed to determine the performance of the others. This concept of 'most important' is, as we shall see, trouble-some. The easiest thing for the moment is to refer to an example, the way in which reasoning dominates in deciding the function of the person (cf. chapter II). At present it is enough that *the* function that is the function of X is in the last resort determined not linguistically, but by reference to the system in which X plays a part.

This move involves at least three assumptions: first, that there will only be one way of interpreting the universe functionally. To this I shall return when considering Plato's views on explanation. Second, that one will always be able to proceed to *some* total functional account. Third, that always when one is justified in talking of a good X short of the total system, this is only justified because one can specify X's function. It is this last that makes the second a plausible assumption at all, and indeed it entails it. Yet if we return to the example of human excellence it comes to look a somewhat dubious assumption. For while it is clearly an intelligible view that the human species should have a non-destructive part to play in the balance of nature, it is also conceivable that one should be able to describe the form of life that character-ises this species and determines the roles required of various members, without there being any answer to the question 'what does the existence of that form of life contribute to the working of the whole?' Perhaps the only difference that would be made by the extinction of the species would be that the world would lack that particular form of life. This might be enough to convince G. E. Moore that it is better that such things exist, but it is not enough for Plato. This point becomes clearer if we widen the range of examples taken. Thus it is perfectly sensible to talk of a good pirouette or a good sprint. While it may be that either has a function, it is not this fact that is relied on in attributing excellence, but the fact that each requires some skill or unusual ability which admits of degrees. Similarly a good anagram poem will be one that manifests considerable ingenuity. In fact Plato interestingly enough hovers be-tween these two ways of determining excellence in *Republic* Book I. We are told that the 'function' of a thing is to be discovered by discovering what that thing does best or what we would do best with it. Suppose we have a species of monkey whose special gift is pirouetting. It does many other things, but only indifferently compared with the performance of other species. In pirouetting, but only in pirouetting, does it excel. Pirouetting must be its function therefore, by the first wording, and its excellence judged by reference to its skill in that performance. But if we now ask what we can do with this monkey better than with any other creature it is not clear that there must be an answer. Plato's examples of a horse and a sickle suggest some end we can accomplish by their means, such as transport or cutting a field of corn. But we certainly cannot pirouette by means of this monkey, and there is no reason to suppose that the pirouetting can be used at all, let alone better than anything else, to produce any further end. Yet the conflation of these two ways of determining excellence is not unimportant to Plato, because the thing that only men do, or do better than anything else is apparently (forgetting the gods?) reasoning. Plato in fact thinks of this in terms of its use in relation to other parts of the person or universe – its function is to rule and care for. But of course it would be possible to assess performance here in terms of ingenuity, or capacity to discover universal truths. It might now be possible to hold that human excellence is determined by reference to the peculiarly human activity of reasoning, while holding that the high flights of its exercise do not serve any further purpose. Higher education is its own justification. If Plato had seen the difference between these two ways of determining excellence he would have realised that his position would need considerable further defence. For it would now be possible to hold over and over again that while the excellence of the parts of a thing is settled by reference to function, the excellence of the whole is determined by reference to the activity that either it alone does or it does best, and these activities do not require any relation to any greater whole for the judging of their merit. Plato might, of course, think that unless these activities have a part to play in some larger whole, then they are worthless, but that is now coming clean with a prejudice, not relying on the conditions that have to be satisfied in order to make sense of attributing excellence.

In fact the situation is somewhat worse than this suggests, as becomes clear if one takes a still wider field of examples. A good toffee may be thought to be judged so in relation to its function of pleasing the eater, but it will not do for Plato's purposes. In order for something to count as having an 'ergon' it has to be the possible subject of some techne. The Gorgias distinction between skills and knacks makes it clear that there could not be a skill covering toffees unless there were an overall account of human taste to be given. 'Satisfying the taste of the eater' no more gives a studiable function than does 'satisfying the fashion of the day'. Since tastes, like fashion, are variable, the expression at best stands for an indefinite range of possible functions. In fact, however, the judgement that a toffee is a good one often carries no implications of a general sort even about the taste of the speaker. Sometimes, according to context, 'good' is equivalent to 'useful', sometimes to 'skilful', sometimes to 'admirable', but sometimes just to 'nice'. Nor is this just a fact about the English word 'good'. Plato would have been familiar enough with a use of the words 'agathos' and 'arete' where it was not performance of a function that was being assessed. When used of men these terms usually indicated a person's position in society and/or his prowess. A person in a position of power capable of keeping it, so long as he was not mean in his exercise of it, would show 'arete' and be, especially if of correct descent, an *agathos*. The argument that he was less useful to the community than various public servants of less social standing would not have been felt to diminish his title to excellence. Just as in England, at one time, who were one's betters was not decided at all on Platonic lines, not even on grounds of ability, so in Greece, who were *agathoi* and had *arete* was not decided in the way Plato wanted. It was, of course, as possible for him as for someone in English to start selecting examples with a view to persuading people that a person cannot really be said to be good unless one can first determine his proper function and then show that he performs it well; but the force of 'not really' would not be that it is not true that he is good in the sense meant.

This only shows that it makes sense to assess the excellence of subjects even when the assessment is not of the subject's performance of its function. Plato might be able to argue that such assessments are parasitic on ones which do satisfy his conditions and that it is this that justifies him in saying that the others do not really assess the subject's excellence. In that case he might be entitled to dismiss the counterexamples while still holding that he is not simply trying to persuade us to change our ways of judging worth. In order to do this he will need a fairly strong form of the claim that the other assessments are parasitic, and he will have to show first that the claim works on assessments of men and second that it is only what is good in the non-parasitic sense that is the object of desire. It will be no use showing that, for instance, the practice of calling things good in virtue of the skilful performance of useless tasks can be seen to be an offshoot of the practice of an interest in the good performance of useful ones. That may be the genesis of the practice, but if it now operates independently then it is quite possible first that men are usually assessed in this way and second that, if it is a truth that all men desire the good, it is only that they desire to be good according to this parasitic form of assessment. Thus Plato's contemporaries could agree that all men desire *arete* and *arete* only, but also claim that excellence is not for these purposes assessed in the way Plato proposes. In that case Plato would have a choice: he would either have to admit that it is false that all men desire the good strictly speaking, or bring separate arguments for supposing that they do, or argue that while the assessment in question does not directly rely on facts about function in the last resort its acceptability does rely on such facts. The first alternative would mean abandoning one of his main props. The second would not be a great deal happier for him. Reliance on the attraction of saying that everyone wants his own good gets into the same problem, but if he baldly declares that everyone wants to be functioning well by some criteria ultimately derived from the economy of nature, then the need for some supporting argument becomes acute. Even if he argued that our own welfare can only be achieved by achieving the good running of the whole he is left with two difficulties: first, that such arguments are highly unconvincing when supposed to apply to every single choice, and throw the burden on the elaborate arguments for immortality and the World Soul. Second, any such move is tantamount to abandoning the possibility of taking it as an obvious premiss that we all want what is best.

Thus, unless Plato is prepared either to abandon the position that all men want the good, or start looking for a complex of empirical support that he does not seem to have much hope of finding, he is left with the third alternative. This might be argued for either on general grounds or on the particular one that with assessments of men, at least, the position holds. Since a refutation of the last will be enough for present purposes I shall confine myself to that. What Plato needs to be able to show is that if you take an interpretation of 'good man' such that it is likely to be admitted that all men want to be good, then it will emerge on examination that men only are, on this assessment, good if they fulfil their human function. That is to say, it will, under pressure at least, become clear that the assessor is taking for granted a view of the human function and making his assessment on this basis. The trouble is that nothing of the sort seems to be true. One can see that in some cases something of the sort might hold. Thus someone might judge that a given detective is a good one on the grounds that he lights his pipe in a certain way and never gives his opinion on a case. Clearly he is either using these as marks of a good detective on imagined empirical grounds or he is not assessing him as a detective at all. If the first, then any explanation of the grounds he uses will have to refer to the detective function and how the marks are marks of its good performance. In this case, of course, to consider someone as a detective is to consider him as fulfilling a given function. But *ex hypothesi* we are considering cases where assessing someone as a man is not in this straightforward way taking account of function performance. Yet Greeks who thought of the successful well-to-do man of good birth as *agathos* were not taking these points as marks of some further excellence. They were taking them as constituting excellence. In part this is a comment on the person's success and position, in part perhaps on his accomplishments. What it does not have is any reference to his usefulness. This is even clearer with someone who, in Thrasymachean vein, admired the man who can put himself above the law and use its institutions for his own purposes. In all this there may be some use of exceptional accomplishment underlying the attribution of excellence, but there is no suggestion of men having a special function. Indeed, such a position is a rejection of the whole picture that Plato is advocating.

It might be objected that Plato is right to say that it is always in order to ask 'what is the good of success, of being a tyrant or whatever it may be?', and this shows that it is always supposed that if something is a good X, then it is a good thing that there should be Xes. Unfortunately a question's being in order does not ensure its answerability, nor does the fact that it cannot be answered render the original statement unacceptable. It may well be that it is appropriate to ask 'what is the good of success?', and to take this as questioning whether success has a role in a wider relationship. Suppose the answer is 'none'. This only says that success does not have a role in a wider relationship. It does not indicate that no sense can be given to saying none the less that it is a good thing without reference to anything further. Only if to say it was good was only sense if it had a function whose performance was being assessed in calling it good would this follow. But that would simply be begging the question at issue. When, as at the beginning of *Republic* Book II, he is equating goodness with desirability, Plato in effect accepts this possibility, but he needs to avoid it when he is treating goodness as determined independently of desirability and related to the Form of the Good.

It seems then, that Plato wants an account of 'good' whereby (i) X can meaningfully be said to be a good Y if and only if 'Y' determines a function that can conceivably be performed by X. (ii) It must be possible to isolate some function or set of functions as the proper function(s) of X. (iii) Proper functions are determined by reference to the system of which X is a part. (iv) All men want the good. We have seen that (i) will not hold. To begin with, for his synoptic view of goodness he needs a clearly functional interpretation of '*ergon*'. His own wording in *Republic* Book I (but not in Book X 601d) allows for a weaker interpretation, but while this might have helped disguise the mistake it does not remove it. If one casts one's net wider it is clear that even these two ways of determining excellence do not exhaust the possibilities. It may be that in the expression 'good as a Y' some limitations have to be set on the possible substitutions for 'Y'. It seems that 'Y' must determine a range of some sort which allows for approximation to some standard, but nothing so narrow as function does justice to the facts. While (ii) exercises some pull with a limited selection of terms, once one strays afield it is clear that it relies upon (iii), underlining *the* system. If one allows of an object's possibly playing a part in a variety of systems then there is the possibility of rival accounts of its function with no means of deciding which is its 'proper' one. Even so, the requirement that one be able to refer to some wider system breaks down once (i) is abandoned. Further, on the face of it, in so far as it seems plausible to say that everyone wants the good (the best life, his own welfare) 'good' does not seem to be operating as part of a functional assessment.

All that Plato may have lost so far is a certain amount of *a priori* defence of his positions. It might still be possible to make out a functional interpretation of the universe and to exhibit the special role of man in the complete structure. That would give sense to talking, in that context, of human excellence in the way Plato wants. It would not follow that there was a single form of excellence for all human beings, but there would at least be a way of talking of human excellence such that the function(s) that constituted it were determined by reference to the wider interplay of nature. It is part of such an interpretation to see things as having a natural tendency towards behaving in the way required of them. Indeed, part of the evidence needed for showing such an interpretation possible would be that things of the various proposed kinds for the most part tended towards their proposed roles, with failures being explained either in terms of interference or by some category of malformation. In that case if the interpretation is possible at all then it must be possible to attribute some nisus towards their own perfection to things of various kinds. In the case of percipient and intelligent human beings such a nisus would take the form of a desire. Consequently, if the universe is susceptible of a functional interpretation then it must be possible to attribute to men a desire for their own perfection, and so say that the good is what they all want. This does, of course, mean opting for a special form of functional explanation. So far I have expounded it as though the analogy with machines would be quite adequate, but that would not yield any temptation to attribute any nisus towards anything. The parts of machines show no tendency towards self-perfection or self-repair. They only deteriorate. The relevant model is an organism, such as a plant or animal, and this is, of course, the one used by Plato in both the *Timaeus* and the *Philebus*. It might indeed be argued that part of the distinction between an organism and a machine is that the former should manifest a tendency to the development and preservation of a certain form of life, whereas the latter only performs under manipulation. If all entities of a given type showed tendencies destructive of the form of life attributed in calling them organisms of such and such a sort, that would be sufficient to refute that particular organic hypothesis. In the case of beings to which intelligence is being attributed, this might amount to saying that such beings must want their own welfare, as complete absence of such a desire would entail probably that they were not organisms and certainly that they were not intelligent ones. If this were accepted then it should be possible to work out certain norms of behaviour that gave the good functioning of the organism, and attribute to it a fundamental desire to operate in that way. In that case it would not, with men, be possible for anyone truthfully (or sanely) to disavow interest in such behaviour. If traditional moral norms can be shown more or less to yield the norms of good functioning, then it would follow that no one who understands about them can reject traditional moral standards as undesirable. That something is a morally good thing will now be a consideration with a special status. Whereas the rejection of other considerations may simply show eccentricity, the rejection of this shows hostility to one's performance as the kind of being one is, which in the case of men means hostility to one's performance as a rational being. In this sense, then, rejection of moral considerations would always show irrationality.

The position now no longer depends on any general thesis about the word 'good' and the presuppositions of its attributability, but partly on the possibility of interpreting the universe in a certain way, partly on the possibility of being able in consequence to attribute to men a certain fundamental desire, and partly on being able to relate traditional moral norms to what answers to that desire. I shall have little to say about the first point. It should be clear that whatever one's initial bias may be, this is really an empirical question and so not a proper subject for philosophical dogmatising. That means that, as I think he realises, Plato would have to do the very considerable work necessary for showing that such an account of nature held. I shall be more concerned with the question of what would follow if we accepted, what does not seem entirely implausible, the view that man is an intelligent organism. In particular one needs to ask what the relevant fundamental desire would be, whether it suffices for Plato's purposes as outlined in the early chapters, and whether we are left with a rendering of 'X is a good thing' that makes it a consideration that it would be irrational to reject, in some interesting sense of 'irrational'. It will then be asked whether anyway this would result in a good account of traditional morality, and indeed what sort of account any such account would be, and what sort of thing it would be an account of.

XV

Desire for Excellence

The argument now to be discussed aims to show that all men must have a desire to function well, so that recognition of the fact that a certain way of life or form of behaviour is incompatible with living well must operate against it. It can consequently be argued that we really want what is in fact (functionally) the best life, though it does not follow that what is by all criteria the best life is really wanted by everyone. To begin with I shall ignore the overall picture of the universe as a quasi-organism, and concentrate on what follows about X's desire for its own excellence or welfare from the fact that X is an organism. The point of doing this is that with this limitation it becomes clear that there is all the difference in the world between saying that every organism must aim at the preservation and continuance of its own life, and saying that it must aim at the development of certain capacities peculiar to it which are not related to its own survival or that of the species. Suppose we take wasps as a species of living thing. It certainly seems that that classification commits one to some general account of waspish life. There would obviously at the very least be complications if for any proposed description of a wasp's form of life, it became clear that the whole tendency of the behaviour of the proposed members of the species was at all times to its destruction. This would amount to showing that no such classification was possible. It might be that one particular entity could for special reasons be considered a member of the species while for a time exhibiting not immediately successful suicidal tendencies – but it would have to be put down as a degenerate member. The norm must be for members to have a self-continuing tendency at least for a large portion of their lives. Suppose we grant this, we might provisionally describe the fact by saying that the norm must be for members of a species to aim at their own welfare. We might also allow for the sake of argument that classification as a species of living thing carries the implication of a tendency on the part of members of the species to perform acts that tend to the continuance of the species. This might be described by saying that not merely do members of a species have a tendency to pursue their own welfare, but also to be good members of the species, where merit is determined by the requirements of species survival. What follows? Not enough, as can be seen by returning to wasps. We are commonly told that wasps have an important role in the economy of nature, that of scavengers. By eating decaying vegetable and animal matter they keep down the spread of disease in plants and animals. Suppose now that the Public Health Department reaches a peak of efficiency whereby all decaying matter usually catered for by wasps is cleared away. Would the wasps worry? Not if someone took care to supply them with fresh meat and vegetables. They would indeed, by the previous argument, have to show a tendency to feed themselves and young, but that argument would yield nothing about a tendency to scavenge. That is an activity that is a useful effect of their taking steps to keep alive, but is an effect dependent on certain circumstances obtaining. In other circumstances the activities necessary for survival could occur without any such effects on the general economy. We should need further additions to the view to produce the result that they have a tendency specifically to scavenge, such as, perhaps, reason for treating them as part of a larger quasi-organism in which that is their part. In that case one would expect some signs of frustration or ill effects if, as in the circumstances imagined above, they were deprived of the opportunity to fulfil this role.

Before developing the implication of this for Plato's views of man, I want to examine a further obscurity about the position outlined. The conclusion is that all men want their own excellence or welfare. We have already noted a lack of obvious connection between these two, but there is also a difficulty over just what the relation is between having a tendency in a certain direction and wanting to go there. We have seen in the example of the wasps that on the whole one would demur at attributing to them a desire to scavenge. The reason is that to attribute it would be to claim that the wasp's behaviour could be seen as a function of what they deemed necessary to the end of removing rotting matter. Two considerations would make us pause at this. First, there is no sign even that the behaviour of wasps varies with the needs of the neighbourhood or the world at large in this respect. Second, even if there were, putting the behaviour down to such a desire would lead to a revision of our views of a wasp's intelligence. For we should have to treat it as recognising certain circumstances as having effects both far exceeding in complexity what we suppose to be within a wasp's compass. No doubt we could tell science fiction stories that would lead to such a revision, but they would be very different wasps. In short, putting down an animal's behaviour to the operation of some desire amounts to claiming that the animal is capable of learning to recognise a piece of behaviour as falling in a certain category, and commonly as leading to some end. Once this is recognised, it of course becomes a good question whether even the survival-directed behaviour that can supposedly be attributed to normal members of a species should be put down to a desire on their part for their survival. Suppose we take eating, which is a necessary activity for most species, it is doubtful whether this should ever, except on rare occasions with some members of the human species, be explained as due to a desire to survive. Hunger is the common stimulus, and with humans it may be simply recognising that it is dinner time, or seeing others at it. Notoriously in the case of one species-required activity, copulation, the effects of the activity have not always been realised, let alone envisaged, by those who have engaged in it. It is one thing to say that behaviour is a function of what is (in general) needed for a certain purpose, and quite another to say it is a function of what is thought on any particular occasion to be needed for it. Either may be true, but it is usually not difficult to think of circumstances where they would call for different behaviour.

Granted these distinctions, it is clear that one could not assume that normally the members of a species want those things that are needed for their own well-being and pursue them because they want it. This is so with rational animals, as the example of sexual intercourse shows. The question arises, therefore, whether Plato can give any reason for supposing that in this instance we can safely attribute such a desire. It should be remembered here that Plato is not in this case attributing a desire for survival but for good functioning. His position on the immortality of the soul makes it impossible to take welfare in the other way. Yet Plato himself is insistent on points which should make the attribution of such a desire difficult. Since he cannot rely on any argument simply from the fact that men are classified as living things, he must fall back on considerations of the economy of nature. Now if one were to succeed in portraying nature as consisting of a set of objects each playing a part in an interrelated whole, then while it may be allowable that some members of a species should fail, and perhaps all members some of the time, a problem arises if pretty well all members, and the species *en bloc*, fail all the time. So long as one can exhibit the proposed function as generally performed by the species then one can take that as confirming the account of nature and take the relevant role to give the nature of the species. But Plato makes no pretence of supposing that men individually or collectively play the ordering role in conjunction with the World Soul that is supposed to be their special feature. On the contrary, he holds that man could only fulfil his function in certain political conditions that have never obtained to date, and are unlikely ever to do so. The results of this are twofold. First, the cosmos has to be seen as a seriously defective organism, and certain operations can only be said to be of man's nature in the sense that it is just possible that he could sporadically perform them and it would be very nice if there were a being capable of performing them regularly. Second, the desire to behave in the appropriate ways is certainly not manifested in most men. Even if we retreated to the position that the desire does not have to be present or manifested in most men – it is only required that the species play its part, and this may be done, as we have seen, by special members only, as the scavenging is not done by queens or males – it would still not do. To begin with, the problem with man is not that not all men play the required role, but that all do not, and largely because the species is ineptly organised. Further, it was part of the attraction of the position being considered that it seemed to argue to a fundamental desire in all men, so that this retreat would mean abandoning one of the position's main attractions. If we do not retreat, then we could only hope to attribute the relevant desire to all men in the rather weak sense that it is a desire that could in principle be developed in all men. But I can certainly disavow a desire of which it is true only that I could acquire it.

Plato might defend himself against this by saying that while few men show a full-fledged desire for proper order, they do all show some intellectual curiosity and they all recognise the desirability of intelligence and the importance of being able to regulate one's life in accordance with one's goals. But the only way of securing the operation of intelligence is to develop it to the full. Any other course leaves one in a position of insecurity because of the power of physical desires. So everyone really wants to have complete rational control of himself, which in turn means wanting disorder brought to order. I have already criticised this view of physical desire in chapter I. I now want to concentrate on the claim that all men really want to control physical desire and so really want the good ordering of the universe. It is the form of the claim that is as interesting as its truth. It is very tempting in a dispute on practical matters to argue that one's opponent does not really want what he claims he wants, and what he is proposing to do. It seems that success here will undermine the whole structure of his practical reasoning. Attractive though this course may be it is one that needs careful watching, for there is a danger of committing a very basic mistake. The mistake is to suppose that 'A really wants X' entails that it is true without qualification that A wants X. It is a familiar enough fact that we are prepared to allow that someone wants something and then qualify the admission. For instance, a man may be described as wanting promotion but not being prepared to work for it, or wanting to become a teacher but not realising what a frustrating and exhausting job it can be, or wanting a chisel but not realising that it is the wrong tool for the job he has in mind. In any of these cases the facts cited after the 'but . . .' can be used to start an argument that he does not *really* want what he is said to want. In other words it is not without qualification true that he wants whatever it is. What he really wants is a leisured life, a life within his tolerance of frustration or a screwdriver. It is now easy to suppose that it is true without qualification that he wants these. Now it may well be doubted whether there is any such thing as its being true without qualification that *A* wants *X*. We should have to suppose that it is possible that none of the intelligible qualifications should hold. While it might be possible to prove that this cannot happen, it is hard to see how one could prove that it can without producing a complete list of intelligible qualifications, and even harder to see how one could be sure that the list was complete. However that may be, it seems clear that in practice, in 'he does not want *X*, he really wants *Y*' the word 'really' does not introduce the claim that it is without qualification true that he wants *Y*. Indeed it is usual that there will indeed be a qualification. To take the example of a man who says he very much wants to be a school-teacher, the grounds for denying that he does really want that will be, for instance, that he is under a misapprehension about what a school-teacher's life is like. He does not realise that the enthusiastic interest that he may arouse in the first few sessions cannot be expected to survive a long series of sessions several times a week. What he really wants is a life that will give him regular contact with groups of students but will ensure that he moves on to a new group before the eagerness of the one before has died down. The reason for saying that this is the sort of life he really wants is that only in this sort of life has he a hope of finding the satisfaction of continued positive response that he plainly needs. For all that, there may be reservations to saying without more ado that he wants such a life, for it may not fit his image of himself as a successful persevering educator, so that he will have nothing to do with it – he really does want to be a regular teacher. The claim that he really wants a life as a roving reserve teacher is tantamount to the claim that that is the life in which he would get the satisfaction his temperament needs. The other is equivalent to the claim that the only career he will countenance for himself is that of a regular teacher. Clearly these are very different, and by no means incompatible. In short, the words 'Jones really wants *X*' can convey any one of a fair number of different claims about Jones in relation to *X*, and it consequently becomes important in any given discussion to discover what the force of it is. In no case can it be assumed that establishing such a claim entails that Jones wants *X* without qualifications.

In most everyday disputes 'he does not want *X* really, he really wants *Y*' serves to draw attention to aspects of the situation considered significant by the speaker and thought to be overlooked by the opposition. At any time, however, the position might become hardened, so that a person uses this form of expression to serve notice that he is not going to accept as genuine examples for his purposes any that do not satisfy the conditions of 'real' wanting. So long as the purposes are clearly defined and the proposed restrictions on 'want' shown to be appropriate to the purposes there can be no objection to this. The possibility, not to say the actuality, of this happening, however, should underline the rashness of supposing that one can safely talk of *the* concept of wanting. This is not, of course, a point that applies only to wanting. A large number of philosophically interesting terms have this feature (e.g. 'knowledge', 'belief', 'action', 'intention', 'understand'). In all these cases talk of the concept of belief, or of Knowledge, with a capital 'k', only serves to raise hopes that can never be satisfied. What is important is not to analyse or discuss the relationships between these mythical units, but to delineate clearly the conditions required for their application in a given area for a given purpose, and then, perhaps, discuss the relationships between these.

It should now be clear that many varied considerations can be brought to support a claim of the form '*A* does not really want *X*, he really wants *Y*', and there is no reason to suppose *a priori* that they all support the same claim. It becomes important therefore to decide what form it has to take to meet a given purpose, and then see whether various considerations offered support it or not. To return to Plato, it emerged in the course of the early chapters that he wants the claim that all men really want 'justice' for one of his purposes to be equivalent to ' "justice" is what all men would acknowledge to be best if they understood what it was' and/or ' "justice" is what all men would choose if they had the wit and the ability'. In the present discussion it seems he could use a claim to the effect that a life with a fully developed, caring, intellect is the only one that securely allows of a life that can be rationally controlled. As I pointed out earlier, these are not equivalent, and what supports the one does not, as Plato needs it to, support the other. How, then, might it seem to? If we turn to two familiar forms of the claim, I think it is possible to understand how what seem very different theses might be thought to be the same.

Suppose we take three examples. First, Elizabeth is proposing to nurse her sick mother, who is in for a lingering illness for some years. While it is agreed to be heroic, it is argued that she cannot really want to do it, on the grounds that it is a course so detrimental to her prospects and her personality. Even when it is agreed that she realises this, it might still be claimed that while she is obviously prepared to do it, it cannot be something she really wants to do. The reason is that it is against her welfare to do it, and so the claim is that people only want to do what is in accordance with their welfare. Second, Thomas is clearly planning to commit some monstrous crime such as introducing a peculiarly virulent germ to wipe out the population of Asia. It is objected that he cannot really want to do that, we must tell him what the effects would be. When it is pointed out that he knows them full well, and the knowledge in fact adds to his determination, then the objector might take refuge in the claim that he must be mad, he cannot 'really' know what he is doing. As he does not really know what he is doing, he cannot really want to do it, properly viewed. In short, no one really wants evil, only what is good. Third, Valerie is a known egoist who never considers anyone else's comfort and openly acknowledges that she only thinks her own convenience worth considering. When she is observed one day patiently reading to a crotchety invalid aunt, it is immediately assumed that she does not really want to. Even if we discover that she is there willingly and will not be deriving any material benefit, but assures us that she has decided that her aunt needs cheering up, we may still be dubious about whether she really wants to console her and give up her own comfort in this way. The objection is not to the interpretation of this particular piece of behaviour, but to any suggestion that it reflects Valerie's considered objectives. This is a passing aberration. Of course, we may be wrong. The point is that the claim that she does not really want to spend time consoling her aunt is equivalent to saying that this is not what on reflection she will consider to be the best way of spending her time.

We have, then, three forms of the claim that A really wants not X but Y, which assume respectively (i) that men only want what is to their own good; (ii) that men only want what is good and (iii) men only want what they consider good. With regard to the first two, it is probable that the objections reflect the objector's difficulty in believing that a person will willingly do the things described under the circumstances described. Certainly in the second type of case talk of moral monsters seems to betray a hope that those guilty of such wickedness will turn out to be clearly insane by independent criteria for insanity. For present purposes, it is enough to recognise these as three ways in which a person might try to back a claim that A really wants X rather than Y Each way seems to involve supposing some connection between desire and good, and indeed any or all of them might be summed up by saying that desire is for what is good.

In the previous part of this discussion I argued that one cannot automatically move from 'this is a good X' to 'it is a good thing that there should be things like this' where 'it is a good thing' has to be interpreted functionally. Still, it might be that whether or not it is a good thing that there be things like X is something for which there must be at least in principle, relevant arguments and even proof. If that is so, then the relationship between 'Jones wants what is good' and 'Jones wants what he thinks is good' will be like that between 'Jones wants an apple' and 'Jones wants what he thinks to be an apple.' If it turns out that what he is after is not in fact an apple, then it will follow that he does not really want it, and similarly, if what he is after turns out not to be in fact good, it will follow that he does not really want it. As Plato thinks that whether or not it is good that there be things like X is open to proof, he will think that this relationship holds. In that case we have him believing the following points: a person wants what he considers on reflection to be best. In fact living a life of competent co-operation with the World Soul is best, and also alone ensures the object of a desire we all have in virtue of being rational. Therefore such a life is what a person wants.

The crucial brick in this bridge, apart from the view of physical desire, is the point that the question of what is best is open to proof. If Plato were allowed his position on the conditions for attributing excellence, this would be plain sailing. It would seem, however, that just as with calling something a good X there is commonly a variety of Y's as which X can be considered good, so with saying that it is a good thing that there be Xes there can be a great variety of respects in which Xes might be considered as candidates for merit. Now it may be that X can only be said to be a good thing in some respect or from some point of view, but that once that respect or point of view is specified it will very likely be possible to show whether or not it is in that way good. In such a case, if someone wanted to claim that something is good while rejecting the need to specify any respect, then either he would ensure the impossibility of any argument by excluding all contexts that might allow of its generation, or he would be saying that it was good in all conceivable respects, which would lead to contradiction.

It might seem that some help could be got here by developing another approach to goodness that is also found embryonically in Plato, the approach through desire. Thus it might be argued that any assertion that it is a good thing that there should be things of a certain sort, or that certain things should happen, asserts some relation, however complex, between the existence or occurrence of these things and some human desire. It is hard to know what to make of someone's saying that it is a good thing that there are motes floating in the sunlight if all connection with human desire is ruled out. 'What is so good about it?' is a request for the spelling out of such a connection. With something like pain, to which we suppose a universal aversion, we immediately suppose that anyone who considers it is a good thing is referring to further effects that might be desired, and would find it very puzzling if someone declared that he thought it was a good thing in itself, irrespective of consequences. There are many desires that we recognise but do not share, and so it often happens that someone's claim that something is good is intelligible but not accepted. There are, however, desires that it is part of being a human being to have, and it is not possible to refuse to accept the goodness of what answers to them. A good man will be a man whose life ensures that these desires are met.

As I have expounded it, this is a rather confused position which allows a number of possibilities between which choices must be made. Suppose we take it that if someone says it is a good thing that certain circumstances obtain, then he is committed to answering the question what desire is met by the occurrence of these circumstances, and that if, therefore, he wants to safeguard himself against the possibility of someone's not caring for what he says is good, he will have to produce a desire which no one can disclaim. A person may still indeed refuse to do what he acknowledges to be good, because he may have desires of various sorts. He will not, however, be able truthfully to say that it is of no interest to him that things be this way, and unless he has over-riding desires then he will in fact be in favour of it.

I propose to waive all difficulties about the relevant concept of desire, and ask what this might yield quite apart from that. It certainly seems possible to select desires that are common to all men, or at least to the vast majority. Thus men are usually subject to hunger, so that they have a recurrent desire for food and a resultant interest in ensuring that there are sufficient stocks available. So by this argument a person could claim that food is a good thing with little fear of sincere opposition. There is also a widespread delight in food that gives rise to an interest in it unrelated to hunger. Indeed, someone who succeeds in satisfying this interest is envied or censured for his good living. Yet this is not what is usually suggested by calling him a good man. It is not usually even included as a constituent part of what is meant. No doubt anyone might campaign for a change in this respect, but there is quite a range of desires like this and neither success nor capacity to satisfy them is commonly even part of what is connoted by the expression 'a good man'. Indeed, it is more plausible to suggest that being good answers to the desires of others than to those of the virtuous man himself. It is more evidently in my interest that other people should be honest and just and truthful than that I should be so myself. Even here it would be safer to insert the caveat 'at least on the whole'. If we are going to try to relate the goodness of a man to the desires of the good man at all, it must be a relation to some special set of desires common to all men, not to all. This point is more obvious with regard to the English expression than with the Greek '*agathos*'. It would probably have been generally acceptable that an *agathos* would be both skilful and successful in pursuing objectives whether shared or idiosyncratic. In so far as the English expression is used in a moral context it is not so generous in its coverage.

We should need, therefore, to select the desires that are to be appealed to in talking of good men. Now suppose we have succeeded in doing that, then no one will be able to disavow all interest in goodness, and the question 'why should I want to be good?' is answered by specifying the desires catered for. But that is as far as the discussion can get. Trouble starts if one asks why it is better to satisfy those desires than other universally shared ones. For presumably saying one thing is better than another requires to be backed by showing either that there are more desires for it, or the desires are greater, or both, or both together with Benthamite considerations of fertility and so on. In view of the generally accepted fact of men's moral weakness it is implausible to say that the desires that the moral life meets are stronger in any sense that implies that strength brings success. It is attractive, therefore, to try Plato's way and claim that it meets more more reliably over a longer period. If we have a good way of counting desires then sense could be given to the claim that it is better to be moral than immoral that is not simply the banal claim that it is more moral to be moral. There are, however, two points to be noted. First, this is reinstating all universally shared desires, which might be all right for some uses of the expression 'good man', but not, as we have seen, for all when used in a context where it is accepted that being good should take priority in a man's life. Second, connected with this, it would not follow that if a man agreed that course (life, act) A is better than course B he would therefore want to embark on it in any sense that might imply action unless prevented. It would not follow, in other words, that it is what he would want if he had the wit and ability in the way in which Plato wishes to interpret that – or at least it would only follow if we could show that a majority or totality of universally shared desires was always effective over any number of idiosyncratic ones. While this would doubtless be an empirical question it does not seem unduly daring to suppose that it could not be shown.

The moral of all this is that one might try to explain how the use of the word 'good' may be justified by reference to desire. In that case one has to isolate the relevant concept of desire (or set of concepts together with a clear account of their interrelationships), and show that the whole task can be done by means of them. There must be no surreptitious reintroduction of goodness to help distinguish between desires that should and those that should not be preferred. Alternatively, one might try to explain what is or should be desired by reference to what is good. In that case a clear account is needed of how to determine goodness that does not rely on appeal to that notion of desire that is up for explanation. One might of course refrain from trying either of these lines. What one cannot do is follow both at once. It in fact seems quite possible to make sense of Plato's proposals for determining excellence, including human excellence, but even if it also turned out to be possible to work them, and even if it was further possible to show that there was some desire for excellence, what is not shown is that all men would want (choose) it if they had the power and realisation.

Granted that of the three examples given earlier (p. 244) the first and second reflect recognisable prejudices as to what a person can willingly or knowingly pursue, there are still three ways of relating wanting and goodness which have a more definitional air. First there is that manifested in the third example, whereby it is only going to be accepted as a genuine ('real') example of wanting if in fact it is an example of what the person takes to be in accordance with what are his settled priorities. For these purposes my sudden itch to wring someone's neck or be extravagantly rude to him does not count as what I want, and to wring his neck or be rude only becomes what I want if other conditions are added. Second, there is the move of saying that to want something is to treat it as a good. This can, of course, simply be a way of putting the first version, but philosophers sometimes seem to take it more widely, so that all cravings and spontaneous diversions from the normal course count as desires. It is not always clear whether there is a limitation to desires that lead to action or not – that is to say, it is not clear whether cigarette smoking becomes a good for me if I crave them or only if I smoke them – but for present purposes this does not matter. The important point is that whereas in the other example wanting is tied to reflection on priorities and only loosely to action, here wanting is widened to include unreflective desires and may be tied closely to action. The third possibility is to start from deliberation and point out that the form of deliberation can be characterised as taking some goal or principle or set of either and trying to work out in the light of them what it is best to do. This may involve reference to the agent's major priorities, but it will be enough if someone is wondering how to defeat his opponent at tiddly-winks and decides it will be best to try to distract him as he is about to flick his counter. In either case his reasoning can be spelled out in a schema ending with 'so it will be best to . . .'. The schema will not be applicable to yearnings nor to unreflective action on them. A person who acts without thinking does not give himself time to decide what he really wants to do (thinks best) in the circumstances. So this leads to restrictions on what is to count as an example of wanting that are more limiting than any that operate in the second example, but still allow of things ruled out by the first. For despite the deliberation in the tiddly-winks case the whole episode may be so out of keeping with the player's accepted priorities as to justify one in claiming that it is not what he really wants to do on the first interpretation of that claim.

I noted the difficulties that Plato gets into by conflating the first and second of these in chapter II. It may be that the possibility of the third helps the conflation. The difficulty mentioned earlier was that if one takes wanting what is best as wanting what one considers overall to be best, then one can start working on these views about what is best, in the way Plato wants, with a hope of pushing a person into more consistent and adequate views. But then one has to drop unreflective impulses and cravings as not being for these purposes desires. Alternatively one can include them, in which case to say that X is considered a good is simply to say it is pursued, and there is no implication about thinking it to be on balance the best thing to do. Indeed, there is not room for the question 'is it really good?' once it is settled what the agent is pursuing. The third example, however, allows for a great many short-term objectives while apparently always being concerned about what is best. One can deliberate on how best to get the gravy passed, and then one is both concerned with an object of hunger or greed, which accommodates Plato's lower desires, and talking in terms of what is best to do, which seems to be raising about it the big question. In fact, however, these are three quite different ways of relating desire to what is good. The distinction is important not only for Plato, but because a popular thesis that we always desire things *sub specie boni* tends to straddle the last two, and if wedded to the first might seem to produce not merely an unbreakable connection between desire and goodness, but also between desiring the good and a deliberate synoptic approach to one's life.

Even if a person does not want to go so far as this, it can still seem tempting to suppose that since all desire is for the good, and all human action properly speaking is governed by some desire, all practical reasoning must be about what is good, and 'this is bad but I want it' must be the practical analogue to contradicting oneself. If one makes the above distinctions it is clear that many actions done from desire are non-deliberative and do not even call for a reason-schema for their description, while many deliberative actions are confined in their goals and the deliberation does not raise any questions about priorities. If we confine ourselves to the deliberative examples then it is of course possible to say that in any deliberation some considerations must be taken as governing ones at least by the end, and this can be expressed by saying that these give what is taken as good for the purposes of this deliberation. In that case it becomes a problem what to make of someone who says 'this is good but I do not want it' because, of course, *in this context* we have to read this as 'this is what I take as to be pursued here but I do not propose to pursue it'. This can only be saved by supposing that he has abandoned the deliberation, or the earlier 'goods', or he is using either 'good' or 'want' in ways suitable to other contexts but not this one. If, on the other hand, we confine ourselves to the example where really to want is to consider it to be in conformity with one's overall priorities, we get a different situation. If a person says now that he does not want what he considers best he is contradicting himself. On the other hand he could fail to want-what-is-best, in other words simply not have any overall priorities and not ever raise or be interested in having any. Such a person could, I suppose, be said to be irrational in the very special sense that he had no general organised view of life in terms of which to raise or answer questions about priorities, but it would be in an equally special sense of 'practical reasoning' that this showed anything to be awry in that area. If, in considering what a person really wants we are wondering what his priorities are, this can be put by wondering what he thinks important in life, what he thinks it best to pursue. But there is no general way of showing that someone is right or another wrong in this respect. If, as Plato supposed, there were, then it would be possible to claim of someone who was mistaken that there had been some breakdown in his practical reasoning and that it was unreasonable to have the priorities he had. As it is, this cannot be done. It could, of course, be claimed of certain priorities that what the man considers a good thing is not so, if the denial is, say, that they are not morally good, and 'morally' is giving a respect in which worth is to be assessed. But once again, in that case it will be possible to ask the general 'what is the good of being morally good?' and hold that there is no good being morally good. It is at this level that there are no canons to enable us to determine that certain reasons are good ones for holding that this or that is good.

This last point needs treating with a little care. It is not true that all statements that 'it is good that X' are immune to criticism, and consequently not true that all desires are equally reasonable. For instance, if someone says it is good, indeed best, to have been potentially what one now is and at the same time holds that everything that actually is was once potentially what it now is, he seems to be offending against one condition for claiming that it is good that X, viz. that it should be possible that not X. So that view would be open to objection. That still leaves a host of views that pass this sort of 'logical' test, but there are still other possibilities of criticism. If a man privately pursues or publicly advocates a life given to taking stupefying drugs, then he is in favour of a course that leads to the destruction or at least debilitation of reasoning faculties. If he is against the having of priorities and in favour of drifting from day to day, following the course that catches his fancy, then, as we have seen, he is taking a stand against a certain use of reason, and if this is carried to the extreme of being in favour of just waiting to see what happens to one and never stirring a finger, it will be a stance against all practical or theoretical uses of reason. Again, if a person is advocating norms for general acceptance, there is a variety of possible criticisms. It may be more than could reasonably be expected that people should keep to a certain norm, as might be complained if one advocated that no one should ever make any physical movement without giving it two seconds' prior thought. Or it might be self-defeating, as an ideal that everyone should give all his property to the poor. Or it might undermine the whole possibility of using reason, as an ideal of complete intellectual dishonesty. Yet while these are all possible criticisms, they are a very varied set. Those which take the form of showing that in one way or another what is advocated or pursued tells against the use of reason can be construed as showing that the position in question is unreasonable, but they do not thereby show it to be bad. It may be better not to have one's life organised according to definite overriding principles. Even when one considers an extreme undermining of human life, it is an intelligible view that human life is so mean a thing, and human reason so incompetent and destructively directed, that it would be better that it be reduced to a low level of operation or destroyed altogether. This is not shown to be wrong by showing it to be anti-rational. So while there are many forms that a criticism of unreasonableness may take, none of them enables one to show of a number of possible positions that one is right. It may be possible to settle that some things cannot be good, but not that some are.

In all this I have repeatedly used the expression 'it is a good thing that . . .', and it might be objected that this is not an acceptable expression at all (cf. Geach, 1967). It is perfectly possible to make sense of talking of a good typewriter, but it makes no sense to talk of a good thing. We have only to suppose someone admitting that his typewriter is a very poor typewriter and then saying 'but that doesn't matter, because it is a frightfully good thing, in fact it is a far better thing than any thing you have got' to appreciate the absurdity of the expression. Once it is rejected, a good deal of what has been said above falls to the ground.

This point may be true or false according to how one takes it. If the point is that nothing can be said to be good *as a thing*, then it is of course true. But then when someone says that it is a good thing to take a holiday from time to time he is not saying that taking a holiday from time to time is good as a thing. The objection seems to assume that 'good' operates like 'efficient'. There are definite restrictions on what can be said to be efficient, and it makes no sense to say things like 'it is an efficient thing that there are women' or 'it is an efficient thing to be able to appreciate music'. But 'good' is more like 'desirable', where, while it is difficult to make anything of 'this typewriter is desirable as a thing', 'it is a desirable thing to have someone around who can make jokes' simply means 'it is desirable to have someone around who can make jokes'.

In chapter XIV I developed some criticisms of Plato's views on determining excellence which resulted in difficulties for his position that everyone wants the good. In the present chapter I have tried to see what could be made of this thesis even granted the criticisms of the previous chapter. It becomes necessary to distinguish between wanting one's own welfare, wanting to operate as a good member of one's species and, perhaps, wanting to be morally good. It is further necessary to distinguish between having a tendency to perform acts with a certain effect and wanting the effect. If we accept all these distinctions, then it seems that Plato is wishing to say that everyone wants to operate as a good member of his species, where excellence is determined by the requirements of the economy of the universe, yet that this is not what everyone realises he wants but what he really wants. It is therefore important to be clear that there is not some one thing that constitutes really wanting, but rather there is a host of forms the claim that *A* really wants *B* might take. Among these there is a variety that might seem to support the view that desire is always of the good, but it emerges on examination that they in fact support a variety of different views. If Plato's position on how to determine excellence were acceptable, then perhaps some of what he says about everyone really wanting the good might be preserved, though even so he could not establish the conclusion that what is best is what everyone who had the wit and ability would choose (or even acknowledge should be chosen). If his view on excellence is abandoned, then so must his ambitions on disputes about how best to live. I ended by considering the possibility that it is somehow irrational or unreasonable to want anything but what is good, and that some positions on what is good are unreasonable. Among all the possibilities considered here there seemed to be nothing that resulted in a position strong enough for Plato's needs. Indeed, most of them Plato would probably have not toyed with. He does, indeed, want to say that only a person who lives producing some good with understanding applies his intelligence to his life, and in particular someone who uses his understanding in helping the operation of the universe. In this restricted sense he can claim that only the knowledgeable man lives skilfully or cleverly. But perhaps it is not good to be too clever.

All this only concerns the possibility of arguing about how best to live and allotting accolades of intelligence or otherwise to those who give certain sorts of answer. It is, as I have said, still possible that someone should consider what are commonly held to be moral norms and wonder what distinguishes good from bad arguments in that area and in what sense if any it might be held to be rational to be moral. If my views on the spirited element of the soul are right then Plato has a position on the status of traditional moral views, and I shall now turn to discussion of them.

XVI

Common Morality

One function of the concept of the spirited element of the soul in Plato's theory is to isolate a type of motivation held to underly common moral attitudes. Now it has been usual for societies to give considerable importance to considerations of justice, truthfulness, loyalty, courage and the like, and to speak of the combination of these as constituting human excellence and making a good man. There have, to be sure, been variations between society and society. Some give more emphasis to one virtue than another, and they vary in the details of the behaviour commended. Still it is plausible to suppose both that there is a similar general pattern and that it reflects a single recurrent ideal. We seem, then, to have a phenomenon to discuss. Further, there are various possible 'accounts' which can be persuasively presented to explain our admiration of the good man, or why we do/should accept the standards of morality, which confirm our hunch that we have a single complex ideal, not a set. It can, for instance, plausibly be made out that the observance of standards of truthfulness, kindness, justice, honesty and the rest make for a happier community, and that we all tend to become doubtful about a practice if it becomes clear that it does not have this tendency, or has the opposite one. Thus we have become doubtful about many norms concerning both sexual matters and punishment as evidence has accumulated that the observance of these norms either has no tendency to further happiness or a tendency to lessen it. This particular example seems to offer a principle underlying moral dispute and argument, and it comes up against the difficulty that moral standards seem to be looked upon as in some way absolute. It seems objectionable to suggest that they are hypothetical, that we should be honest only if honesty leads to general happiness. We should surely be honest not because of the consequences, but because it is right to be honest. Now this can only be a problem for someone who is hoping that his utilitarian principle will yield the same results as common morality, even if it also brings order into what otherwise seems chaotic. Granted someone has that hope, then he has to explain the apparent absoluteness of moral rules in a way that allows that their 'point' is still utilitarian. Thus Nowell-Smith (1954) appeals to the fact that the purpose of the rules has a very complex relationship to the rules, but that it is nevertheless important that the rules be taught at an age when people do not have the intellectual ability to understand how they serve their point, or even in any detail what the point is. They have therefore to be taught dogmatically, and consequently 'it is wrong to kick people who have kicked you' will not be accompanied by any explanation and will be viewed as having some special authority, as being categorical rather than hypothetical.

Now Plato does not have any such rationalising story about the genesis of moral standards. Indeed, at one level he does not think that they are looked on as having this sort of absoluteness. He is struck rather by the fact that rules like 'it is wrong to steal', 'it is wrong to lie' are not usually looked upon as absolute at all. While people give 'but that is a lie' as a reason for not saying it, and also reject an appeal to good effects as justifying it, they nevertheless commonly accept that in other circumstances it is the right thing to lie, and 'but that is the truth' would be a reason for not saying it. There is, indeed, something that in his view does tend to operate as an absolute answer. 'It is the manly thing to do' operates always in favour, 'it is unmanly' against. People do not consider that manliness is pursued for any further purpose or requires any justification. But it is characteristic of appeals to manliness that not only do they, without it being clear why, seem usable to support different types of action on different occasions, but also to produce a conflict of view about the same behaviour. 'Argument' about whether a certain action or style of life is manly, when conducted by appeal to images of manliness, is an irretrievably messy business, and does not really deserve the name of argument at all. One may raise the question of what the proper ideal of manliness is, but that, as we have seen, is not viewed by Plato as uncovering the forgotten or half-recognised purpose for which the rules of conduct have been devised. Instead, his claim is that most people's positions on how to live are based on some image of manly behaviour. We are all susceptible to the appeal to manliness and will tend to accept such ideals without any question of what purpose, if any, they serve. Further, whatever may be true of the proper ideal, it is clear that there is no common purpose aimed at by the various ideals that Plato would allow. While a man brought up on the approved ideal will accept norms of behaviour which are in fact conducive to the good ordering of the community, someone who is brought up on the plutocratic ideal will be accepting standards geared to the wealthier section of the community, while someone who, like Callicles in the *Gorgias,* admires the man who wins mastery over others will not be attracted by any ideal of service to the community at all. So Plato offers a psychological account of how morality arises which makes no appeal to any purposes it serves. It will, indeed, account for a variety of 'moralities', and reference to purposes only comes in at all at the level of justifying the acceptance of one.

In one respect Plato's account seems to me superior to those of many others. It does seem that frequently one's objection to or advocacy of styles of behaviour is based on some ideal image, and that such images tend to be taken as unquestionably acceptable and lead to spluttering uncertainty in just the way Plato supposes. There are, however, three assumptions that need questioning: (i) that such images can be reduced to a single style, differences being accounted for as variations (and in some cases degenerations) on a theme; (ii) that a given person will be influenced by just one such image at any given period of his life; (iii) that all familiar moral appeals are based on some such image – where 'familiar' means 'not Platonically philosophical'.

There is some plausibility in treating the images of manliness envisaged by Plato as being roughly out of the same stable. They are all connected with ideas of success, power, position, honour, and differ only in what they take to constitute these. But it is possible to think of ideals that reject these notions. People have been moved by the picture of a supposed St Francis, meek, gentle, self-effacing, talking with the birds, welcoming the contempt of society. Whatever one may think of such an ideal, it militates not only against pandering to physical desires, but also against admiration for the sorts of character that would count as manly. One can see that granted the sorts of position discussed in the last two chapters Plato would have some antecedent expectation of a tendency to admire the right ideal that would lead to the possibility of confining us to a limited set that could be seen as manifestations of this tendency. This might explain a selective view of the facts, which might also have been helped by the actual conditions prevailing. Once those other views are abandoned, however, and a wider selection of facts taken into account, Plato's position seems altogether too restrictive. Even if it is true that children tend at a certain stage to manifest some aspirations that fit Plato's requirements, that would only be a fact about child development. It would not show that it was either true or desirable that various features of that stage linger on into adult life. It would certainly not alter the fact that people are capable of aspirations that do not fit that pattern.

Once this is recognised it becomes obvious that in practice there is a host of varied such images to which people are accustomed to appeal. Day in day out attitudes and behaviour are castigated as immature, illiberal, bourgeois, materialistic, fascist, unfeminine and so on and so on. All typically result in the sort of uncertain relation to specific behaviour that Plato thought characteristic of ideals of manliness; they all take the ideal appealed to as unquestionable; they are all liable to come into conflict with the pursuit of the satisfaction of 'physical' desires; yet few fit easily into the pattern of variations on or deviations from, the Platonic model of manliness; at the same time they are commonly used to bolster positions as to what it is right or wrong to do. People are, in fact, far more varied than Plato's picture allows, and a far more complicated account of the human person is called for, even if the complication only takes the form of a disjunction of possible types. We have already seen that even this would remove one valued prop from Plato's polemic.

This review of the variety of images to which appeals can be made starts arousing suspicions about the second assumption, that any given person is under the influence of one such image at any period of his life. It is, of course, not quite fair to attribute this assumption to Plato in this bald form. A man whose gentlemanly ideals are becoming eroded in favour of moneymaking ones will no doubt go through a period when he finds himself pulled both ways. He would like to give vent to his admiration for the successful financier but is still hampered by the feeling that the profession is vulgar and not suitable for a gentleman. There is no reason why Plato could not allow for this. He is aware enough that conversions rarely take place overnight. Any such state of divided ideal, however, has to be seen as a stage in a progress from domination by one to domination by another. The democratic-style personality is no exception to this, for he is not open to a variety of ideals, but only sporadically open to one. What Plato does not allow for is the apparently common situation of being open to a considerable variety of such appeals, without any being clearly dominant, and without it being true that the subject is in process from one to another. Thus many people find that they react to complaints that their behaviour is spineless or bigoted or bullying or out of date. They find they do not wish to seem any of these things. They wish to be acceptable. But their lives are not dominated by any of the ideals underlying these complaints, they cannot be described as aspiring to live up to any of them, nor can they be described as an arena of ideals jostling for supremacy. The fact rather seems to be that few of us like to be thought of as out of the swim. Various circles have their terms of praise and condemnation that roughly catch the acceptable and unacceptable styles of behaviour in those circles. We may find ourselves attracted by the standard images of the groups we come in contact with, without ever reconciling them, or we may simply be influenced by the wish to be accepted by the group we are at the time in contact with. Fashion is very powerful. Even in

philosophy there are schools and resultant fashionable and unfashion-
able views, so that argument by '-ism' can often be more effective than
valid argument from true premisses.

If this is so, then Plato's picture of a typical man as influenced, if by
any at all, by one ideal image, is quite unacceptable. Proliferation of
tendencies is almost as common in the second 'part of the soul' as in the
third. The result is that differences in ideal cannot all be looked upon as
differences as to what constitutes manliness. Once the position has dis-
integrated this far, one is ready to wonder whether all familiar moral
objections are based on such ideal images anyway. While it is possible
for someone to have an ideal of manliness that looks upon just and
upright dealing as noble and manly, and the kind of behaviour advocated by Thrasymachus as ignoble and mean, it does not follow, and is
by no means obvious, that everyone who acknowledges the claims of
justice considers such behaviour manly or in conformity with any other
rival image appealing to some emotion. Once this is recognised, and
various other parts of Plato's position are abandoned, it is possible to
distinguish between two activities in which Plato is engaged. On the
one hand he is trying to bring a number of virtues, such as self-restraint
and justice, under the heading of manliness, and on the other he is
trying to determine what manliness really is and concluding that it does
involve the others. Granted other parts of his position these might not
seem to be different. Without them the difference is apparent. It is
helpful to compare his procedure with that of late nineteenth-century
struggles with the title 'gentleman'. There were clearly many conditions
to be satisfied to justify a claim to that title. There was birth, position
and also a range of behaviour. This last included what was considered
honourable behaviour, but while much of what was required here was
recognisably moral (e.g. honesty, truthfulness, loyalty), many things
would be held to be demeaning and dishonourable which people would
also want to consider morally admirable. This develops a strain. No
gentleman can be expected to swallow an insult to his honour, and yet
some moral ideals would seem to require it, and justice might even
seem to demand an apology to someone of a lower station in life to
whom a gentleman would not be seen speaking let alone apologising.
In such circumstances moral considerations are likely to lose out unless
their advocates can redraw the lines of gentlemanly behaviour so that
anything that goes against the relevant moral requirements can be
represented as ungentlemanly. If this is successful, then a moralist can
avail himself of the strongest support current. But success here is a
matter of persuasion, and while the dispute is over what a real gentleman will do, 'real' is a term of insinuation and does not bring with it
the possibility of proof as commonly when used of bicycles, Rem-
brandts or mistakes.

Now in the situation envisaged above it is not that considerations of justice have no weight unless they can be brought within the ambit of what is gentlemanly, but that they can be assured of success if they are. There is in fact liable to be a strain between an individual's recognition of what justice requires and his feeling for what is gentlemanly conduct, and while in any particular case these may be reconciled by a modification of one or both, it is also possible that the strain will lead to a rejection of one in favour of the other or to their being allowed to continue in uneasy and unresolved conflict. One has, in short, the possibility of certain considerations being recognised as important even though they do not come as part of an ideal of manliness or any similar ideal image. Considerations of justice, of course, may be part of an ideal as to the form of society, but it may be an ideal of a society which allows of a variety of ideals of man to flower among its members and even admits of members with no such ideal. This co-existence of rival values is not only possible, but was the situation that obtained in Plato's day. The battle was over who could win the title to manliness for his standards.

At the same time, Plato thought that one could settle the question of what really constituted manliness, so that he would not think that he was simply engaged in a competition of rhetoric. The 'really' of 'really manly' carried for him a claim to truth, a claim that relied on the possibility of isolating a particular tendency to admiration, one that looks like being common at least at some stages of development to all men, and one that can be shown to be a requirement of the 'nature of man', part of his true excellence. So while he is embroiled in a propaganda battle he sees it as a dispute about the facts. The result is a distortion of the actual situation. In practice we most of us find ourselves admiring a wide range of traits and capacities in an unco-ordinated way. Thus most people admire the ability to master fear, the power to be indifferent to hunger and thirst, a flair for a witty turn of phrase and so on. These tend to win our respect regardless of the context of their manifestation, though that may well, of course, influence our final judgment. For in various contexts it becomes desirable to have these capacities regulated. Thus in a battle indifference to danger may be as much a liability as an asset, and a degree of austerity that may be useful in expeditions to the North Pole might be off-putting in someone required to run a social club. There is therefore a criss-cross of needs and objectives leading us not always to commend what we admire, and a variety of things that win our admiration in a way that may also leave us confused. Plato hopes to be able to determine human excellence by reference to the needs of the whole. He thinks that that will yield some characteristics that are required in each member of the species, the same ones constituting the excellence of each. Thus each member has an identical constitution and observance of the norms has to be shown to flow from a single element of the personality, whose good operation accounts for it. We have seen that none of this is necessary, and the whole picture prevents him from canvassing any view that human excellence be determined by reference to the needs of the community and the individual in relation to the community, not by reference to any balance of elements within the person. This possibility is closed to him because he does not think they can be separated.

I said earlier that it would be possible for someone to have an ideal of a society which allowed for the development of very different types of personality and different ideals not just of manliness but of the other sorts mentioned earlier. There may well be limits on the forms of ideal that can co-exist, but it is obviously possible to prefer a varied to a uniform society in this respect. Earlier this was mentioned as a possibility for an ideal of justice, but clearly it would be a mistake to identify considerations of justice with an ideal for a pluralistic society. It is quite possible to have an ideal of a society where everyone shares the same view of what society and men should be like while nevertheless acknowledging that everyone should be accorded equal rights before the law and have equal political rights. One might even allow that justice requires that variations of moral view should be tolerated if they occur, while still holding that their occurrence is a regrettable evil. While a belief in justice may put limits on the forms of society one would find acceptable it does not necessarily determine which out of a number is to be preferred. So one set of familiar moral considerations is not dependent on any particular ideal of manliness or society. Though they may serve to modify many, they entail none. Indeed, there is nothing to prevent a person who has no interest in such ideals recognising these obligations. In other words, such recognition does not even require some ideal or other of manliness or something else. Plato, therefore, may be right in suggesting that some ideal of manliness could accommodate an admiration for self-restraint and concern for justice, but he is wrong to hold the converse that these two suppose some ideal of manliness.

In all that has gone so far I have spoken in cavalier fashion of 'common morality', 'moral considerations', 'familiar moral notions' and so on. There is, I think, no doubt that we all tend to think that we can do this. Even if we acknowledge that there are variations from society to society, we feel that within our own society, or at least our own group, we can identify something that we can refer to as its shared morality. While Plato does not have a word for 'morality' he certainly supposes that when we speak of human excellence we are always basically talking of the same thing and that justice, courage and the rest form part of a single complex of values – 'single' in the sense that all are facets of one ideal. This is shown in the case of the philosopher, assumed by the ordinary upright man, and I think that Plato at least feels that someone like Thrasymachus shares the admiration but is wrong about the details of its object. Yet this is a very dubious assumption and brings one up against one of the thorniest problems in moral philosophy, the question of what its subject-matter is. Since one of Plato's major shortcomings is a failure to clarify this I shall now turn to it, but whereas on some of the other topics there has been a fair amount of progress since Plato wrote, this one is in little better condition now than it was then. What follows will therefore be mainly a weak attempt to map the problem rather than a set of constructive proposals. That in itself, however, will help one see Plato's limitations more clearly.

In the previous two chapters it emerged that it is possible to raise the question 'how is it best to live?' while refusing to specify any special respects in terms of which the answer is to be given. As there are no overall respects the result is that no set of considerations has any title to be considered as those that give *the* reason for calling one form of life good over and against others. Plato, of course, with his views on how to determine excellence, does not accept this and consequently will not accept the division of subject-matter that follows. Granted this point, however, it is now possible to discuss the status of discussions on how best to live, whether they are irretrievably *ad hominem*, whether asking the question is a mark of a rational approach to life and so on. Plato, for instance, clearly thinks it is the most important question one can ask. One may well feel that it is, but having asked it decide that it is a bad idea to have views on how best to live that govern one's decisions and lead to a planned organised life: it is better to take decisions as they come and live from day to day. It is of interest to ask whether there is any strong sense of 'reasonable' in which such an approach to life is not reasonable, or even in which refusing to raise the question altogether is not reasonable. This is one subject that moral philosophers have been interested in. Hume's discussion of the relation of reason and the passions is partly concerned with it. It leads people to talk of any answer to this question as a moral decision and any resultant approach to life as the subject's moral view. Now this is a very generous use of 'moral'. It allows one to speak of someone's view that it is best to keep himself to himself and only consider others in so far as it is in his interest to do so as being his moral position. Yet many find this counter-intuitive. Such a view seems to them not moral at all, but a different sort of position altogether. One reason for refusing it the title 'moral' would be that the man concerned is simply interested in how to live his own life. His view is not about how it is good for a man to live. This is the form that a view has to take to count as a moral one.

Now it is quite possible, so far as one can see, to hive off a set of views about life that have this characteristic that they are not about how some individual is to live, but how it is best for a man to live. It is now pertinent to ask whether and in what sense it is reasonable to have views about how everyone should conduct his life, whether it is something everyone should do or just some favoured prophets, what the possibilities of argument are with regard to such views granted that they are desirable and so on. It is also possible to take discussions of morality to be about views of this sort, so that they constitute the subject-matter of moral philosophy. Yet this, too, is a generous definition of 'moral'. For it allows as moral a view that it is best for a man to live so far as possible on his own, independent of the rest of mankind. Once more, many people would consider it counter-intuitive to count this as a moral view, though doubtless with hesitation in so far as they supposed it to embody some ideal of the rugged independent individual cutting his own swath. The trouble is that it is not a view about how to govern human interrelationships, but an admonition to abandon them. To meet this point one might add in a further condition that to be a moral one a view has to concern how the mutual treatment of each other by human beings should be governed. This is a somewhat imprecise formulation, but I hope clear enough in the context of what has gone before to give sufficiently the gist of the development.

So far, then, we have three possible topics for discussion (i) views on how to live (ii) views on how it is best for men to live (iii) views on how it is best for men to conduct their interrelationships. Plato is discussing all three in discussing human excellence. If we grant that they are distinct, then it might be worth keeping them apart. Suppose that we agree that so far as (i) is concerned there is no way of determining what is the best way for an individual to live, it does not follow that there are not special possibilities when we come to discuss (ii). There might, for instance, be special problems in advocating ways of life to which the majority of men are unsuited. It will always be worth asking whether the view is of the form 'it is good that any man who can should . . .' or 'it is good that all men should'. Those of the second form are vulnerable to types of objection to which the others are immune. Once one comes to (iii) it might well be possible to show that what is advocated must lead to the cessation of human interrelationships. The principle that all men should at all times do their best to mislead each other would be an extravagant example, but arguments in this direction would always be relevant objections to views of this sort. So questions about reasonableness, the possibility and forms of relevant argument and so on would very likely receive different answers according to which of these three topics we were talking about.

Another set of confusions arises once we reach (iii). This can cover positions on what men's mutual obligations and duties should be, but it is also true that in many societies or groups within society there are well acknowledged norms on these subjects in terms of which it is not difficult to decide what obligations and duties impinge on whom. It is not uncommon to consider the morality of a society or group, meaning by that the sub-legal obligations and duties operative in the group. Sometimes a discussion of morality is a discussion of what it is to have a moral view and the importance of having one. The stress is on the individual. But sometimes 'morality' is taken to cover a set of norms recognised in a group or society. Even here all is not plain sailing, for it is often uncertain whether any restrictions are to be put on what norms count as moral. Suppose that in a given group being up in the latest folk music and attendant terminology is the condition and sign of being in with the group. This will result in certain behaviour and pursuits being required of members of the group, and the group will certainly have a distinctive ethos. Similarly in any given society there may be a generally shared admiration for the extrovert or tough or cultured person, with a resultant pressure on the members of the society to conform on pain of being outsiders. Does this constitute part (or all) of the morality of the society? or is the morality confined to the accepted mutual duties and obligations? If we make the mistake of relying on intuitions we shall most of us be caught hovering.

If one discusses the accepted norms of a society under the title of its morality, one is liable to meet the objection that these conventions have nothing to do with morality at all. You can have a society where everyone unquestioningly accepts a clear code of conduct, which may well serve to bind the society together, but where no one behaves or is treated as a moral agent. They none of them take responsibility for the way they live or question why it is best to live so, and all they require of others is their conformity to the norms. They discourage moral thought altogether as dangerous and have no conception of moral responsibility or a moral agent. In such a society morality is not in evidence. Morality is a matter of the subject thinking for himself about the conduct of his life and being prepared to take responsibility for the way he lives.

There are doubtless further complexities that could be devised if one set one's mind to it. For the moment it is enough to see that one has at least three avenues of approach, one through the question of what makes a view a moral view, one through an interest in what makes a group or society hang together, and one through the question of what constitutes a moral agent. Each of these approaches is liable to yield a number of different phenomena for discussion. When I say they are different phenomena I mean that they are theoretically separable. Of course in practice an individual may give his view on how best to live in terms of how it is best for a man to live in a way that shows an interest in the norms that should govern mutual dealings and embodies an ideal both of man and society, and the view he gives be the one current in his society, which is one where great stress is put on the importance of self-determining moral agents. So in any given case one may be concerned with an example that includes all the elements mentioned. It remains that they give theoretically different ways of defining what morality is, and often the real life example one is discussing may qualify under one head and fail under another. In these circumstances no one is entitled to say to anyone discussing one of these topics 'but that has nothing to do with morality' except as a pompous and misleading way of declaring a preference for another topic. Nor is there anything to prevent a person from selecting some combination of these features for discussion, as, for instance, those views that an individual might hold about the desirable ways of governing interpersonal dealings which lay stress on the importance of the subject's accepting those ways as his own and taking responsibility for that acceptance. Nor is it clear that these topics have no interconnections which it may be important to draw out. But, once more, although we all use the word 'moral' with varying degrees of familiarity and comfort, and more or less share intuitions on when it is and when it is not straightforwardly appropriate to apply it, it is a mistake to infer that there is a single clearly specifiable subject for analysis that underlies this usage. It is essential, therefore, to make it clear what one proposes to talk about first, and, if one thinks there are important relationships between one or more topics, to spell these out. If one is engaged, say, in sociological description, then it will be necessary to get clear what concept of morality one needs for the purposes in hand. Having done that, one should be quite unabashed that one offends a few intuitions. With a term like this any precise usage can be expected to offend an intuition or two.

If we turn to Plato, it is fairly clear that for better or worse he does not in fact make these sorts of distinction. He thinks that the most important question an individual can ask is how best to conduct his life, takes this as equivalent to asking how it is best for a man to live, thinks this must yield norms governing interrelationships in society and that these norms will be bound up with an admiration for a style of life that will give a dominating ethos to the society. It is true that he is not interested primarily in describing societies, but in legislating for them, though he seems to have a use of 'justice' (*dikaiosune*) such that the rules current in a society are its *dikaiosune*. At the same time there are topics that tend to receive considerable attention in twentieth-century moral philosophy that receive little notice if any in Plato. It is difficult to determine to what extent it would have been possible for him in the context of Greek society to isolate these concerns, but he would certainly not be helped by an equivalent to the assumption that morality is morality.

Many present-day philosophers are clearly concerned to emphasise the importance of the subject's making his own decisions particularly on fundamental questions of how to conduct his life. There is a contrast to be made between the man who follows the conventions of his society without thinking about them and allows himself to be weighed down by the dead wood of other men's lack of thought, and the man who exercises his freedom to decide whether or not it is best to live this way and embraces his way of life with open eyes and in full freedom. The contrast is generally in favour of the latter. This is a far cry from a conception of morality as the sublegal conventions that help society operate, with a consequent use of 'moral man' to refer to anyone who abides by those conventions. Now Plato in fact came across a man who made a point of asking why one should accept the standards on which one was brought up and who is reported in dialogues like the *Gorgias* as declaring that the important thing is to follow where the argument leads. The suggestion is that the important thing is to think matters out as thoroughly as one can and conduct one's life in accordance with the conclusions. The complaint about the opposition is as much as anything that they do not take the question of how to live seriously enough. The implication is that being right is not any more important than being serious. This may indeed have been what Socrates thought, but if so it does not seem that Plato was prepared to go along with it. There is no doubting his admiration of Socrates, and in particular for his determination to think things out for himself and his preparedness to act accordingly. He was not, however, ready to hold that it is in general an admirable thing to be captain of one's soul. For most people it is ridiculous and highly dangerous. Raising questions for oneself on how to live would mean engaging in dialectic, and while dialectic is an honourable profession, it is not one to be embarked on except under proper supervision. It is better to be a member of a properly governed community, accepting the standards laid down by those in authority and not presuming to raise questions about them, than to be an incompetent thinker, however sincere, managing one's life for oneself. What is good is to behave as an excellent man, and while an excellent man must be able to think, a thinking man will not necessarily be excellent. This is because it is important for acting well that one knows how it is best to act. Thinking is needed to achieve knowledge, and knowledge is needed for the high point of excellence. On its own, thinking can equally well be deplorable or valuable. Favoured modern characteristics such as integrity, sincerity, self-reliance are only valued in the well-educated. This is a direct result of his views on excellence and his belief that it is an object of knowledge.

Something similar emerges if we consider a point that tends to be taken for granted in modern western philosophical circles, that a person is to be commended in so far as he does what he thinks is right, even if he openly disagrees with the rest of us, and that it is a paradigm of immorality to try to persuade someone to do what he thinks is wrong. This is often taken as axiomatic. It is a condition of moral as opposed to other forms of praise or blame of the agent, rather than his act, that they are apportioned in accordance with whether or not he did what he did because he thought it was right. This is not simply a philosophical position, of course, but reflects a fairly widespread moral view in western society. What is not so often observed is that these conditions for allotting praise and blame make queer bed-fellows for some accounts of morality. Suppose, for instance, that it is held that the purpose of morality (moral standards and conventions) is to produce a happier society. In that case, certain forms of behaviour are to be considered virtuous, certain duties and obligations recognised, because they lead to greater happiness in society at large. It is puzzling to see why, in this case, one should want to absolve from blame those who acted with a view to general happiness, and be unprepared to pressure them into acting against those beliefs if one thought them misguided. The likely result of everyone acting on his own ideas of what might lead to greater happiness is a considerable reduction in that commodity. In no other area where long-term harmonising results are in view does one run such a risk. The law, for instance, does not allow any general extenuation on the grounds that the accused thought his way of acting the best for achieving the general aims of the law. Those aims are best served by conformity, not by everyone thinking for himself. This sort of consideration leads people to separate the questions (i) what determines whether or not X was the right thing to do and (ii) what procedures should people follow in deciding what to do? As it seems that there is a greater hope of approximation to the happy society if we do not rely on individual speculation, it is held that when it comes to deciding what to do people should refer to rules. The result will be occasional undesirable actions, but the overall result will be preferable to that of a free-for-all.

If we accept this move, it might seem that we can now explain the insistence on people's doing what they think is right, for this can now be interpreted as insisting that people do what they consider to be in conformity with the conventions, not what they think will best advance the general purposes that the conventions are devised to serve. If a person was trying to keep the rules it is surely reasonable to count that to his credit, and not to try to persuade him to contravene them, as he thinks. Yet even this yields a justification of a more limited practice than that which obtains. One can see that a misconception as to what the rule is might in many institutions exculpate someone, but there are at least three points to be made. First, many institutions with harmonising goals are understandably reluctant to give much rein to this excuse. They throw the burden on the agent to know what the rules are. 'He thought it was in accordance with the rules' is an excuse with very limited prospects of success. Second, the very model supposes a discoverable set of rules, and limits the excuse to the person who is understandably ignorant of one of them. It does not envisage the situation where there are no agreed rules and there is disagreement as to what they should be. Indeed, one would expect pressure to put an end to that situation as soon as possible for the production of harmony. There can be no excusing the person who flouts the rules because he thinks they should be different. Yet it is commonly recognised that moral disagreement may extend to the type of norm considered desireable, and that still a person is to be praised for adhering to the norms he advocates, and should not be persuaded to decide in contravention of them. No doubt there will still be limits on what may count as moral advocacy of a norm, but if a person thinks that a property system is inevitably a system of exploitation and ought not to be condoned, while one might think that his thefts should be legally restrained, and disagree with his objection, it is still possible to hold that morally his behaviour does him some credit and that it would be to his discredit if as a result of social pressure he conformed while restraining his beliefs. This, however, takes us back to praising people for acting on the norms they think best, and involves abandoning the view that people should just use agreed rules in their decisions. Third, it remains irretrievably an empirical point that there is a particular motive such that if it is encouraged either a certain goal will be achieved, or obedience to the rules whose observance will achieve it will be secured. But if it is an empirical point that this motive is of considerable importance, then it cannot be treated as axiomatic. Quite apart from whether or not it is at all plausible as an empirical position, it is in fact commonly taken as a hallmark of morality that praise and blame should be allotted on these conditions.

Now there are moral views in which this insistence on motive is no problem. For instance, views that hold up an ideal of the brotherhood of man, or the family of man, and make this the basis of moral injunctions. For in effect such views are putting forward friendship as the model for the way in which interpersonal dealings should in general be viewed. In this context the question of why a person does what he does takes on at least as much importance as the question of what he does. It is a friendly disposition that is sought, and the reasons for which the act is done are important indicators here. It is signs of this disposition that win a friendly response. It would be inimical to a friendship to persuade someone to do something that he considered unfriendly. A view that takes friendship as the model for the way we should consider other men must put the familiar emphasis on the reason for which the act is done, for it must put a value on good will and not just smoothness of operation.

Such a model, especially when applied to mankind in general, will allow of thought about proper ways to treat each other but will also for the most part discourage the use of coercion in getting one's views accepted. So long at least as a person's heart is in the right place, the presumption will be strongly in favour of persuasion rather than force. Even when it is in the wrong place a devotee of the ideal might understandably prefer to go to considerable lengths to prove his sincerity before taking steps to ensure some last ditch conformity. There doubtless comes a stage, however, when minimal conditions for following the model at all have to be safeguarded, and people's views on when that point is reached may differ even if they have an equal enthusiasm for the ideal.

Some such ideal has been influential in much moral thinking, but if it is taken as definitional of morality it is worth noting that it is a special concept of morality that is being considered. If we start by taking 'morality' to refer to a set of standards put forward to govern interpersonal dealings at sub-legal level, then the new concept would only refer to a subset of moralities. It would collect its own problems with regard to argument and reasonableness. For instance, a moral person, in this more limited sense of the word, is committed to a large extent to eschewing force and pressure and leaving the acceptance of his moral positions to discussion (reason?). On the other hand he will be interested in the acceptance of norms that favour friendship-type relations, rather than domination by sections of the community. Success would mean the recognition of general canons to which to appeal in practical discussions, canons that did not necessitate constant reference to the particular ambitions of individuals. But proposals would be open to the objection that it would be unreasonable to expect anyone to agree. They would, like other norms, be open to the criticism that it is unreasonable to expect anyone to be able to abide by them – as, perhaps, a requirement that everyone give up all demands for possession – but also to one that it is unreasonable to expect people to agree to what is proposed, e.g. the view that you always treat people with trust, even total strangers.

I have gone on about this at some length because some such model seems to underlie quite a lot of moral thought, and it is a model that was familiar to Plato. Indeed he insists that friendship is the cement of a well run state. Although he confines the model to relationships within a particular society, it is there nevertheless, and one might expect it to play a governing role. It does, as we have seen (cf. chapter VI), play its part in justifying the view that no one willingly does wrong. Those who do wrong and are not incurable should, if possible, be persuaded. They are, after all, our friends. Even if we have to resort to punishment this must be viewed as an attempt to benefit them, that is as an act of friendship. Yet Plato does not take the model any further. Friendship seems to be valued as ensuring more willing co-operation in the conduct of the state, but when a person turns out to have deviant views on the state and cannot be persuaded from them, friendship will stand him in little stead. What is paramount is the proper running of the state to preserve the good condition of its members. It would, no doubt, have been difficult for Plato to isolate and discuss a moral ideal in conformity with this model and distinct from the state. It would have been difficult in part because of the set of positions discussed in the last two chapters, but partly also because of the climate of thought at the time and the fact that the nearest words he has for 'moral virtue' are '*sophrosune*' and '*dikaiosune*'. The first mainly connotes self-control and so does not draw attention to relations to others. The second has strong political connotations and it would call for special effort to detach it from these to describe standards and obligations that are considered to be neither legally enforced nor confined to one's fellow citizens. He might have come nearer to it if he had developed his heterodox views on the nature of the soul and its function, the consequences of this for the role of all men, and then applied it in discussing morals and politics. In practice men seem to be considered capable of performing their role only in a political context, and it is always assumed that if they ever succeed at all it will only be in a minority of states among a majority of poor ones, and 'justice' will operate within the state.

If one holds a moral ideal based on a model of friendship, then one will doubtless deplore most of Plato's views on how best to live. Even if one is neutral on this it remains that Plato runs together topics that ought to be kept distinct, and that, no doubt for understandable reasons, he fails to distinguish other topics that have since taken their places under the generous umbrella of moral philosophy. He shows no awareness of the nobility of facing the loneliness of self-declarative decision, that spiritual analogue of the ideal of *arete* with which he was familiar and to which he was opposed. Knowing how to live he considered admirable. Assertion of freedom and of responsibility for one's life he thought usually deplorable. In so far as any ideal on the model of friendship began to bud, it soon withered before the demands of psychic development. So while he shows signs of putting some stress on the motives of those who do wrong, this leads him to pity them, not to pardon them. It is not developed to set up a special category of moral praise or censure. Consequently on morality in accordance with some possible definitions Plato has nothing to say, though one can infer that he would often have little time for morality so defined.

In this chapter I have argued that while Plato's account of nonphilosophical adherence to moral norms has its merits, it involves an unduly uniform view of human motivation involving failure to note the vast variety of ideal images in fact operative or to distinguish these from other considerations that involve appeal to no such image. The truth seems to be that characteristics like fearlessness, self-control, wit, good humour, are widely admired, but without agreed limits on the form in which they are admired. A desire for justice might well lead one to wish them to be admired only with restrictions, and it will doubtless be tempting to try to dub admiration of these characteristics in unrestricted form as a distortion, as admiring what is not *naturally* admirable. One way of doing this would be to show that it is not what by nature we admire. By nature we admire courage restricted by the requirements of justice. If one abandons hope of success here one is left with competing ideals, fears and other considerations, and a question of how to determine which of them are to be deemed moral. At this point Plato shows a failure, common in moral philosophy, of not presenting us with any precise concept of morality as the topic of discussion. To illustrate this point I have tried to bring out how there are several theoretically distinct topics that come together under this heading, that any given phenomenon is liable to qualify under one or other or some combination, but not necessarily on the same counts as some other. There is no harm in discussing some one of these topics, or some combined topic, but it is important to be clear what one is doing and keep to it. At the very least one might be saved some argument at cross purposes.

XVII

Preferred Explanations

In the last three chapters I have been criticising Plato's views on the relation between desire and goodness, and I now wish to turn to the other side of his position, the relation between knowledge and goodness. In Plato's mind, of course, these two sides to his position are closely related, but even if one jettisons the thesis about desire and goodness, it could still be that in some preferred sense knowledge is tied to functional excellence. This is not a view that has any great attraction for a twentieth-century reader, but as there are, I think, points of interest about it I propose to pursue it a little further.

As we have seen, a great many terms that interest philosophers are used over a fair range of phenomena in a way that makes it easy to start insinuating that some do not really deserve the description in question. This gives the impression that there is some preferred strict sense of the term, yielding some privileged subset of phenomena covered by it which are the only really genuine examples. In the cases considered so far this seems pretty dubious practice. There are ones, however, that have a special feature. Take the notion of proof, for instance. Notoriously, in many empirical areas, the evidence brought for believing that P leaves open the theoretical possibility that not P. For any given set of evidence it is possible to point out the gap, and demand more. In day-to-day life we commonly accept as adequate evidence which we acknowledge that we should consider inadequate if anything of great importance hung upon the issue. Normally a person will take it as good enough reason for believing that his car is in a parking lot that he left it there half an hour ago. If he has had to leave a case full of high denomination bank notes in it he is liable to step up his standards of adequate evidence. More frequent checks will be needed to induce a more secure frame of mind. In this example constant unblinking observation of the open case possibly constitutes a high point of perfection, but there is an obvious possibility of varying degrees short of that. In other cases, as for instance generalisation over open-ended classes, there is no such satisfying end term. While it is always possible to fix a level for satisfactory evidence, it is always possible to demand more, claiming that what one has so far does not really prove anything. Either way 'real proof' is a step higher up a recognisable ladder, and while one may in the second case consider it unreasonable to take a position of demanding a point higher than every point, it does not seem obviously unreasonable to require, of any given point, some point higher, so long as this is not higher than some highest conceivable point. With 'knowledge' too it is possible to start a progress up a recognisable ladder. One can, for instance, chisel away on the question of certainty and room for doubt and so discourage people from saying that they really know anything that falls short of the standards set. As I have said, this is not the route that Plato follows, but he undoubtedly does want to appeal to some ladder and persuade us to contemplate the top rungs. As he thinks there is a top rung his position is not the obviously unreasonable one of demanding a highest point on an infinitely ascending scale. The ladder, on the other hand, is not one that naturally occurs to a speaker of English. Plato seizes on the fact that, truistically, knowledge is of what is the case. If the question at issue is what beauty is, then any proposition that can express our knowledge of the answer must tell us just that. It must not give us what is beautiful in some respects only, or in some contexts only, or on some occasions only, or to some degree only. If that is all we know we still do not know what beauty is.

This is, clearly, not a single ladder, but rather a collection of them. In the early dialogues they constitute, with one or two other conditions, the requirements laid down for an adequate answer to a Socratic question. As time went on Plato became increasingly sensitive to the possibility of using the objections to proposed answers to Socrates against the possibility of any *episteme* at all. This led to an increasing interest in the question of what conditions have to be satisfied for *episteme* to be possible. This shift, from an interest in what makes an adequate answer to a question to one in what is needed for *episteme* to be possible, directed attention to *episteme*. Here the standard examples of the earlier dialogues suggest a tie with goodness. This further influences the requirements for an adequate answer. Knowledge is concerned with knowing what things really are, but this means knowing their true nature, which will enable one to distinguish between the good and the bad. The change is not unimportant. In the early dialogues we need to know what X is in order to tell whether or not something really is an X. The knowledge enables us to tell genuine from bogus examples. It does not enable us to tell good from bad specimens. This difference does not emerge when we are asking what justice or holiness are, but it is clear if we ask what man is. It is one thing to be able to judge between genuine, borderline and inadmissible cases, and quite another to be able to distinguish between good and bad genuine specimens. It is this last that is a condition of *episteme*. This can be thought of as having as its object either goodness or being. Its object is goodness in that it is a matter of knowing how it is best that things should be. Its object is being, in that it is of the nature of things, and that is a matter of knowing what sorts of thing it is best there should be, where the sorts admit of degrees of performance. Not all terms will stand for something of which it is possible to give an *ousia,* they will not stand for *onta,* because they will not be part of the explanatory system which tells us how things really are and so give us the unqualified truth. So goodness influences the way being is thought of. But the approach through being leads to a demand for changeless 'is'-es, to a static pattern of how things should be to which the changing world approximates and so affects the account of goodness. 'Real' *episteme* is possible only if there is a system of inter-related functions for things to perform and the behaviour of things can be interpreted as an approximation to their performance. Plato's interest in knowledge, in fact, is an interest in the proper way to conduct scientific enquiry and the proper form of the end result. In so far as it is philosophical it is philosophy of science.

Knowing what *X* is, then, is either knowing what something like largeness is, or what something like man is. In the first case it is a matter of knowing what determines proper size in fields where there is a proper size, in the second of knowing the proper function in terms of which to settle the question of proper size etc. These are two sides of the same penny. Anyone possessed of this knowledge should be able to explain why certain characteristics are, when they are, part of what makes a man good, in what contexts they are so, to what extent etc. In other words, knowing what *X* is is inextricably bound up with being able to explain certain facts and the advocacy of real knowledge is also the advocacy of a certain style of explanation as the only real explanation. We can, of course, establish the antecedent conditions necessary for the occurrence of a certain event, but in Plato's view that is not 'really' explaining it, and if that is all that can be done, the event is inexplicable. True science produces the real explanation, and that is a matter of showing how it is best for things to be.

All this sounds blatantly dogmatic, an expression of a unilateral determination to refuse to accept anything but a certain pattern of explanation. To some extent, however, it seems blatant simply because we are most of us at present disinclined to accept the model of explanation that Plato proposes. That does not make it clear just where if anywhere Plato's mistake lies. It is not obvious and arrant nonsense to complain that suggested explanations do not really explain, nor does the fact that a proposal is uncongenial show it to be false. It is necessary, therefore, to get at least a sketchy idea of the form objections to inadequacy of explanation might take, in order to see where to locate Plato's. Unfortunately the topic is of a complexity far beyond the scope of the present volume and my aim will be adequacy for immediate purposes rather than completeness.

There is fairly clearly a variety of ways in which explanations may be felt to fail to explain short of flagrant irrelevance. For instance, faced with a man who has become a whole-time member of a gang that indulges in armed robbery, we might try to explain his present activities by reference to his poverty-stricken and unaffectionate home background. But it might be complained that while this might explain his being a delinquent it does not explain the particular form of his delinquency, so it does not really explain his going in for armed robbery rather than pick-pocketing. Poverty and lack of affection are no doubt relevant, but they are not sufficient. In a slightly different way, if someone explains a fire by pointing out that an oil stove was knocked over, it is possible to object that there had to be air in the atmosphere and inflammable material to hand. It is usually a tiresome objection, for we usually take for granted this sort of thing when offering such an explanation. Whereas the previous objection points out a lack of detailed power in the explanation offered, the second draws attention to a reliance on unmentioned factors. In both cases the objection assumes that a certain style of explanation is to the point, but not enough in that line has yet been done. In either case it is supposed that certain additions will produce an adequate explanation.

A more radical objection might take the form of saying that in neither of these cases do we get the real explanation, even when they have been touched up. Notoriously, explanations of the poverty to delinquency type only hold for the most part, so that they cannot give us what really makes the man go delinquent. In the example of the fire the conflagration is really explained in chemical terms. Words like 'flame' and 'air' are too crude. The real reason why everything goes up in flames is given in terms of chemical interactions. We are then given a precise account of the conditions that give rise to the effect. What are originally offered as explanations are good enough as rough signs of when to expect certain effects, but they never get to the heart of the matter.

There are no doubt many forms that this objection might take, and many different things wrong accordingly. I want to concentrate on one common form. It is often supposed that if A is the cause of B then whenever A then B and conversely, allowing for time order. This seems natural enough. After all, if A occurs without B, that shows that A is not sufficient for B. In other words, some other condition must be added if B is to be produced. If, on the other hand, B occurs without A, that shows that A is not necessary for B, and so in giving A we have not given all the conditions for B. So if the regularity is broken we have to admit that we do not yet have the conditions for B's occurrence. But that is surely what we claim in giving A as the cause. Therefore we must have admitted that A is not the cause. This is why 'on the whole' explanations must be inadequate. Further, a cause, in producing its effect, must be responsible for all the effect. This seems a necessary truth since nothing unaccounted for can be *its* effect. So the cause must account for every detail of the effect. This is why reference to fire and air does not really explain what happened. For a full explanation we have to resort to a more detailed account. Granted that real explanations have to be full ones, this is why talk of flames and air has no prospect of final success.

To start with I shall suppose that if A is the cause of B then whenever A, B and conversely. What, then, is meant by explaining the whole of the effect? To begin with a simple point, it is doubtful whether at one level it makes any sense to talk of any such thing. What the effect is is determined by such things as the context in which it is being considered and the sort of explanation being offered. Suppose a man serves his guest poisonous mushrooms, and the guest dies. We should probably divide off the eating as the cause and death as the effect. If we had a more minutely physiological interest we might take the contact of the fungus with the tongue as the cause and count the consequent physiological reactions as the effect. Which is *the* effect of his putting the mushrooms in his mouth? Both are pertinent ways of describing the results, according to context, but they make a different selection of the situation. So it might be tempting to suggest that the whole effect is covered by the totality of possible descriptions of it. But to this there is no limit, nor any clear way of curbing the possible expansion of the effect. We may be viewing the episode in an historical perspective, so that the guest's death is the result of a conspiracy, but the conspiracy explains the overthrow of a government of which the guest's death is but a small part. This can lead to the hunt for the minimal events that are 'really' related as cause to effect. But this is an illusion. If any way of characterising events is to be declared *a priori* arbitrary, then they all are. There is no *it* that really comprises *the* event such that all the other descriptions are covertly referring, say, to relations between this and other things. In fact, when we talk of A being the cause of B, 'A' and 'B' already give ways of determining the items to be correlated, and there is no way of determining *the* event that is somehow privileged over others. Neutral descriptions are only neutral relative to competitors. If, then, we required of an explanation that it explained all the details of what is explained, and allow that all permissible ways of describing the effects are allowable, then we should never know whether we in fact had an explanation of anything since we could never have good reason to suppose that the explanation yielded all these results, nor that we had a complete account of the results.

This, however, may be considered an unimportant point. Suppose we take a chess-playing computer. If it has been well programmed then numerous moves will be explicable in terms of threatening its opponent's king or defending its own, taking a knight and so on, and these items will be explicable as parts of a strategy such that once we have grasped it we shall be able to predict future moves, and even establish correlations between situations and events, such as 'whenever its king is threatened it moves to defend it'. Now each such defensive move will involve some physical alteration on the board, and each will be physically describable and correlatable, in terms of that description, with its antecedents as physically described. But there will be no correlation between any sort of physical antecedent and moves defensive of the king, nor between situations of threat and physical descriptions of what follows. Now we can, of course, explain certain physical changes by reference to the need to defend the king, and also the move to defend the king by reference to the antecedent physical state. But these are, as Aristotle might say, accidental explanations, and they only operate at all because there is a system of correlations, or, in other words, there is a way of describing the events whereby correlations can be set up. Strictly the physical antecedents do not explain why the defensive move is being made, but why certain physical changes are occurring. As, in context, these can be identified via the description 'move to defend the king' we can, but loosely, speak of it being explained by them. Once this is realised it can be seen that any explanation is only offered of items in so far as they qualify for some given description. One would thus expect the antecedent physical conditions to explain all the resultant physical condition, and the reference to defence of the king to explain all about the move, but one would hardly expect them to do each other's explaining. So while accidental explanation can hardly be expected to explain much, proper explanation will always be complete with respect to the sort of item explained.

Yet even this does not seem quite right. Suppose we have an item A and a second item B consisting of elements (123) in that order. The effect of the impact of A on B is to produce swivel-B. This is a well-established law, but unfortunately swivel-B is either (132) or (213), and there is no way of predicting which. In this case, impact of A on B will explain the occurrence of swivel-B, but will not explain why this form and not that. So it will not explain everything about the effect even as properly described.

Now the earlier move of rejecting accidental explanation could be seen as an attempt to preserve the rule that an explanation must take the form of a universal law, under which the explanandum can be brought. But this last point could look like breaking that rule too. For after all, in any given case, the impact of A produces swivel-B, and each impact produces the swivel-B it produces. It must therefore explain that swivel-B. In other words, the impact of A sometimes produces swivel-B' and sometimes swivel-B''. That is another way of saying that the same cause produces different effects in a non-lawlike way. This result, however, might be thought an illusion born of a confusion. The confusion is in the passage from 'A causes B' where 'A' and 'B' stand for individuals to where they stand for types. Suppose that we allow that the statement taken this second way is always a universal correlation, then this law will, granted the occurrence of some A, determine the future to the extent of the claim that something will qualify as B. The actual A, of course, will bring about the actual B, with whatever actual features that has. In that sense it will explain their occurrence, but that is a far cry from saying that from the fact that an A has occurred it is possible to determine anything beyond the fact that some B will occur. So while any particular impact of A will, in the example above, produce some particular swivel-B, the law does not determine things so far and does not cover the form of swivel-B.

That being so, the universal law thesis can be retained with the limitation that any explanation, properly formulated, specifies the respect in which the items are correlated, and in that respect the correlation must be universal. It is, however, worth wondering what its status could be. The view that a cause determines the whole of the effect can be preserved even in the limited form now given it only if the causal law concerned is universal. Otherwise it would be of the form 'Usually (or often, or all things being equal) when A, B', which does not allow us to determine the effect but allows it to be on occasion undetermined. It is often felt that nothing in this form could ever explain, and certainly not causally. For it is surely one of the distinguishing marks between a causal and a statistical law that the one is, and the other is not, universal. At least, not being universal is a sufficient condition of not being causal. It might be allowed that often our formulations are careless and incomplete, but they always suppose the possibility of completion. While we mention the flame as the cause of the conflagration, we all recognise the assumption of the presence of other factors, and if they serve to explain it is because whenever the combination of factors is present the result follows. The discovery that it does not would be proof that we did not yet have the explanation.

For all its attraction, this seems to be nothing but dogma, a dogma in favour of the world being a certain way. Suppose that things were different and that if we wanted a fire there were, we knew, just two things we could do: we could pour water on a stone and we could rub two dry sticks together. Now of course often when we have quite dissimilar causes we discover a way in which, despite appearances, they are alike, and sometimes this might be done by means of some theoretical structure in terms of which they can be put in the same category. It is of interest, here, that the move is not to refuse to call them causes until this can be done. We start off with the datum that they are causes and search for a similarity in the interests of a unified system. It is not, therefore, that it makes no sense to talk of different causes of the same effect, nor that it is inaccurate. The same is true of the same cause having varied effects. In the example above, it would be perfectly possible to speak of the impact of A giving rise to two sorts of effect. Indeed, the distinction between taking 'A' as referring to a particular event and as referring to a type of event could be used in the opposed direction. It might be claimed that what gives plausibility to the assumption that if events of type A cause events of type B then any cause A must completely determine its effect, is the very confusion mentioned. Once the distinction is made the possibility of one type of cause having different possible effects seems clear. In either case we should no doubt hunt for a way of avoiding the situation, and this is the main cause of the trouble. For once we have succeeded we are liable to say that the real explanation is the one given in terms that allow of a universal law, even if one hedged with a *ceteris paribus*. The real explanation of the kettle's boiling is not that it was put on this hotplate, but one given in terms of thermal energy. Yet the other only becomes, if at all, not the real one, if this one is available. It would not follow that often/often causes were never the real explanations if they were all that was available. The refusal in special circumstances would not be based on some failure on their part to explain, but on their failure to be part of the more comprehensive explanatory system. It could, then, be that the world was as suggested above, and it proved impossible to find any way of incorporating the causes of fire into a single category, except the unhelpful one 'dry-sticks-or-water-on-stone'. If this is good enough we never need to start any interesting scientific investigation. It could also be that causes only on the whole produced their effects. It is not clear that in such a world all talk of what made certain things happen would collapse. Indeed, most non-scientists at least operate as though causes are non-uniformly related to their effects. In situations where we had poured water on a stone to produce a fire, this would be how we had produced it, even if it were known that every now and then, for no known reason, it failed. If, in the absence of any further theory making it possible to establish universal correlations, someone refused to call this the real explanation, this could only amount to indicating that it failed to comply with some so far as we know unrealisable ideal. Of course, once some such theory is in the wings, the situation is different.

For the theory might be atomist in form, postulating rigid laws of behaviour for atoms under varying conditions. It may be that granted such a theory it must always be possible to give a single account of apparently disparate causes. Now refusing to call pouring water on a stone the real explanation of the fire will mark one's devotion to the theory. But supposing the most likely theory is not of a form to have such consequences?

Sometimes, then, the refusal to allow that a proposed explanation really explains amounts to no more than an expression of preference for a certain ideal for the form of an explanation, or of adherence to a particular theory. The preference or adherence may, or course, be perfectly sensible, granted the world is as it is, but it has nothing to do with the conditions that have to be satisified if explanations are to be possible. The preference may be so well embedded that, as in the case of universal causal laws, one may fail to see it for what it is. Yet it is important to see it in its true light since otherwise one may unjustifiably try to turn round and refuse the name of explanation to adequate explanations. In this context refusing a name can amount to refusing attention.

I have gone at some length into this because it is an example that has some pull in the twentieth century. Yet it is the same sort of mistake as Plato made in what is now less attractive garb. Before going on to that, however, I want to take up another point that emerged in this discussion: that just as explanations vary, so does what is explained. If we return to the example of the chess-playing computer it seems fairly clear that the problem of how to explain moves is different from that of how to explain movements. Puzzled by a move, we may try the hypothesis that it is a subtle feint, or shows that this must be one of the computer's first games. The assumption is that we have a machine capable of adaptation in a certain direction. Certain forms of behaviour become hard to explain on that hypothesis, but they do not become any easier to explain if we can point out that granted these physical conditions this physical movement was to be expected. Of course, if it turned out that the assumed physical laws were not holding, that would be relevant, but being assured that they are is not to the point. It is doubtless assumed that they are, and it was on that assumption that the machine was constructed. What is at issue is whether we have a fault in design, or a happy and unforeseen bonus from design, or perhaps even, very radically, no machine at all. Whether or not the workings of a machine comply with the laws of physics, and whether or not the machine is capable of playing chess are two quite independent questions, and each involves trying to apply different sorts of description to what is going on and establish different correlations.

This is not to say that such questions are always quite independent.

I have chosen this example because it illustrates the point without getting entangled with problems about free will. It is not easy to see how things stand when one takes other examples. It seems that the question of whether an argument is to be taken seriously or as a satire is independent of questions of the physiological conditions leading to the production of such and such marks on paper, but it is not so clear what the connection is between being able to attribute the power to deliberate and being able to predict the same subject's physical movements from physical data alone on some agreed account of 'physical'. There is no *a priori* reason for supposing that proposed patterns of explanation cannot come into competition.

So far I have taken examples which in some more or less familiar sense explain events. But explanations are not always in this straight-forward way explanations of events. Some forms of linguistic theory, for instance, do not purport to explain why John Smith produces the particular guttural noises he does when he tries to speak. The aim is rather to devise certain theoretical categories and laws in terms of them such that one can derive what would generally be recognised as accept-able utterances and reject what would be recognised as unacceptable. Leaving aside problems about acceptability, the result is that instead of having, for any new utterance, to rely on trying it out, one would be able to judge its acceptability in terms of the laws discovered. This would not enable one to explain or predict the utterings of individuals, though those utterances would have to tend for the most part to abide by the rules proposed if the theory was to be acceptable. The theory, however, would be an idealisation, not a description or a causal account. At most it would explain why utterances *tend* to take certain forms and be related in certain ways, and not how on occasions they come to be.

What is to be explained, then, may be very varied indeed, and this fact makes even starker the claim that only one form of explanation really explains. Really explains what? Even if we stick to explaining events one could only claim that one pattern of explanation alone really explained what was going on if one could show that there is some privileged way of determining what is going on. When one moves further afield not even this will do.

All these examples are ones that might be familiar to a twentieth-century reader. Plato, of course, is not enamoured of the sort of causal explanation that I have been considering, and has no inclination to suppose that only such explanations are really explanatory. On the contrary, he seems to consider them not really explanatory at all. The style of mistake that he makes, however, is very similar to those dis-cussed, the main difference being that he opts for a different preferred candidate. I now want to return to Plato and indicate how this is so. The similarities are partly in the demand for a certain completeness and partly in the strong preference for a certain model of explanation.

To begin with it is worth remembering that Plato is in one respect like certain linguistic theorists, in that he is not concerned to explain particular events or how things come about, but at most why things tend to happen in the way they do. The Forms give an idealisation to which things as a whole only approximate, though the tendencies of things should, of course, be towards compliance. Even his views about the Demiurge are no exception, for there is here no interest in the mechanics or the fact of original production, but in asserting that the universe is to be interpreted as intelligently organised. The result, of course, will be that we shall be better able to cope if we understand the organisation, but the explanation takes the form of revealing the organ- isation. Some facts may well be recalcitrant, and Plato, indeed, recog- nises that they will be. Some occurrences will have to be described as malfunctions and put down to the intractability of the material. This is a common feature of this sort of explanation. For instance, if one is trying to interpret a piece of writing as an argument to the effect that only the moral life answers to all a man's desires, one is offering a purpose to the satisfaction of which the actual product can be seen to approximate. There are, however, ready to hand, a number of categories for saving the hypothesis. Thus, there will be parts of the argument that fail in fact to tell in this direction and have to be interpreted as fallacious. 'Fall- acious' is in this context a term for coping with material that is recal- citrant, allowing us to preserve the attribution of intention through the supposition of mistake. For more flagrant failure to fit there are cat- egories like those of 'aside' and 'digression'. These serve to admit that the material falls outside the proposed purpose – it does not even purport to come under it – while retaining that purpose as the dominant factor for interpreting the work. These categories have, of course, to be used with circumspection. I do not mean simply that certain facts are relevant to their applicability, but also there are limits to how extensively they can be applied without wrecking the thesis they were supposed to preserve. If the whole of a work has to be interpreted as a digression from its main purpose it would be better to try to construe it some other way, and if every argument has to be taken as fallacious it is worth toying with the idea of a different intended conclusion or purpose in writing. Similarly the sort of linguistic theory mentioned earlier has to allow for some tolerance of deviant performance. Deviations con- stitute prima facie counter evidence, but it takes more than one deviation to make a fall. Similarly, Plato allows that the cosmos is not a perfect embodiment of the system. He does not attempt to explain why Aristarchus' appendix is not functioning properly, but he does aim to show that the world operates in a way that makes it possible to speak of the proper function of the appendix. Things will go wrong, of course, because of the nature of the material of which the world is constructed. It may also be possible to discover under what conditions this tends to happen, but that is not explained by the Forms. His theory, therefore, does not have to explain everything if that means explaining why everything happens as it does. On the other hand he does suppose it can cover everything in that there should not be items that neither conform to the system nor come under some form of deviation. A linguistic theory will fail to cover a great many noises that come in the midst of speech, such as groans, sneezes and the like. But there had best not be acknowledged utterances which are neither correct nor incorrect. As the theory of Forms is out to explain the cosmos it cannot allow part of the cosmos to fall outside its competence in the way in which linguistic theory can with some noises. If we suppose a world in which there were several unrelated systems of entities then the theory of Forms could not account for such a world, for the Forms comprise an interrelated system. The same goes for a world in which large areas had to be treated as functionless background against which other items did, but did not need to operate.

This requirement of Plato's is analogous to the prejudice that says that we do not have an explanation of phenomena until we have a system of universal laws to explain them. It may be very well as an objective, but cannot be taken as a requirement. Similarly, one can understand anyone who is attracted by the project of showing the whole universe to be a balance of interrelated parts but feel less sympathy when he shows signs of demanding that the project shall be successful. To be fair, Plato does not quite do this. He seems to allow that it is an empirical question whether or not the world is a system of the sort he supposes. For he thinks that the way we describe it presupposes that it is, but allows that our language may be ill-devised. In other words, the presupposition might be unjustified. If it is unjustified, however, then it is impossible to show that it is best that things be as they are, no *episteme* of the universe is possible, and it is impossible to explain why things are as they are. In short, the world would be unaccountable and unintelligible. All this seems to follow from the role of the Form of the Good in making knowledge possible. It is tantamount to saying that only one form of explanation really explains. For of course, if that sort of explanation is not available, then things cannot be explained that way and no branch of knowledge that used that form of explanation could be established. But that would be a very mild conclusion and would not justify one in saying that no branches of knowledge could be established. Plato is prepared to reject as in any genuine sense a branch of knowledge any discipline that does not employ this mode of explanation. So he claims both that any genuine explanation must take a certain form, and that to be an adequate one it must be part of an all embracing system.

The reason for Plato's believing the first is partly that the members of a typical list of *epistemai* invite such an account, partly that successful sciences in his day followed this pattern, but partly, too, that he thought there was good reason for believing that the total account was there to be found. Trust in the overall theory would lead him to reject other proposed explanations as not 'real' because they did not explain in its terms. They could not therefore be complete or comprehensive. In his time there was as good reason to believe in the possible success of Plato's style of account as in that of atomist or similiar ones. After all, these last were not so formulated as to yield precise empirical tests or be capable of explaining phenomena in any satisfactory way. They served rather to meet very general difficulties about change and give a plausible sounding account of the basic constitution of the world. Compared with the progress of medicine and music they were not getting very far in dealing with particular phenomena. Once one starts on the Platonic route of looking for interconnections between the objects of various branches of study, the chances of success look good. Whereas it is not easy to see what experiments arc going to help decide between one Greek atomist theory and another, nor easy for the proponents to devise tests, the sort of situation that would count against the Platonic story seems fairly clear, although a great deal of work would have to go into either establishing or refuting it. Further, the model of the world as a giant organism, which strikes us as fantastic, would itself have explanatory advantages. I have tended to speak as though Plato's views on goodness can be understood if we take machines and artefacts as examples, and certainly he uses artefacts himself. But if we take an artefact as our model for the working of the universe the very model will immediately give rise to certain questions. For the universe will have to be seen either as a machine or as an implement under constant manipulation. Either way it is a very extraordinary artefact since it does not run down or fall apart. The model of an organism at least helps explain this to some extent, since it is charcteristic of an organism to be to some degree self-repairing and have, as it were, a set of mutually supporting parts. When I say that it helps to some extent I do not mean that it gives the chemical structure that explains the organism's operation. But granted that it can be interpreted as an organism, then in virtue of that characterisation one would expect it to be to an extent self-perpetuating, so that the fact that it was would not be an objection to that interpretation, and so would not have to be accounted for in order to preserve it. If we suppose that ordinary organisms tend to degenerate because of their interaction with their environment, then in the case of the whole universe that cause of degeneration would be lacking. Further, the degeneration of ordinary organisms might be seen now as part of the life of the whole. They are now to be looked on as parts of an organism, to fade out and be replaced according to the way of organisms. In that case the cosmos is the only proper organism, and some features of actual ones can now be interpreted as really being features of organs. Consequently some of the obvious mocking questions to ask, such as where it gets its food, might be met with a proper agnosticism because it is only an obviously good question if our ordinary examples are to be taken as genuine examples. Consequently the organism model can seem explanatorily helpful, seem a likely starter, and also reinforce and be reinforced by considerations drawn from Plato's views on the determination of excellence, which seem to drive one to an overall account on penalty of having to drop all the intermediary ones.

All this, however, only serves to explain how Plato came to make his mistakes, it does not stop them being mistakes. It remains quite possible that the world should contain some items that call for description as organisms and so allow of explanations of the general trend of certain events in terms of what is needed for the subject's welfare, while also containing other areas where no such account can be made to stick. Also, in such a world, not only might these other areas be susceptible of other modes of explanation, but the operations of those items susceptible of Platonically favoured accounts might be subject to other types of explanation possibly explaining different facts about them, as with the chess-playing computer. It is one thing to be in favour of a particular mode of enquiry, quite another to go to the lengths of rejecting all others or treating them as not worth the attention of a serious and well-developed mind.

There are two further points about Plato's view that are of some importance, one concerning the possibility of rival accounts, the other on the difficulty raised earlier that Plato has what might be called a static account of the good condition for a thing to be in. To take the first first: it is not clear why Plato should be confident (justifiably confident) that if there is any way of construing the universe on the model of an organism, then there is only one. Suppose we turn back to the ideal of explaining phenomena by bringing them under universal causal laws, and also indulge in a little make-believe for expository purposes. Suppose that we can establish a perfect correlation between contact of flame and wax on the one hand and sputtering of flame and melting of wax on the other. We might still wonder what it is about the flame and wax that make them behave this way, and develop a theory about their constitution. The theory says that flames are made up of sharp atoms and wax of round ones, and when the sharp atoms meet the round ones they prize them apart, producing the phenomenon known as melting, while the impact chips pieces off the sharp ones, producing the phenomenon known as sputtering. Let us further suppose that we can verify the presence of particles of these different shapes. In that case, one would expect a similar correlation between the impact of a collection of sharp particles on a collection of round ones and the resultant separation of the round ones and chipping of the sharp ones. One would therefore have two laws of the desired kind, and since every flame is a collection of such and such atoms, and conversely, and similarly with wax, there will also be correlations between a flame approaching a collection of round atoms and the separation of the atoms and so on. In other words, there would be two parallel accounts of events, with nothing to choose between them so far as appeal to universal laws went, although different facts would have to be established to establish them. Showing that wax melted and showing that round atoms were separating would be two different exercises, although it would emerge that whenever the one was true so was the other. The question now is whether similar duplication would be possible with Plato's ideal of explanation. The answer is, I think, that it is, but it is perhaps more tempting to suppose that it is not.

To start with let us take the example of a tool discovered by an archaeologist. The point of choosing such a supposedly ancient tool is that it rules out the possibility of referring to the maker for his intention, which is fair enough as Plato does not envisage appealing to the Demiurge – we are supposed to be able to determine his intentions by reviewing the operations of his products. Now there may be reason enough for supposing that what the archaeologist finds is a tool, as it might show signs of workmanship and only occur on what are independently known to be sites of workshops. It may be possible to conceive of it as being used either as a last for shaping shoes or as a tool for shaping ornaments, and experiment might show it to be equally adequate for either task. There are therefore two equally possible hypotheses as to its function and the role it played in the life of this culture – equally plausible that is, supposing that shoes and ornaments were made in the same place. It may be, however, that according to which hypothesis one adopts one will select different specimens as being well made. Each hypothesis, however, fits the facts equally well.

Plato might, I suppose, reject this example, and on the grounds that it is of artefacts. It will perhaps be part of the point of taking an organism as an example that it should show some tendency towards the sort of activity appropriate to the characterisation. So if we took two organism accounts, presumably offering different defining functions, Plato would perhaps be able to say that we had a choice. It may be that we simply do not have, with either, a sufficiently complex description of the function, or else on at least one hypothesis the things will fail to show the requisite tendency towards the defining activity. In the first case we should not have a parallel account, and in the second we should not have an analogue of the tool example just because the interpretation will only be justified if there is a noticeable tendency towards the required behaviour.

Now this might be so if we are dealing with supposedly pretty well faultless examples, but it does not look at all so plausible when we suppose the case only to approximate to the defining performance. While Plato hopes to explain what happens by exhibiting the universe as constructed on a system which gives how it is best for things to be, he is quite clear that whatever may be true of occasional phenomena, the cosmos as a whole only approximates to the ideal system. As a general rule an account which involved less resort to categories of malfunction would cover the phenomena better than one that had more. Certainly once such categories are in use the question is raised whether there is not some alternative account, for items that require their use are prima facie evidence against the account offered. In the case of the cosmos not only does Plato acknowledge a general condition of approximation, but also, as we have seen, one whole species, man, is, on his account, in a constant serious state of malfunction. It would not seem difficult to suggest alternative accounts of the universe involving no more serious attributions of defective operation. The human species is defective because it fails to order its life by reason and so fails to play its part in the direction of the universe. But if we are offering an idealisation to which the world we know can be seen to approximate, the very facts which Plato has to take as showing defective operation might be taken to show that while some members of the species may be capable of some rational development, care and government are not the function of the species, and there is no special role for the maverick members who do develop that way: they have to be content to be spectators. The role of the human species might be that of flexible predator, ready to step in and reduce any surplus left by a more specialised predator. For the performance of this function a wide variety of interests with consequent proliferation of crafts and a desire to explore and experiment can be seen to be useful, though pure mathematics and philosophy might have to be seen as just offshoots. 'Offshoot' is doubtless a category for accommodating phenomena which do not directly fit the hypothesis, but the reliance on it would seem no more serious than what Plato has to put on his own accommodating categories. Of course, any such suggestion would have to stand the test of whether or not it illuminated the facts. The point is merely to illustrate the difficulty of supposing that one set of phenomena must only be susceptible of one interpretation of the sort proposed. There is no *a priori* reason for supposing that it must be possible to settle which of these fits better. Of course, it will make a difference to what one thinks will make the world run better, but that is not what is at issue. The point is that they would be equally systematic structures giving how it is best for things to be, with neither being more adequate than the other as an account of that to which the world can be seen to approximate. So Plato cannot assume that only one such account will be findable, nor that it will be possible to settle the issue between two.

There are two defences Plato might offer, not on the general point, but against the sort of alternative proposed, one based on facts about desire, the other on facts about intelligence. Thus he might claim that men have in fact a desire for the truth and to order things properly, so that a tendency this way is discernible in the species. We have already seen, especially in chapter XV, that this claim gets into difficulties. It is especially weak in the present context. For if we observe men's pursuits, or tabulate their professed or operative ideals, it is fairly clear that there is too much variety and plasticity for Plato's comfort. It is no use at this point having recourse to the general system of which men are a part, and arguing that as this is their role it is legitimate to postulate some nisus in this direction, for of course the nature of that system is precisely what is at issue, and consequently what role we could justifiably attribute.

At this point some help might be looked for from the second consideration. After all, men do have intelligent capacities, however limitedly they are commonly developed. As Plato points out, it is in possession of these capacities that man comes nearest to the gods, and it is only sensible to determine man's function by reference to them. Whatever the inherent attractions of this move, however, it involves the abandonment of other points if taken. For in effect this is taking characteristic performance rather than function as the determinant of excellence, thus potentially abandoning the thesis that there is a system of functions, and certainly abandoning its importance. Further, it amounts to selecting a particular special performance as the most important. After all, language, artistic performance, moral concern, political life and so on can all be taken as special to man. Consequently, it has to be taken that one sort of performance is more important than others, and that the performance of this activity is important in itself quite apart from the question of the part it plays in any wider whole. In fact Plato seems to be holding that it is better to be intelligent than not, better to be a god than a man, a man than an oyster and so on, a view that perhaps surfaces in the *Philebus* at least (21). But any such view cuts across the middle dialogue position on the determination of excellence and the whole project of showing the excellence of X in part to depend on its relation to the total system.

In short, even if we suppose that it will always be possible, if one can sensibly talk of the excellence of some items in the universe, to find some total system of which they can be seen to be a part, it does not follow that there will only be one such account devisable. So the actual situation could be equally well covered by two accounts, without it being possible to determine which was right. Barring appeal to the Demiurge, indeed, it would not follow either that one must be right. If one once allows for a considerable degree of plasticity in human nature in the matter of desires it might be possible to see the universe as a determinable system that can to some extent be given by this species a different determining centre of its operation and so of the excellence of its parts.

This suggestion would, of course, be quite abhorrent to Plato, and this brings me to the last aspect of his position I wish to discuss, what I have called his static assumption. This expression has tended to cover two distinct points, first, the position that men are in some basic respects uniform, and second, that development is not allowed for. Each of these ties in with the general position on knowledge. The conclusion on uniformity is probably the result of a number of factors. To begin with, an early interest in moral matters would lead Plato to feel that considerations of justice and ideals of courage and temperance bear on all men equally as these virtues are part of what makes a good man, and being a man is common to all men. At the same time, the attempt to use the analogy of health to make it clear how the virtues make a good man, led to talking of a psychic constitution common to all men, and this no doubt made it easy to overlook the possibility of a species function not performed by all, or even any, members of the species individually. As I have suggested, the analogy with health, even if accepted, does not obviously compel the conclusion of uniformity, unless one also accepts some theory about health which itself provides a uniform account. Failing that, or supposing a theory which allowed for the specification of a number of 'ill' conditions that made a wide range of typical necessary activities impossible, but also for a range of 'healthy' conditions when normal life was not interfered with, no such conclusion would even be encouraged by the analogy. Such a looser position would raise doubts as to whether there is an *episteme* of medicine or of the human soul, and would certainly suggest the possibility that there was no need for such *epistemai* to have precise accounts of proper order and proportion with the consequent use of mathematical techniques.

Perhaps more serious is the point about lack of development. Plato's position on the Forms constituting a system, and there being just one such system, allows for progress and development on our part in the acquisition of knowledge, but not for development on the world's part which would involve a change in the idealisation to which it approximated. The most that could be admitted in this direction would be the view that the cosmos at present was analogous to an embryo or a child, but even this would involve an account of the fully developed state on the way towards which this was a stage. The main responsibility for this lies with the restrictions put on the object of *episteme,* and consequently on what is to count strictly as the truth. For it emerges that if a proposition is to count as giving what is, and so as giving *episteme,* then it must be for ever true, but also carry no time reference, and further be not simply a definition of some concept, but an account of what constitutes being X, where being X is part of the system to which the world does eternally approximate. But just as there is no *a priori* reason to suppose the universe could not develop so that a physical theory adequate to its present state was inadequate to a later one and vice versa, so there is no *a priori* reason to suppose that it could not develop so that a Platonic style account now applicable becomes inapplicable, and such development be not to a term. Yet any such suggestion is clearly repugnant to Plato, and consequently there are unjustifiable elements in his position preventing him from envisaging possibilities even within his own preferred style of approach.

This limitation has also serious effects on his moral position. Taking this to start with as a view on the desirable ideals of man, his position on *episteme* not only rules out the possibility of an indefinite range of ideals that would be desirable according to developing circumstances, but also rules out the possibility of men's adapting to such an indefinite range. He would consequently be predisposed to a restrictive position on the issue of whether or not and to what extent it is possible to talk generally of human nature. He would, for instance, be predisposed to reject the suggestion that primitive man is radically different from ourselves in the sort of ideal he has or is capable of and in most of the basic motives that rule his life, and that this is true in varying degrees of men in different societies. Similarly he would not readily envisage the possibility that future generations might be quite unmoved by considerations of toughness or manliness but not either dominated or even from time to time harried by lechery, greed and intemperance. Yet his opposition would not be based on a reasonable scepticism merely, founded on well interpreted data, but also on the feeling that if all this were true, then there would be no *episteme.*

It might be felt that if we freed Plato of the analogy between virtue and health matters might be better. After all, he could now allow for indefinite plasticity of personality, but that would not matter. He would still be right that justice is invariable, and he could maintain this even while allowing for variations of other sorts in society. For if man ceases to be a social animal there will be grounds for saying we have a different species, but so long as he is a social animal there will have to be limits on what is acceptable behaviour, ruling out such things as unrestricted killing and lying, so Plato will still be able to maintain a basic unchanging set of restrictions and will be right to resist the suggestion of plasticity at least in this area.

This would, of course, be a fairly radical retreat, but even so it involves at least one of two serious confusions. The first arises if we suppose the argument to concern social rules or laws. Considering Plato's assimilation of law and morality this would not be unreasonable. In that case the argument is that since certain types of behaviour would tend to the destruction or debilitation of society it is clearly right to say that there should be a law forbidding them. Yet clearly there would be no reason for having a law forbidding them unless there was some tendency on the part of some members of the society concerned to go in for the objectionable behaviour. If no one had any such inclination it would be absurd to have a law, and possibly objectionable on the grounds that one should not suggest to people evil possibilities that they had not thought of. Only if one could establish some general thesis about human nature, such as that all men had a strong inclination to all forms of anti-social behaviour, could one draw the conclusion. But that would take us back to the previous point.

The argument might, however, be that although a law may not be necessary it must be generally recognised by a group of social beings that anti-social behaviour is undesirable. Consequently one could expect that in a society where no one has some particular anti-social inclination it would still be acknowledged that such behaviour was undesirable. Even if it was not recognised it would still be possible to show that it was undesirable, and that would be enough for Plato. It would not, however, be anywhere near enough. For the argument only establishes that there are limits beyond which behaviour is unacceptable, it does not rule out infinite possibilities of variation within those limits. Euclidean parallel lines impose a limit on an area in two directions but do not constitute a figure. It would be quite possible, therefore, to hold that the forms of behaviour desirable in a given society, which constituted just behaviour in that society, were partially determined by the various capacities of the members of the society. There may be limits on what could count as just, but also infinite variations between societies that resulted in infinite variations on the forms of behaviour to be considered just, and so on the norms. There would consequently be no *episteme* of justice. In this case it would not either be in order to search for the ideal form of society in general, made up of men brought up in the ideal way, after the manner of both Plato and Aristotle.

It would, of course, be open to Plato to argue these points. My purpose has been to show how he is pushed into taking positions on them because of unnecessary and largely unattractive elements in his views on knowledge. These lead to restrictive views on what are acceptable forms of enquiry, and to prejudices as to what views can reasonably be held even in areas where Plato's method of enquiry no longer seems unduly bizarre.

XVIII

Innate Knowledge and the Corrigibility of Language

Plato's belief that there is only one way of explaining things and that there could not be two rival idealisations to which phenomena might approximate, might have seemed both to support and be supported by another element in his position. He was clearly struck by the fact that although, as he supposed, the use of terms like 'good', 'equal', 'just' commits their users to a view of the world of which they are only dimly, if at all, aware, and which they can certainly not justify, nevertheless these terms are in very common use, and from an early age. Not only are the terms used, but people show, under questioning, an ability to see that certain proposed accounts of what constitutes justice, knowledge or whatever are inadequate, and in a way that suggests familiarity of some sort with some standard against which the proposed answers are measured. Under questioning we become clearer about the standard, but from early on it is operative. It therefore seems a good question to ask how people know what justice, knowledge and the rest are, i.e. what they consist in. They cannot have gained this knowledge by observation of phenomena, for the use of the terms is already an implicit judging of the phenomena relative to some standard. Further, it is not just the terms 'good', 'fine' and their like that carry this implicit world view, but also the terms that embody classifications of things in terms of functions and thereby allow of qualification by the first set of terms. We start, then, with a ready acceptance of a language which, considered as a whole, supposes the world to be structured in a certain way. Yet how could we know that it is so structured, when establishing that it is is so obviously an extremely complicated matter requiring a lifetime of investigation and argument? The only answer is that we start life with this knowledge.

This last is, of course, true only if it is in fact knowledge, that is to say if the world is in fact structured in the way supposed. Plato does seem to allow, in the *Cratylus,* that our language might be wrong, and this is a very plausible thing to suppose. After all, if we consider a language as a whole it would seem to reflect the way in which those who use the language view the world. They will express what they consider their discoveries about the world in the language they have, but that already takes it for granted that it is right to classify and describe things in the ways laid down in their language. If their language embodies a misrepresentation of reality then that is just repeated or perhaps magnified in their further speculations. A language which sorted things into kinds according to differences in shape and colour, say, takes reality to be different from one that sorts them according to difference of function. Yet they cannot both be right. The world must be one way or the other (or neither) and there must be a correct way to sort things. An essential precondition of all science must be the construction of a language which reflects reality accurately. There can be two correct languages only in the sense that there can be two different sets of sound-types in which each member of one set is matched with one of the other by identity of sense, and no member of either fails to reflect reality. If we have two languages whose items fail to match in this way, then they must 'divide up reality' differently, and at least one of them must be wrong. The combination of some such view about language with a belief that we approach the world with some knowledge of what constitutes knowledge, excellence and the rest, would create a prejudice in favour of thinking that there is only one true account of the world and that it is an overall functional account. Alternatives are misrepresentations.

In all this there are just two points that I propose to discuss: first, the plausibility of suggesting that we approach the world with some innate knowledge of its structure, and second, the view that our language could be mistaken. These two are related in Plato because it is naturally assumed that the great majority of words in a language are taken to have some application, and if the majority of them are such that their application presupposes some theory, then the possibility of the theory's being false entails the possibility of the language's needing revision. To some extent, however, they raise different problems and to that extent I shall treat them separately. For the purposes of what follows I shall suppose that Plato is right about the word 'good' as expounded earlier. After all, any particular language could have a word which was confined to functions in the way Plato would like, and whose use of any particular item was only justifiable if certain facts about the whole held. At the same time this word might operate as the basic term of praise. While *we* might be able to describe the word as performing different functions, it would not be possible to ask, in the language, what the 'good' was of being in a state required by the system. I do not mean by this that it would not be possible in the end to make this initially bizarre question intelligible, but that until success here was achieved it was taken as a condition of having learned the term that one should reject the question as unaskable. Pretending that this is true of the Greek word '*agathos*' I want to see how Plato's view would stand with regard to our innate knowledge and the corrigibility of language. For Plato is not alone in holding some such view, and it is not immediately clear whether and if so why it should be deemed objectionable, at least in principle.

The starting-point of such views is that there are certain assumptions integral to our knowledge which cannot be justified in certain accepted ways. One choice is to say we do not know them, and so perhaps know nothing, another is to say that we do, but in that case it seems a good question to ask 'how?' In Plato's case the important steps in the argument seem to be these: (i) we all use terms like 'good', 'fine', 'equal' and the rest; (ii) we all know that there is a difference between Good and the good things we come across; (iii) the use of the terms is an implicit use of a standard to which the things described as good are referred or compared. It now seems a good question to ask how we know the standard. Phenomena do not yield it, they yield to it, and we approach them armed with it. In Plato's presentation the question is 'how do we know equality?', but in the form 'where did we acquire our knowledge of it?' Put this way it is really not very clear what we are being asked, nor whether it is at all a good question.

To begin with, that we all know the difference between Good and good things, Equal and equal things and so on, may in part seem acceptable because we interpret it as admitting that it is one thing to talk about good things, and another to talk about what it is to be good. One could accept this while not distinguishing between talking about what 'good' means and talking about what constitutes being good, so that even if one thought there was no general answer to the second question, one could still accept the original distinction. So a failure to distinguish clearly between discussing meaning and discussing what being *F* consists in can make it seem more readily acceptable that we know the difference between Equal and equal things. Further the very fact that we use the terms suggests that we know what 'equal' means, and so know Equal. So the failure to distinguish may make it easier to get accepted the conclusion that we know Equal than it would be if this was seen clearly as knowing the standard. Because of the possible dual interpretation of knowing Equal, the apparent appositeness of asking 'how do we know?' can seem to get support from two quite different angles. First, if one has a view that the possession of certain concepts is non-problematic, since after all we have come across those things to which they undoubtedly apply, one might be inclined to think that there is a problem about how we acquired certain other concepts when we have never come across anything to which they undoubtedly apply, and they cannot be seen as constructions of elements of which this is true. Second, if in the use of a certain concept one is comparing the things of which one uses it with a standard, it seems appropriate to wonder how we came to know about the standard.

Plato's problem, however, does not arise primarily from a difficulty as to how we acquired the concepts, even if that helped the confusion. The important point is that we readily apply the concepts, and that is taken to imply a belief that things really do only approximate to some standard. Further, the belief is right, with all its ramified implications about a total system of interpretation, and it becomes very puzzling how we could have known all that from the beginning. Yet even granted that the knowledge is not explicit and articulated, it seems clear that it is somehow implicit there from the word 'go'. In order to sort out the confusions of this position, some of which also have their part to play in other theses concerning innate knowledge, it will be necessary to make a few points about knowledge and belief, in the hope of seeing more clearly when and why 'how do you know?' is a good question.

To begin with 'belief': this is a term that commonly occurs in interpretations of the behaviour of animals, human or otherwise, as intelligent and exhibiting learning. Commonly behaviour that manifests intelligence also shows some form of error, but we still want to interpret it as a piece of intelligent behaviour although one which shows a less than perfect state of learning as yet. Thus we characterise the blunderings of the novice at bridge as aimed at achieving his contract, and put down the flight of pigeons from a man with a walking stick to their knowledge of guns. There is clearly a place for a term which is non-commital as to the correctness or otherwise of the subject's views and so as to the range and extent of the subject's knowledge. Terms like 'believe' and 'think' fill this place, and the resultant concept applies indifferently to verbal and non-verbal behaviour, and to the behaviour of beings with or without language. The concept is such that it is not a condition of A's believing that P that A should either know or believe that he believes that P. In other words, in a formal system covering arguments for this concept of belief, it would not be a theorem either that Bap→BaBap, or that Bap→KaBap (where 'B' is rendered 'believes' and 'K' 'knows'). The conditions that are sufficient for the truth of 'A thinks there is a rabbit down that hole' are quite insufficient for the truth of 'A thinks that A thinks that there is a rabbit down that hole.'

This is not, however, the only concept of belief. When we are dealing with human beings we are frequently interested in discovering what propositions people will sincerely declare their assent to. I do not mean which they will publicly assent to, but which ones they will assent to, if only privately, when they face up to them. In the case of refusal to declare themselves openly, behaviour is taken as evidence, as it is also, no doubt, of the sincerity of public declarations. The important point is that it is now taken as a necessary condition of the truth of 'A believes that P' that A sticks by his assent to P. It is not of course necessary that the words used to express P, in the proposition attributing the belief, should be understood by A, nor that he should assent to the proposition so expressed. It is necessary that he should have some means of expressing it such that in accordance with that means of expression it is true that he assents to it. Clearly this concept cannot apply to any being not possessed of any form of language, and is probably the concept in operation when people declare that animals do not really have *beliefs*. It is also manifest in refusals to say that a person can be said to believe, say, that the government ought to be trusted, if he has never considered the question (and so cannot be said to have assented to the proposition), even if he clearly acts in a way suggesting that that is taken for granted. If one is devising a formal system to cover arguments using this concept it is at least plausible to require that it be a theorem that Bap→BaBap, and possibly, though less obviously, that Bap→KaBap. I say 'plausible' only, because there are complexities which I will just mention, though I do not wish to go into them. It might be that A's sincere assent to P is necessary for the truth of 'A believes that P' but that it is also necessary that A be prepared to act on the supposed truth that P either by accepting P as a premiss in discussions or in more practical ways; but it may at the same time be that A's sincere assent to P is sufficient for the truth of 'A sincerely assents to the proposition that A sincerely assents to P' and that that is all that is required to manifest belief in that proposition. On the other hand it might not be all, and the arguments pro and con there will, it is hoped, bring out what the concept is required for, and probably also that the above talk of *the* concept, in the singular, is premature. These difficulties bear also on the question of the inference to knowledge, with the added problem of deciding on the relevant concept of knowledge. For the moment it is enough to remark that if we are operating with a concept of belief such that assent of the subject to P is a condition of the truth of the attribution of belief in P to the subject, then it is at least tempting to suppose that the subject must have some reason, albeit a bad one, for believing P. Consequently it can seem that 'how does he come to believe that P?'/'why does he believe that P?' are questions to which there must be an answer other than 'nohow'/'for no reason' if 'he believes that P' is to be true.

In order to discuss Plato more clearly we now need one further slight modification of the broad distinction of uses of 'believe'. As I have outlined the first concept above the use of 'believe' is limited so that if A believes that P, then A has (mis)learned that P in learning to do the sort of thing he is engaged in. This limitation was convenient for the purposes of exposition, but clearly when we are trying to interpret a piece of behaviour as intelligent the interpretation might require us to take the subject as acting on the supposition that P even though there is no question of (mis)learning that P in the course of learning to do what is being done or anything else. Thus it may be that in describing the behaviour of the young of a given species as seeking the protection of their mother we have to attribute a belief that their mother is a source of protection, even if that belief cannot be said to be acquired as part of the (mis)acquisition of some learning.

To turn now to knowledge: there seems to be a fairly well accepted usage whereby if we can attribute a settled belief, where this is the modified version of the first concept discussed, and the belief is right, then the subject is said to know. Thus animals that hibernate show that they think winter is approaching by preparing stores of food or warm dens, and as they are characteristically right they are said to know that winter is approaching irrespective of whether they have learned any signs or whatever. Similarly, suppose we have a primitive people who believe that the earth is a sphere and but one of a vast number of mainly larger bodies in a state of constant motion relative to each other. It would be perfectly natural to describe these people as knowing a number of facts about the universe long before they were discovered in western Europe, even if it is accepted that, so far as we know, these facts were never discovered by their ancestors, nor did they even think that they had good reasons for their belief. If it turned out that there were many similar beliefs among this people, then it would be an interesting fact about them that they knew a great many things about the world for which they had no evidence. If this concept is in question it is obviously quite wrong to infer from 'A knows that P' either that A believes that he knows that P or that he knows that he knows that P.

Once again, however, this is not the only concept of knowledge current. There is the familiar objection that the subjects described above do not really *know* that winter is approaching or that the earth is a moving member of a solar system, and those deploying the objection are displaying a preference for a different concept of knowledge. For present purposes it is worth distinguishing between two different extra conditions that might be added. First, the objection might be that in order to know that P the subject must have learned that P. In the case of the animals we have to distinguish between instinct, which leads them to go in for hibernating behaviour, and knowledge, which comes from learning. Similarly with the supposed primitive people, although since we do not know any such, there is no category available for describing their beliefs, they clearly do not constitute knowledge – according to the example not even knowledge by hearsay.

In this case, as in the previous one, if one were producing a formal system to cover arguments where an operator mirrors this concept one could not allow either Kap→BaKap or Kap→KaKap as theorems. But in one respect there is an important difference. With the previous concept, while it might often be a sensible question to ask 'how do they know?', and in that sense a good one, it would not have any air of devastating challenge, for it may well be that there is no way in which they got to know. Clearly, however, this is not so with the second concept. For there it is a condition of the truth of 'A knows that P' that A should have somehow got to know that P. Consequently 'how do they know?' delivers a direct challenge to the original statement, and unless there is some true answer to it the statement is false.

The second condition that might be added is one that requires that if someone is to be said to know that P he must be in possession of sufficient reason for P. To be in possession of sufficient reason for P is for these purposes something which requires the power to assess evidence and to have it in a form in which it can be presented in a justification of the assertion that P. This rules out non-language users, but it is once again a condition of the truth of 'A knows that P' that there should be a satisfactory answer to the question 'how does he know?' The feeling that some such condition should apply lies behind many common refusals to attribute knowledge. For instance, many country people are credited with the ability to prophesy the weather with a fair degree of accuracy. They look at the clouds and sniff the air and make their pronouncements, and for some of us this is good enough. By the previous concept the man knows it is going to rain, and the question how he knows is answered by reference to his long experience. On the other hand, it is sometimes claimed that he does not really know whether or not it is going to rain, on the grounds that he cannot justify his prophecy in any way or bring forward any evidence. Since the power to produce the justification is a condition of the truth of the attribution of knowledge and on the assumption that if someone in this sense knows that P then he believes that P, it seems very likely that one can infer from the truth of 'A knows that P' that A believes that A knows that P, and perhaps also that A knows that A knows that P. Kap→BaKap and Kap→KaKap seem to be very much more hopeful candidates for theoremhood.

If we now return to Plato and the knowledge of Equal, Good and the rest, it is clear that he wishes to deny that we know Equal in anything like this last sense. Indeed, the fact that we cannot justify our initial attributions of equality or goodness, let alone any implicit beliefs about the total system, is positively traded upon. At the same time he wants to say that in some sense our use of these terms betrays our knowledge of the wider system. Consequently he is committed to distinguishing two senses in which a person can be said to know Equal and Good, one for which it is required that he be able to explain and justify his attributions and the other for which it is not. He wants this second sense, however, to be such that it is a condition of the truth of 'A knows that P' (or 'A knows Equal, etc.') that A should have got to know that P (or got to know Equal, etc.). Granted that Plato is right about the implicit beliefs in the use of these terms, and granted that those beliefs are true, the most that would follow, in the way of knowledge, is that we know these things in a sense which requires no such condition. So while it may be appropriate to ask how we got to know, there is no need to expect that there must be some way in which we did. Faced, then, with Plato's question how we know, we have a choice. We could answer that for all we know it is simply the fact that our linguistic behaviour can only be interpreted as supposing the world to be ordered in a certain way, and that the supposition is true. If Plato objects that if that were all, then we should not count as knowing Equal, etc., we could apologise for misunderstanding, and say that in that case for all we know we do not know, if it is a condition of knowing that we should have learned. If this is the concept of knowledge that Plato is employing, then it is up to him to show that we do know in the required sense, and for that he will of course have to bring non-question-begging reasons for supposing that we (must) have learned.

There is, then, no reason why the question 'how does A know?' should have an answer, and this is true not only in the case in which Plato admits it, but also in the one in which he wants to deny it. The same sort of point holds in the case of belief. It can seem a good question to ask 'why does A believe P?'/'how does A come to believe P?', and once again it is no doubt a question that is usually worth asking. The feeling that there is more to it that that, that there must be an answer to it, comes from conflating different concepts of belief. If we are using a concept where assent is a condition, then it would seem that it will at least be the norm that A should have a reason for his belief, and one could have a concept so closely tied to learning that it only applies if there is some answer to 'how did A come by the belief?' But Plato's case must be weaker than either of these, at least in the sense that the most he offers grounds for is belief on some interpretation which does not demand these conditions.

If we do not make any of the above distinctions, but do accept Plato's views on 'good' and the rest, then we may well feel driven by the question 'where do we get our knowledge of Good, Equal and the rest?' into supposing that we must have acquired it in some mysterious way before birth. After all, we must have acquired these concepts somehow and as we approach phenomena with some standard in mind, we have to explain our familiarity with the standard and why we suppose it, or how we know it, to apply. There are familiar concepts of belief and knowledge which would incline us to accept the appropriateness of these various demands, especially as they are concealed under the appearance of a single demand. Once the distinctions are made, however, the invitation to accede to the demands has no attraction at all.

For clarity, perhaps the point being made here needs distinguishing from another that can sound like it, and with which it can therefore be confused. A person may, and possibly for good reasons, hold a general theory according to which whenever we have behaviour that can be explained in terms of belief it is possible to give an account of the acquisition of the belief in terms, say, of stimulus and response. Such a theory might be supplemented so as to allow for genetically transmitted beliefs, but the point is that anyone holding such a theory will of course feel, as Plato felt, that if A believes that P, it must be possible to give an account of the genesis of that belief. But his position is in one important respect unlike Plato's. For he feels the need to make this demand because of a general theory which is in the last resort to be accepted or rejected according to whether it does or does not account for what it purports to account for. But Plato makes his demands because he feels they have to be met if the concept is to be applicable, quite apart from any such theory. In other words, he feels that it just would not make sense to say that A knows or believes that P, while denying that the conditions are met, while the other man should hold that while it is conceivable, they are ruled impossible by his theory, and so if we had to accept that they occurred, we should at the very least have to modify the theory.

This is an important distinction, for a person who does not make it and bear it in mind might well feel that his theory has the benefit of some antecedent obviousness because the alternatives are not only contrary to the theory but also offend his prejudices that they are conceptually impossible. So if he fails to make the above distinctions concerning knowledge and belief, he might feel that it is anyway obvious that a belief can only be attributed if there is some account discoverable as to how it was acquired, and so his theory, which also makes this demand quite generally, has some strong *a priori* claim to acceptance. The conceptual confusions can thus intrude to make difficult the envisaging of alternative theories.

The distinction is also important because there are in fact two quite distinct disputes about innate knowledge that failure to make this distinction only helps one to fudge. The first is a dispute as to whether any account of learning requires the postulation of certain contributions from the side of the learner which are, so to speak, disproportionate to the input. This is a dispute that a philosopher is for the most part well-advised to steer clear of. It is primarily at least a dispute as to the adequacy of certain types of theory to a range of phenomena. The other is whether the use of certain terms commits one to beliefs beyond one's powers of justification. The puzzling nature of this description is at least partly intended, in that it is supposed to cover some possibly interesting differences. If we accept Plato's account of 'good', then it will follow that any justification of any statement of the form 'X is good' is exceedingly complex, and clearly in fact beyond the powers of most of us. This result is based on an (in this case incorrect) analysis of the meaning of 'good', and if the analysis were right the correctness or otherwise of the implicit assumptions would in principle be checkable. There are, however, arguments of a more far-reaching kind to the effect that certain assumptions are implicit in the very use of language or conduct of argument. Plato's argument in the *Theaetetus* might be taken as of this sort, in so far as it suggests that if there is to be any judgment there must be a judger capable of reviewing perceptions. For if the argument holds it seems to show that if we know anything at all, even about our present perceptions, then we know more than that, viz. that there is a being capable of comparing perceptions. Nor is it open to anyone to object that the proper conclusion is that we do not even know about our present perceptions. For either he is producing an objection or he is not. If he is, then he is using terms with a certain sense, and if the argument is right this presupposes that there is a being capable of comparing perceptions, since that is held to be a presupposition of the acquisition of concepts. Alternatively, he is not producing an objection, and so there is no argument. Now if this kind of argument can be made to stick, it could be claimed that we all believe that there are persistent subjects capable of comparing their own various perceptions, that this belief cannot be established empirically, and yet it cannot be treated as a mere assumption, that one could reasonably drop. It is already assumed if one supposes one is reasoning, dropping assumptions and so on. Unless we know this we know nothing, and unless this is true we are not going in for reasoning. To say that we all believe it is not to say that we all understand and assent to the proposition, but that the interpretation of behaviour as intentionally and intelligently linguistic requires taking it as performed on this assumption. To claim that we know it would be to claim it is right, or simply that it has the status outlined of not being capable of being put in question. Clearly, if true, this is a far stronger position than Plato's, and it would rule out *a priori* the possibility of saying how we came to know it in the first place, and since developing or hearing about an argument of the above sort would be the only way of establishing it, not everyone has got to know it if that is what is required for knowing it. So this thesis would discourage one from setting up a particular empirical project, and if not a confusion would be an example where the two concerns about innate knowledge might make contact. It is, of course, worth noting that if one decided to say that such basic propositions are true and therefore known, the concept of knowledge employed is somewhat different from any outlined above. To begin with, the truth of these propositions cannot be established, as can the beliefs of animals about approaching winter, and this has led some, like Collingwood, to refuse the title of truths and call them absolute presuppositions. At the same time, if the thesis holds, there is no question of our being wrong about them, and those who agree with what they take to be Wittgenstein's view, that we can only know what we can be mistaken about, will therefore refuse to say we know them: they are, rather, the background that makes possible the acquisition of knowledge. If one prefers not to strike attitudes over the words but get clear about the concepts, declaring them known will seem neither repugnant nor exciting.

If a language has the sort of feature Plato holds that Greek has in respect to a range of terms, it remains possible to drop those terms, substitute others without that feature, and still have a learnable language. If the *Theaetetus* style argument is right one could not have a learnable language without the assumption in question. There would be no possibility of discovering the assumption not to be borne out by the facts. Between these two there is at least one further possibility. It is often, for instance, argued that the use of any language by human beings, any human language, presupposes the possibility of identifying perceptible persistent independent particulars by the users of the language. While such an argument does not purport to show this to be a presupposition of all rational activity that might in any world count as use of language, the argument is likely to rely on the supposed fact that no such language is conceivable by us. The fact that the use of any language usable by us carries this assumption does not on the face of it entail that the use of every language does. But it does seem to entail that we could not introduce any specimen terms of any such language, so that while we might be able to allow for the possibility of such a language, since the supposition does not lead to contradiction, we should not be able to conceive of a language that would qualify. I have no wish to go into the question of whether any such argument can be sustained. It is enough if there are two possibilities that a person might be taken to be arguing for, and that they differ from Plato's example.

None of the above is intended as a complete account of knowledge, belief or whatever, if such a thing is possible. It does not take very much ingenuity to devise examples where we might be tempted to attribute knowledge or belief, and which fall outside or on the borders of the above accounts, or suggest further refinements. This might, but also might not, suggest that the earlier sketch did not isolate separate concepts, but it is not in general a very important fact, as it is always likely to be true, however successful one's distinctions. It is, I hope, enough to indicate that while there is not necessarily anything very exciting about suggesting that there might be innate knowledge, and that if Plato were right about the Greek language and the nature of the universe the ancient Greeks would have possessed some, Plato's more exciting conclusions would not follow.

Plato's own view on what we innately know is one that attributes to us an assumption that might well turn out to be mistaken. The discovery of such a mistake should lead to a revision of the original language. The terms that are in this way vulnerable are very common terms of everyday life, so that this admission makes one wonder uneasily how far the rot might have spread. As we have seen, Plato seems to allow that it might be to all. It takes skill to devise a language, and while even a dialectician no doubt has to start with the language he is brought up with, it seems that by criticism he could set it to rights. This in turn suggests that there is a right way for language to be, and that disastrous results follow if we have one not constructed aright. If we have the wrong tools, or badly constructed ones, we have no hope of describing reality as it is.

It is not clear how radical Plato is prepared to be with regard to language, but it is clearly not possible for someone to set about criticising *in toto* all the concepts available to him, since the criticism can only be made in terms of some. So while he can set about criticising one language he speaks, or one spoken by someone else, he can only do so by taking the terms of another as not, for the period of critique, open to question. While he can no doubt repeat this exercise indefinitely, he cannot do it without reserving some items in relation to each operation. Whether or not Plato thought he could depends partly on how seriously he took the analogy with tools that we find in the *Cratylus*. It is a seductive analogy which may within limits be helpful, but it is important to note that the criticism of tools requires that one knows what they are for. Granted that, one can start working out whether this design of object in this material is suitable. If one looked on words as conveying their sense in virtue of the sort of sound made, as Cratylus wants, then one could criticise all words, but only on the supposition that one understood the task they were to perform. But having that knowledge would be being in possession of the relevant concepts, and so already supposing that we knew how to 'divide up reality'. Plato himself, of course, destroys the Cratylus position which would make a more exact analogy with tools possible. Yet if we move to asking whether our words do what they are meant to do, i.e. divide up reality correctly, it is hard to see how we could set about answering that question as one about all our concepts. For what is it to observe what reality is like but not observe that it is thus and so?

This only shows a certain sort of radical critique to be impossible, however. It would be a mistake to infer that language cannot be subjected to criticism of any kind, but it is of some help in assessing

Plato's position to get some idea of the different forms such criticisms can take. For in some cases it seems possible to talk of false assumptions, in some to use the tool analogy, while in others the project of showing inadequacy looks absurd from the start. I shall start with some that fit Plato's view and move on to others which seem less happy. These reveal the underlying assumptions of Plato's position. Until these different cases are considered it might seem still possible that although we cannot criticise our concepts *in toto,* still there is no subset of concepts that is not in principle subject to criticism in the way Plato wants.

To begin with, there does seem to be the clear possibility of areas of language being in theory corrigible in the way in which a good deal of Greek would be if Plato were right about that language. Thus in our society we get taught words for inanimate objects in a way that embodies a contrast with animate ones, and so renders unacceptable literal interpretations of 'the river is angry' or 'this oak tree is feeling sorry for itself'. A society of animists could have a language where the 'equivalents' of 'river' and 'tree' were taught with no such implied contrast, and so the above sentences would be taken seriously on their literal interpretations. The use of the terms so learned carries the assumption that certain other concepts will hold of what these terms are true of, and further experiences might lead the members of the society to reject the assumption. For this to be possible it is important that the members of the class of rivers, say, can be identified without having to establish that the further concepts apply to them, so that the term can be taught by references to examples, although what is taught as truistic of the examples goes beyond what is taught as sufficient to identify the examples. The discovery that the assumption should be rejected would lead to a revision of the language so that a set of terms for kinds of thing would now be so taught that the above sentences were unacceptable on a literal interpretation. The use of the terms would still carry an assumption, but the opposite one. In this sense the languages are alternatives and there could be argument as to which if either was correct.

With this sort of example one can see some point in talking of a language being true, and granted that one function of language is to enable us to express the truth about the world, one could speak of one criticised on this score as containing or consisting of a set of ill-devised tools. There is, however, no way of so specifying the task beforehand that one can then directly test the tool for success. That would necessitate already having the correct concepts, for the judging of whose correctness there is no such possibility. There are, however, cases where one can specify a task and then judge the adequacy or otherwise of a term with a given sense for performing it. Philosophers have, for instance, hoped to find some way of characterising acts for which the agent can be held responsible and ones for which he cannot. They then select some pair of terms, such as 'free'/'compelled', 'willing'/'unwilling' 'intentional'/'unintentional', 'voluntary'/'involuntary' and proceed to describe all acts for which the agent is responsible by the first of one of these pairs, those for which he can escape responsibility by the second. Of course, it is always possible to declare them technical terms and so define 'free', say, that it is a necessary and sufficient condition for its application to an action that the action be such that the agent can be held responsible for it. Usually, however, it is hoped that without such manhandling the terms chosen will turn out to be satisfactory. Consequently it is pertinent to test any pair out by trying to devise examples where the action would normally be said to be free but the agent absolved of responsibility, or the action not free but the agent held responsible. The purpose is to see whether the terms as commmonly understood are adequate for the task proposed for them. Even when it is acknowledged that the use is technical there can be dispute as to whether a given pair is more or less misleading than another and so a better or worse pair for the extension in question. Commonly, as Aristotle began to discover with the Greek words '*hekon*' and '*akon*', familiar terms fail to live up to one's hopes. Similiar questions of adequacy arise about collections of expressions, as for instance as to whether a given number system is adequate for dealing with certain equations, or whether a truth-functional calculus is good enough for testing the validity of modal arguments. In all these cases the tool analogy can once more seem apt, but now it is possible to specify beforehand what the term or set of terms have to be able to do and see whether as defined they are capable of it; and this, as we have seen, is just what is not possible with the earlier examples. The tool analogy can therefore be taken more strongly with these cases than the former ones. There is, however, no temptation to talk of them as somehow inaccurate or not true. It is not that their use carries an assumption that might be falsified, but whether, with whatever assumptions their use carries, they can be used in their normal sense to deal with specifiable problems. So despite the misfortune that the tool analogy seems appropriate in both cases, the form of criticism is different, and only with the first is there any colour at all to talking of a language or part of a language being misleading, inaccurate, not quite true or whatever. The second, on the other hand, is certainly a very common topic of philosophical discussion. Often, the dispute is over whether a given term, 'alienation', say, or 'determined', as defined at the beginning of an argument, is capable of doing the work required of it by the end, and whether any term could possibly perform the function in question. This fact may explain in part the perennial attraction of the tool analogy.

This should not, however, be confused with another fate that can befall a term, and be put down to its being of no use. Thus the *Oxford*

Dictionary contains the word 'giglet'. 'Giglet' means 'a giddy romping girl'. It is not a term any longer in common use, and so far as I know no equivalent has emerged to take its place. The reason is not, I take it, that such things have ceased to exist, nor that it was discovered to be of no use for the task assigned it, but rather that the task has ceased to exist. No doubt in a different social context and climate the identification of giglets was both possible and important at least to parents. If one wished one could still no doubt identify them, but with a change of mores the urge has passed. Whatever may be true of our society, our present language at least is not less (nor more) adequate or accurate for the loss. 'She is a giglet' may be a truth, but it is a truth in which people no longer have any interest, and so a piece of information for which people no longer have any use. Once again one can talk of the word as a discarded tool, but in this case it is discarded not because of any inadequacy on the part of the tool, but because the craftsman has decided to take up other hobbies. The aptness of the tool analogy here gives rise to no case for talk of the inaccuracy or inadequacy of the language.

With this last example it is not clear what the suggestion that the term was inaccurate could amount to, and this is a point that holds of large numbers of words. Different languages may have non-matching sets of colour words, and may even cut the spectrum up differently, but there is no answer to the question 'which is right?' It is quite possible that a colour vocabulary found useful in a certain climate and for certain purposes will cease to be useful in other climates or for other purposes, but even so the questions of truth or accuracy do not arise. Any supposed check would involve use of some alternative concepts which would themselves be in the same competition. It would be like letting one of two disagreeing members of a quiz competition decide which answers were right. The point here is not that we could never know which was right, but that no proposed candidate could have the status of being *the* right one. God himself would be of no avail, for claiming that his omniscience extended to settling the question would be to suppose, for no reason, that there was something for him to know.

So far, then, we have three sorts of criticism, and in relation to each it is not unnatural to talk of words as tools. First, the use of some terms may carry an assumption that is in principle falsifiable; second, there may be specifiable purposes for which terms with a given sense may be assessed as adequate or inadequate; third, we may cease to pursue the purpose or have the interest of which the term's use was a part. In the second case the tool analogy is at its strongest. Indeed, with some of the possible criticisms in this area, such as vagueness, the metaphor of sharpening the term up comes readily to mind, together with the idea of measuring the performance of the tool against the reality. It is this that

Plato wants, but which seems hard to supply in the other two sorts of case. It is of no help that matters are not so clear-cut as I have suggested. I have spoken of a colour vocabulary as though it were not possible there to specify a task against which the words can be measured. If we take individual items, such as 'red', this seems plausible enough. The natural task to mention is something highly general, like describing, and here it will be no better or worse than another. But if one has the whole colour vocabulary in mind, then one might hit on a non-linguistic category for giving the purpose, such as 'distinguishing and identifying things by sight'. Now one vocabulary may be more apt than another according to circumstances, so that one's descent into disuse may be due to more than just change of interest on the part of the population. A vocabulary that distinguishes minutely across the spectrum may be less effective in a country of bright sunshine and harsh colour-contrast than one which concentrates on depth and lightness of colour.

The borderline between changes of interest and adequacy to purpose may become blurred here. One might therefore be tempted to take advantage of the blur to point out that one can clearly query the adequacy to purpose of areas of language. And surely the purposes of the different areas are just part of the general purpose of language, against which the purpose of the whole is judged. As we have seen in discussing Plato's views on the determination of excellence, from the fact that each member of a set of items has a function it does not follow that the set has a function. The temptation in the case of language is, however, notorious. After all, it seems pretty well definitional that it is the function of language to help us communicate. If we ask 'communicate what?' the answer seems to be 'ideas' with the general purpose of discovering the truth. So the predominant function of language must be to express the truth. How tempting the latter parts of this progress are depends very largely on what one's predominant interests are. If they are in knowledge, and that and language are thought to distinguish men from animals, it will doubtless be strong. For the moment I shall suppose that this is right. It certainly seems to be assumed by Plato. Yet he, as we have seen, wishes to go a good deal further than that. For an interest in the truth turns out to be an interest in the discovery of propositions expressed in unqualified 'is'-es. Sometimes people so use the term 'true' that if 'the cat is on the mat' is true, the sentence 'the cat is on the mat' has to be taken as short for 'the cat is on the mat at t_n' for some value of 'n', and when it is said that this is true, the 'is' in 'is true' has no such time restriction. Others are inclined to treat 'the cat is on the mat' as true on some occasions, not on others. In this case, the 'is' in the sentence 'the cat is on the mat' in ' "the cat is on the mat" is true' is without time restriction, but not that in 'is true'. This latter must hold either for all or some times. Now Plato may seem nearer to this last, for he thinks of eternal truths as propositions that are true at all times. But in fact both these accounts concentrate on propositions, whereas Plato thinks primarily of the objects of which the propositions hold. If we take 'the cat is on the mat' the trouble is not with the proposition but with the cat. Its mode of being in relation to the mat is such that 'is' does not really apply. Consequently 'the cat is on the mat' is not strictly true ever, and the attempt to insert time references into it would simply underline the reason why.

This, as we have seen, puts severe restrictions on what propositions even have a chance of being true, and further restrictions result from the demand that the subject be without qualification what it is said to be. By the middle dialogues, however, it seems to be supposed that only Forms are proper subjects of such propositions, so that reaching the truth is giving something's *ousia* which in turn will be a functional account. These severe restrictions are intelligible if we take Plato to think that the main function of language is to be a tool for the dissemination of the truth, for telling us how things really are, and to suppose that it is only when we understand the system of Forms that we know how things really are. Only a language which makes this possible is a proper tool for its purpose. That means only a language where things are classified according to function is capable of expressing the unchanging reality which can be described in unqualified 'is'-es. To say that such a language, or those parts of a language are apt for giving the truth about how things are, reflects the belief that the real explanation of the universe takes a form for which these terms are proper vehicles. For on Plato's view any proper explanation of the universe must be couched in terms of interrelated functions. So in Plato's view the purpose of language is not simply, in the vulgar sense, to convey truths, but to convey the correct explanation. Thus the main classificatory terms can be criticised as failing to fulfil their proper part, and the ragbag of day-to-day terms, even in a language which has the right classifications, are simply not, on these Draconian terms, concerned with the truth, and therefore are not fulfilling language's proper role.

While the particular form the prejudice takes is influenced by Plato's views on explanation, the style is the same as that which leads people to think that ordinary language is radically inadequate in that its terms are not suitable for expressing the nature of reality, for which we need a precise technical vocabulary. Ordinary language is well enough for the rough and tumble of everyday affairs, but will not do for those concerned for the strict truth. Everyday life allows for imprecise terms and inaccurate ways of speech, and we manage well enough with them there, but those are characteristics which impede the pursuit of truth, something which can only be achieved by the use of a proper scientific vocabulary geared to the reality it is to describe. In either case there is a simple bias in favour of a certain sort of information, and because it seems so useful or so clear or so unchanging it is considered a more respectable sort of information than other sorts. It alone constitutes the real truth, and so only terms capable of conveying it properly fulfil the function of language, and only languages that contain them have any title to adequacy.

There are certain points here that are true, but most of them are not. If we confine ourselves to the question of which propositions are/can be true, the answer is that ones formulated in scientific terminology have no monopoly. The fact that what I am sitting on can be correctly described in the vocabulary of atomic physics does not imply that describing it as a chair, or a four-legged wooden object, is inaccurate or untrue. Nor is the first of these at least imprecise. Or perhaps it would be better to say that precision and imprecision are relative to requirements, and although any of these ways may be for certain purposes imprecise, for others they may give precisely what the object is. The sorts of context in which they can variously be used to convey precise information will vary, and this is because of the variation of interest and purpose which their use is suited to serve. Limiting the accolade 'real truth' to propositions that can form part of a scientific description or account is just an underhand way of insinuating some propaganda in favour of one set of interests and pursuits over others.

It is, however, true that often when people say such things as 'this chair is really a configuration of electrons in constant motion' their claim is that that is the correct account of the physical constitution of the chair. Common macroscopic descriptions, such as that it is stationary or solid, may satisfy some purposes but are quite misleading as to the real nature of the object. Consequently these descriptions are rejected as not being altogether true. All this is unobjectionable, but only so long as it is remembered that the context is an interest in the physical constitution of things, not in the descriptions that are true of them. Without this restriction the question 'what is the real nature of reality?' is as bogus as it is big.

Even when we confine discussion to the communication of facts, then Plato is trying to impose restrictions on what is to count as a truth which in fact, for all their appearance of being strict uses, amount to no more than a smuggling in of a preference for information about the way the universe is constructed. If we do not so confine the discussion it emerges as a bias in favour of passing facts rather than joking, writing poems, exhorting, making promises and the host of other things for which language tends to be used. While few have shared Plato's choice of candidate for real truth, it has not been uncommon for philosophers to suppose that in some way the real purpose of language is for the conveyance of information. Even if it is acknowledged that we do go in for these other activities and use language for them, it is felt that in some way they are not the basic function of language. This may once more be a simple prejudice in favour of truth-finding activities over others, but it may also be based on a feeling that in some way these other activities are parasitic upon an interest in facts, so that while it could exist without them, they could not exist without it. This has in the present context to be taken not as a thesis about human psychological capacities, but to the effect that the attribution of these other activities to any subject whatever presupposes the attribution of factual interests, while the converse does not hold.

At this point it is important to distinguish between two theses. First, it might be held that any language in which it was possible to express commands, say, must also contain the means of stating some facts. To say that it must have these means is to say that there must be recognised constructions for doing just this, or there must be recognised ambiguities of construction. In the latter case any user of the language must be able in principle to make it clear, e.g. by tone of voice, in which way the construction was to be interpreted. This, it seems to me, would be a very difficult thesis to establish. Second, it might be held that if we are to have a language that can be taught, then anyone capable of learning it must be able to recognise the circumstances when its various terms are appropriate and distinguish them from those when they are not. Thus, suppose we could have a language where 'nouns' were commonly used alone, but only in a limited range of tones of voice. According to tone, 'lion' could mean 'fetch me a lion', 'beware lion' and so on, but there was no way of making factual statements about lions. It would still arguably be necessary for anyone learning the language to learn to identify lions and to know the difference between approaching and running away. He could now be described as knowing that that is (or is not) a lion, knowing that lions are different from tigers and so on according to his degree of expertise. Such descriptions, however, would be a comment on his powers of differentiation, and would carry no implication as to his linguistic capacities for stating facts. Once one has mentioned the two theses the difference is obvious, but the latter seems far more plausible than the former, and may well, if not distinguished, seem to strengthen the position that the statement of facts is a basic linguistic activity. Unfortunately it is the first thesis that Plato wants, and once it is seen to differ from the second it is clearly badly in need of unsupplied defence. Even the second thesis would need more precise formulation and argument before one could be sure whether it should be accepted or not.

Plato's views on the corrigibility of language, then, seem to embody a prejudice in favour of, roughly, the descriptive function of language over others, and within descriptions in favour of those in terms that play a part in a true account of the structure of the universe. In part this is plain prejudice, in part a result of not getting clear on the different ways in which the tool analogy may be appropriate. The prejudice is closely related to the other prejudice on types of explanation and what constitutes real knowledge, and in conjunction with them leads to a very cramping view on reputable intellectual activities, as well as on what activities are reputable for intellectual beings. Further, he talks as though a radical revision of language was a theoretical possibility. It seems that total revision of one's current concepts is out of the question. When we turn to examples where the tool analogy seems apt, it emerges that it is so for a variety of reasons, that only in some cases is it at all plausible to talk of truth or accuracy, and only in some of adequacy to a task. If theses of the sort mentioned at the end of the discussion on innate knowledge can be established, there will be terms in any human language whose use implies assumptions that are not in principle checkable, whose adequacy is not open to criticism (at least in the sense that some such terms *must* occur), and which belong to a class such that the class must always be represented. The tool analogy ceases to have any great pull in such cases, and the relevant arguments for innate knowledge or belief would rule out the possibility of revision in the respects mentioned. The tool-picture of language, taken as a simple model for the whole of linguistic activity, with its utter separation between language and reality, looks like being too simple by more than half.

In these last five chapters I have been trying to criticise what I take to be a set of central Platonic positions. The attraction of the synthesis is also its weakness. It is attractive because so many apparently disparate topics are brought together. Men will find the answer to their deepest desires if they pursue scientific enquiry to the end. Within the context of a complete understanding of the universe they will discover what the ideal life for man is, and with that discovery the desire to live it will develop. The combined comprehensiveness and structural simplicity of the position make it attractive. At the same time it is in all sorts of ways unduly restrictive: in its view of the human person, on the use of 'good', on knowledge, explanation and truth, on the use of language. As an ambition it has a certain grandeur, as a set of limitations within which to operate it is claustrophobic.

Bibliography of Modern
Works Referred to in the Text

Ackrill, J. (1965) 'Plato and the copula: *Sophist* 251–9' in *Studies in Plato's Metaphysics*, ed. R. E. Allen, Routledge & Kegan Paul, London.

Adkins, A. (1960) *Merit and Responsibility*, Clarendon Press, Oxford.

Bentham, J. (1789) *An Introduction to the Principles of Morals and Legislation*.

Burnet, J. (1911) *Plato's Phaedo*, Clarendon Press, Oxford.

Collingwood, R. G. (1940) *An Essay on Metaphysics*, Oxford University Press.

Cornford, F. (1935) *Plato's Theory of Knowledge*, Routledge & Kegan Paul, London.

Crombie, I. (1962) *An Examination of Plato's Doctrines* (two vols), Routledge & Kegan Paul, London.

Diels, H. (1954) *Die Fragmente der Vorsokratiker*, Weidmannsche, Berlin.

Frede, M. (1970) *Prädikation und Existenzaussage*, Vandenhoeck & Ruprecht, Göttingen.

Geach, P. (1967) 'Good and Evil' in *Theories of Ethics*, ed. Philippa Foot, Oxford University Press.

Gosling, J. C. B. (1960) 'Republic Book V: *Τὰ πολλὰ καλά*, etc.', *Phronesis* 5 (2).

Gosling, J. C. B. (1968) '*Δόξα* and *Δύναμις* in Plato's *Republic*', *Phronesis* 13 (2).

Lorenz, K. (1954) *Man Meets Dog*, trans. Marjorie Kerr Wilson, Methuen, London.

Lyons, J. (1966) *Structural Semantics*, Blackwell, Oxford.

Murphy, N. R. (1951) *The Interpretation of Plato's Republic*, Clarendon Press, Oxford.

Nowell-Smith, P. H. (1954) *Ethics*, Penguin, Harmondsworth.

Moravcsik, J. (1962) 'Being and meaning in the *Sophist*', *Acta Philosophica Fennica* 14.

Robinson, R. (1953) *Plato's Earlier Dialectic*, 2nd ed., Clarendon Press, Oxford.

Runciman, W. (1962) *Plato's Later Epistemology*, Cambridge University Press.

Taylor, A. (1926) *Plato, the Man and his Work*, Methuen, London.

Taylor, C. C. W. (1967) 'Plato and the mathematicians', *Philosophical Quarterly* 17 (68).

Wedberg, A. (1955) *Plato's Philosophy of Mathematics*, Almquist & Wiksell, Stockholm.

Index

080402